Harmonising Regulatory and Antitrust Regimes for International Air Transport

Harmonising Regulatory and Antitrust Regimes for International Air Transport addresses the timely and problematic issue of lack of uniformity in legal standards for international civil aviation. The book focuses on discrepancies within the regulatory and antitrust framework, comprehensively reveals the major legal limitations and conflicts, and presents possible solutions thereto. It discusses potential strategies for multilateralisation and defragmentation of air law, and for international harmonisation of airline economic regulation with fair competition standards. This discussion extends to competition between air transport law and other legal regimes as well as to specific regulatory problems related to air transport. The unique feature of the book is that it reconciles distinct perspectives on these issues presented by renowned aviation and aerospace experts who represent the world's key air transport markets and air law academic centres.

By providing unbiased solutions that could serve as a base for future international arrangements, this book will be invaluable for aviation professionals, as well as students and scholars with an interest in air law, economic regulation, antitrust studies, international relations, transportation policy and airline management.

Jan Walulik has a PhD in law; Head, Civil Aviation Laboratory, Centre for Antitrust and Regulatory Studies, Faculty of Management, University of Warsaw; corporate attorney (Warsaw bar).

Routledge Research in Competition Law

Available titles in this series include:

The Internationalisation of Competition Rules
Brendan J. Sweeney

Antitrust Federalism in the EU and the US
Firat Cengiz

Competition and Regulation in the Airline Industry
Puppets in Chaos
Steven Truxal

Forthcoming titles in this series include:

Merger Control in Post-Communist Countries
EC Merger Regulation in Small Market Economies
Jurgita Malinauskaite

Merger Control in Europe
The Gap In The ECMR And National Merger Legislations
Ioannis Kokkoris

Harmonising Regulatory and Antitrust Regimes for International Air Transport
Jan Walulik

Collective Redress and EU Competition Law
Eda Şahin

Competition Policy and Network Industries
Structural Separation in the Telecommunications Sector
Pierluigi Congedo

Harmonising Regulatory and Antitrust Regimes for International Air Transport

Edited by Jan Walulik

Routledge
Taylor & Francis Group
LONDON AND NEW YORK

First published 2019
by Routledge
2 Park Square, Milton Park, Abingdon, Oxon OX14 4RN

and by Routledge
52 Vanderbilt Avenue, New York, NY 10017

First issued in paperback 2020

Routledge is an imprint of the Taylor & Francis Group, an informa business

British Library Cataloguing-in-Publication Data
A catalogue record for this book is available from the British Library

Library of Congress Cataloging-in-Publication Data
Names: Walulik, Jan, editor.
Title: Harmonising regulatory and antitrust regimes for international air transport / Jan Walulik.
Description: Abingdon, Oxon ; New York, NY : Routledge, 2019. |
Series: Routledge research in competition law
Identifiers: LCCN 2018037228 | ISBN 9780815353867 (hbk)
Subjects: LCSH: Aeronautics, Commercial—Law and legislation. |
Antitrust law.
Classification: LCC K4095 .H356 2019 | DDC 343.09/7—dc23
LC record available at https://lccn.loc.gov/2018037228

ISBN 13: 978-0-367-58306-4 (pbk)
ISBN 13: 978-0-8153-5386-7 (hbk)

Typeset in Galliard
by Swales & Willis Ltd, Exeter, Devon, UK

Contents

Tables

Abbreviations

ACAC	Arab Civil Aviation Commission
ACI	Air Connectivity Index
AF	Air France
AOC	Air Operator Certificate
ASA	Air Services Agreement
ASCM	WTO Agreement on Subsidies and Countervailing Measures
ASEAN	Association of South East Asian Nations
AST	Associate Administrator for Commercial Space Transportation
AT	Royal Air Maroc
CAB	US Civil Aeronautics Board
CCDev	Commercial Crew Development
CFR	US Code of Federal Regulations
CJEU	Court of Justice of the EU, previously Court of Justice of the European Communities
CO_2	carbon dioxide
CORSIA	Carbon Offsetting and Reduction Scheme for International Aviation
COTS	Commercial Orbital Transportation Services
CRS	computerised reservation systems
DOT	US Department of Transportation
EAS	Essential Air Services
EASA	EU Aviation Safety Agency, previously European Aviation Safety Agency
EC	European Community
EEC	European Economic Community
ECJ	European Court of Justice
ECAC	European Civil Aviation Conference
EEA	European Economic Area
EIA	Environmental Impact Assesment
ETS	Emission Trading Scheme
EU	European Union
FAA	US Federal Aviation Administration
FTC	US Federal Trade Commission

FTE	full-time equivalent
GATS	General Agreement on Trade in Services
GATT	General Agreement on Tariffs and Trade
GDP	gross domestic product
GDS	global distribution system
IAG	International Airline Group
IATA	International Air Transport Association
IATFCPA	US International Air Transportation Fair Competitive Practices Act of 1974
ICAO	International Civil Aviation Organization
ICJ	International Court of Justice
ILO	International Labour Organization
ISS	International Space Station
LCC	Low Cost Carrier
MALIAT	Multilateral Agreement on the Liberalisation of International Air Transportation
MFN	Most-Favoured-Nation
NASA	US National Aeronautics and Space Administration
OECD	Organisation for Economic Co-Operation and Development
OST	Outer Space Treaty
Pan Am	Pan American World Airways
PSO	Public Service Obligation
SARPs	Standards and Recommended Practices
TFEU	Treaty on the Functioning of the European Union
UAE	United Arab Emirates
UK	United Kingdom
UN	United Nations
UNTS	United Nations Treaty Series
UNCOPUOS	United Nations Committee on the Peaceful Uses of Outer Space
UNFCCC	United Nations Framework Convention on Climate Change
UNOOSA	United Nations Office for Outer Space Affairs
US	United States
USC	US Code
WTO	World Trade Organization

List of legal acts

International agreements

Convention Relating to the Regulation of Aerial Navigation, signed in Paris on 13 October 1919, entered into force on 29 March 1922, 11 LNTS 173.

Ibero-American Convention on Air Navigation, signed in Madrid on 1 November 1926, never came into force.

Pan-American Convention on Commercial Aviation, signed in Havana on 20 February 1928, 129 LNTS 223.

Convention for the Unification of Certain Rules Relating to International Carriage by Air, signed at Warsaw on 12 October 1929, entered into force on 13 February 1933, 137 LTNS 11.

Convention on International Civil Aviation, signed in Chicago on 7 December 1944, entered into force 4 April 1947, ICAO Doc. 7300/9, 15 UNTS 295.

International Air Services Transit Agreement, signed in Chicago on 7 December 1944, entered into force on 30 January 1945, ICAO Doc. 9587, 84 UNTS 389.

International Air Transport Agreement, signed in Chicago on 7 December 1944, entered into force on 8 February 1945, ICAO Doc. 9587, 171 UNTS 387.

Agreement between the Government of the United Kingdom and the Government of the United States of America relating to Air Services between their Respective Territories (with Annex), signed in Bermuda on 11 February 1946, entered into force by signature, 3 UNTS 253, UKTS 3 (1946) Cm. 6747.

General Agreement on Tariffs and Trade, signed in Geneva on 30 October 1947, applied provisionally since 1 January 1948, 55 UNTS 194, incorporated in the General Agreement on Tariffs and Trade part of the Multilateral Agreements on Trade in Goods – Annex 1A of the Marrakesh Agreement Establishing the World Trade Organization, done in Marrakesh on 15 April 1994, entered into force on 1 January 1995, 1867 UNTS 187.

Convention on Damage Caused by Foreign Aircraft to Third Parties on the Surface, done in Rome on 7 October 1952, entered into force on 4 February 1958, ICAO Doc. 7364, 310 UNTS 181.

Treaty on the Functioning of the European Union (TFEU), signed on 25 March 1957 in Rome, entered into force on 1 January 1958 (then Treaty establishing the European Economic Community, later Treaty establishing the European Economic Community, consolidated version OJ C 202, 7.6.2016, pp. 47–199.

Air Transport Agreement between the Government of the United States of America and the Government of the Kingdom of the Netherlands, signed in Washington on 3 April 1957, provisionally applied by signature, 410 UNTS 193,

Agreement on First and Second Freedoms of the Air for Arab Civil Aircraft, signed in Cairo on 25 March 1963.

Convention on Offences and Certain Other Acts Committed on Board Aircraft, done in Tokyo on 14 September 1963, entered into force on 4 December 1969, ICAO Doc. 8364, 704 UNTS 219.

Treaty on Principles Governing the Activities of States in the Exploration and Use of Outer Space, including the Moon and Other Celestial Bodies, done in London, Moscow and Washington on 27 January 1967, entered into force on 10 October 1967, 610 UNTS 205.

Agreement on the Rescue of Astronauts, the Return of Astronauts and the Return of Objects Launched into Outer Space, done in London, Moscow and Washington on 22 April 1968, entered into force on 3 December 1968, 672 UNTS 119.

Vienna Convention on the law of treaties, concluded at Vienna on 23 May 1969, entered into force on 27 January 1980, 1155 UNTS 331.

Convention for the Suppression of Unlawful Seizure of Aircraft, signed at The Hague on 16 December 1970, entered into force on 14 October 1971, ICAO Doc. 8920, 860 UNTS 105.

Convention for the Suppression of Unlawful Acts against the Safety of Civil Aviation, signed at Montréal on 23 September 1971, entered into force on 26 January 1973, ICAO Doc. 8966, 974 UNTS 177.

Convention on International Liability for Damage Caused by Space Objects, done in London, Moscow and Washington on 29 March 1972, entered into force on 1 September 19729, 61 UNTS 187.

Convention on Registration of Objects Launched into Outer Space, done in New York on 14 January 1975, entered into force on 15 September 1976, 1023 UNTS 15.

Agreement between the Government of the United States of America and the Government of the United Kingdom of Great Britain and Northern Ireland concerning Air Services (with Annexes and Exchange of letters), signed in Bermuda on 23 July 1977 ('Bermuda II Agreement'), entered into force by signature, 1079 UNTS 21.

Protocol relating to the Air Transport Agreement between the Government of the United States of America and the Government of the Kingdom of the Netherlands of 1957, as amended, signed at Washington on 31 March 1978, entered into force by signature, 1123 UNTS 345.

Protocol to Amend the Convention on Damage Caused by Foreign Aircraft to Third Parties on the Surface signed at Rome on 7 October 1952, done in Montréal on 23 September 1978, entered into force on 25 July 2002, ICAO Doc. 9257, 2195 UNTS 370.

Agreement Amending the Air Transport Services Agreement of 1946, as amended, signed on 12–14 December 1978, United States–Belgium, TIAS No 9207.

Non-scheduled Arab air services are also ruled by Agreement for Non-Scheduled Air Transport between Arab States, signed in Tunis on 15 December 1978.

Protocol Relating to an Amendment to the Convention on International Civil Aviation (Article 83 *bis*), signed at Montréal on 6 October 1980, entered into force on 20 June 1997, ICAO Doc. 9318, 2122 UNTS 321.

Agreement for Facilitation and Promotion of Trade among Arab States, signed in Tunis on 22 February 1981, entered into force 1 January 1998.

United Nations Convention on the Law of the Sea, done in Montego Bay on 10 December 1982, entered into force on 16 November 1994, 1833 UNTS 3 and 1835 UNTS 261.

Agreement between the Government of the United States of America and the Commission of the European Communities regarding the application of their competition laws, done at Washington on 23 September 1991, entered into force on 23 September 1991, OJ L 95, 27.4.1995, pp. 47–52; 2872 UNTS 1.

United Nations Framework Convention on Climate Change (UNFCCC), signed in New York on 9 May 1992, entered into force on 21 March 1994, 1771 UNTS 107.

Agreement between the United States of America and the Netherlands amending the Air Transport Agreement of 3 April 1957 and the Protocol of 31 March 1978, as amended, signed in the Hague on 14 September 1992, entered into force on 11 May 1993, 2246 UNTS 169.

Agreement on Subsidies and Countervailing Measures, part of the Multilateral Agreements on Trade in Goods – Annex 1A of the Marrakesh Agreement Establishing the World Trade Organization, done in Marrakesh on 15 April 1994, entered into force on 1 January 1995, 1869 UNTS 14.

General Agreement on Trade in Services – Annex 1B of the Marrakesh Agreement Establishing the World Trade Organization, done in Marrakesh on 15 April 1994, entered into force on 1 January 1995, 1869 UNTS 183.

Agreement for the creation of Arab Civil Aviation Commission, signed in Cairo on 15 September 1994, entered into force on 7 February, 1996.

Kyoto Protocol to the United Nations Framework Convention on Climate Change (UNFCCC) signed in Kyoto on 11 December 1997, entered into force on 16 February 2005, 2303 UNTS 162.

Convention for the Unification of Certain Rules for International Carriage by Air, done at Montréal on 28 May 1999, entered into force on 4 November 2003, ICAO Doc. 9740, 2242 UNTS 350.

Multilateral Agreement on the Liberalization of International Air Transportation (MALIAT), done at Wellington on 1 May 2001, entered into force on 21 December 2001, 2215 UNTS 33.

Protocol to the Multilateral Agreement on the Liberalization of International Air Transportation, done at Wellington on 1 May 2001, entered into force on 21 December 2001, 2215 UNTS 402.

Agreement between the Government of New Zealand and the Government of Australia relating to Air Services, done at Auckland on 8 August 2002, entered into force on 25 August 2003, 2003 ATS 18; 2003 NZTS 13; 2258 UNTS 177.

Treaty establishing a Constitution for Europe, done in Rome on 29 October 2004, never entered into force, OJ C 310, 16.12.2004, pp. 1–474,

Agreement for Collective Negotiations with Regional and Sub-Regional Groups, signed in Damascus on 19 December, 2004.

Agreement on Liberalisation of Air Transport between the Arab states done in Damascus on 19 December 2004, entered into force on 18 February 2007.

Maritime Labour Convention done in Geneva on 23 February 2006, entered into force on 20 August 2013, UNTS, Vol. 2952, No. 51299.

Multilateral Agreement between the European Community and its Member States, the Republic of Albania, Bosnia and Herzegovina, the Republic of Bulgaria, the Republic of Croatia, the former Yugoslav Republic of Macedonia, the Republic of Iceland, the Republic of Montenegro, the Kingdom of Norway, Romania, the Republic of Serbia and the United Nations Interim Administration Mission in Kosovo on the establishment of a European Common Aviation Area, signed on 5 July 2006 in Luxembourg, entered into force on 1 December 2017, OJ L 285, 16.10.2006, pp. 3–46.

Euro-Mediterranean aviation agreement between the European Community and its Member States, of the one part, and the Kingdom of Morocco, of the other part, signed on 12 December 2006 in Brussels, applied provisionally, OJ L 386, 29.12.2006, pp. 57–88.

Air Transport Agreement between the United States of America and the Republic of Austria, the Kingdom of Belgium, the Republic of Bulgaria, the Republic of Cyprus, the Czech Republic, the Kingdom of Denmark, the Republic of Estonia, the Republic of Finland, the French Republic, the Federal Republic of Germany, the Hellenic Republic, the Republic of Hungary, Ireland, the Italian Republic, the Republic of Latvia, the Republic of Lithuania, the Grand Duchy of Luxembourg, Malta, the Kingdom of The Netherlands, the Republic of Poland, the Portuguese Republic, Romania, the Slovak Republic, the Republic of Slovenia, the Kingdom of Spain, the Kingdom of Sweden, the United Kingdom of Great Britain And Northern Ireland, and the European Community, done at Brussels on 25 April 2007 and at Washington on 30 April 2007, provisionally applied as from 30 March 2008, OJ L 134, 25.5.2007, pp. 4–41.

Treaty of Lisbon amending the Treaty on European Union and the Treaty establishing the European Community, done in Lisbon on 13 December 2007, entered into force on 1 December 2009, OJ C 306, 17.12.2007, pp. 1–271.

Convention on Compensation for Damage Caused by Aircraft to Third Parties, done at Montréal on 2 May 2009, not in force, ICAO Doc. 9919.

Convention on Compensation for Damage to Third Parties, Resulting from Acts of Unlawful Interference Involving Aircraft, done at Montréal on 2 May 2009, not in force, ICAO Doc. 9920.

Agreement on Multimodal Transport of Goods between the Arab States, signed in Cairo on 9 September 2009.

Protocol to amend the Air Transport Agreement between the United States of America and the European Community and its Member States, signed on 25 and 30 April 2007, signed on 24 June 2010 in Luxembourg, provisionally applied as from the date of signature, OJ L 223, 25.8.2010, pp. 3–19

Protocol Supplementary to the Convention for the Suppression of Unlawful Seizure of Aircraft, done at Beijing on 10 September 2010, entered into force on 1 January 2018, ICAO Doc. 9959.

Convention on the Suppression of Unlawful Acts Relating to International Civil Aviation, done at Beijing on 10 September 2010, not in force, ICAO Doc. 9960.

Multilateral Open Skies Agreement for the Member States of the Latin American Civil Aviation Commission (*Acuerdo Multilateral de Cielos Abiertos*), done at Punta Cana, Dominican Republic, on 5 November 2010, LACAC Assembly Resolution No. A19-03.

Euro-Mediterranean Aviation Agreement between the European Union and its Member States, of the one part, and the Hashemite Kingdom of Jordan, of the other part, signed on 15 December 2010 in Brussels, applied provisionally, OJ L 334, 6.12.2012, pp. 3–30.

Common Aviation Area Agreement between the European Union and its Member States and the Republic of Moldova, signed on 26 June 2012 in Brussels, applied provisionally as of the date of signature, OJ L 292, 20.10.2012, pp. 3–37.

Euro-Mediterranean Aviation Agreement between the European Union and its Member States, of the one part, and the government of the State of Israel, of the other part, signed on 10 June 2013 in Luxembourg, applied provisionally, OJ L 208, 2.8.2013, pp. 3–67.

Protocol to Amend the Convention on Offences and Certain Other Acts Committed on Board Aircraft, done at Montréal on 4 April 2014, not in force, ICAO Doc. 10034.

Paris Agreement signed in Paris on 12 December 2015, entered into force on 4 November 2016.

EU legislation:

Regulation No. 4057/86/EEC of the Council of 22 December 1986 on unfair pricing practices in maritime transport, OJ L 378, 31.12.1986, pp. 14–20.

Regulation No. 2671/88/EEC of the Commission of 26 July 1988 on the application of Article 85 (3) of the Treaty to certain categories of agreements between undertakings, decisions of associations of undertakings and concerted practices concerning joint planning and coordination of capacity, sharing of revenue and consultations on tariffs on scheduled air services and slot allocation at airports, OJ L 239, 30.8.1988, pp. 9–12.

Regulation No. 2407/92/EEC of the Council of 23 July 1992 on licensing of air carriers, OJ L 240, 24.8.1992, pp. 1–7.

Regulation No. 1617/93/EEC of the Commission of 25 June 1993 on the application of Article 85 (3) of the Treaty to certain categories of agreements and concerted practices concerning joint planning and coordination of schedules, joint operations, consultations on passenger and cargo tariffs on scheduled air services and slot allocation at airports, OJ L 155, 26.6.1993, pp. 18–22.

Decision of the Council and the Commission of 10 April 1995 concerning the conclusion of the Agreement between the European Communities and the Government of the United States of America regarding the application of their competition laws, OJ L 95, 27.4.1995, pp. 45–52.

Regulation No. 1523/96/EC of the Commission of 24 July 1996 amending Regulation (EEC) No 1617/93 on the application of Article 85 (3) of the Treaty to certain categories of agreements and concerted practices concerning joint planning and coordination of schedules, joint operations, consultations on passenger and cargo tariffs on scheduled air services and slot allocation at airports, OJ L 190, 31.7.1996, pp. 11–12.

Regulation No. 1/2003/EC of the Council of 16 December 2002 on the implementation of the rules on competition laid down in Articles 81 and 82 of the Treaty, OJ L 1, 4.1.2003, pp. 1–25.

Regulation No. 139/2004/EC of the Council of 20 January 2004 on the control of concentrations between undertakings, OJ L 24, 29.1.2004, pp. 1–22.

Regulation No. 261/2004/EC of the European Parliament and of the Council of 11 February 2004 establishing common rules on compensation and assistance to passengers in the event of denied boarding and of cancellation or long delay of flights, and repealing Regulation (EEC) No 295/91, OJ L 46, 17.2.2004, pp. 1–8.

Regulation No. 411/2004/EC of the Council of 26 February 2004 repealing Regulation (EEC) No 3975/87 and amending Regulations (EEC) No 3976/87 and (EC) No 1/2003, in connection with air transport between the Community and third countries, OJ L 68, 6.3.2004, pp. 1–2.

Regulation No. 802/2004/EC of the Commission of 7 April 2004 implementing Council Regulation (EC) No 139/2004 on the control of concentrations between undertakings, OJ L 133, 30.4.2004, pp. 1–39.

Regulation No. 868/2004/EC of the European Parliament and of the Council of 21 April 2004 concerning protection against subsidisation and unfair pricing practices causing injury to Community air carriers in the supply of air services from countries not members of the European Community, OJ L 162, 30.4.2004, pp. 1–7.

Regulation No. 1459/2006/EC of the Commission of 28 September 2006 on the application of Article 81(3) of the Treaty to certain categories of agreements and concerted practices concerning consultations on passenger tariffs on scheduled air services and slot allocation at airports, OJ L 272, 3.10.2006, pp. 3–8.

Regulation No. 1008/2008/EC of the European Parliament and of the Council of 24 September 2008 on common rules for the operation of air services in the Community, OJ L 293, 31.10.2008, pp. 3–20.

Directive No. 2008/101/EC of the European Parliament and of the Council of 19 November 2008 amending Directive 2003/87/EC so to include aviation activities in the scheme for greenhouse gas emissions allowances trading within the Community, OJ L 8, 13.1.2009, pp. 3–21.

Regulation No. 428/2009/EC of the Council of 5 May 2009 setting up a Community regime for the control of exports, transfer, brokering and transit of dual-use items, OJ L 134, 29.5.2009, pp. 1–269.

Regulation No. 487/2009/EC of the Council of 25 May 2009 on the application of Article 81(3) of the Treaty to certain categories of agreements and concerted practices in the air transport sector, OJ L 148, 11.6.2009, pp. 1–4.

Decision No. 377/2013/EU of the European Parliament and of the Council of 24 April 2013 derogating temporarily from Directive 2003/87/EC establishing a scheme for greenhouse gas emission allowances trading within the Community, OJ L 113, 25.4.2013, pp. 1–4.

Regulation No. 421/2014/EU of the European Parliament and of the Council of 16 April 2014 amending Directive 2003/87/EC establishing a scheme for greenhouse gas emission allowance trading within the Community, in view of the implementation by 2020 of an international agreement applying a single global market-based measure to international aviation emissions, OJ L 129, 30.4.2014, pp. 1–4.

Regulation 2017/2392/EU of the European Parliament and of the Council of 13 December 2017 amending Directive 2003/87/EC to continue current limitations of scope for aviation activities and to prepare to implement a global-market based measure from 2021, OJ L 350, 29.12.2017, pp. 7–14.

African Economic Community legislation:

Decision Relating to the Implementation of the Yamoussoukro Declaration concerning the Liberalisation of Access to Air Transport Markets in Africa of 14 November 1999, United Nations Economic and Social Council, Economic Commission of Africa, ECA/RCID/CM.CIVAC/99/RPT, Annex 1. The Yamoussoukro Decision, which has entered into force on 12 August 2000.

West African Economic and Monetary Union legislation:

Regulation No. 24/2002/CM/WAEMU of 18 November 2002 establishing the conditions of access by air carriers to the WAEMU community air routes.

National legislations:

Australia:

An act about space activities, and for related purposes, No. 123 of 1998, assented to 21 December 1998.

Austria:

Federal Law on the Authorisation of Space Activities and the Establishment of a National Space Registry (*Bundesgesetz über die Genehmigung von Weltraumaktivitäten und die Einrichtung eines Weltraumregisters (Weltraumgesetz)*), 6 December 2011, Federal Law Gazette of 27 December 2011.

Belgium:

Law on the Activities of Launching, Flight Operations or Guidance of Space Objects, 17 September 2005.

Denmark:

Law on activities in outer space (*Lov om aktiviteter i det ydre rum*), 3 May 2016, Parliament Gazette, 2015–17, No. L 128.

Finland:

Act on space activities, 63/2018, of 23 January 2018.

France:

Law on Space Operations (*Loi relative aux opérations spatiales*), Loi no. 2008–518 du 3 juin 2008.

Germany:

Law to Ensure Proof of Ownership and Control of Air Carriers for the Maintenance of Air Transport Management and Air Transport Rights' (Gesetz zur Sicherung des Nachweises der Eigentümerstellung und der Kontrolle von Luftfahrtunternehmen für die Aufrechterhaltung der Luftverkehrsbetriebsgenehmigung und der Luftverkehrsrechte – Luftverkehrsnachweissicherungsgesetz), 5 June 1997, Bundesgesetzblatt I S. 1322.

Japan:

Law Concerning the National Space Development Agency of Japan, No. 50 of 23 June 1969, as amended in 1998.

Kazakhstan:

Law of the Republic of Kazakhstan on Space Activities, of 6 January 2012, 2012 No. 528-IV.

The Netherlands:

Law Incorporating Rules Concerning Space Activities and the Establishment of a Registry of Space Objects, 24 January 2007, 80 Staatsblad (2007).

The Republic of South Africa:

Space Affairs Act No. 84 of 1993, assented to 23 June 1993.

Russian Federation:

Law About Space Activities (Закон о космической деятельности) of August 20, 1993, No. 5663-I.

Sweden:

Act on Space Activities, 1982: 963.

Decree on Space Activities, 1982: 1069.

UK:

Outer Space Act, 18 July 1986, 1986 Ch. 38.

Space Industry Act, 15 March 2018, 2018 Ch. 5.

US:

The Sherman Antitrust Act of July 2, 1890, Ch. 647, 26 Stat. 209.

The Clayton Antitrust Act of October 15, 1914, Ch. 323, 38 Stat. 730.

Securities Exchange Act of 1934, Pub.L. 73–291, June 6, 1934, 48 Stat. 881.

The Robinson-Patman Antidiscrimination Act of 1936, Pub. L. No. 74–692 – June 19, 1936, 49 Stat. 1526.

An act to amend the Act creating the Federal Trade Commission, to define its powers and duties, and for other purposes, Pub. L. 75–447 – March 21, 1938, 52 Stat. 111.

The Civil Aeronautics Act of 1938, Pub. L. 75–706 – June 23, 1938, 52 Stat. 973.

The Federal Aviation Act of 1958, Pub. L. 85–726 – August 23, 1958, 72 Stat. 731.

International Air Transportation Fair Competitive Practices Act of 1974, Pub. L. 93–623, January 3, 1975, 88 Stat. 2102.

The Airline Deregulation Act of 1978, Pub. L. 95–504 – October 24, 1978, 92 Stat. 1705.

Export Administration Act of 1979, Pub. L. 96–72 – September 29, 1979, 93 Stat. 503.

The International Air Transport Competition Act of 1979, Pub. L. 96–192 – February 15, 1980, 94 Stat. 35.

Civil Aeronautics Board Sunset Act of 1984, Pub. Law 98–443 – October 4, 1984, 98 Stat. 1703.

Commercial Space Launch Act, Pub. L. 98–575 – October 30, 1984, 98 Stat. 3055.

Commercial Space Act of 1998, Pub. L. 105–303 – January 27, 1998, 112 Stat. 2843.

Commercial Space Launch Amendments Act of 2004, Pub. L. 108–492 – December 23, 2004, 118 Stat. 3974.

European Emissions Trading Scheme Prohibition Act of 2011. Pub. Law 112–200, November 27, 2012, 126 Stat. 1477.

Commercial Space Launch Competitiveness Act, Pub. L. 114–90 – November 25, 2015, 129 Stat. 70.

List of court rulings

CJEU:

United Brands v. Commission of the European Communities, CJEU judgment of 14 February 1978, Case 27/76.

Hoffman-La Roche, CJEU judgment of 13 February 1979, Case 85/76.

Ministère Public vs. Lucas Asjes and Others, CJEU judgment of 30 April 1986, Cases C-209-213/84.

Ahmed Saeed Flugreisen and Silver Line Reisebüro v. Zentrale zur Bekämpfung unlautern Wettbewerb E.V., CJEU judgment of 11 April 1989, Case 66/86.

French Republic v. Commission of the European Communities, CJEU judgment of 9 August 1994, Case C-327/91.

CJEU judgments of 5 November 2002: Case C-466/98 – *Commission v. United Kingdom of Great Britain and Northern Ireland*, Case C-467/98 – *Commission v. Kingdom of Denmark*, Case C-468/98 – *Commission v. Kingdom of Sweden*, Case C-469/98 – *Commission v. Republic of Finland*, Case C-471/98 – *Commission v. Kingdom of Belgium*, Case C-472/98 – *Commission v. Grand Duchy of Luxemburg*, Case C-475/98 – *Commission v. Republic of Austria*, Case C-476/98 – *Commission v. Federal Republic of Germany*, ('Open Skies').

Yassin Abdullah Kadi and Al Barakaat International Foundation v. Council and Commission, CJEU (Grand Chamber) judgment of 3 September 2008, Cases C-402/05 and C-415/P.

Ryanair v. Commission, CJEU (Court of First Instance) judgment of 17 December 2008, Case T-196/04.

The Air Transport Association of America, American Airlines Inc., Continental Airlines, Inc., United Airlines Inc. v. The Secretary of State for Energy and Climate Change, CJEU (Grand Chamber) judgment of 21 December 2011, Case C-366/10.

European Commission and others v. Yassin Abdullah Kadi, CJEU (Grand Chamber) judgment of 18 July 2013, Cases C-548/10 P, C-539/10 and C-595/10.

CJEU (General Court) judgments of 16 December 2015: Case T-9/11 – *Air Canada v. Commission*, Case T-28/11 – *Koninklijke Luchtvaart Maatschappij v. Commission*, Case T-36/11 – *Japan Airlines v. Commission*, Case T-38/11 – *Cathay Pacific Airways v. Commission*, Case T-39/11 – *Cargolux Airlines v. Commission*, Case T-40/11 – *LAN Airlines and LAN Cargo v. Commission*, Case T-43/11 – *Singapore Airlines and Singapore Airlines Cargo PTE v. Commission*, Case T-46/11 – *Deutsche Lufthansa and Others v. Commission*, Case T-48/11 – *British Airways v. Commission*, Case T-56/11 – *SAS Cargo Group and Others v. Commission*, Case T-62/11 – *Air France – KLM v.*

Commission, Case T-63/11 - *Air France v. Commission*, Case T-67/11 – *Martinair Holland v. Commission*, ('Air Cargo Fuel Charges').

ICJ:

Nuclear Tests (New Zealand v. France), ICJ judgment of 20 December 1974, ICJ Reports 1974, p. 457.
Gabčikovo-Nagymaros Project (Hungary v. Slovakia), ICJ judgment of 25 September 1997, ICJ Reports 1997, p. 7.
Pulp Mills on the River Uruguay (Argentina v. Uruguay), ICJ judgment of 20 April 2010, ICJ Reports 2010, p. 14.
Certain Activities Carried Out by Nicaragua in the Border Area (Costa Rica v. Nicaragua) and *Constitution of a Road in Costa Rica along the San Juan River (Nicaragua v. Costa Rica)*, ICJ judgment of 16 December 2015, ICJ Reports 2015, p. 665.

US Courts:

United States v. Alcoa, 148 F.2d 416 (2nd Cir. 1945).
Brown Shoe, 370 US 294, 344–45 (1962).
U.S. v. Philadelphia National Bank, 374 US 321, 362 (1963).
Matsushita Elec. Indus. Co. v. Zenith Radio Corp., 475 US 574, 598 (1986).
FTC v. Indiana Fed'n of Dentists, 476 US 447 (1986).
Cargill, Inc. v. Monfort of Colo., Inc., 479 US 104, 117 (1986).
Atlantic Richfield Co. v. USA Petroleum Co., 495 US 328, 338 (1990).
Palmer v. BRG of Georgia, Inc., 498 US 46 (1990).
Brooke Group Ltd. v. Brown & Williamson Tobacco Corp., 509 US 209, 212 (1993).
California Dental Assn. v. FTC, 526 US 756 (1999).
Virgin Atlantic Airways Ltd. v. British Airways PLC, 257 F.3rd 256, 264 (2nd Cir. 2001).
Continental Airlines v. United Airlines, 277 F.3rd 499 (4th Cir. 2002).
Bell Atlantic Corp. v. Twombly, 550 US 544 (2007).
Delta/AirTran Baggage Fee Antitrust Litigation, 733 F. Supp. 2nd 1348, 1360 (N.D. Ga. 2010).
Malaney v. UAL Corp., 2010 U.S. Dist. Lexis 106049 (N.D. Cal. 2010).

List of administrative decisions

Germany:

Bundeskartellamt Entscheidung B9-190/16, *Lufthansa darf Flugzeuge von Air Berlin leasen*, 30.1.2017.

EU:

Decision No. 88/589/EEC of the Commission of 4 November 1988 relating to a proceeding under Article 86 of the EEC Treaty (IV/32.318, London European – Sabena), OJ L 317, 24.11.1988, pp. 47–54.

Decision of the Commission of 13 September 1991 declaring a concentration to be compatible with the common market (Case No IV/M.130 – Delta Air Lines/Pan Am) according to Council Regulation (EEC) No 4064/89, OJ C 289, 7.11.1991, p. 14.

Decision No. 92/213/EEC of the Commission of 26 February 1992 relating to a procedure pursuant to Articles 85 and 86 of the EEC Treaty (IV/33.544, British Midland v. Aer Lingus), OJ L 96, 10.4.1992, pp. 34–45.

Decision No. 95/364/EC of the Commission of 28 June 1995 relating to a proceeding pursuant to Article 90 (3) of the Treaty, OJ L 216, 12.9.1995, pp. 8–14.

Decision No. 95/404/EC of the Commission of 19 July 1995 on a procedure relating to the application of Council Regulation (EEC) No. 2407/92 (Swissair/Sabena), OJ L 239, 7.10.1995, pp. 19–28.

Decision No. 1999/641/EC of the Commission of 25 November 1998 declaring a concentration to be compatible with the common market and the functioning of the EEA Agreement (Case No IV/M.1225 – Enso/Stora), OJ L 254, 29.9.1999, pp. 9–21.

Decision No. 1999/198/EC of the Commission of 10 February 1999 relating to a proceeding pursuant to Article 86 of the Treaty (IV/35.767 – Ilmailulaitos/Luftfartsverket), OJ L 69, 16.3.1999, pp. 24–30.

Decision No. 1999/199/EC of the Commission of 10 February 1999 relating to a proceeding pursuant to Article 90 of the Treaty (Case No IV/35.703 – Portuguese airports), OJ L 69, 16.3.1999, pp. 31–39.

Commission notice of 30 October 2002 concerning the Alliance between KLM Royal Dutch Airlines and Northwest Airlines, Inc., (case COMP/D-2/36.111 – procedure under Article 85 (ex Article 89) of the EC Treaty), OJ C 264, 30.10.2002, p. 11.

Commission notice of 30 October 2002 concerning the alliance between Lufthansa, SAS and United Airlines (cases COMP/D-2/36.201, 36.076, 36.078 – procedure under Article 85 of the Treaty (ex Article 89)) (Text with EEA relevance), OJ C 264, 30.10.2002, pp. 5–9.

Air France/KLM, Commission decision of 11 February 2004, COMP/M.3280, SG-Greffe(2004) D/200549.

Sociètè Air France/Alitalia Linee Aeree Italiane S.p.A., Commission decision of 7 April 2004, COMP/38.284/D2, C(2004) 1307 final.

Lufthansa/Austrian Airlines, Commission decision of 28 August 2009, COMP/M.5440.

Iberia/British Airways, Commission Decision of 8 September 2010, COMP/M.5747.

Continental/United/Lufthansa/Air Canada, Commission decision of 23 May 2013, COMP/AT.39595, C(2013) 2836 final.

US Airways/American Airlines, Commission decision of 5 August 2013, COMP/M.6607, C(2013) 5232 final.

Swissport/Servisair, Commission decision of 18 December 2013, COMP/M.7021, C(2013) 9666 final.

Hyundai Merchant Marine Co., Ltd., Commission decision of 21 December 2015, AT/39.850.

Airfreight cartel, Commission decision of 17 March 2017, COMP/39.258.

Lufthansa/Certain Air Berlin Assets, Commission decision of 27 October 2017, M.8633, C(2017) 7355 final.

US:

CAB Order No. 78-9-2 (1978).

Acquisition of Northwest Airlines by Wings Holdings, Inc., DOT Order No. 89-9-51 (1989).

In the Matter of Defining 'Open Skies', DOT Order No. 92-8-13 (1992).

DOT Order No. 91-1-11 (1993).

Applications of American Airlines et al., DOT Order 97-2-26 (1997).

Application of United Airlines et al., DOT Order 97-6-30 (1997).

American Airlines and the Taca Group Reciprocal Code-Share Services Proceeding, DOT Order 97-12-35 (1997).

Application of American Airlines et al, DOT Order 99-6-6 (1999).

Joint Application of United Air Lines, Inc., and All Nippon Airlines, Ltd., DOT Order 99-8-14 (1999).

Application of American Airlines et al., DOT Order 2000-4-22 (2000).

Application of American Airlines et al., DOT Order 2000-5-13 (2000).

SkyTeam, Docket OST-2004-19214, DOT Show Cause Order 2005-12-22.

DOT Order No. 2008-4-17 R 2 (2008).

Expanded Star Application, DOT Order 2009-4-5 (2009).

Expanded Star Application, DOT Order 2009-7-10 (2009).

Joint Application of American Airlines, Inc; British Airways Plc; Finnair OYJ; Iberia Líneas Aéreas De España, SA; Royal Jordanian Airlines; Under 49 USC §§ 41308-41309 for approval of and antitrust immunity for alliance agreements, DOT Show Cause Order 2010-2-13.

Joint Application of American Airlines and Qantas Airways, DOT Order 2016-11-16 (2016).

Joint Application of Delta Air Lines and Aerovias de Mexico, DOT Order 2016-11-2 (2016).

Foreword from the editor

The limitations of the system of international air transport law have been discussed since deregulation in this sector began. However, recently the development of airline international activities has revealed several critical structural problems in air law. When the deregulated airline markets seemed to achieve equilibrium after a lengthy process of consolidations and privatizations, the rising competition, especially from state-owned Middle East carriers, has brought about doubts concerning uniformity of legal standards for airlines worldwide. These reservations have already triggered governmental actions, including the European Commission proposal for a regulation on safeguarding competition in air transport published in June 2017. Additionally, Brexit[1] and possible US isolationist policy have posed further questions regarding fragmentation of air law and unilateralism in aviation relations.

Given any consideration, it was high time to study potential ways for bringing this scattered legal environment together. With this aim, in 2017 I invited a group of renowned aviation and aerospace experts to the Airline Antitrust and Regulatory Conference[2] at the Centre for Antitrust an Regulatory Studies, Faculty of Management, University of Warsaw, Poland. The employed approach was to discuss and reconcile distinct perspectives on air law issues and provide possibly unbiased solutions, which could serve as base for future harmonisation of international arrangements. As a post-conference project, this book presents to the reader the results of this vivid debate.

This publication also endeavours to harmonise aviation regulatory and antitrust regimes in that it gathers and addresses the most timely legal questions in these spheres within one volume. It focuses on discrepancies within the regulatory and antitrust framework for civil aviation, comprehensively reveals the major legal limitations and conflicts, and presents solutions thereto. This debate starts with general problems and moves to more specific matters.

Discussed are possible strategies for multilateralization and defragmentation of air law (Part 1) and for international harmonisation of airline economic regulation

1 The impending withdrawal of the UK from the EU. More on Brexit and aviation law see Walulik 2019.

2 www.arac2017.wz.uw.edu.pl.

with fair competition standards (Part 2). What is more, this book exceeds the traditionally addressed regulatory–antitrust relationship and includes the aspect of competition between air transport law and other legal regimes (Part 3). It also contributes to some specific problems related to air transport regulation and liberalisation that are less often discussed in aviation literature, such as avoiding counterproductive liberalisation and regulating space tourism under air law. The presented specific regulatory problems also include airline ownership and control, regional liberalisation and connectivity gaps (Part 4).

Finally, this publication symbolically harmonises and reconciles views on current legal problems in air transport by gathering opinions of various experts originating from different regions. Notably, the contributing authors represent the most important air transport markets (EU, US, UAE) and air law academic centres worldwide.

Jan Walulik

Contributors

Shadi A. Alshdaifat is Assistant Professor of Public International Law, College of Law, University of Sharjah, Sharjah, UAE; SJD, Golden Gate University School of Law, 2012.

Elena Carpanelli holds a PhD in International Law; Post-doctoral Research Fellow in Public International Law, Centre for Studies in International and European Affairs (CSEIA), University of Parma (Italy).

Paul S. Dempsey is Tomlinson Professor Emeritus of Global Governance in Air and Space Law and Director Emeritus of the Institute of Air and Space Law, McGill University.

Piotr P. Dziubak is a PhD Candidate and Affiliated Member, Civil Aviation Laboratory, Centre for Antitrust and Regulatory Studies, Faculty of Management, University of Warsaw; Official at the Ministry of Infrastructure of the Republic of Poland.

Elmar M. Giemulla is Honorary Professor of Aviation Law, Berlin Institute of Technology, Attorney at Law (Berlin).

Peter P.C. Haanappel is Professor Emeritus and former Head of International Institute of Air and Space Law Leiden University; former Professor and Associate Director of Air and Space Law Institute, McGill University; former Director, European Aeropolitical Affairs at the International Air Transport Association.

Agnieszka Kunert-Diallo holds a PhD in law; Affiliated Member, Civil Aviation Laboratory, Centre for Antitrust and Regulatory Studies, Faculty of Management, University of Warsaw; academic teacher; legal counsel at LOT Polish Airlines.

Bashar H. Malkawi is Dean and Professor of Law at the University of Sharjah, UAE; SJD American University, Washington College of Law and LL.M in International Trade Law from the University of Arizona.

Pablo Mendes de Leon is Professor of Air and Space Law and Director, International Institute of Air and Space Law, Leiden University.

Małgorzata Polkowska is Professor of Law and Chair, Law of War Institute, National Security Department, War Studies University, Warsaw; Former representative of Poland to the ICAO Council.

Andrea Trimarchi is a PhD Candidate and Research Assistant, International Institute of Air and Space Law, Leiden University.

Frans G. von der Dunk is Harvey and Susan Perlman Alumni/Othmer Professor of Space Law, University of Nebraska-Lincoln, College of Law.

Jan Walulik holds a PhD in law; Head, Civil Aviation Laboratory, Centre for Antitrust and Regulatory Studies, Faculty of Management, University of Warsaw; Corporate attorney (Warsaw bar).

Paweł Zagrajek PhD in economics; Affiliated Member, Civil Aviation Laboratory, Centre for Antitrust and Regulatory Studies, Faculty of Management, University of Warsaw; Assistant Professor, Warsaw School of Economics.

Marek Żylicz is University of Warsaw Professor Emeritus; former Head of Legal Department LOT Polish Airlines; former Deputy Director of Polish Civil Aviation Administration; representative of Poland to ICAO Assembly and Legal Committee; representative of LOT Polish Airlines to IATA.

Part 1

Multilateralisation of international civil aviation relations and defragmentation of international air law

This part of the book will show how the lack of a global framework for the economic regulation of international air transport has contributed to the emergence of multiple closed aviation regimes, which led to fragmentation of international air law within bilateral aviation relations. It will be indicated that deregulation and liberalisation of these regimes, although economically significant, has not constituted a comprehensive and complete regulatory reform. It has not translated into the long-awaited unification and globalisation of air transport law. Conversely, it has brought about new legal problems in relation to competition law and other regimes that are applicable to the international air transport activity. Finally, in response to these problems, this part will present the multilateralisation and defragmentation strategies at the airline and governmental level.

1 The seven decades of scattered skies

Marek Żylicz

It is a great pleasure and an interesting task to write this short introduction to this book. New regulatory challenges, multilateralisation, defragmentation of aviation law regime, redefining spatial and substantive boundaries of this regime against other legal systems and foremost balancing this legal collage with competition law and policy. This all amounts to a fascinating tale, which shows how complicated air law can be and how far its evolution has progressed in just one century. It is especially exciting for me to observe this process, since during the seven decades of my practice and studies in air law, at least five decades coincided with the domination of the Chicago-bilateral system, leaving no, or very little, room for airline competition.

Starting from the general principle of closed skies adopted by the Chicago Convention, the so-called freedoms of the air exchanged between the states concerned were in fact exceptions to the restrictive principle. Under these freedoms, air transport market access was strictly controlled. Access was granted to a restricted number of national air carriers on strictly defined routes, with limited or predetermined capacities, with strict tariffs regulations and so on. In addition, the governments conferred authority to the IATA[1] to establish the minimum level of airline tariffs and the maximum level of on-board services provided, the maximum distances between passenger seats, the maximum level of agency commission and so on; everything that was needed to prevent effective competition between airlines. From the meetings of the IATA Legal Committee, I remember the discussions on the possible ways of opposing the antitrust policies of the US authorities.

During the second half of the past century, that restrictive system was subject to the process of liberalisation and deregulation. This process did not go smoothly. The government policies were not always consistent. For instance, it took the US government and Poland three decades to move from the most restrictive to the most liberal open skies bilateral air services agreement. In contrast, the Bermuda I agreement between the US and the UK was replaced after four decades by Bermuda II, which was even more restrictive in some respects than its predecessor.

1 International Air Transport Association.

Although there was no progress in terms of the liberalisation of international air transport at the multilateral (ICAO[2] and WTO[3]) level, regional arrangements proved to be more successful, particularly in the European Community (EC). While the room for airline competition gradually broadened, the international aviation society has faced an increasing number of new problems that need to be solved to ensure not only free but also fair competition. Once again it has not been possible to create a multilateral system until now as both the ICAO's and the WTO's actions failed. The relevant regulatory systems that have been created within regional frameworks and the existing bilateral agreements and national legislations differ largely.

The liberalisation of market access was a relatively uncomplicated process affecting bilateral relations between governments and airlines. It was sufficient to remove the restrictive rules and there was no need for assistance from global international organisations. In case of regulations concerning airline competition, more efforts on the side of governments are needed. What is more, the unification or at least harmonisation of the relevant rules has to be achieved at the multilateral level. However, defragmentation and multilateralisation of air transport legal regime is much more difficult than the simple liberalisation and deregulation of market access.

2 International Civil Aviation Organization.
3 World Trade Organization.

2 Multilateralization of international civil aviation relations and defragmentation of international air law

Peter P.C. Haanappel

2.1 Introduction

It is characteristic of economic regulation in air transport that it never lent itself to easy agreement between states. North *versus* South, East *versus* West, rich *versus* poor, large *versus* small, traffic generating *versus* traffic receiving, domestic air transport *versus* international. All these factors play a role in determining the policy of individual states and their airlines, even in a world where, on the whole, affluence is increasing and free market doctrines seem to win over other theories.

That is one thing, a pragmatic one. On top of that, or underneath it, are economic doctrines: the public utility doctrine, the regulated industry doctrine, the deregulation doctrine, the liberalization doctrine. Or more generally: free market doctrines as opposed to socialist, centrally planned economy doctrines. This is perhaps best seen through the history of national, bilateral and multilateral economic regulation of air transport.

That is, therefore, the reason that this chapter starts with a historical survey of its topic, followed by a piece of economic theory, further followed by an analysis of what is happening with airline and governmental multilateralization, as defined here. Europe and some other regions will follow as examples. The attention will then turn to the world, with, as centrepiece, the reform of ownership and control of airlines, the quest for global multilateralization,[1] and the concomitant defragmentation,[2] through existing multilateral intergovernmental organizations or otherwise.

1 Multilateralization, as used here, may occur at two levels. First, multilateralization between airlines, because they begin to cooperate in cross-border airline alliances, mergers or takeovers. Second, in the intergovernmental arena, where states may move from bilateral to multilateral or even supranational ASAs. This can happen, amongst other things, to back up their airlines, involved in commercial cooperation or integration.

2 Defragmentation indicates the result of multilateralization where differing national or bilateral rules give way to a more global system of economic regulation of air transport, at the regional, inter-regional, or eventually even the global level.

2.2 History

Three periods are distinguished: from the beginning of commercial air transport at the end of the First World War in 1919 to the end of the Second World War in 1944–1945. Next, the first 30 years after the War, where tremendous growth and progress were accomplished, under a regime of strict governmental economic control of airlines. Finally, from 1975 onwards, the period of deregulation and liberalization of air transport, in which we still find ourselves today. It is noteworthy that the third and last period has now lasted longer than the two other ones! The question in this chapter, with regard to chronology, then remains whether this period will – sooner or later, but rather sooner than later – be replaced by a period of global and stable multilateralism and defragmentation.

2.2.1 1919–1944: the interbellum

Where one consults Wikipedia's list of airlines by foundation date (1909–1929), one sees that some air transport enterprises actually predate the end of the First World War, 1914–1918. Generally, however, one takes the year 1919 and the inauguration of daily air services between Paris and London as the beginning of commercial (international) air transport. The International Air Traffic Association (old or pre-war IATA) was founded in the same year in The Hague. Significantly, again in the same year, international air transport entered the world of multilateral intergovernmental agreements: the conclusion of the Paris Convention of 1919.[3] Articles 1 and 15 thereof made the performance of international air services subject to prior intergovernmental agreement. The same applied to its Spanish language counterpart, the Madrid Convention of 1926.[4] Significantly different was the Havana Convention of 1928.[5] In principle its Article XXI allowed international air services to be developed without prior intergovernmental agreement. The year 1939 and Pan American World Airways (hereafter Pan Am) (1927–1991) heralded the opening of truly regular transatlantic air service. The outbreak of the Second World War in 1939 would soon interrupt that.[6]

The *interbellum* shows no true or predominant economic policy. Most airlines were established as privately-owned and operated enterprises. Only with the great economic depression of the 1930s, did a wave of airline nationalizations begin, especially in Europe. America would never go that way. Postal subsidies, however, in the *interbellum* in the US, made possible the emergence of a solid American domestic air transport market. Prior to the Second World War, both Pan Am and

3 Convention Relating to the Regulation of Aerial Navigation, signed in Paris on 13 October 1919, entered into force on 29 March 1922, 11 LNTS 173.

4 Ibero-American Convention on Air Navigation, signed in Madrid on 1 November 1926, never came into force.

5 Pan American Convention on Commercial Aviation, signed in Havana on 20 February 1928, 129 LNTS 223.

6 See Haanappel 2003, pp. 3–5, 15–17.

German air transport enterprises invested significantly in the South American air transport system. For European countries with colonies on other continents, air transport was an important means of shortening the travel time between the metropolis and its overseas territories. Imperial Airways (1924–1939) in the UK was probably the best example.

The early period also shows some bilateral air services agreements (ASAs), such as in 1913 between Germany and France, which would obviously not have a long life because of the Great War, and in the *interbellum* between Canada ('Paris Convention' territory through Mother country, the UK) and the US ('Havana Convention' territory). There was certainly no tradition of bilateral agreements in the *interbellum*. There were probably quite a few less than formal bilateral arrangements, and direct concessions by governments to foreign airlines.[7]

2.2.2 1945–1975: the regulatory period

Whereas there was little uniformity during the *interbellum*, the regulatory period was highly structured. It was the period of reconstruction, the period of the introduction of jet engine, and the period of the introduction of wide-bodied aircraft. America ruled the international skies, with Pan Am, Trans World Airlines and the major aircraft manufacturers.

The Chicago Convention[8] was, and still is today, the basic regulatory document. Successful as it has always been in the technical, safety and later security fields, it has never meant much in the field of economic regulation. Article 6 makes the conduct of scheduled international air services subject to the consent of states, whether given by multilateral or bilateral agreement, or granted unilaterally.

The Chicago Convention does not address commercial issues such as airline pricing, capacity or routing. The US was actually in favour of free competition in these areas, but its major partner, the UK, was in favour of government regulation. Foreseeing pricing as the major problem area, as early as at the end of 1944, Pan Am took the initiative and proposed to set up a new IATA and to equip that association with Traffic Conferences to discuss and agree upon international air fares and rates, subject to government approval. The model in mind was the one of maritime Shipping Conferences. The new IATA was set up in Havana in April 1945 and established in Montreal soon thereafter, the same city where the International Civil Aviation Organization (ICAO), created by the Chicago Convention, would be housed. The ICAO and IATA were actually co-located in the same building for many years.

The building blocks further moved into place with the adoption by the US and the UK, in February 1946, of a bilateral ASA between themselves – the Bermuda

7 Ibid.

8 Convention on International Civil Aviation, signed in Chicago on 7 December 1944, entered into force on 4 April 1947, ICAO Doc. 7300/9, 15 UNTS 295.

I Agreement,[9] which would deal with routes, capacity and pricing. Airline routing was determined in the agreement itself. Pricing was delegated to IATA, subject to governmental approval. Capacity, that is frequency of flights and the type of aircraft used, was left to airline management to decide.

This system of 'regulated competition', in American thinking, and then transposed upon the international market, consisted in: pricing by industry agreement but subject to governmental approval; freedom of capacity, subject to a number of *ex post facto* controls. The model of Bermuda I was copied in the great majority of bilateral ASAs in the regulatory period, subject to variations in the area of capacity. Significantly, in the Bermuda I Agreement itself, the Americans pledged to immunize the IATA Traffic Conferences from the effect of the US antitrust laws, which they did by immunizing the machinery as such and individual tariff (pricing) agreements coming out of the machinery. The antitrust star was the former US Civil Aeronautics Board (CAB), which did its work admirably well.

Other states at the time did not show much, if any, interest in antitrust matters. The IATA was pretty much an imperfect cartel, in charge of pricing only, but not supply (capacity), subject to government control. The IATA was also arrogant, which would soon become evident in the area of non-scheduled services, charter services and their pricing. During the regulatory period, most IATA member airlines were also fully or majority owned by their governments. A snapshot in the year 1975 showed 88 active IATA member airlines,[10] of which 39 airlines were entirely state-owned, 24 were 50% or more state-owned, four more than 50% privately owned, and 21 were entirely privately owned.[11]

What IATA did not wish to acknowledge and what it did not want to cater for was that, as of the 1960s, there was new money, new wealth, in the Americas and in Western Europe, interested in inexpensive leisure travel. That demand had to be satisfied by charter airlines and charter services of scheduled airlines, outside the structure of the IATA. By 1973, some 50% of intra-European international air traffic (mostly North–South) travelled charter, inclusive of tour charter. In the same year, about one third of transatlantic traffic moved on various charter types, mostly the affinity charter. There was a lot of illegal discounting on IATA tariffs and IATA agency fees came under great strain. In 1975, the IATA's then largest member airline, Pan Am, walked out, leaving the IATA organization in great trouble. After a couple of years, Pan Am came back, but not before IATA had restructured.

9 Agreement between the Government of the United Kingdom and the Government of the United States of America relating to Air Services between their Respective Territories (with Annex), signed in Bermuda on 11 February 1946, entered into force by signature, 3 UNTS 253, UKTS 3 (1946) Cm. 6747.

10 The other 24 being associate (i.e. domestic) member airlines, for a total of 112 member airlines.

11 See Haanappel 2003, pp. 153–155, footnote 8.

In 1978, it became essentially a voluntary, imperfect cartel. Member airlines no longer had to participate in tariff coordination activities.[12]

2.2.3 1975–today: deregulation and liberalization

Whereas charter competition killed off the old regulatory period in the 'international arena', the US 'domestic' situation, the world's largest domestic air transport market, was in a bit of a different situation. There was no large-scale dissatisfaction with US domestic air fares: there was not much choice (basic First, basic Coach and Early Bird – night fares), but successive CAB Domestic Passenger Fare Investigations kept the otherwise distance-based (with distance taper) price levels low, as compared to international scheduled air fares. Dissatisfaction was related to the CAB's lack of willingness to license new domestic carriers and routes. The last significant pre-deregulation domestic entry was the merger of Northeast Airlines with a local Mississippi delta airline, in 1972, into what is now Delta Air Lines. US deregulation of domestic air transport – free entry, free pricing, free exit – took place *de facto* between 1975 and 1978, and *de jure* as of the year 1978 with the Airline Deregulation Act.[13] The year 1978 also heralded the beginning of US international airline deregulation by introducing so-called liberal bilateral ASAs. US domestic and in part US international air transport deregulation was complete in 1984.

It was around that time that air transport liberalization started in Europe with the European Commission's communication to member states in 1984. The first phase of liberalization began in 1986, the third and final one has finished in 1993. Again, free entry for European Community (EC) air carriers, free pricing and free exit. Whereas the European Commission was an ardent advocate of air transport liberalization, European 'flag carriers' were generally not overly enthusiastic. What eventually carried the day in EU air transport liberalization was the maverick role played by low-cost carriers, such as Ryanair and EasyJet.

Both in the US and in Europe antitrust and competition laws played a significant role in air transport deregulation and liberalization. In the US antitrust laws were used to control carrier dominance with high prices at major hub airports, in addition to ensuring that airline mergers and takeovers would not stifle new entry into the industry. In Europe, competition laws were principally used to remove barriers between EU member states in order to create a level playing field in the single market. On both sides of the Atlantic deregulation and liberalization made new air passenger consumer protection necessary, perhaps even more strongly so in Europe than in the

12 More on the regulatory period see Haanappel 1984a, Ch. 2.

13 The Airline Deregulation Act of 1978, Pub. L. 95–504 – 24 October 1978, 92 Stat. 1705.

US, with the name EU Regulation 261/2004[14] having become famous as Europe's most litigated piece of air transport legislation.

Europe has also begun to deregulate, to liberalize, its air transport relations with third countries, but this process is not as advanced as in the case of its counterpart in the US. Nevertheless, important open skies agreements now exist between the EU and such jurisdictions as the US and Canada. The Russian Federation, China and Japan would be important markets for the EU to follow up, along with the large air transport service provision countries on the Arab Peninsula. Single air transport markets between the EU and non-EU Eastern Europe,[15] and between the EU and the Mediterranean basin[16] are also in the making.[17]

2.3 Economic theory and practice

Although practical reasons such as rich *versus* poor, East *versus* West, North *versus* South and large *versus* small have probably played a dominant role in practice, theoretical doctrines cannot be ignored and indeed were not, especially not in North America. Under the Civil Aeronautics Act 1938,[18] and the Federal Aviation Act 1958,[19] and until the Airline Deregulation Act of 1978, a system of 'regulated competition' prevailed in the US, as mentioned before. It also expressed the generally held view that transport, including air transport, was a 'public utility', best performed by a regulated number of suppliers (airlines), under regulatory control (the CAB until 1984), at least with regard to entry and

14 Regulation No. 261/2004/EC of the European Parliament and of the Council of 11 February 2004 establishing common rules on compensation and assistance to passengers in the event of denied boarding and of cancellation or long delay of flights, and repealing Regulation (EEC) No 295/91, OJ L 46, 17.2.2004, pp. 1–8.

15 Multilateral Agreement between the European Community and its Member States, the Republic of Albania, Bosnia and Herzegovina, the Republic of Bulgaria, the Republic of Croatia, the former Yugoslav Republic of Macedonia, the Republic of Iceland, the Republic of Montenegro, the Kingdom of Norway, Romania, the Republic of Serbia and the United Nations Interim Administration Mission in Kosovo on the establishment of a European Common Aviation Area, signed on 5 July 2006 in Luxembourg, entered into force on 1 December 2017, OJ L 285, 16.10.2006, pp. 3–46.

16 Euro–Mediterranean aviation agreement between the European Community and its Member States, of the one part, and the Kingdom of Morocco, of the other part, signed on 12 December 2006 in Brussels, applied provisionally, OJ L 386, 29.12.2006, pp. 57–88; Euro–Mediterranean Aviation Agreement between the European Union and its Member States, of the one part, and the Hashemite Kingdom of Jordan, of the other part, signed on 15 December 2010 in Brussels, applied provisionally OJ L 334, 6.12.2012, pp. 3–30; Euro–Mediterranean Aviation Agreement between the European Union and its Member States, of the one part, and the government of the State of Israel, of the other part, signed on 10 June 2013 in Luxembourg, applied provisionally, OJ L 208, 2.8.2013, pp. 3–67.

17 For more on the liberalization period see Haanappel 2003, Ch. 6, footnote 6.

18 The Civil Aeronautics Act of 1938, Pub. L. 75–706 – 23 June 1938, 52 Stat. 973.

19 The Federal Aviation Act of 1958, Pub. L. 85–726 – 23 August 1958, 72 Stat. 731.

prices. This translated into a system of federal regulatory control of a privately-owned airline industry.

The main architect of US deregulation in air transport was Professor Alfred Kahn of Cornell University, who specialised in industry regulation and deregulation. He did not regard air transport as a public utility and thought it best to leave it as much as possible to free competition. He was appointed chairman of the CAB in 1977, and remained so until the passage of the Airline Deregulation Act one year later. The CAB itself was 'sunsetted' (abolished) in 1984–1985, after a transitional period, and its remaining functions have been transferred to the Department of Transportation (DOT).

But even the US deregulation never firmly answered the question of whether air transport is a regulatory and/or a natural oligopoly industry. The implication hereof will return at the end of this section on economic theory.

In Europe and in other parts of the world public utility notions would never be as pronounced as in the US, principally and probably because, following the great depression of the 1930s, the state-owned or predominantly state-owned 'flag carriers' would become the accepted model in the regulatory period, as already shown. This was even more true for airlines from the former socialist nations of the world and, more generally, from centrally planned economies.

In the end, though, in most countries of the world airline liberalization, if not deregulation, has had a profound influence on the air transport world. Motives have not always been the same. Consumerism and free trade have more often than not been in the forefront, and should be, it is submitted. But liberalization, at least to an extent, can also be the consequence of incoming tourism in certain, often developing nations, being one of the major sources of national income and foreign currency earning power. National security and national prestige may also still be factors to give regulators an extra interest in the airline industry, which normal economic theory would perhaps not warrant.

To conclude: whatever economic theory and practice, whether oligopoly or not, public utility or not, air transport seems to operate best in deregulated and liberalized markets when there is some measure of antitrust/competition law control so as to avoid anticompetitive agreements and practices, especially in the capacity (supply) and pricing fields. Where such agreements or practices are not controlled, there is the risk of under capacity and high prices.

2.4 Airline privatization and multilateralization

Especially in Europe, airline liberalization was often combined with airline privatization, whether total or partial. The biggest privatization was probably that of British Airways in 1987. The airline had been created in 1974 out of a number of airlines, the biggest ones being nationalized British Overseas Airways Corporation and British European Airways. But there are important examples of privatization also outside Europe, such as Air Canada and Qantas (Australia). It seems to be a misconception to say that an airline, in order to be efficient and profitable, needs to be private or privatized. State-owned airlines can very well be profitable, as long as they are run and managed on sound commercial principles. A disadvantage of a state-owned airline is, however, that it may be more easily prone to accusations of state aids and subsidies, whether true or not. Where a state-owned airline may have a commercial disadvantage, is where it wishes to cooperate with an airline from another country, especially where close cooperation is concerned and where the state-owned airline has a corporate structure other than one under general commercial or civil law. In that case, prior privatization may be necessary before international cooperation.

Airline multilateralization is a bit of a difficult concept to grasp. It is probably quite old, if one includes commercial pooling agreements between airlines, that is the joint operation of an air route or air routes by two (or more) carriers, whereby the revenues of the joint operation are divided between the participating airlines, and where, especially later, forms of code-sharing were used between participating airlines. The oldest code-share, however, already goes back to the year 1947, when Air France (AF) and Royal Air Maroc (AT) began to designate their jointly operated flight as AF/AT (AF aircraft) or AT/AF (AT aircraft).

Commercial pooling was frowned upon by the US CAB as being anticompetitive, and seldom or never approved.[20] Although quite common in Europe and other parts of the world, EU competition law authorities began to look unfavourably upon commercial pooling as of the late 1980s. In the early 1990s, round about the two Gulf Wars, multilateralization between airlines entered a new era. That period was characterized by declining traffic and revenues. The same happened in the aftermath of the terrorist events of 11 September 2001, and the world banking crisis of 2008. Airlines reacted by entering into a variety of alliance cooperation agreements, tolerated by US and EC competition law authorities, in a wish to help ailing airlines through difficult periods. Within a decade, at the end of the last century, however, airline alliances, bilateral but especially multilateral, would change the air transport world.

It is not so easy to say what these new inter-airline multilateral agreements were and are. One thing is certain: they stand outside the IATA. But what is their substance, what is their purpose? Initially, the inter-airline agreements dealt with matters of economies of scope and network such as joint advertising, common frequent flyer programmes and joint passenger lounges. They then branched out into matters of scale, route, market access, through code-sharing agreements, blocked space agreements and soon also joint venture agreements.

It is probably helpful to try to delineate general alliance agreements and more specific joint venture agreements. Although there are no official definitions, it seems, it is proposed to reserve the expression 'joint venture agreement' for a bilateral or multilateral arrangement between participating carriers where agreements are made that would normally require antitrust/competition law approval, whether such

20 An exception was the commercial agreement between Pan Am and Aeroflot. This agreement was necessitated by politics when services between Moscow and New York started. See Haanappel 2003, p. 128, footnote 104.

control is exercised in fact or not: agreements on division of markets, on capacity/frequency/type of aircraft and, very importantly, on pricing. In fact, joint ventures have a lot in common with 'old fashioned' commercial pooling agreements and have come under criticism for the same reason: too much restriction of competition, to the (potential) detriment of the aviation consumer, the user, in respect of choice of carrier, frequency of service and pricing.[21]

Oligopoly or not, there have been a lot of mergers, takeovers and worldwide airline alliances. In the US, unhindered by special rules on national ownership and control of airlines, to which this chapter will have to revert later, airline concentration has led to the creation of three large legacy or network carriers, in alphabetical order American, Delta and United. Outside the US, and exactly because of national ownership and control requirements, worldwide alliances have been created. The three largest now are: Star Alliance, created in 1997, with Lufthansa and United as main carriers; Oneworld, created in 1999, with American and British Airways as main carriers; and SkyTeam, created in 2000, with Air France-KLM and Delta as main carriers. All three are worldwide; all three have European and American carriers as main participants. It should also be noted that British Airways operates within the International Airline Group (IAG), created in 2011, along with, amongst others, Iberia of Spain and Aer Lingus of Ireland. Air France and KLM operate as working companies of the holding company Air France-KLM SA, created in 2004. The Lufthansa Group, finally, owns quite a few formerly independent European air carriers, now owned by the Group, such as Austrian, Brussels and Swiss International Airlines (still operating under their own names).

All in all, there are now three levels of multilateralization: domestic mergers and takeovers such as in America;[22] international alliances such as Star; and international (financial) holding companies such as IAG and Air France-KLM SA. The foregoing is a lot of multilateralization of airlines, concomitant, outside the US, with multinationalization of airlines, all of which would not have been possible without the support of governments, which leads us into the next subject.[23]

2.5 Intergovernmental multilateralization

2.5.1 The United States

As of the year 1991, the US government, recognizing the poor financial health of Northwest Airlines, allowed its European partner airline, KLM, to acquire 49% of the equity stock in Northwest, instead of the statutory limit of 25%, provided that

21 For more on inter-airline cooperative arrangements and their legal status see Chapter 5 of this book.

22 For a European example in the 1990s: the Groupe Air France consisting of Compagnie Nationale Air France, Union des Transports Aériens (UTA; privately owned French international airline, incorporated into the Groupe); Air Inter (publicly owned French domestic airline, incorporated into the Groupe).

23 For airline alliances see also Chapters 3 and 4 of this book.

no more than 25 of the 49% were voting stock. In addition, the US and the Netherlands entered into the first US open skies agreement in 1992, specifically allowing cooperative marketing agreements between designated airlines, such as in the then existing Wings alliance, a predecessor of the aforementioned Sky-Team. The joint venture agreement between KLM and Northwest received antitrust approval from the US DOT in 1993.[24]

In this way, the following system has emerged as a governmental policy in the US, without changing basic aviation or antitrust law, but thereby favouring multilateralization of airlines: provided that there is an open skies agreement in force with open entry into US-foreign markets, a broad array of marketing agreements between US and foreign carriers is allowed; foreign investment in US airlines may go up to 25% of voting stock and up to 49% of equity stock; joint venture agreements may be approved by the DOT so as to immunize them from the antitrust laws; in the case of pricing agreements in joint ventures, participating airlines may then not participate in IATA tariff coordination and intra-alliance pricing at the same time.[25]

Where the US has been less flexible, as the following will show, is in changes in national ownership and control rules beyond the already mentioned maximum of 49% equity stock. Similarly, the US is not showing signs of wishing to abandon the system of bilateral ASAs in favour of a global multilateral ASA. The US–EU open skies agreement of 2007/2010 is essentially, at least economically, a bilateral agreement between the single largest aviation country and the single largest economic block in the world.[26]

2.5.2 The European Union

Whereas the US, in the area of intergovernmental multilateralization, seems to have acted principally with the interests of its airlines and air transport users in mind, the emphasis in the EU and associated bodies, such as the European Economic Area (EEA), seems to have been somewhat different in the sense that Europe's political and economic unification was the principal motive, the 'level playing field' already alluded to earlier in the context of Section 2.3 of this chapter.

24 See Chapter 3 of this book. See also Haanappel 2003, pp. 147–149, 285.
25 Ibid. For the DOT policy toward airline alliances see also Chapter 4 of this book.
26 To date, the UK belongs to that block. The EU and its single air transport market, with its own external air transport relations, seemed pretty stable until Brexit came along in 2016. There is risk that EU air carriers may lose their rights to perform stand-alone air services between the UK and the US, unless there is some new tripartite deal between the EU, the UK and the US; obviously the same would apply to any current stand-alone services of UK airlines from points on the continent to the US. At this point in time, it is too early to tell how the EU and the UK will negotiate some new air transport deal before March 2019, if at all. This chapter will give some more examples of possible fragmentation, disintegration of the current EU air transport regime after Brexit.

Concretely, in the context of the third and final EU air transport liberalization package of 1993,[27] the Community or EU air carrier concept was adopted.[28] Such an air carrier must have its principal place of business in an EU/EEA state that has licensed it according to common European criteria, and it must be more than 50% owned and effectively controlled by one or more EU/EEA states and/or by their nationals.[29]

This has, perhaps indirectly, made the multilateral, multinational European carrier possible. The aforementioned Lufthansa Group, with fully Lufthansa-owned carriers such as Austrian, Brussels and Swiss International Airlines in it, is perhaps the best example. Lufthansa, the largest carrier in the group, can then, again as an example, have alliance agreements within the Star Alliance, inside Europe, with or without code-sharing,[30] or outside Europe.[31]

2.5.3 Elsewhere

Elsewhere in the world governments have also been busy creating multilateral agreements or arrangements for their carriers. What they seem to miss is the political and economic power of the US, or the institutional power of the EU. This chapter cannot contain a full survey of such agreements or arrangements throughout the world. Two examples will suffice to show two different tendencies: The Association of South East Asian Nations (ASEAN) Single Aviation Market came into force, on paper, in 2015/2016, and is also a potential partner for the EU in a collective, comprehensive ASA. Except that, little or nothing seems to be happening in practice: ASEAN carriers do not seem interested in multilateralizing or multinationalization, probably because there is still enough internal growth within individual carriers in the region.[32]

On the other end of the spectrum, there is South America with the success story of LATAM. Inter-airline cooperation and multilateralization were urgently needed in the market in order to survive commercially. Chile's LAN and Brazil's TAM Airlines decided to merge in the period of 2010–2012. They did so subject to the necessary governmental approvals and agreements, which only started to come out in the period of 2011–2013. Now, five years later, by the beginning of 2018, a whole web of agreements and arrangements is in place to sustain the multinational, multilateral LATAM, with principal hubs in Brazil, Colombia and Chile, and with no less than ten subsidiary airlines in various South American

27 See also Section 2.2.3.

28 See consolidating Regulation No. 1008/2008/EC of the European Parliament and of the Council of 24 September 2008 on common rules for the operation of air services in the Community, OJ L 293, 31.10.2008, pp. 3–20.

29 For airline ownership and control in the EU see Chapter 11 of this book.

30 For example, without code-sharing with SAS, with code-sharing with LOT.

31 For the full list of Star Alliance see www.staralliance.com/en/member-airlines.

32 But see, almost as a repeat exercise, ASEAN 2017. A similar problem may be observed in the Arab region. See Chapter 13 of this book.

countries. The LATAM Airlines Group is the holding company of the multilateral structure and is based and incorporated in Chile.

2.6 Ownership and control of airlines

With the exception perhaps of the US, multilateralization has not yet led to great defragmentation of a divided global air transport market, and that is probably because no basic reform has yet been adopted in the area of national ownership and control of airlines.

There is a rather cynical expression in air transport circles that 'an alliance is a poor man's merger'. What is meant is that in cross-border, multinational arrangements between airlines, full mergers and takeovers are legally impossible or at least very difficult because of multilateral, bilateral or national requirements that a designated airline be substantially owned (usually more than 50%) and effectively controlled by the designating state or its citizens. In Europe this has changed through the above-mentioned liberalization with its Community air carrier concept,[33] but that does not bind third countries, unless there is a so-called 'horizontal' agreement in force between the EU and the third country in question.

The point is that full scale mergers and takeovers are 'final' and 'complete', once approved, if necessary, by transport, competition and/or antitrust authorities, whereas alliances are inherently unstable: they can fall apart, they may be subject to periodical antitrust/competition law review. The best one can reach in this situation today is the multinational financial holding company concept, such as the aforementioned Air France-KLM SA or the IAG.[34]

In various quarters proposals for change have been made or *ad hoc* accommodations found, in a period of now some 30 years. The most authoritative proposal has, it seems, been made by the European Civil Aviation Conference (ECAC), early this century: a designated airline must be incorporated in the designating country and have its principal place of business in that country.[35]

But, is even the foregoing ECAC proposal too 'stringent', too restraining for airlines that want to be truly global and multinational? Should either 'incorporation' or 'principal place of business' suffice as criterion, and what if there are in fact several principal places of business? And again: if one looks at the above-described LATAM, what if only the country of incorporation seems to count for the corporate structure of the whole LATAM Airlines Group?

33 This rule will also be affected by Brexit. Ryanair, an Irish air carrier, which is currently the largest airline at London's Stansted Airport may lose the right to fly to EU destinations from Stansted, except if it becomes British; EasyJet, a UK carrier, may lose its hubs on the European continent from which it performs domestic or international continental air services, unless there is some kind of new deal on the right of UK carriers to establish themselves in the EU.

34 However, after Brexit the IAG may no longer be a comfortable home as holding company for British Airways (UK's largest carrier) and EU airlines.

35 See Haanappel 2003, pp. 145–151.

And in order to give another example of the complexity of ownership and control of airlines: in September 2017, Delta Air Lines, Air France-KLM SA, China Eastern and Virgin Atlantic announced a billion-dollar mega transaction whereby Delta and China Eastern each purchase 10% of AF-KLM SA (new capital), and whereby AF-KLM SA purchases 31% of Virgin (in which Delta already own 49%).[36] Virgin Atlantic thereby becomes 80% non-British owned, of which nevertheless 51% is in EU hands (Franco–Dutch and British, it seems).[37]

2.7 Global reform

The question may be legitimately asked whether the entire system of bilateral ASAs ought not to be abandoned or seriously reformed to accommodate multilateralism in air transport through multinationalization of air carriers. Can ICAO be instrumental here, or the World Trade Organization (WTO)?[38]

2.7.1 The International Civil Aviation Organization (ICAO)

ICAO's principal vocation has no doubt been in the area of safety and security of (international) civil aviation, but it has also done work, mostly studies and conferences, in the commercial arena, especially between 1944 and 1947, and since 1974, with the Special or First (Worldwide) Air Transport Conference in 1977. There have now been a total of six Worldwide Air Transport Conferences, the last one in the year 2013. Ownership and control of airlines is high on ICAO's agenda, especially since the last Conference in 2013, but concrete worldwide agreement is hard to reach, given the already noted policy divergences between the states of this world.[39] However, it is interesting to see in ICAO's guidance materials a recommended Template Air Services Agreement, which, in its 'full liberalization option', makes air carrier designation only subject to 'effective regulatory control' by the designating state, which, according to the commentary, means safety and security control.

36 See Zhang 2017.

37 Provided that Brexit does not disturb the equation in 2019. After Brexit, Virgin Atlantic, some 80% owned by Delta Air Lines and Air France-KLM, and today 51% owned and controlled by EU interests (Franco–Dutch and British), as permitted by the EU–US open skies agreement, would no longer be 'British' enough to operate under a new UK–US agreement if that agreement requires more than 50% British 'content'.

38 It should be noted that two other intergovernmental organizations have shown an interest in restructuring the regulatory framework, within which international air transport operates: United Nations Conference on Trade and Development for the developing nations, and Organisation for Economic Co-operation and Development for the all-cargo air market. See Haanappel 2003, pp. 151–153.

39 See *Air Carrier Ownership and Control Clauses in Bilateral Air Services Agreements, (presented by Ireland on behalf of the EU and ECAC)*, ICAO AT Conf/6-WP/49, 14.2.2013; *Outcome of the Sixth Worldwide Air Transport Conference (Presented by the Council of ICAO)*, ICAO A38-WP/56, EC/6, 31.7.2013.

But then, does the ICAO analysis, quite understandably by the way, still take as a starting point the existing, mostly bilateral practice of airline designation? Does this help multinational multilateralization of airlines adequately, whilst at the same time defragmenting the old bilateral and regional regulatory systems enough in favour of a single system? Or should one, for that purpose, turn to a single, multilateral solution within the WTO? If none of the two, ICAO and WTO, work, one, that is states and airlines in co-operation, can always turn to more or less *ad hoc* plurilateral arrangements, of which LATAM seems to be a good example. But let's first look at the WTO.[40]

2.7.2 The World Trade Organization (WTO)

In the mid-1990s, WTO, the successor to the GATT[41] Secretariat, sponsored the General Agreement on Trade in Services (GATS) of the year 1994.[42] Air transport is governed by a special Annex to GATS. The general rules of GATS apply to air transport, unless the Annex on Air Transport Services excludes this, which is more often the case than not. Notably GATS does not apply to the exchange of traffic (route) rights, at least not for the time being. The Annex applies to three distinct areas only, not of much interest to this chapter: aircraft repair and maintenance (off-line), computerized reservation systems (CRS) and the marketing (but not pricing) of air transport services.[43]

It is submitted that applying GATS more broadly to air transport than is the case now would promote multilateralization and multinationalization of international air transport, whilst at the same time helping defragmentation. International trade law, including WTO/GATT/GATS matters, is a highly specialised area going beyond the scope of this chapter. However, it seems that the following Articles in the GATS could be of assistance: Article II on the Most-Favoured-Nation (MFN) Clause, Article VIII on Monopolies and Exclusive

40 Although ICAO itself and its Assemblies and Worldwide Air Transport Conferences are of the opinion that ICAO is the preferred forum for matters of (commercial) international air transport.

41 General Agreement on Tariffs and Trade, signed in Geneva on 30 October 1947, applied provisionally since 1 January 1948, 55 UNTS 194, incorporated in the General Agreement on Tariffs and Trade part of the Multilateral Agreements on Trade in Goods – Annex 1A of the Marrakesh Agreement Establishing the World Trade Organization, done in Marrakesh on 15 April 1994, entered into force on 1 January 1995, 1867 UNTS 187. GATT applies to trade in goods (as opposed to services). GATT is relevant to air cargo transport. In February 2017 WTO Agreement on Trade Facilitation entered into force (as a part of the Multilateral Agreements on Trade in Goods – Annex 1A of the Marrakesh Agreement Establishing the World Trade Organization). This agreement applies to air cargo services and, amongst other things, allows e-payments and electronic documentation.

42 General Agreement on Trade in Services – Annex 1B of the Marrakesh Agreement Establishing the World Trade Organization, done in Marrakesh on 15 April 1994, entered into force on 1 January 1995, 1869 UNTS 183.

43 See Haanappel 2003, pp. 151–153.

Service Providers, Article X on Emergency Safety Measures and Article XIV*bis* on Security Exceptions,[44] Article XV on Subsidies,[45] Article XVI on Market Access, Article XVII on National Treatment, Articles XIX–XXI on Progressive Liberalisation, and Article XXIII on Dispute Settlement and Enforcement.[46] The application of these GATS Articles to air transport would also have to cater, someway, to national security concerns (Article XIV*bis*), safeguards (Articles XIX–XXI) and essential or public service obligations (Article VIII, it seems).

Multilateral, multinational airlines could possibly function more easily in this system than in the present one, with nationality of the airline residing in its country of incorporation, which would then also be responsible for safety and security under the Chicago/ICAO system, possibly combined with the option to delegate the safety/security functions to another ICAO member state – but this option would have to be examined in much greater detail than this chapter allows.[47] Such a system would perhaps also fit in well with the full liberalization option in the Template Air Services Agreement, developed by ICAO and briefly described earlier.

All this does not seem to be for the future. The GATS Annex on Air Transport Services is now more than 20 years old; it has been periodically reviewed but not modified. On the one hand, as the approximately 120-member GATS is still growing, it should perhaps apply increasingly to air transport services. On the other hand, there are some important hold outs such as the US, which still often thinks that bilateral trade agreements serve its interests better than multilateral ones and that, because of internal size, national companies do not necessarily have to expand into multilateral, multinational ones. Time will tell.

2.8 Conclusions and prospects for multilateralization and defragmentation

The term 'multilateralization' has had two meanings in this text: inter-airline and intergovernmental. In addition, the term 'multinationalization' has been added, indicating inter-airline multilateralization at the multinational level, whether leading to a merger or takeover between airlines of different nationalities (a rarity because of

44 Possibly reflecting the safety and national security concerns that international air transport tends to raise.

45 Perhaps helping to solve the perennial problem of subsidies and state aids in the air transport sector. See, for example, *Proposal for a Regulation of the European Parliament and of the Council on safeguarding competition in air transport, repealing Regulation (EC) No 868/2004*, COM(2017)289 final, 8.6.2017.

46 Hopefully, as in the case of aircraft manufacturing, being more efficient than the dispute settlement provisions in Articles 84–88 of the Chicago Convention or in bilateral ASAs.

47 One complication is that safety and security of an airline should not be confused with the safety and security of an aircraft and its personnel: the former would depend on the country of incorporation of the airline; the latter on the country of the nationality of the aircraft (including the possible application of Article 83*bis* of the Chicago Convention). See also Chapter 10 of this book.

national ownership and effective control clauses) or to a variety of international airline alliances.

There is evidence that inter-airline multilateralization has the better chance of producing practical results than intergovernmental multilateralization, with the notable exception of the EU. Intergovernmental multilateralization, however, can fulfil an important supporting role, in order to create the regulatory climate and framework within which inter-airline multilateralization can function. Absent such intergovernmental multilateralization, states and airlines may have recourse to plurilateralism (plurilateral instead of bilateral agreements) or simply to taking an inter-airline multinational initiative and letting the (inter)governmental multilateralization follow, hopefully.

There is also evidence that multilateralization, at the two levels, leads to defragmentation in the sense of a reduction in bilateral agreements in favour of fewer multilateral or supranational, or for that matter plurilateral, agreements, but, to date, that has not gone further than the regional level. Defragmentation towards the global level, one agreement, real unification of economic regulation of air transport in the world, can, it seems, only be solved through a solution for the airline ownership and control issue, at the ICAO or WTO level, or absent that through state practice.

It is to be noted that a move away from bilateral agreements towards an eventual single multilateral agreement does not include unification of national transportation and antitrust/competition laws. Unification of competition and antitrust laws would be particularly difficult. All that one may expect is conformity between national laws and the new, single international law. At any rate, such single international law is still a while away, because not all states are ready for it.[48]

A little bit more with regard to detail: there seems to be evidence that inter-airline multilateralization and multinationalization do not necessarily require airline privatization. National corporate or company laws governing state-owned airlines may, however, need to be adjusted to fit into different forms of multinational inter-airline cooperation.

As far as the application of transportation, consumer and antitrust/competition law is concerned, it seems that so-called joint venture agreements are the boundary beyond which competition/antitrust law begins to fulfil a dominant role. This would also seem to apply to agreements creating financial holding companies within which airlines operate.

Finally, as long as there is not a stable worldwide agreement leading to defragmentation to the detriment of a system of divided national, bilateral or multilateral regimes, there is the risk of disintegration. Let Brexit serve as an example.

48 For international harmonization of competition regimes see Chapter 3 of this book.

Part 2

Balancing air policy and fair competition in international air transport

The second part of the book will be devoted to the troublesome relationship between public policy goals arising from air services agreements and national competition law regimes. The conflict between economic regulation and competition policy will be explained, as well as possible discrepancies between the competition regimes themselves. This will be illustrated based on airline and governmental viewpoints. The first perspective will include a discussion of limitations on airline international cooperative arrangements laid down in market access regulations and competition laws and will indicate that these activities may be treated differently in various competition law systems. The government point of view will refer to the EU competition policy as applied in its external aviation relations, a particularly representative case, given the fact that Brussels creates fair competition and a level playing field with its prerequisites for third-party market opening. This part will also search for harmonised solutions that would provide a proper balance between competition policies and air transport law.

3 Airlines as allies

How to manage the market?

Pablo Mendes de Leon

3.1 The trend towards international alliances

The formation of international alliances is a trend pertaining to deregulation and liberalisation of aviation policies, and of privatisation of airlines and other parties involved in international civil aviation at national, regional, trans-regional and global levels. Hence, international alliances are seen as a direct consequence of these movements.

The nature of cooperative agreements including alliances and joint ventures is diverse: it may vary from 'simple' interline agreements and joint frequent flyer programmes, to the joint operation of catering and maintenance services, joint purchasing, schedule coordination, revenue sharing, fuel and insurance pooling agreements, blocked space agreements, code-sharing, franchising, equity investments and exchange of management board members.

The establishment of an alliance consists in the maintenance of two separate companies that share their core strengths with each other. A joint venture is a legal partnership between two or more companies pursuant to which they create a new entity for competitive advantage. Mergers and acquisitions involve a more intensive partnership between two companies as they decide to set up a single new company rather than remain separately owned and operated. Even if international cooperation in air transport is not as strong as in other sectors, alliances may cause anti-competitive effects under applicable competition regimes. With the exception of the special case of the EU, international mergers are difficult to achieve under the present regulatory regime.

The present contribution will pay attention to significant aviation cases and assess the relations between competition and trade. Next, the kind of conduct of airlines that is liable to produce anti-competitive effects will be examined. This section will be followed by an analysis of competition regimes. The last part looks at possible solutions for the lack of coherence of competition law and policies, and is designed to promote cooperation between competition authorities and convergence of competition law regimes, with special reference to the cross-border nature of air transport. Progress will be anticipated realistically, considering the prevailing trade interests and the jurisdictional powers.

3.2 The first significant case: KLM–Northwest airlines

The move towards more comprehensive airline cooperation was set in 1993 by the Wings alliance between KLM Royal Dutch Airlines (KLM) and Northwest Airlines. The alliance was judged by the US and Dutch governments who permitted the airlines in question to exclude competition among them. Charged with the task to investigate anti-competitive effects of agreements between airlines that affect international air transport, the US Department of Transportation (DOT) granted an antitrust immunity. The European Commission did not take any action because at the time it did not have competence in external aviation relations.

In 1989 KLM had acquired a non-voting share of 56.74% and less than 5% voting interest in – then ailing – Northwest Airlines. Moreover, KLM was entitled to nominate one out of twelve board members of Northwest Airlines, as well as to advise its US partner on financial matters through a special committee. Thus, the legal requirements of US citizenship had been met, because KLM owned less than the statutory 25% of Northwest Airlines' voting stock and appointed less than one third of its directors.

However, DOT was so concerned with the many institutional links between the two airlines that KLM's control of Northwest Airlines was judged to be more effective than it would seem on the basis of the facts and figures relating to the arrangement. DOT persuaded the holding company of Northwest Airlines and KLM to overcome DOT's concerns. After KLM reduced its investment in Wings alliance, the three parties agreed terms.[1]

The DOT's decision held that foreign equity in the airline could not be more than 49% and that voting shares could not exceed 25%.[2] The DOT applied a control test, which required that the airline remain under the authority of US citizens. The DOT has seen 'no potential for the foreign interest represented by KLM to exert control, given the structure of these corporate mechanisms and the remaining restrictions retained in this order.'[3]

Since the DOT examines airline transactions on a case-by-case basis, it looks at other factors in addition to the 'control' test. An important consideration is the aviation relationship between the US and the home country of the foreign airline. For instance, in the case of the KLM–Northwest Airlines alliance the DOT expressed that it had 'reached these decisions in the context of the liberalised aviation relationship that prevails between the United States and KLM's homeland.'[4]

Indeed, this liberalised environment was based on the first air transport agreement between the Netherlands and the US of 1957.[5] Under it, the US designated carriers

1 *Acquisition of Northwest Airlines by Wings Holdings, Inc.*, DOT Order No. 89-9-51 (1989).

2 Ibid. §§21–22.

3 Ibid. §18.

4 Ibid.

5 Air Transport Agreement between the Government of the United States of America and the Government of the Kingdom of the Netherlands, signed in Washington on 3 April 1957, provisionally applied by signature, 410 UNTS 193.

enjoyed unlimited market access opportunities. In 1978, a Protocol amended the agreement of 1957.[6] This Protocol was concluded only one year after the conclusion of the restrictive Bermuda II Agreement between the US and the UK.[7] The US was looking for an 'ally' to shape a more competitive international air policy, reversing the restrictive policy underlying the Bermuda II Agreement.[8] This goal was in part achieved. However, the Protocol of 1978 formed an open-ended compromise, which was designed to be further liberalised in the years between 1978 and 1992 when the very first 'open skies' agreement was concluded between these two countries.[9] This agreement also yielded an effect on the second competition case involving KLM and Northwest Airlines. Thus, the Netherlands–US open skies agreement of 1992 is not a new agreement. The previous agreements encompassed the substantive conditions on which the agreement of 1992 could be concluded.[10]

The KLM and Northwest Airlines venture not only raised nationality questions but also antitrust and competition concerns. The two carriers had decided to expand their commercial relationship by engaging in joint selling and marketing, joint scheduling of flights, coordination of pricing, joint baggage handling and combining logos so as to promote a single identity for the two carriers to the public. The potential antitrust issues resulting from the joint ventures between KLM and Northwest Airlines were resolved in the context of the mentioned open skies agreement of 1992.

The aforementioned cases involving carriers from different sides of the Atlantic Ocean demonstrate the intrinsic relation between government policy including trade and aviation policy, on the one hand, and the way competition is handled in an air transport market. Section 3.3 will concisely explain this relation.

3.3 Competition and trade in air transport

Clearly, airline behaviour may affect competition. However, government actions may also influence airline competition, but such behaviour is connected with the broader subject of trade policy and regulation. Examples of such government behaviour are state aid, grant of antitrust immunity, taxation or exemption of

6 Protocol relating to the Air Transport Agreement between the Government of the United States of America and the Government of the Kingdom of the Netherlands of 1957, as amended, signed at Washington on 31 March 1978, entered into force by signature, 1123 UNTS 345.

7 Agreement between the Government of the United States of America and the Government of the United Kingdom of Great Britain and Northern Ireland concerning Air Services (with Annexes and Exchange of letters), signed in Bermuda on 23 July 1977 ('Bermuda II Agreement'), entered into force by signature, 1079 UNTS 21.

8 See Wassenbergh 1978, pp. 160–161.

9 Agreement between the United States of America and the Netherlands amending the Air Transport Agreement of 3 April 1957 and the Protocol of 31 March 1978, as amended, signed in the Hague on 14 September 1992, entered into force on 11 May 1993, 2246 UNTS 169.

10 See *Memorandum of Consultations concerning the US-NL Open Skies Agreement*, 1992. See also §12 of this Agreement – 'Airlines of both countries can fly from any point in either country to any point in the other, via any intermediate point, and beyond to any point.'

taxation, and the question of foreign ownership and control limitations. Those issues are not examined in this section.

However, competition and trade are closely related in that they have similar objectives of raising standards of living, the volume of real income and effective demand, promoting efficient use of economic resources, opening markets and maximising consumer choice. Consequently, it may be questioned whether a certain dispute falls under a competition or a trade regime. Again, the quest for a solution to this question may be inspired by political rather than legal motives.

That said, this chapter principally focuses on market behaviour in relation to competition. Before paying attention to competition law regimes, airline behaviour that may be subject to such regimes will be identified in Section 3.4.

3.4 Airline behaviour affecting competition

For the present purpose, two types of airline behaviour must be distinguished: the cooperative agreements and unilateral conduct involving the abuse of a dominant position.

Cooperative agreements, designed to achieve fleet rationalisation and network efficiencies, are widespread among airlines; they form an essential part of airline operations and are used as an instrument of cost reduction and risk spreading. Cooperation between airlines includes but is not limited to: consultation on and coordination of tariffs, joint operations, including pooling of services and capacity, interline agreements, route planning, fleet rationalisation, including code-sharing, blocked space agreements and similar mechanisms, coordination of schedules, joint frequent flyer programmes, Global Distribution Systems (GDSs) formerly known as Computerised Reservation Systems (CRSs), airport scheduling and slot allocation. A number of these coordinated and concerted activities were exempted under the former EU competition regime, but those exemptions have been lifted.[11]

The problem of abuse of dominant position is also relevant in the air transport sector. Obviously, many airlines, especially 'flag carriers,' have inherited their dominant positions from the traditional regulatory and policy regime. Dominance may lead to abuse, that is, monopolisation and predatory behaviour. This may occur especially in the areas of scheduling, pricing, capacity (dumping), slots and GDSs. However, no case law has yet been made on 'flag carriers' abusing their dominant position. Meanwhile, 'flag carriers' are not so dominant anymore due to the rise of low-cost carriers and the liberalisation of international markets, which allow for multiple entry.

The above-mentioned practices have been and are scrutinised under competition law regimes of various jurisdictions. Section 3.5 will concisely elaborate on the application of these regimes to international air services.

11 This will be further explained in Section 3.5.2. For this issue see also Chapter 5 of this book.

3.5 Competition regimes in air transport

National legislation is not the most convenient basis for handling competition in international air transport. In international trade, national competition regimes lead to problems such extra-territorial application of national law, uncertainty about competence, lack of transparency regarding the applicable rules, conflicts of jurisdiction, long lasting procedures and, last but not least, high costs for the parties involved.[12]

Until the end of the 1970s, national competition laws, if present at all, were not, or at best were not scarcely, applied to domestic and international air transport. Air transport was seen as a public utility, which should not be made subject to market forces. Moreover, this is explained by the choice in favour of protectionism rather than facilitating competition.

3.5.1 The US law and policy

The first changes at the national level occurred in the US with the introduction of the Airline Deregulation Act of 1978[13] and the International Air Transport Competition Act of 1979.[14] The latter statute has been designed 'to amend the Federal Aviation Act of 1958 in order to promote competition in international air transportation, provide greater opportunities for United States carriers, establish goals for developing United States international aviation negotiating policy, and for other purposes.'

However, at that time no 'greater opportunities' were created for foreign air carriers in order to promote the availability of a variety of adequate, economic, efficient, and low price services by air carriers and foreign air carriers without unjust discrimination, undue preferences or advantages, or unfair or deceptive practices, the need to improve relations among, and in coordination by, air carriers.[15] Although, this has changed with the introduction of the open skies policy and the implementation of the ASAs following it.

The US DOT has the power to exclude from the application of antitrust laws, that is, principally, the Sherman Act[16] and the Clayton Act,[17] certain behaviour, including unfair methods of competition or unjust or deceptive acts in air transportation or the sale of air transportation.[18] Exemptions must be justified on the grounds of public interest. Joint venture agreements must be submitted to the DOT for assessment under antitrust laws.[19]

12 These frictions will be alluded to in Section 3.6 below.

13 The Airline Deregulation Act of 1978, Pub. L. 95–504 – 24 October 1978, 92 Stat. 1705.

14 The International Air Transport Competition Act of 1979, Pub. L. 96–192 – 15 February 1980, 94 Stat. 35.

15 Cf. 49 USC 40101(a).

16 The Sherman Antitrust Act of 2 July 1890, Ch. 647, 26 Stat. 209; 15 USC 1 et seq.

17 The Clayton Antitrust Act of 15 October 1914, Ch. 323, 38 Stat. 730; 15 USC 12 et seq.

18 See 49 USC 41308.

19 49 USC 41720. For more on the US antitrust law and policy in air transport see Chapter 4 of this book.

3.5.2 The EU regime

Following US deregulation and decisions rendered by the European Court of Justice (ECJ), now Court of Justice of the EU (CJEU) in the well-known *Nouvelles Frontières*[20] and *Saeed* cases,[21] the – then – European Economic Community (EEC) Transport Council decided to integrate the European air transport market, including the European Economic Area (EEA). A single competition regime was to be applied to air transport within the EEC. This regime has been designed to prevail over national competition legislation and bilateral competition clauses.[22]

The application of the EU competition regime, with special reference to Articles 101 and 102 of the Treaty on the Functioning of the European Union (TFEU),[23] is monitored by the European Commission. The investigations under Article 101 TFEU include the cooperative arrangements between airlines, in particular the formation of airline alliances. The Commission has published myriad decisions in this field.[24]

The alleged anti-competitive conduct has to be determined in relation to a particular relevant market. This market has been divided into two categories: the relevant product, or in this case air services market, and the geographic market. The geographic market has been defined as 'an area where the objective conditions of competition applying to the product in question are the same for all traders.'[25] The above-mentioned concepts have been fine-tuned by the European Commission and the CJEU in case law where they have distinguished between business/time sensitive and leisure/price sensitive passengers in relation to the behaviour of airlines on these markets.

If needed, airlines participating in an alliance are requested to remedy their potentially anti-competitive behaviour by surrendering slots at hub airports, freezing capacity and/or fares and granting interline opportunities to new

20 *Ministère Public v. Lucas Asjes and Others*, ECJ judgment of 30 April 1986, Cases C-209–213/84.

21 *Ahmed Saeed Flugreisen and Silver Line Reisebüro v. Zentrale zur Bekämpfung unlautern Wettbewerb E.V.*, ECJ judgment of 11 April 1989, Case 66/86.

22 For bilateral competition clauses see Section 3.6.

23 Treaty on the Functioning of the European Union (TFEU), signed on 25 March 1957 in Rome, entered into force on 1 January 1958 (then Treaty establishing the European Economic Community, later Treaty establishing the European Economic Community, consolidated version OJ C 202, 7.6.2016, pp. 47–199.

24 See, for instance, Commission notice of 30 October 2002 concerning the alliance between Lufthansa, SAS and United Airlines (cases COMP/D-2/36.201, 36.076, 36.078 – procedure under Article 85 of the Treaty (ex Article 89)) (Text with EEA relevance), OJ C 264, 30.10.2002, pp. 5–9; Commission notice of 30 October 2002 concerning the Alliance between KLM Royal Dutch Airlines and Northwest Airlines, Inc., (case COMP/D-2/36.111 – procedure under Article 85 (ex Article 89) of the EC Treaty), OJ C 264, 30.10.2002, p. 11. See also: Mohan 2014 and Milligan 2017.

25 See *United Brands v. Commission of the European Communities*, ECJ judgment of 14 February 1978, Case 27/76.

entrants. Generally speaking, the European Commission supports consolidation, with due regard for global developments in this field.

The anti-competitive effects of alliance agreements must now be self-assessed by airlines pursuant to EU law.[26] Regulation 1/2003[27] as amended by Regulation 411/2004[28] extends the EU competition rules to air transport between the EU and third countries.[29] As a result, the European Commission has enforcement powers concerning air services between points in the EU and points outside the EU. The Commission may, thus, wish to invoke the 'effects' doctrine.[30] Consequently, all airline behaviour, including the operation of air transport services between the EU and third countries,[31] falls under the scope of EU competition law. No exemptions currently apply.

There is little case law applying Article 102 TFEU on the abuse of a dominant position in the relevant market to air transport services. Dominance per se is not prohibited; its abuse is. According to the CJEU, abuse is an 'objective concept.'[32] In one case, namely, *British Midland v. Aer Lingus*,[33] the Commission found that Aer Lingus had infringed, mainly, Article 82 of the Treaty establishing the

26 See Simon 2014.

27 Regulation No. 1/2003/EC of the Council of 16 December 2002 on the implementation of the rules on competition laid down in Articles 81 and 82 of the Treaty, OJ L 1, 4.1.2003, pp. 1–25.

28 Regulation No. 411/2004/EC of the Council of 26 February 2004 repealing Regulation (EEC) No 3975/87 and amending Regulations (EEC) No 3976/87 and (EC) No 1/2003, in connection with air transport between the Community and third countries, OJ L 68, 6.3.2004, pp. 1–2.

29 Regulation No. 487/2009/EC of the Council of 25 May 2009 on the application of Article 81(3) of the Treaty to certain categories of agreements and concerted practices in the air transport sector, OJ L 148, 11.6.2009, pp. 1–4, is the only air transport specific competition law regulation still in place. It empowers the European Commission to exempt specified practices from the scope of Article 101 TFEU on the prohibition of concerted practices. So far, the Commission has not adopted any specific exemption and there are no indications that it intends to do so. Hence, the operation of air services is fully subject to the general competition law regime of the EU, and airlines and other undertakings have to manage their competitive behaviour themselves, under compliance procedures. If not, they may be exposed to *ex post facto* review by the European Commission or national competition authorities, with the risk of imposition of fines.

30 See Section 3.7.1.

31 See Regulation 411/2004.

32 See *Hoffman-La Roche*, ECJ judgement of 13 February 1979, Case 85/76, §38:

> the dominant position … relates to a position of economic strength enjoyed by an undertaking which enables it to prevent effective competition being maintained on the relevant market by affording it the power to behave to an appreciable extent independently of its competitors, its customers and ultimately of the consumers.

33 See Decision No. 92/213/EEC of the Commission of 26 February 1992 relating to a procedure pursuant to Articles 85 and 86 of the EEC Treaty (IV/33.544, *British Midland v. Aer Lingus*), OJ L 96, 10.4.1992, pp. 34–45.

European Community (now Article 102 TFEU) by refusing to interline with British Midland on the London–Dublin route.

Article 102 TFEU may also involve airline and airport behaviour,[34] principally in relation to pricing of airport services, that is, airport or landing charges, or access to CRSs, now termed GDSs.[35]

The EU competition rules also include provisions on state aid, which have been applied many times to EU air carriers in the 1990s and in the first decade of the 21st century. This has contributed to, among others, the disappearance of former flag carriers such as the Belgium carrier Sabena and Swiss Air. The EU state aid rules apply also to airports, which must behave as 'commercial undertakings' and are, hence, not allowed to favour certain carriers.[36]

As said, mergers go one step further than alliances as the two parties get more closely involved, among others, by deeper integration of corporate structures and of joint activities. The level of integration will of course vary from one merger to another; it will depend on the circumstances and conditions under which it is concluded whether one speaks of a cooperative agreement, an alliance or a merger. Mergers are examined under the EU Merger Regulation.[37] In the past 15 years, the Commission and the CJEU have scrutinised mergers concerning, among others, Air France–KLM, Lufthansa–Austrian Airlines, and British Airways–Iberia, and approved them subject to conditions.[38]

34 See Decision No. 1999/198/EC of the Commission of 10 February 1999 relating to a proceeding pursuant to Article 86 of the Treaty (IV/35.767 – Ilmailulaitos/Luftfartsverket), OJ L 69, 16.3.1999, pp. 24–30; Decision No. 95/364/EC of the Commission of 28 June 1995 relating to a proceeding pursuant to Article 90 (3) of the Treaty, OJ L 216, 12.9.1995, pp. 8–14; Decision No. 1999/199/EC of the Commission of 10 February 1999 relating to a proceeding pursuant to Article 90 of the Treaty (Case No IV/35.703 – Portuguese airports), OJ L 69, 16.3.1999, pp. 31–39.

35 As to predatory (below cost) pricing by KLM on the Amsterdam–London route see the case EasyJet/KLM. This case was settled between the parties with the intervention from the Commission in 1997, see easyJet (1996). In the *London European/Sabena* case of 1992 London European who used to operate on the Luton–Brussels route lodged a complaint against the then Belgian national flag carrier (Sabena) as Sabena denied the complainant access to its own CRS, called Saphir, on the grounds that London European fares were too low. Consequently, London European was denied access to 80% of the market and, in practice, was kicked out of that market. In 1988, the European Commission obliged Sabena to display these flights on Saphir. See Decision No. 88/589/EEC of the Commission of 4 November 1988 relating to a proceeding under Article 86 of the EEC Treaty (IV/32.318, London European – Sabena), OJ L 317, 24.11.1988, pp. 47–54.

36 See the well know Charleroi case *Ryanair v. Commission*, CJEU (Court of First Instance) judgement of 17 December 2008, Case T-196/04.

37 Regulation No. 139/2004/EC of the Council of 20 January 2004 on the control of concentrations between undertakings, OJ L 24, 29.1.2004, pp. 1–22 as implemented by Regulation No. 802/2004/EC of the Commission of 7 April 2004 implementing Council Regulation (EC) No 139/2004 on the control of concentrations between undertakings, OJ L 133, 30.4.2004, pp. 1–39.

38 See *Air France/KLM*, Commission Decision of 11 February 2004, COMP/M.3280, §36; *Lufthansa/Austrian Airlines*, Commission Decision of 28 August 2009, COMP/

A merger between two undertakings holding a market share above 60% means dominance.[39] The behaviour of an undertaking in a dominant position may influence the structure of a market and weaken the level of competition if this undertaking takes recourse to measures that are different from those that create normal conditions of competition. Such behaviour may impede market growth.[40]

So far, the EU competition regime is the most advanced one to regulate competition at a multilateral level. After all, the – now – 28 member states are sovereign states in international civil aviation. However, since the EU effort is restricted to the regional level, inconveniences and frictions arise. These include extra-territorial application of competition law, lack of coherence with trade partners and lack of transparency for airlines. These problems may only be solved by global efforts.[41]

3.5.3 Other countries

Apart from the US and the EU, a number of countries have enacted national competition laws, which in varying degrees apply to air transport. Examples may be found in Canada, Australia, Mexico, Chile, South Korea, Japan, Singapore, Brazil, South Africa and other African countries.[42]

3.6 Frictions between competition law and bilateral ASAs

In practice, national law is not a vehicle for the promotion of competition internationally. The degree to which competition is allowed internationally and the conditions under which air carriers compete, equally depend on the bilateral relationship between the 'home' states of the airlines designated under ASAs.

Bilateral ASAs (also referred to as bilateral agreements) are not very clear on the matter of international airline competition. This may be explained by the fact that they are, or in some regions were, the most effective instrument for states to participate in the system of international air transport that is understood as

M.5440, §29; *Iberia/British Airways*, Commission Decision of 8 September 2010, COMP/M.5747, §41.

39 See Decision No. 1999/641/EC of the Commission of 25 November 1998 declaring a concentration to be compatible with the common market and the functioning of the EEA Agreement (Case No IV/M.1225 – Enso/Stora), OJ L 254, 29.9.1999, pp. 9–21, §§84–97.

40 Dominance includes the possession and use of a 'leading position,' 'substantial market power,' or the power to 'increase prices.' See *Guidance on the Commission's enforcement priorities in applying Article 82 of the EC Treaty to abusive exclusionary conduct by dominant undertakings*, Communication from the Commission, OJ C 45, 24.2.2009, pp. 7–20.

41 See Section 3.8.

42 For updates on the various jurisdictions, see Balfour and Bisset 2016; Meneghetti and Perrotta 2017.

'public utility.'[43] Again, the creation of new market environment by open skies agreements is changing this picture.

This tension between the bilateral and the competition law regimes is explained by the ICAO Secretariat, which has noted that 'the traditional approach in many bilateral agreements favouring airline cooperation on issues like capacity and pricing is squarely at odds with competition laws that strictly prohibit price fixing, market division and other collusive practices by market competitors.'[44] This is evidenced, among others, by the *Air Freight Cartel* cases.[45]

Most of the traditional bilateral agreements contain a very general, and, consequently, rather vaguely worded provision, which speaks of 'a fair and equal opportunity to operate' on the agreed routes, and, later, of 'a fair and equal opportunity to compete' – and, in some instances 'a fair and equal opportunity to effectively participate in the international air transportation as agreed.' The formula has never been interpreted legally in arbitration or other legal procedures. Hence, it is not an easy task to apply this clause to the alleged anti-competitive behaviour of airlines. This is because ASAs are not designed to promote competition, unless they are shaped as open skies agreements.

Under more liberal ASAs, including open skies agreements, the operation of international air services is moving away from *a priori* regulation with respect to competition-related issues such as market access, including the matter of single or multiple designation, capacity limitations, tariff setting and code-sharing. The most well-known agreement of this kind is the EU–US open skies agreement concluded in 2007[46] and amended in 2010.[47] This agreement lays down that

43 See *Report of the World Wide Air Transport Conference on International Air Transport Regulation: Present and Future, Montréal 23 November – 6 December 1994*, ICAO ATConf/4 1994, ICAO Doc. 9644.

44 *Fair Competition in International Air Transport (Presented by the Secretariat)*, ICAO ATConf/6-WP/4, 4.12.2012, Section 4.4.

45 See Section 3.7.2.

46 Air Transport Agreement between the United States of America and the Republic of Austria, the Kingdom of Belgium, the Republic of Bulgaria, the Republic of Cyprus, the Czech Republic, the Kingdom of Denmark, the Republic of Estonia, the Republic of Finland, the French Republic, the Federal Republic of Germany, the Hellenic Republic, the Republic of Hungary, Ireland, the Italian Republic, the Republic of Latvia, the Republic of Lithuania, the Grand Duchy of Luxembourg, Malta, the Kingdom of The Netherlands, the Republic of Poland, the Portuguese Republic, Romania, the Slovak Republic, the Republic of Slovenia, the Kingdom of Spain, the Kingdom of Sweden, the United Kingdom of Great Britain And Northern Ireland, and the European Community, done at Brussels on 25 April 2007 and at Washington on 30 April 2007, provisionally applied as from 30 March 2008, OJ L 134, 25.5.2007, pp. 4–41.

47 Protocol to amend the Air Transport Agreement between the United States of America and the European Community and its Member States, signed on 25 and 30 April 2007, signed on 24 June 2010 in Luxembourg, provisionally applied as from the date of signature, OJ L 223, 25.8.2010, pp. 3–19.

'Government Subsidies and Support may adversely affect the fair and equal opportunity of airlines to compete in providing the international air transportation.' Should a party believe that support or a subsidy is being considered or granted it may submit its observations to the other party and can request a meeting of the Joint Committee to formulate 'appropriate responses to concerns found to be legitimate' (Article 14).

The EU–US open skies agreement also stipulates that competition is important for achieving the goals of the agreement, but it does not speak of 'fair competition'. Competition matters should be dealt with and mutual understanding reached through consultations between the European Commission, the US Department of Justice (DOJ) and the DOT. Annex 2 to the Agreement specifies areas of and procedures for cooperation.

The three global alliances – Oneworld, SkyTeam and Star Alliance – have been judged by the said authorities working in concerted action; the same is true for the mergers affecting the relevant market of the other party, but not under a 'converged regulatory regime'. This situation is illustrated by the merger between Air France and KLM in 2003, which the DOT approved the day after the approval made by the European Commission.[48]

3.7 Implications of cross-border service provision

3.7.1 The 'effects' doctrine

The Chicago Convention[49] principles proceed from the idea of territorial jurisdiction in national airspace. Among others, this follows from the combined effect of Article 1[50] and Article 2[51] of this convention. Thus, extra-territorial application of competition laws should be avoided. However, this opinion is not undisputed, especially in the US.[52] The extra-territorial application of

48 See *Air France/KLM*, Commission Decision of 11 February 2004, COMP/M.3280. For decisions on mergers and alliances in aviation see also Chapter 4 of this book.

49 Convention on International Civil Aviation, signed in Chicago on 7 December 1944, entered into force on 4 April 1947, ICAO Doc. 7300/9, 15 UNTS 295.

50 Article 1, *Sovereignty*: 'The contracting States recognize that every State has complete and exclusive sovereignty over the airspace above its territory.'

51 Article 2, *Territory*: 'For the purposes of this Convention the territory of a State shall be deemed to be the land areas and territorial waters adjacent thereto under the sovereignty, suzerainty, protection or mandate of such State.'

52 See, for example, Fox and Ordover 1994, p. 22. These learned authors have indicated that, absent a seamless international anti-competition code, global allocative efficiency is better served by overlapping jurisdiction, f.i., based on the 'effects' doctrine, than gaps in jurisdiction which would allow anti-competitive conduct to fall between 'the cracks of domestic competition regimes.' Extra-territoriality is said to become even more desirable if its major disadvantages – the potential for inefficiency and system friction – are effectively moderated by comity, which the OECD has described as 'an important principle underlying competition policy and its enforcement.'

competition,[53] environmental, safety and other regulations may give rise to frictions as evidenced by cases on aircraft emissions on this matter.[54]

Under the 'effects' doctrine, which is applied by the CJEU, anti-competitive behaviour, for instance, price fixing by undertakings that are established outside the EU, may be subject to the EU competition regime if such behaviour affects intra-EU trade.[55] The case of merger between Boeing and McDonnell Douglas[56] and the Delta Airlines (Delta)/Pan American World Airways (Pan Am) case also illustrate the application of this doctrine. Delta took over the Pan Am routes crossing the Atlantic Ocean, the intra-German operations of Pan Am and Pan Am's US East coast shuttle operations. The resulting concentration, however, did not jeopardise intra-Community trade, because the parties had a relatively little market share and because of important competitors in the relevant market.[57]

In the US, the effects doctrine has even been codified. It is established that a 'direct, substantial and reasonably foreseeable effect on US commerce justifies US jurisdiction.'[58]

3.7.2 The Air Cargo Fuel Charges *cases*

The *Air Cargo Fuel Charges* cases exemplify the extra-territorial application of competition laws, including the EU competition rules. The alleged anti-competitive acts were carried out outside the EU. The investigation started in 2006 with dawn raids, also involving non-EU airlines who had been accused of colliding with respect to coordinated imposition of surcharges on the prices for the carriage of cargo shipments and other trading conditions, which was supposed to be in breach of Article 101 TFEU. On 9 November 2010, the European Commission imposed fines of almost EUR 790 million on 11 airlines for operating a cartel on cargo fuel and security charges.[59] Hence, price fixing has been punished severely because pricing must be made in an independent fashion by the undertakings.

The European Commission warned that 'the existence of an alliance agreement cannot give a blank cheque for naked price coordination among the members.'

53 See the efforts of the EU to apply its rules on state subsidies to services from non-EU states to points in the EU, as explained in *An Aviation Strategy for Europe*, Communication from the Commission to the European Parliament, the Council, the European Economic and Social Committee and the Committee of the Regions, COM(2015)598 final, 7.12.2015.

54 See, for instance, in the environmental field: Mendes de Leon 2012; Havel and Mulligan 2012.

55 Because Article 101 TFEU does not require that the 'undertakings' have an 'EU nationality' or that they have an establishment with the EU: the principal condition for application of the said article is that trade between member states is affected, irrespective of nationality criteria.

56 See Section 3.7.4.

57 See Decision of the Commission of 13 September 1991 declaring a concentration to be compatible with the common market (Case No IV/M.130 – Delta Air Lines/Pan Am) according to Council Regulation (EEC) No 4064/89, OJ C 289, 7.11.1991, p. 14.

58 See Section 7 of the Sherman Act. See also *United States v. Alcoa*, 148 F.2d 416 (2d Cir. 1945).

59 See *Airfreight cartel*, Commission Decision of 17 March 2017, COMP/39.258.

On the other side, the Commission showed comprehension for the existence of the regulatory regime prevailing in international air transport encouraging, under specified conditions, airlines to behave in an anti-competitive manner because of government dictated trade in air services laid down in bilateral and other international ASAs. This comprehension resulted in some cases in a 15% reduction of fines.[60]

All of the airlines apart from Qantas appealed the decision.[61] The appealing airlines claimed that:

- the level of the fines was disproportionate to the relatively low profitability of the airline sector,
- the European Commission's decision did not comply with the principle of equal treatment in applying different standards of proof,
- the European Commission's decision failed to correctly define the relevant market,
- the European Commission's decision violated the principles of non-interference or comity between states,
- the European Commission exceeded its jurisdiction with respect to activities regulated and managed outside the EU jurisdiction,[62] and
- the European Commission's decision infringed the principle of proportionality as it only reduced the fines by 15% on account of the prevailing principles of cooperation in the established regulatory framework.

The airlines/claimants also used procedural arguments.[63] Moreover, airline managers who have been involved with these cases have faced imprisonment, especially in the US and the UK where cartel offences are classed as criminal offences. Moreover, the DOJ is conducting a criminal price fixing investigation of certain airlines.

The investigation has resulted in 17 guilty pleas and over USD 1.6 billion in fines to date, the largest fine ever imposed in a single criminal antitrust investigation. Following the announcement of criminal investigations, purchasers of air cargo services filed antitrust class actions seeking treble damages from the airlines for price fixing.[64]

On 16 December 2015, the CJEU (General Court) annulled the European Commission's decision, which fined 21 carriers for their alleged collusive

60 See, Clyde & Co 2003. The problematic relationship between the *ex ante* bilateral ASAs and the *ex post* competition law regimes is sharply articulated in an article by Truxal and Harris 2013.

61 Appeals brought in January 2011.

62 Cf. the above-mentioned comments on the 'effects doctrine.'

63 Concerning the admissibility of the evidence; breach of the rights of defence and breach of the right of fair trial.

64 See Katten Muchin Rosenman LLP, *Air Transport in 40 Jurisdictions Worldwide* 247 (2011).

conduct.[65] The Court found that the grounds of the decision were inconsistent with the operative part of the Commission's decision, which it found insufficiently clear. The grounds contained substantial internal inconsistencies infringing the defence rights of the carriers. Hence, the court emphasised that the principle of effective judicial protection required that the decision made by the Commission should comply with the standard of legal certainty, which it did not. As a result, the decision was overturned.[66] Following this decision of the CJEU, the Commission took a new decision under Article 101 TFEU on 17 March 2017.[67] In it, the Commission maintains its standpoint that the airlines mentioned in this decision committed cartel behaviour prohibited by this provision on routes between airports within the European Economic Area (EEA), between airports in the EAA and third countries, and between airports in the EU and Switzerland. As a consequence, the EU Commission fined the accused airlines for their anti-competitive behaviour. In December 2017, airlines appealed from this Commission appealed yet again from this Commission Decision before the CJEU which is studying the cases. A new decision from the CJEU is expected for 2019.

At the same time, the freight forwarders and shippers, and their customers, that is, the undertakings whose goods were carried, are also seeking compensation of their civil damages before courts in Germany, the Netherlands, Norway, the US and the UK. Liability claims amount to several hundred million Euro. The procedures include questions on the admissibility of the claimants and secrecy of information held by the European Commission.[68]

3.7.3 Multilateral efforts in harmonising competition laws

The efforts to regulate the economic side of air transport at the Chicago Conference in 1944 failed. The Chicago Convention does not go much further than stipulating that unreasonable competition should be prevented.[69] However, ICAO pays attention to the role of 'fair competition' in air transport and promotes cooperation between competition authorities across the world. It also attempts to establish understanding principles governing competition by

65 CJEU (General Court) judgements of 16 December 2015: Case T-9/11 – *Air Canada v. Commission*, Case T-28/11 – *Koninklijke Luchtvaart Maatschappij v. Commission*, Case T-36/11 – *Japan Airlines v. Commission*, Case T-38/11 – *Cathay Pacific Airways v. Commission*, Case T-39/11 – *Cargolux Airlines v. Commission*, Case T-40/11 – *LAN Airlines and LAN Cargo v. Commission*, Case T-43/11 – *Singapore Airlines and Singapore Airlines Cargo PTE v. Commission*, Case T-46/11 – *Deutsche Lufthansa and Others v. Commission*, Case T-48/11 – *British Airways v. Commission*, Case T-56/11 – *SAS Cargo Group and Others v. Commission*, Case T-62/11 – *Air France KLM v. Commission*, Case T-63/11 *Air France v. Commission*, Case T-67/11 – *Martinair Holland v. Commission*, ('Air Cargo Fuel Charges').

66 See General Court of the European Union 2015.

67 Case AT.39258 – Airfreight No. C(2017) 1742 final.

68 For price fixing on fuel charges see also Chapter 4 of this book.

69 See Article 44(e) of the Chicago Convention.

conducting research.[70] In this respect, the ICAO Assembly has broadly endorsed the recommendations of ATConf/6.[71]

While not all of its member states share this view, it seems that ICAO has embraced the concept of 'fair competition', and urged its members to view it as 'an important general principle in the operation of international air services'.[72] The ICAO Assembly has also called the ICAO Council to monitor developments on 'fair competition' by updating policies and guidance materials, and serving as a forum for the exchange of information. State aid or public subsidies have not been addressed.

3.7.4 Achievements on convergence of competition law and policy

At least yet, there is no consensus to apply GATS principles to air transport so as to facilitate operation of air services, and to create a more levelled playing field between airlines by the introduction of MFN treatment, the enhancement of the freedom of establishment of undertakings, the reduction of tariff barriers and the establishment of a dispute resolution mechanism.

Progress on harmonisation of competition rules including state aid rules and procedures can be observed in the general economic field. For instance, the 1991 ground-breaking agreement between the government of the US and the European Commission regarding the application of their competition laws (re-approved in 1995)[73] sets forth the principle of positive comity, according to which each side must notify the other side and give weight to competition law and policy of the other side in any instances where enterprises of the latter are involved.

70 See *Addressing Competition Issues: Towards a Better Operating Environment*, ICAO Air Transport Symposium, Montréal, 30–31.3.2016. See also Shelton 1999.

71 See *Outcome of the Sixth Worldwide Air Transport Conference (Presented by the Council of ICAO)*, ICAO A38-WP/56, EC/6, 31.7.2013.

72 See *Consolidated statement of continuing ICAO policies in the air transport field*, ICAO Assembly Resolution A38-14, Appendix A, Section II.

73 Agreement between the Government of the United States of America and the Commission of the European Communities regarding the application of their competition laws, done at Washington on 23 September 1991, entered into force on 23 September 1991, OJ L 95, 27.4.1995, pp. 47–52; 2872 UNTS 1. The fact that the Commission had concluded the agreement was challenged by some member states, especially France. It argued that the Council of Ministers should have concluded the agreement. The European Court of Justice judged in favour of France and the Agreement has been rendered invalid, see *French Republic v. Commission of the European Communities*, CJEU judgment of 9 August 1994, Case C-327/91. Meanwhile, the EU Council has re-approved the agreement on behalf of the Community in 1995, see Decision of the Council and the Commission of 10 April 1995 concerning the conclusion of the agreement between the European Communities and the Government of the United States of America regarding the application of their competition laws, OJ L 95, 27.4.1995, pp. 45–52. This point is, again, a matter of competence in external relations.

The agreement is designed 'to promote cooperation and coordination and lessen the possibility or impact of differences between the parties in the application of their competition laws.' Neither air transport nor any other economic activity is exempt from the application of this agreement. So far, there are no instances in which the agreement has been applied to potential anti-competitive conduct of airlines, although the settlement of the proposed British Airways–American Airlines alliance theoretically could have been brought under the umbrella of the agreement.

The regulatory regime is different in other sectors, including the aircraft manufacturing industry where a significantly higher degree of harmonisation exists. Transatlantic ventures and disputes arise there as well, albeit under different rules and procedures. The *Boeing and McDonnell Douglas* cases of 1997[74] and the on-going *Boeing–Airbus* cases[75] are instances in which the subsidy rules and related procedures of the World Trade Organization (WTO) have been applied to the aircraft manufacturers due to their alleged subsidisation by governments. However, the subsidy rules, and related procedures, do not apply to airlines as the operation of air services falls outside the scope of the WTO framework.[76]

3.8 Conclusions and recommendations

At the time when access to foreign markets in air transportation is being liberalised and when the airline industry is becoming subject to the market forces, airlines need to face increasing competition. This leads to a continuing pressure on tariffs. For that reason, the current airline industry, in order to become and stay profitable, is forced to economise – that is, to look for cost reductions – and to increase market coverage. Competition from the low-cost market has to be answered by lowering fares on scheduled services. Moreover, the growing number of and ever-higher taxes and duties, as well as the many delays resulting from airport and airspace congestion, must be off-set by higher airline revenues.

Under these circumstances, airlines engage in cross-border joint ventures and other cooperative agreements in order to rationalise their operations, increase their market coverage and strengthen their competitive position on the market. In this process, they face different competition regulations and policies applied by individual states and inter-governmental organisations.

74 See *Statement of Chairman Robert Pitofsky and Commissioners Janet D. Steiger, Roscoe B. Starek III and Christine A. Varney in the Matter of The Boeing Company/McDonnell Douglas Corporation*, FTC Matter No. 971–0051, 5 Trade Reg. Rep. (CCH), 24,295, 1.7.1997.

75 See, for instance, *United States – Measures Affecting Trade in Large Civil Aircraft (Second Complaint): Recourse to Article 21.5 of the DSU by the European Union*, Report of the Panel, WT/DS353/RW, 9.6.2017.

76 See also Chapter 2 of this book.

Thus, liberalisation of international air transport goes hand in hand with the application of competition regimes in different jurisdictions. These developments require a reset of the regulatory approach towards the operation of international air services in order to overcome the loss of traditional protection, which has prevailed under the traditional, restrictive bilateral ASAs.

In practice, competition law provisions laid down in national law are not an ideal vehicle for the promotion of airline competition internationally. The degree to which competition is allowed internationally, as well as the conditions under which air carriers compete, very much depend on the bilateral relationship between the 'home' states of the airlines designated under the bilateral agreements. The simultaneous application of competition law regimes and bilateral provisions may lead to uncertainty and questions about prioritisation of policies and rules.

Based on the analysis in this chapter it is concluded that convergence of competition regulations and policy should be promoted, to begin with in the transatlantic area, and be extended to other areas in the world. In the long term, important benefits can be derived from a converged approach towards competition.

Convergence shall create a coherent and transparent framework giving guidance for inter-airline activities. Airlines should know who are the competent authorities and which rules apply to what kind of conduct. This would facilitate cross-border joint ventures and alliances. Consumers should benefit from optimised competition. If no attempt is made to find a common approach, the danger of unilateral actions, leading to uncertainty and frictions, will arise.

Realistically, harmonisation, let alone unification of competition law and policy, would be a few steps too far at this stage. Nevertheless, absent worldwide consensus on how to regulate competition internationally, EU member states and other regional groupings such as Mercosur in South America, Australia, New Zealand and ASEAN countries in East Asia are seeking to realise greater benefits by the exploitation of geographic adjacency, political and cultural affinity, and, last but not least, economic interests, thus contributing to the growing importance of regions in international air transport.

Looking at the EU and the US, with their close trade and commercial relationships, it must be acknowledged that there are fundamental differences of opinion between the two parties on what constitutes free trade and free market. A willingness to intensify cooperation in the above fields is presumed, but practice learns that even this presumption may sometimes be questioned. The fear of compromising policy objectives and giving up jurisdictional powers may prevent the setting of ambitious goals.

The most advanced ASA, namely, the mentioned EU–US open skies agreement of 2007/2010 focuses on cooperation between the competition authorities rather than convergence of competition law of the two parties. The formal and informal cooperation on transatlantic anti-competitive practices and mergers between the competition authorities of the two sides may produce a harmonised approach and create mutual understanding. This is, however, insufficient to cope with the challenges of globalisation, which are particularly relevant in the airline industry as manifested by the air cargo fuel cartel cases.[77]

In order to promote a freer exchange of air services throughout the world under a globalised open skies framework consisting of harmonisation of regional arrangements, a regulatory framework that helps to realise that objective must be established. Creation of a 'Common Aviation Area' should be promoted. This applies, in the first place, to the EU-US aviation market, but also to emerging regional markets (Tasman, Andean, Mercosur, ASEAN), and inter-regional markets.

In this 'Common Aviation Area,' both the procedures, including jurisdictional questions, and the standards to be applied to competitive behaviour involving cross-border, 'inter-area' and 'intra-area' alliances should be streamlined in order to create transparency for airlines and consumers, as well as coherence between separate jurisdictions. The standards to be applied should preferably be of a corrective (*a posteriori*) rather than a pre-emptive (*a priori*) nature in order to assure maximum degree of freedom. To that end, it is essential that the rules that govern inter-airline behaviour are clearly defined.

In order to ensure a smooth and speedy solution to handling differences, an adequate dispute settlement mechanism should be part of such an inter-regional and, finally, global framework. The broader purpose is to arrive at a seamless travel system, in the interest of world trade and tourism. This is only possible if accompanied by a seamless, converged competition regime, applicable world-wide, which serves airlines and consumers.

77 See Section 3.7.2.

4 Regulatory schizophrenia

Mergers, alliances, metal-neutral joint ventures and the emergence of a global aviation cartel*

Paul S. Dempsey

4.1 Introduction

Airlines are a high fixed-cost, safety- and labour-intensive industry prone to destructive competition.[1] Demand is fickle and fuel prices are volatile. In a manner consistent with Garrett Hardin's insight into the *Tragedy of the Commons*,[2] after deregulation, airline management has behaved in an individually rational and collectively irrational manner, competing away airline profits in order to fill seats that otherwise would fly empty.[3] Destructive competition emerged from airline deregulation,[4] eventually causing every US major pre-deregulation interstate airline to collapse into bankruptcy.[5] This led to massive cost-cutting

* Originally published by the *Journal of Air Law and Commerce* (83 J. Air L. & Com. 3). Reprinted in amended form with permission from the *Journal of Air Law and Commerce* and Southern Methodist University.

1 Dempsey 1990 and 2008a, p. 421.

2 Hardin 1968.

3 Dempsey 1991.

4 Commercial airlines were deregulated by the the Airline Deregulation Act of 1978, Pub. L. 95–504 – 24 October 1978, 92 Stat. 1705. This was followed by the Civil Aeronautics Board Sunset Act of 1984, Pub. Law 98–443 – 4 October 1984, 98 Stat. 1703, which terminated the CAB and transferred its remaining responsibilities to the DOT. One prominent deregulation apologist expressed why the deregulation movement gained bipartisan support in Congress:

> Deregulation succeeded against industry opposition because it was supported by a coalition of academics able to highlight concrete examples of lower fares with less regulation, consumer groups, politicians looking for an anti-inflation or pro-free-market issue, public disgust with scandals, and charismatic individual spokesmen, all of which excited a media blizzard that lasted for several years.
>
> (see Levine 2006, p. 291)

5 Dempsey 2003. Former American Airlines CEO Bob Crandall observed:

> Our airlines, once world leaders, are now laggards in every category, including fleet age, service quality and international reputation ... [T]he financial health of the industry, and of the individual carriers, has become ever more precarious. Most have been through the bankruptcy process at least once, and some have passed through on multiple occasions

and service deterioration.[6] Financial distress also corroded management–labour relations. Once the finest commercial aviation industry in the world, and the launch customer for every new aircraft that Boeing, Douglas or Lockheed produced pre-deregulation, today the US airlines no longer stand first in line for deliveries, nor are they viewed as the world's finest. Businesspeople who fly across oceans tend to avoid the US airlines whose service levels have deteriorated enormously vis-à-vis their foreign counterparts.[7]

The |US Department of Transport (DOT) posts data on several measurements of consumer abuse (e.g., delays of more than 15 minutes, flight cancellations, denied boarding, lost bags). Also, consumer ratings of airlines reveal that the ultra-low-cost carriers (ultra LCCs) have the worst approval ratings. To thwart ultra LCC inroads, the majors have also skimmed service amenities off the basic economy fares (which have been lowered to ultra LCC levels or thereabouts) – and imposed *a la carte* supplemental pricing on reserved seating, checked and carry-on bags and items for which there were historically no separate charges. Consumers appear to have resigned themselves to poor quality service and, by and large, have stopped complaining except when their adverse treatment is extreme. At the same time, passenger rage appears to be growing, as incidents of unruly passengers increase.[8] That rage is probably a reflection of consumer frustration. In response, consumer protection legislation and regulation are proliferating worldwide.[9]

To offset this unsustainable financial distress, and to avoid re-regulation, the US Department of Justice (DOJ) abdicated while the industry consolidated. Further, the US DOT injected airlines with antitrust immunity so they could establish global alliances whereby competitors collude on pricing and service. The US government jettisoned both economic regulation and antitrust oversight, which institutionally protected the public interest, in favour of airline self-regulation, without meaningful government oversight. We are left with an industry characterised by collusion, monopolisation, consumer exploitation and predation, with skeletal consumer protection.[10]

> ... I feel little need to argue that deregulation has worked poorly in the airline industry. Three decades of deregulation have demonstrated that airlines have special characteristics incompatible with a completely unregulated environment. To put things bluntly, experience has established that market forces alone cannot and will not produce a satisfactory airline industry, which clearly needs some help to solve its pricing, cost and operating problems.
>
> (see Remarks of Robert L. Crandall, The Wings Club (New York 10 June 2008), available at All 2009)

6 Dempsey 1994a, 1994b, 1995.

7 Dempsey 1989.

8 More than 10,000 incidents of unruly passengers worldwide were reported by airlines in 2015, up from 9,316 the year before. See IATA 2016.

9 See *Consumer Protection and Definition of Passenger Rights in Different Contexts (Presented by the Secretariat)*, ICAO ATConf/6-WP/5, 7.12.2012.

10 Dempsey 2002a, 2002b.

Of late, though, airlines may have learned something from the capacity and fare wars of the first several decades of deregulation. If they refrain from fighting for market share, yields generate more sustainable revenue. Keeping capacity levels relatively stable facilitates yield maximisation, as does government-sanctioned price and service collusion.

This chapter examines the tortious path from economic regulation, to deregulation and liberalisation, to consolidation and collusion. It examines several elements of antitrust and competition law and policy, including mergers and acquisitions, collusion on pricing and service between competitors, and the failure of governmental institutions to advance a coherent transportation policy.

4.2 The metamorphosis of air transport agreements

The Chicago Convention[11] laid the foundation for the bilateral negotiation of traffic rights. Article 1 of the Chicago Convention affirms the 'complete and exclusive sovereignty' of every state over 'the airspace above its territory.' Article 5 provides certain traffic rights for non-scheduled flights, though potentially restricted by 'such regulations, conditions or limitations' as the underlying state may deem desirable. Article 6 prohibits scheduled international flights over the territory of a state, 'except with the special permission or other authorization of that state, and in accordance with the terms of such permission or authorization.' Article 7 allows a state to restrict foreign airlines from engaging in for-hire domestic (cabotage) air transport, and prohibits the discriminatory authorisation of cabotage rights to a foreign airline.[12]

The post-World War II era experienced a proliferation of bilateral air transport agreements, beginning with the so-called Bermuda I Agreement between the US and the UK in 1946.[13] For four decades, the Bermuda I Agreement was the model for bilateral air transportation agreements concluded worldwide, though many states departed from the US insistence on an explicit prohibition of capacity predetermination and pooling.[14] Government oversight then was largely promotional and protectionist in emphasis, focusing on avoiding 'destructive

11 Convention on International Civil Aviation, signed in Chicago on 7 December 1944, entered into force 4 April 1947, ICAO Doc. 7300/9, 15 UNTS 295.

12 'Cabotage involves permitting foreign carriers to operate commercial segments of their flights within another country. This can be part of a routing which takes the foreign carrier back to its own country or the operation of a purely domestic flight within a foreign country' (Foerster 2001, p. 181, n. 32).

13 Agreement between the Government of the United Kingdom and the Government of the United States of America relating to Air Services between their Respective Territories (with Annex), signed in Bermuda on 11 February 1946, entered into force by signature, 3 UNTS 253, UKTS 3 (1946) Cm. 6747.

14 As we shall see, the DOT has since insisted on 'metal-neutral joint ventures' as the price for conferring antitrust immunity. Those joint ventures usually include pooling of revenue or profits.

competition' and on achieving a balance of carrier economic health for airlines and safe, efficient and reasonably priced service for consumers. In the three decades following World War II, the US pursued a bilateral negotiating policy that emphasised an equitable exchange of economic benefits (i.e., a trading of operating rights having approximately equal market value).[15] During this era, intercarrier agreements on tariffs under the auspices of the International Air Transport Association (IATA) were the norm.[16]

Pricing and entry were regulated in the US with the creation of the Civil Aeronautics Board (CAB) in 1938, and would continue until deregulation in 1978.[17] Deregulation was designed to encourage price and service competition between airlines. Yet, as we shall see, antitrust immunity enables competitors to collude on pricing, capacity and other components of the service product.

In the wake of the Airline Deregulation Act of 1978,[18] the US concluded the first of its 'liberal' bilateral air transport agreements.[19] Pricing provisions in these new first generation open skies bilaterals placed an emphasis on the encouragement of low fares set by individual carriers on the basis of forces in the marketplace, without reference to the IATA ratemaking machinery.[20] These bilaterals were characterised by their opportunities for pricing flexibility,[21] unrestricted capacity,[22] multiple designations,[23] access to interior US markets for foreign-flag carriers,[24]

15 Loy 1968.

16 Dempsey 1987, pp. 40–43.

17 Dempsey 1979.

18 The Airline Deregulation Act of 1978, Pub. L. 95–504 – 24 October 1978, 92 Stat. 1705.

19 Liberal bilateral air transport agreements were concluded during 1978 between the US and the Netherlands, Belgium and Israel. Between 1978 and 1980, the US concluded and signed 11 new 'open skies' Benelux-type bilaterals or amendments to existing bilateral air transport agreements. Their tariff provisions encouraged low tariffs, set by individual airlines on the basis of forces of the marketplace without reference to the ratemaking machinery of IATA. See: Haanappel 1980, pp. 261–262; Majid 1983, p. 299.

20 Haanappel 1984a, p. 42.

21 See Rosenfield 1982, p. 478; Klem and Leister 1979, pp. 573–574. The pricing regimes of the first generation liberal bilaterals are of two principal types. 'Country-of-origin pricing' (concluded originally in the bilaterals between the US and the Netherlands, and the US and the Federal Republic of Germany), allows the nation in whose territory the flight originates to set the rate. The most liberal provision, 'double disapproval pricing' (concluded first in bilaterals between the US and Belgium, Korea and Israel) allows the carrier's proposed rate to go into effect unless both nations object. Layered on top of this regime was a Memorandum of Understanding concluded between the US and the European Civil Aviation Conference (ECAC), which established a zone of reasonableness within which market conditions will set the rate.

22 'The right to fly any number of seats on any number of frequencies would be determined by the carrier, based solely on market conditions' (Rosenfield 1982, p. 478).

23 Multiple designation consists of the ability of a state to designate more than one of its flag carriers to serve a particular route.

24 For example, direct access to Miami, Atlanta, Dallas/Ft Worth, San Juan, Anchorage and San Francisco was given to Germany; Atlanta and three additional cities were conferred to Belgium;

new fifth-freedom rights,[25] country-of-origin charter rules[26] and elimination of discrimination and unfair methods of competition.[27] They typically provided for either country-of-origin[28] pricing (under which a fare may be unilaterally disapproved only by the state from which the flight originates), or mutual disapproval[29] pricing (under which new fares may be freely inaugurated unless both states disapprove them), the latter being the most liberal of the two. Prior to the sunset of the CAB in 1984, the US also threatened revocation of IATA's antitrust immunity, causing it to divide itself in two – a trade association for non-tariff activities, and a traffic conference for ratemaking activities.[30]

The major Benelux states (i.e., the Netherlands[31] and Belgium[32]) were the first to embrace the pro-competitive approach of the US by entering into liberal bilateral air transport agreements that surrendered restrictions on numbers of carriers, capacity and rates, in exchange for access to lucrative interior US markets.[33] Of course, airlines that focus on sixth freedom[34] traffic would naturally favour liberal access to markets, and small states with few major airports face little risk to their flag carriers in trading unlimited access. By expeditiously

and rights between Korea–New York, Korea–Los Angeles and Tokyo–Los Angeles were given to South Korea. See William T. Seawell statement in *A Review of US International Aviation Policy*, Hearings Before the House Committee on Public Works and Transportation, 97th Cong, 1st and 2nd Sess. 574, 1982–82. Another commentator summarised examples of foreign access to interior US points even more generously, by saying that 'Germany has rights to 12 US cities and has named 10 thus far, the United Kingdom has rights to name 20 US cities and has listed 17 so far on their major route.' See testimony of Donald C. Comish in these hearings.

25 Fifth freedom rights enable an airline to carry to carry traffic between two countries outside its own state as long as the flight originates or terminates in its own state. See Rosenfield 1982, p. 478.

26 Under this provision, charter flights are governed by the rules of the nation in which the flight originates.

27 Dempsey 1978, pp. 411–415; Klem and Leister 1979, pp. 573–574; Majid 1983, pp. 299–300.

28 Under country-of-origin pricing provisions, governmental authorities can unilaterally disapprove a fare proposed by a carrier only if the route in question originates within its own territory.

29 Under mutual disapproval pricing provisions, neither state may disapprove and suspend a proposed rate unless the other also disapproves the rate in question. In the event that the two states fail to agree, the carrier's proposed rate becomes effective.

30 Dempsey 1987, p 42.

31 Protocol relating to the Air Transport Agreement between the Government of the United States of America and the Government of the Kingdom of the Netherlands of 1957, as amended, signed at Washington on 31 March 1978, entered into force as of the date of signature, 1123 UNTS 345.

32 Agreement Amending the Air Transport Services Agreement of 1946, as amended, signed on 12–14 December 1978, United States–Belgium, TIAS No 9207.

33 CAB Order No. 78-9-2 (1978) at 6.

34 Under sixth freedom rights, an airline has the right to carry traffic between two foreign countries via its own state (sixth freedom can also be viewed as a combination of third and fourth freedoms secured by the state from two different countries).

authorising multiple US-flag entrants, the CAB hoped to put pressure on other European governments in close geographic proximity to jump aboard the competitive bandwagon so as to avoid the loss of tourists and business travellers to Brussels and Amsterdam, and the loss of sixth freedom traffic flown over these cities by Sabena and KLM, respectively.[35]

In 1977, President Jimmy Carter appointed economist Alfred Kahn as Chairman of the CAB. That set in motion promulgation of the Airline Deregulation Act of 1978, which deregulated domestic pricing and entry, and liberalised international markets as well. Kahn responded to the British refusal to embrace the US open skies ideology with an approach of, 'let's stick it to the Brits – let's put pressure on the Germans through Amsterdam.'[36] With the opportunity to engage in pricing competition and serve interior US points, Sabena and KLM began to draw traffic away from their neighbours and obtain significant increases in market shares and tourist revenue.[37]

By the mid-1980s, the US had concluded liberal bilaterals with Belgium, Costa Rica, Finland, Israel, Jordan, Jamaica, South Korea, Thailand, Taiwan and Singapore.[38] But still, major European states were resistant; and meanwhile, the European Commission began to liberalise air transport by regulatory fiat, from Brussels.[39]

- In 1992, the DOT began to pursue a second generation of even more liberal open skies agreements rather indiscriminately. In a reprise of its 1978 strategy, the US would begin, again, with the Dutch, in a rebounded effort to open the skies with Europe's Big Three – Germany, France and the UK. DOT identified the basic elements that constitute the essential components of an open skies bilateral air transport agreement: Open entry on all routes.
- Unrestricted capacity and frequency on all routes.

35 CAB Chairman Marvin Cohen subsequently noted the success of this approach in *A Review of US International Aviation Policy*, Hearings Before the House Committee on Public Works and Transportation, 97th Cong, 1st and 2nd Sess. 574, 1982–82.

36 Sampson 1984, p. 145. Brenner, Leet and Schott noted that

> the US government saw [the new liberal pro-competitive bilaterals] as a means of putting pressure on recalcitrant governments in the same geographic area. The US, under this 'encirclement' theory, the United Kingdom was to be pressured by expansion of air service to and via Belgium and The Netherlands. Not too much later a new agreement with South Korea was intended to put pressure on Japan.
>
> (Brenner, Leet and Schott 1985, p. 13 [citations omitted])

37 *A Review of US International Aviation Policy*, Hearings Before the House Committee on Public Works and Transportation, 97th Cong, 1st and 2nd Sess. 574, 1982–82, p. 100, n 1. In 1977, Sabena was given the right to fly to Atlanta. No British carriers could begin service under Bermuda II to this important sunbelt city until 1980. Gray 1978, p. 21.

38 Haanappel 1984b, p. 52.

39 Dempsey 1992, 2001.

- Unrestricted route and traffic rights, that is, the right to operate service between any point, including no restrictions as to intermediate and beyond points, change of gauge, routing flexibility, coterminalisation, or the right to carry fifth-freedom traffic.
- Double-disapproval pricing in third and fourth freedom markets, and price leadership in third country markets to the extent that the third and fourth freedom carriers in those markets have it.
- Liberal charter arrangement (the least restrictive charter regulations of the two governments would apply, regardless of the origin of the flight).
- Liberal cargo regime (criteria as comprehensive as those defined for the combination carriers).
- Conversion and remittance arrangement (carriers would be able to convert earnings and remit in hard currency promptly and without restriction).
- Open code-sharing opportunities.
- Self-handling provisions (right of a carrier to perform/control its airport functions going to support its operations).
- Pro-competitive provisions on commercial opportunities, user charges, fair competition and intermodal rights. Explicit commitment for non-discriminatory operation of and access for computer reservation systems.[40]

In November 1992, DOT gave Northwest–KLM preliminary antitrust immunity to create the first integrated international intercarrier alliance.[41] Final approval was given only days before the inauguration of Bill Clinton as President in January 1993.[42] The alliance enabled these two airlines to draw enormous traffic from their rivals in the transatlantic market. The aim was strategic. If KLM bled enough traffic from its nearby rivals, they might lobby their governments to conclude open skies agreements with the US so that they too could enjoy antitrust immunity with US airlines.

The strategy began to work. By 1995, the US had concluded open skies agreements with nine additional European countries. Germany fell in 1996, followed by the Czech Republic, Italy, Portugal, the Slovak Republic, Malta and Poland, and in 2002, France. With a conclusion of an open skies agreement with India on 15 January 2005, the US had achieved open skies agreements with 67 states worldwide, including 15 of the 25 EU members.[43] By 2017, the US had concluded open skies bilateral air transport agreements with more than 120 states.[44]

40 *In the Matter of Defining 'Open Skies'*, DOT Order No. 92–8-13 (1992).

41 Some speculated the decision was predicated on the USD 100,000 contribution Northwest co-chairman Gary Wilson had made to Bush's committee to re-elect the President in August 1992. In contrast, four years earlier he had contributed to Democrat Michael Dukakis' Presidential campaign. See Airline 1992, p. A8; Northwest 1992, p. 15A.

42 DOT Order No. 91–1-11 (1993).

43 Byerly 2004.

44 Dempsey 2017, pp. 698–699.

Although a public interest rationale for approving the first alliance antitrust immunity between Northwest and KLM had been to 'promote competition by furthering our efforts to obtain less restrictive aviation agreements with other European countries',[45] the DOT continued to grant antitrust immunity profligately long after all the major European dominos had fallen. Antitrust immunity no longer became a means of facilitating open skies bilaterals; curiously, it became a way of facilitating creation of anticompetitive alliances of a particular type: 'metal-neutral joint ventures'. More about that in a moment.

4.3 Airline alliances

Since the dawn of commercial aviation, airlines have engaged in cooperative relationships. In part, these arrangements are necessary to move passengers and freight beyond airline route systems. Interlining has long been an essential component of international air travel. For many decades, IATA served as facilitator of fare and capacity coordination between airlines. In recent decades, however, antitrust scrutiny has forced IATA to retreat in areas of parallel routes, though it continues to facilitate end-to-end coordination.

Intercarrier agreements take many forms, including:

- ticketing and baggage agreements,
- joint-fare agreements,
- dry leases,
- wet leases,
- reciprocal airport agreements,
- blocked space relationships (capacity purchase agreements),
- computer reservations systems joint ventures,
- joint sales offices and telephone centres,
- e-commerce joint ventures,
- frequent flyer programme alliances,
- code-sharing,
- coordination of pricing and scheduling,
- pooling of traffic and revenue, and
- metal-neutral profit-sharing joint ventures.

Figure 4.1 depicts the hierarchy of intercarrier agreements, with those at the left end being less integrated vis-à-vis those on the right.

4.3.1 Antitrust and competition: a succinct summary of US and EU laws

Competition and antitrust laws attempt to ensure that competitors compete fairly so that price and service levels are responsive to consumer demand,

45 DOT Order No. 2008–4-17 R 2 (2008).

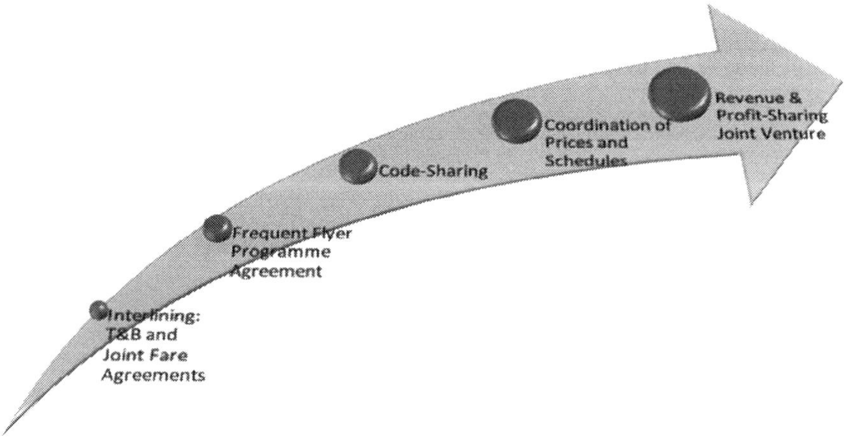

Figure 4.1 Hierarchy of intercarrier agreements

prices drop to marginal costs and consumer welfare is enhanced. Law in this area seeks to:

- prohibit collusion between competitors that restrain trade, such as price fixing,
- prohibit monopolisation through mergers, and
- prohibit monopolisation through anticompetitive means, such as predation or abuse of a dominant position.

The US has promulgated several such laws:

- Sherman Antitrust Act of 1890.[46]
- Clayton Act of 1914.[47]
- Robinson-Patman Act of 1936.[48]
- Federal Trade Commission Act of 1938 (Wheeler-Lea Act).[49]
- Civil Aeronautics Act of 1938 (Federal Aviation Act of 1958).[50]

46 The Sherman Antitrust Act of 2 July 1890, ch. 647, 26 Stat. 209; 15 USC 1 et seq.

47 The Clayton Antitrust Act of 15 October 1914, ch. 323, 38 Stat. 730; 15 USC 12 et seq.

48 The Robinson-Patman Antidiscrimination Act of 1936, Pub. L. No. 74–692 – 19 June 1936, 49 Stat. 1526; 15 USC 13 et. seq.

49 An act to amend the Act creating the Federal Trade Commission, to define its powers and duties, and for other purposes, Pub. L. 75–447 – 21 March 1938, 52 Stat. 111; 15 USC ch. 2.

50 The Federal Aviation Act of 1958, Pub. L. 85–726 – 23 August 1958, 72 Stat. 731.

Similarly, Article 101 of the Treaty on the Functioning of the European Union (TFEU)[51] prohibits 'all agreements between undertakings ... which may affect trade ... and which have as their object or effect the prevention, restriction or distortion of competition'.[52]

Examples include:

- price fixing,
- limitation or control of production,
- shared markets or sources of supply,
- applying dissimilar conditions to equivalent transactions, placing other trading parties at a competitive disadvantage, and

51 Treaty on the Functioning of the European Union (TFEU), signed on 25 March 1957 in Rome, entered into force on 1 January 1958 (then Treaty establishing the European Economic Community, later Treaty establishing the European Economic Community, consolidated version OJ C 202, 7.6.2016, pp. 47–199.

52 Article 101 provides:

1 The following shall be prohibited as incompatible with the common market: all agreements between undertakings, decisions by associations of undertakings and concerted practices which may affect trade between member states and which have as their object or effect the prevention, restriction or distortion of competition within the common market, and in particular those which:

(a) directly or indirectly fix purchase or selling prices or any other trading conditions;
(b) limit or control production, markets, technical development, or investment;
(c) share markets or sources of supply;
(d) apply dissimilar conditions to equivalent transactions with other trading parties, thereby placing them at a competitive disadvantage;
(e) make the conclusion of contracts subject to acceptance by the other parties of supplementary obligations which, by their nature or according to commercial usage, have no connection with the subject of such contracts.

2 Any agreements or decisions prohibited pursuant to this Article shall be automatically void.

3 The provisions of §1) may, however, be declared inapplicable in the case of:

- any agreement or category of agreements between undertakings;
- any decision or category of decisions by associations of undertakings;
- any concerted practice or category of concerted practices,

4 which contributes to improving the production or distribution of goods or to promoting technical or economic progress, while allowing consumers a fair share of the resulting benefit, and which does not:

(a) impose on the undertakings concerned restrictions which are not indispensable to the attainment of these objectives;
(b) afford such undertakings the possibility of eliminating competition in respect of a substantial part of the products in question.

- making the conclusion of contracts subject to approval by others without commercial justification.

In the EU companies found guilty of such activities may face a fine of as much as 10% of annual turnover.

4.3.2 Restraint of trade

It is unlawful in many countries around the world for competitors to agree to fix prices or divide territory. In the US, section 1 of the Sherman Act prohibits combinations and conspiracies in restraint of trade. To prevail on a claim that a horizontal agreement among competitors restrains trade, the plaintiff must prove that defendants engaged in a conspiracy that restrained trade in the relevant market, and competitors suffered injury.

The US Supreme Court has identified three methods of assessing whether a horizontal agreement violates section 1:

1) the ***per se analysis***, for restraints which are obviously anticompetitive, such as price fixing, territorial allocations, group boycotts or tying arrangements,
2) ***quick-look analysis***, for restraints with some pro-competitive justification, and
3) the ***rule of reason*** test, for restraints whose net impact on competition is difficult to determine.[53]

An aggrieved party must prove the restraint is unreasonable or, in other words, harmful to competition. The purpose of the antitrust laws is to protect competition, not to protect individual competitors.[54] Thus, it is not enough to show that the restraint caused a competitor to suffer economic injury. To determine whether the agreement has an adverse effect on competition, courts examine such factors as reduced output, increased prices and decreased quality.[55] In the US, horizontal collusion can result in criminal prosecution by the DOJ, or a civil suit in which treble damages are potentially recoverable by the aggrieved party.

As an example of unlawful collusion in the aviation sector, the air cargo fuel surcharge litigation proved enormously expensive for airlines. The conspiracy to fix fuel prices began in 1996 when IATA passed Resolution 116ss

53 See *FTC v. Indiana Fed'n of Dentists*, 476 U.S. 447 (1986); *Palmer v. BRG of Georgia, Inc.*, 498 U.S. 46 (1990); *California Dental Assn. v. FTC*, 526 U.S. 756 (1999). See also *Continental Airlines v. United Airlines*, 277 F.3rd 499 (4th Cir. 2002).

54 See Markhvida 2017.

55 See *Bell Atlantic Corp. v. Twombly*, 550 U.S. 544 (2007); *Brooke Group Ltd. v. Brown & Williamson Tobacco Corp.*, 509 U.S. 209, 212 (1993); *Cargill, Inc. v. Monfort of Colo., Inc.*, 479 U.S. 104, 117 (1986); *Matsushita Elec. Indus. Co. v. Zenith Radio Corp.*, 475 U.S. 574, 598 (1986); *Atlantic Richfield Co. v. USA Petroleum Co.*, 495 U.S. 328, 338 (1990); *Virgin Atlantic Airways Ltd. v. British Airways PLC*, 257 F.3rd 256, 264 (2nd Cir. 2001). See also Ghoshal and Bush 2008.

on fuel surcharges. However, DOT denied antitrust immunity. Nevertheless, a number of air carriers continued to coordinate fuel surcharges. But since the charges were not tied to distance flown, they were not correlated with fuel consumption. Although fuel prices fell in 2001, the surcharges continued.

In the early years of the new millennium, Lufthansa and its subsidiary Swiss International turned 'state's evidence', so as to enter the corporate leniency programme. They revealed that a number of airlines (including Lufthansa, Lan Chile, Air France, British Airlines, Japan Airlines, Korean Airlines, American Airlines, SAS, Asiana Air, Polar Air, Cathay Pacific, Atlas Air and Cargolux) had conspired to impose uniform fuel and security surcharges. In 2006, law enforcement officers raided the offices of several airlines. Twenty airlines and four executives pleaded guilty and paid fines. British Airways and Korean Airlines paid fines of USD 300 million each in settlement of a DOJ investigation.[56]

As of 2011, 22 airlines and 21 airline executives had been charged with unlawful price fixing. More than USD 1.8 billion in criminal fines were imposed and four executives were sent to prison. More than 100 civil class action lawsuits were filed by private plaintiffs in the US alone, resulting in settlements of nearly half a billion dollars.[57] By 2012, fines totalled almost USD 2 billion. As Table 4.1 reveals, the European Commission imposed fines of EUR 776 million on 11 air cargo carriers that participated in the scheme from December 1999 to February 2006.[58]

However, the conscious parallelism defence did not fare well in a case alleging collusion between Delta Airlines and AirTran to fix prices on baggage fees. The court noted:

> Plaintiffs need not allege the existence of collusive communications in 'smoke-filled rooms' in order to state a §1 Sherman Act claim. Rather, such collusive communications can be based upon circumstantial evidence and can occur in speeches at industry conferences, announcements of future prices, statements on earnings calls, and in other public ways. ... [U]nlawful conspiracies may be inferred when collusive communications among competitors precede changed/responsive business practices, such as new pricing practices.[59]

Nonetheless, the court concluded:

> Even when viewed in the light most favorable to plaintiffs, the evidence in this case simply does not permit a reasonable factfinder to infer the existence

56 For price fixing on fuel charges See also Chapter 3 of this book.
57 terralex.org/calendar/event/4083c84eea/downloadfile?fileid=27c52bf9a3 (visited 9.5.2018).
58 European Commission 2017.
59 In re *Delta/AirTran Baggage Fee Antitrust Litigation*, 733 F. Supp. 2nd 1348, 1360 (N.D. Ga. 2010).

Table 4.1 Fines imposed by the EU on airlines for price fixing on fuel surcharges

	Fine (€)	*Reduction under the Leniency Notice*
Air Canada	21,037,500	15%
Air France	182,920,000	20%
KLM	127,160,000	20%
Martinair	15,400,000	50%
British Airways	104,040,000	10%
Cargolux	79,900,000	15%
Cathay Pacific Airways	57,120,000	20%
Japan Airlines	35,700,000	25%
LAN Chile	8,220,000	20%
SAS	70,167,500	15%
Singapore Airlines	74,800,000	0
Lufthansa	0	100%
Swiss International Air Lines	0	100%

of a conspiracy, as it does not tend to exclude the possibility that the alleged conspirators acted independently.[60]

4.3.3 *Mergers and consolidations*

Mergers raise antitrust concerns as well. Market concentration may reduce competition, causing consumers to suffer higher prices and poorer service. Approximately 100 nations around the world have promulgated pre-merger notification legislation. Requirements range from simple notification to intensive investigations. Typically, jurisdictional thresholds are determined by the size of the transaction. Reviews may include transaction suspension, non-suspension or hybrid approaches depending upon the potential impact of the transaction on the economy. The principal concern is whether, post-merger, the entity will have market power to raise prices. Cross-border ownership is constrained by nationality rules in many states. Foreign ownership in US airlines has been limited to 25% voting stock since the 1920s.[61] In the EU, foreign ownership by non-EU citizens is restricted to 49%. Most bilateral air

60 Delta/AirTran Baggage Fee Antitrust Litigation, case number 1:09-md-02089 in the US District Court for the Northern District of Georgia, summarised at www.law360.com/articles/907594/delta-airtran-score-win-in-bag-fee-mdl (visited 9.5.2018).

61 To qualify as a US flag carrier, US citizens must: (1) hold at least 75% of the voting equity; (2) hold at least 51% of non-voting equity; and (3) effectively 'control' the airline. Foreign ownership restrictions are not unique to aviation, and exist in broadcasting, telecommunications, electric and nuclear power production, shipping and banking.

transport agreements also allow a state to prohibit another state's airlines from enjoying traffic rights under the bilateral if the airline is not 'substantially owned and effectively controlled' by its nationals.[62] However, these rights are often waived.[63] Table 4.2 reveals foreign ownership restrictions in several states.

But domestic airline mergers are possible. Prior to 1985, airline mergers and acquisitions in the US required approval from the CAB. Approval automatically conferred antitrust immunity. Between the sunset of the CAB on 31 December 1984 and 1989, airline mergers were regulated by the DOT. Thereafter, airline mergers would be handled like mergers in any other industry, scrutinised by the Federal Trade Commission (FTC) and DOJ under the Clayton Act. Since 1989, airline mergers have been subject to section 7 of the Clayton Act (15 USC 18).

But for the few years the DOT had jurisdiction, the DOT never met a merger it didn't like, approving each of the 21 merger applications submitted to it, even those to which the DOJ vigorously objected (i.e., Northwest–Republic and TWA–Ozark). Though the pace of airline mergers slowed after the DOJ obtained jurisdiction, it picked up again as financial distress and bankruptcies increased after the turn of the 21st century.

The Clayton Act prohibits a person 'engaged in commerce or in any activity affecting commerce' from acquiring 'the whole or any part' of a business if the

62 Section 5 of the International Air Services Transit Agreement, signed in Chicago on 7 December 1944, entered into force on 30 January 1945, ICAO Doc. 9587, 84 UNTS 389, and Section 6 of the International Air Transport Agreement, signed in Chicago on 7 December 1944, entered into force on 8 February 1945, ICAO Doc. 9587, 171 UNTS 387, provide:

> Each contracting State reserves the right to withhold or revoke a certificate or permit to an air transport enterprise of another State in any case where it is not satisfied that substantial ownership and effective control are vested in nationals of a contracting State

Like their predecessors, modern open skies bilaterals require that 'substantial ownership and effective control' be vested in the nationals of the State designating the airline, and that failure to meet this requirement would entitle either nation to revoke, suspend or limit the operations of the offending airline. See Dempsey 2006.

63 The US has waived the nationality requirements for airlines registered in states that met FAA Category I safety/security requirements, and that have concluded an open skies bilateral with the US. When Iberia gained control of Aerolinas Argentinas, the US did not object to the fact that Spanish citizens owned and control the Argentine carrier after Argentina opened the bilateral to expand traffic rights for US carriers. Conversely, when British Airways sought to gain effective control of USAir, the US stalled on grounds that Bermuda II limited US access to Heathrow. The US denied Virgin Nigeria operations between Lagos–New York on grounds that the carrier was substantially owned and effectively controlled by British citizens (e.g., Richard Branson). The US initially denied Virgin America an operating certificate on grounds it was not controlled by US citizens. Hence, the presence of an ownership and control restriction can be an effective lever to pry loose concessions that would be unattainable absent formal renunciation of the bilateral.

Table 4.2 Status of foreign ownership restrictions for airlines in selected countries[64]

EU	49%
Australia	49% for international (25% single); 100% for domestic
Canada	25% of voting equity (15% single)
Japan	33.33%
New Zealand	49% for international; 100% for domestic
United States	25% of voting equity; 1/3 of board at maximum; cannot be chairman of board

acquisition may substantially 'lessen competition or tend to create a monopoly' (15 USC 12–27; 29 USC 52–53). The FTC and DOJ evaluate the relevant geographic and product market, using reasonable interchangeability or cross-elasticity of demand analysis. Although market share and concentration levels are relevant, they are not conclusive. Instead, courts examine the market's structure, history and future, the characteristics of the customers, trends toward concentration or concentration, the existence of competitors and barriers to entry.[65] Will the merger or acquisition create or enhance market power? This is more likely where the merging entities are direct competitors (known as horizontal mergers). The FTC and DOJ have developed Horizontal Merger Guidelines.[66]

Table 4.3 lists the major US airline mergers that have transpired since airline deregulation in 1978.

The merger of United and Continental Airlines drew antitrust fire from a number of concerned citizens. During the trial, their expert witnesses identified three alternative relevant markets:

- network carriers competing for business travellers,
- airport-pairs, and
- the US airline industry as a whole.

As to the first category, the court concluded:

> because the plaintiffs have failed to show why LCCs should be excluded from a market for business passengers ... network carriers catering to business passengers simply does not fly as a viable relevant geographic and produce market for purposes of Section 7 analysis.[67]

64 Cosmas, Belobaba and Swelbar 2011, p. 21.

65 For example, *Brown Shoe*, 370 U.S. 294, 344–345 (1962); *U.S. v. Philadelphia National Bank*, 374 U.S. 321, 362 (1963). See Sitkol and Vorrasi 2012.

66 *Horizontal Merger Guidelines*, DOJ/FTC, 19.8.2010. See also Hylton 2011.

67 *Malaney v. UAL Corp.*, 2010 U.S. Dist. Lexis 106049 (N.D. Cal. 2010), at 30.

Table 4.3 US major airline mergers since deregulation

Date	*Acquired airline – acquiring airline*
1979	National – Pan Am
1980	Seaboard – Flying Tigers
	Hughes Airwest – Republic
1982	Continental – Texas International
1985	Frontier – People Express
	Muse – Southwest
1986	Pan Am – United
	Republic – Northwest
	Ozark – TWA
	Eastern – Texas Air
	People Express – Texas Air
1987	Air Cal – American
1988	Flying Tigers – Federal Express
1997	AirTran – ValuJet
1998	Reno Air – American
2001	TWA – American
2004	US Airways – America West
2008	Northwest – Delta
2009	Midwest – Republic
	Frontier – Republic
2010	Continental – United
2011	AirTran – Southwest
2013	American – US Airways
2015	TNT Express – FedEx
2016	Southern Air – Atlas Air
	Virgin America – Alaska Airlines

As to airport-pairs, the court found that 'competition from adjacent airports disciplines pricing and must be considered when defining the relevant market. … [G]iven the substantial evidence suggesting city-pairs [may be the appropriate market], plaintiffs' effort to establish anything else never leaves the gate.'[68]

As to the third alternative proffered by plaintiffs (the 'national market') the court noted that it was unclear how a flight from San Francisco to Newark competed with a flight from Seattle to Miami.[69] The pound of flesh

68 Ibid. at 41–42.
69 Ibid. at 42.

surrendered for DOJ acquiescence in the merger was for the carrier to lease slots for 18 round-trip flights to Southwest Airlines at Newark International Airport.

In August 2013, the DOJ and six state Attorney Generals filed suit to block the merger of US Airways and American Airlines. They noted that after the Delta–Northwest and United–Continental mergers, American, Delta and United ceased challenging the others' nonstop fares with lower connecting fares; they also marched in lock-step on ancillary fees. US Airways provided connecting price competition. Concentration at Washington Reagan Airport, where the combined carrier would hold 68% of the landing slots, also was of concern.[70]

By October, a settlement had been reached with the DOJ. The pound of flesh surrendered by the carrier for antitrust acquiescence was the sale of 104 slots at Washington Reagan Washington International Airport, a promise to maintain service to small and mid-size cities from Reagan, the sale of two gates at Chicago O'Hare International Airport, and the maintenance of hubs at New York Kennedy, Charlotte, Chicago, Los Angeles, Miami, Philadelphia and Phoenix for three years.

Since 1991, the US and the EU have coordinated regulatory review on transatlantic mergers, acquisitions, and alliances. For example, Boeing's acquisition of McDonnell-Douglas was reviewed by the European Commission.[71] Under the EU Merger Control Regime:

> A concentration which would significantly impede effective competition, in the common market or in a substantial part of it, in particular as a result of the creation or strengthening of a dominant position, shall be declared incompatible with the common market.[72]

Although transatlantic mergers are prohibited by the statutory restrictions on foreign ownership, discussed earlier, major cross-border airline mergers (e.g., Air France–KLM, British Airways–Iberia, Lufthansa–Austrian) have been concluded within the EU. Middle Eastern air carriers also have purchased significant minority stakes in a number of European carriers (e.g., Etihad Airways acquired significant equity in Air Berlin and Alitalia).[73]

Table 4.4 reveals several of the major non-US airline acquisitions:

Singapore Airlines has launched new airlines targeting various market niches – Scoot, Tiger Airways and Silk Air. Some Southeast Asian airlines (e.g., Tiger

70 Fones 2015.

71 See Dempsey 2004, pp. 118–126.

72 Regulation No. 139/2004/EC of the Council of 20 January 2004 on the control of concentrations between undertakings, OJ L 24, 29.1.2004, pp. 1–22.

73 James and Michaels 2013 p. B7. However, by 2017 Etihad began to retreat from its profligate investment strategy as it lost $1.87 billion, much of which was attributable to writing down its collapsing investments in Air Berlin and Alitalia. Wall 2017, p. B3.

Table 4.4 Major non-US airline acquisitions

Date	*Acquired airline*	*Acquiring airline*	*Percentage*
2000	Canadian Airlines	Air Canada	100%
	Ansett Australia	Air New Zealand	100%
2001	JAS	Japan Air Lines	100%
2004	KLM	Air France	100%
2005	Swiss	Lufthansa	100%
2008	JetBlue	Lufthansa	19%
	Brussels Airlines	Lufthansa	45%
	BMI	Lufthansa	100%
2009	Austrian Airlines	Lufthansa	100%
	Germanwings	Lufthansa	100%
	Brussels Airlines	Lufthansa	45%
2010	British Airways	Iberia	200%
2011	TAM	LAN	100%
	Iberia	British Airways	100%
	Air Berlin	Etihad	29%
2012	Air Seychelles	Etihad	40%
	Aer Lingus	Etihad	3%
2013	Air Serbia	Etihad	49%
	Jet Airways	Etihad	24%
	Darwin Airlines	Etihad	34%
2014	Alitalia	Etihad	49%
	Darwin Airline	Etihad	34%
	Aer Lingus	British Airways	100%
2016	Virgin Australia	Etihad	22%

Airways and Air Asia) also are setting up branded affiliates in nearby countries. Thus, ownership and nationality are becoming increasingly blurred, despite the ownership and control provisions in air transport agreements and in domestic laws.[74]

74 Examples: 1) Alliances: Star, SkyTeam and Oneworld; 2) Metal Neutral Joint Ventures: for example, United–Air Canada–Lufthansa; 3) Multiple Hubs: for example, Lan hubs in Argentina, Ecuador, Peru and Chile; TACA hubs in El Salvador, Costa Rica and Peru; Lufthansa Italia hubs in Milan; EasyJet hubs in Geneva, Madrid, Milan and the UK; 4) Mergers and Acquisitions: for example, Lufthansa acquired Austrian, Swiss, BMI, Brussels; 5) Minority Ownership: for example, Delta in Virgin Atlantic; Lufthansa in JetBlue; Etihad in Air Berlin, Alitalia and Jet Airways; 6) Joint Ventures: for example, Qantas established Jetstar in Singapore; Singapore Airlines established Tiger in Australia; Air Asia operates affiliates in Thailand, Malaysia and Indonesia.

4.3.4 Airline alliances and antitrust immunity

Intercarrier agreements have long been a feature of international aviation. Airlines routinely agree to share ticketing, boarding, baggage handling, catering and maintenance services, as well as gates, lounges and reciprocal frequent flyer programmes. Interline relationships also require an agreement on ticketing and baggage, as well as end-to-end pricing agreement. In recent years, however, airlines have sought, and regulators have conferred, antitrust immunity on agreements in competitive markets addressing issues that otherwise would be deemed collusive and unlawful, such as:

- coordination of routes and scheduling,
- coordination of pricing and inventory management,
- joint marketing and distribution, and
- revenue, cost and profit sharing.[75]

The European Commission may exempt a restrictive alliance if it concludes that the overall benefits of the transaction outweigh its anticompetitive effects, and if those benefits will be enjoyed by consumers. Specifically, the EU evaluates the following criteria:

- Does the agreement contribute to improving the production and distribution of goods or promote technical or economic progress?
- Do consumers receive a fair share of the resulting benefits?
- Are the restrictions imposed by the agreements indispensable to the attainment of these objectives?
- Do the agreements afford the parties the possibility of eliminating competition in respect of a substantial part of the products or services in question?[76]

Recognising that alliances may reduce competition, the European Commission focuses on potential barriers to new competitive entry. These include:

- regulatory barriers, such as government pricing restrictions for indirect flights or the unavailability of necessary traffic rights,
- slot shortages at congested airports,
- increased frequencies resulting from the cooperation,
- network effects resulting from joint frequent flyer, travel agency or corporate customer incentive schemes or reduced third carrier access to transfer passengers, and

75 Markhvida 2017 pp. 317–318.

76 *Transatlantic Airline Alliances: Competitive Issues and Regulatory Approaches*, A report by the European Commission and the United States Department of Transportation, 16.10.2010. See also Stragier 1999.

- 'behavioural' barriers arising from possible predatory pricing or predatory capacity tactics.[77]

In reviewing the Star Alliance relationship between United, Lufthansa and SAS, the European Commission concluded that indirect flights could constitute suitable alternatives to nonstop services on long haul routes and the alliance partners offered to surrender slots at Frankfurt airport to allow new (direct or indirect) air services on the routes concerned. In addition, new entrants using the slots and operating a nonstop service will be admitted to the parties' frequent flyer programme and offered interlining facilities.[78]

While collusion (e.g., price fixing) and mergers are subject to the jurisdiction of the DOJ, the DOT may confer antitrust immunity for airlines in international markets. It appears that antitrust immunity for the three members of the international aviation cartel relieves carriers from the consequences of violation at least two of the three major targets of antitrust law: collusion, monopolisation and predation.

Airlines have several motivations for creating alliances. These include:

- The desire to achieve greater network economies of scale, scope and density.
- The wish to reduce costs by consolidating redundant operations.
- The need to improve revenue by reducing the level of competition wherever possible as markets are liberalised.
- The desire to skirt around the nationality rules (which prohibit multinational ownership) and cabotage (which prohibits foreign carriers from flying domestic traffic).
- The ability to provide more capacity and enter new markets without having to make large capital expenditures for aircraft purchases or airport infrastructure.
- The capability to generate thousands of new online city-pair combinations.
- The ability to extend the reach and scope of their frequent flyer programmes to enhance consumer loyalty.
- The capacity to generate additional passengers per flight.
- The means to enhance market power at hub airports making it more difficult for new entry into the network's markets.
- The ability to sell and market jointly to corporate customers.
- The potential to steal market share from non-aligned competitors.
- The capability to fix prices with competitors in dominant markets.
- The ability to reduce competitive capacity in key markets to improve yields.
- achievement of a reduction in the costs of equipment and services from third-party vendors as a result of greater bargaining power of pooled purchases.
- The means to reduce airport handling, airport operations, selling and ticket costs as a result of economies of scale and the sharing of support services.

77 Gremminger 2003.
78 European Commission 2002.

- The ability to reduce travel agent and GDS costs as a result of enhanced oligopsony market power.
- The potential to pool costs and revenue to share risks and reward.[79]

Yet many of these alleged benefits can be obtained without immunity. End-to-end ticketing, baggage and joint-fare agreements preceded alliances by decades, and do not pose the concerns that horizontal agreements pose. Reciprocal sharing of lounges and frequent flyer programmes also likely can be accomplished without antitrust immunity. The nefarious conduct immunity adds is collusion on fares, frequency and capacity in competitive markets, all of which are manifestly anticompetitive. Alliances also can drain traffic from non-aligned competitors, which further reduces consumer choice.

Three global alliances have emerged – Star, SkyTeam and Oneworld. As of May 2017, these three alliances accounted for 76% of US–Europe seat capacity. Table 4.5 provides data on their respective market shares.

Under the Federal Aviation Act of 1958, the DOT may exempt an agreement from the antitrust laws 'to the extent necessary to allow the person to proceed with the transaction' if DOT determines the exemption is required in the public interest.[80] Pursuant to the statute, the DOT is required to conclude that the alliance will not eliminate actual or potential competition that might enable the allied carriers to raise prices above, or reduce services below, competitive levels.[81] However, the DOT may approve an intercarrier agreement that substantially reduces or eliminates competition if it is necessary to meet a serious transportation need or to achieve important public benefits, which cannot be attained by reasonably achievable alternatives that are materially less anticompetitive.[82] Among the public benefits recognised are international comity and foreign policy considerations.[83]

In determining whether to issue immunity to an intercarrier agreement, the DOT ostensibly asks the following questions:

- Would the agreement substantially reduce or eliminate competition? Would it facilitate the exercise of market power? Would it increase market concentration? The burden of proof on these issues lie with the opponent.
- If so, is the agreement necessary to meet a serious transportation need or achieve important public benefits? The burden of proof on this issue lies with the applicant.
- If so, can those needs or benefits be satisfied by reasonably available alternatives that are materially less anticompetitive? The public benefits require

79 Light 1998 pp. 30–31. See also Tiffany Co. 2000, p. 32.

80 49 USC 41308–41309.

81 *American Airlines and the Taca Group Reciprocal Code-Share Services Proceeding*, DOT Order 97-12-35 (1997), at 58.

82 49 USC 41309(b)(1)(A),(B); 14 CFR Part 212.

83 49 USC 41309(b)(1)(A).

Table 4.5 Airline alliances relative size

	Star			*SkyTeam*			*Oneworld*		
Year	2005	2010	2015	2005	2010	2015	2005	2010	2015
Airlines	n.a.	26	27	n.a.	13	20	n.a.	12	14
Passengers (million)	348	545	641	321	384	665	223	298	557
Countries	139	181	192	137	169	177	135	145	161
Destinations	795	1,130	1,330	685	815	1,062	599	679	1,016

consideration of ***inter alia***, international comity and foreign policy factors. The burden of proof here lies with the opponent.

- Is the agreement required by the 'public interest'? The DOT may exempt the agreement from the antitrust laws 'to the extent necessary to allow the person to proceed with the transaction' if it concludes the exemption is required by the 'public interest.' The DOT insists upon an 'open skies' agreement as a prerequisite to antitrust immunity.
- Will the alliance benefit travellers by enabling applicants to offer better and more efficient service? Will the alliance enhance competition by providing new online services? Will the allied carriers be able to improve the efficiency of their operations?[84]

If the agreement contemplates a joint venture similar to a merger, DOT purports to use Clayton Act analysis:

- Will antitrust immunity substantially reduce competition and facilitate the exercise of market power?
- Will the alliance substantially increase market power?
- Will the alliance cause potential competitive harm?
- Will new entry into the market be timely and sufficient to deter or counteract competitive harm?

In reviewing these statutory criteria, the DOT has found that:

> the pro-competitive effect of global alliances is particularly evident in the case of the behind- and beyond-markets where integrated alliances with coordinated connections, marketing, and services can offer competition well beyond mere interlining. Integrated alliances can, in short, offer a multitude of new on-line [*sic*] services to thousands of city-pair markets, on a global basis.[85]

84 *Expanded Star Application*, DOT Order 2009-4-5 (2009). 49 USC 41309(b)(1)(A). 49 USC 41309. *Expanded Star Application*, DOT Order 2009-7-10 (2009). 49 USC 41308.
85 *Application of American Airlines et al*, DOT Order 2000-4-22 (2000).

They do this by 'code-sharing', whereby they put their flight number on another airline's flight.[86] DOT has lauded code-sharing as 'an important source of new entry, new service, lower fares, and competition' and praised 'the pro-competitive and pro-consumer features of code-share agreements'.[87]

Of course, code-sharing connections are not actually online services at all, though they masquerade as such; they are instead glorified interlines. Moreover, preferential interlines effectively eliminate a multitude of non-preferential interlines to thousands of city-pair markets, thereby reducing competition and consumer convenience.

The DOT has also found solace in the opportunity for new entry presented by open skies bilaterals as well as the 'competitive discipline afforded by competing US hubs and existing competition from one-stop and connecting services'.[88] In one case, DOT sanguinely predicted that, 'Because of the open-skies accords, any US carrier may serve any of these foreign markets from any point in the United States.'[89]

What the DOT ignores is that despite the theoretical opportunity for new entry afforded by the open skies bilaterals, the reality is that the ability of a new airline to provide sustainable competitive service is severely hampered where it does not have a connecting hub at least at one end of the spoke. Surely too, the DOT must recognise that one-stop and connecting services are distinctly inferior alternatives to nonstop operations. But according to DOT, 'a significant element in antitrust analysis is the extent to which facilitating airline integration (through antitrust immunity or otherwise) can enhance overall competitive conditions.'[90]

If such agreements are indeed pro-competitive, why then do they need antitrust immunity? According to DOT, though unlikely to be found to violate the antitrust laws, the approved alliances 'might be exposed to liability under the antitrust laws if we did not grant immunity'.[91] Well then, if they were exposed to antitrust liability, it would be because their activities violated the antitrust laws, and not because they were pro-competitive.

The DOT has acknowledged that, 'the practice of excluding airlines from participating in a particular code-share arrangement can have adverse public consequences because code-sharing can provide a primary, if not the only, method of entering or expanding service in many international aviation

86 A list of DOT approved code-shares as of 31 July 2016, is available at: www.transportation.gov/sites/dot.gov/files/docs/July%202016%20Code%20Share%20Report.pdf (visited 9.5.2018).

87 *Joint Application of United Air Lines, Inc., and All Nippon Airlines, Ltd.*, DOT Order 99-8-14 (1999). See also: Whalen 2007; Ito and Lee 2007; Park and Zhang 2000. Other studies suggest that code-sharing has resulted in consumer price increases. See, for example, Armantier and Richard 2006; Gayle 2008.

88 DOT Order 99–8-14 (1999), at 23.

89 DOT Order 97–12-35 (1997), at 64.

90 *Application of United Airlines et al.*, DOT Order 97–6-30 (1997), at 53.

91 *Applications of American Airlines et al.*, DOT Order 97–2-26 (1997), at 42.

markets.'[92] Nevertheless, DOT believes that open skies bilateral transport agreements are the panacea for the anticompetitive consequences of alliances. Thus, DOT concluded:

> while we continue to have concerns about the impact of exclusivity provisions in markets that are not governed by open-skies agreements, we are satisfied ... that code-share exclusivity provisions would not inhibit competition or otherwise adversely affect the public interest.[93]

In order to ameliorate some of the more blatant anticompetitive consequences of alliances, the DOT has sometimes imposed certain conditions upon them, and limited them to five-year terms so that they could be reviewed every half-decade. For example, to protect time sensitive nonstop travellers, DOT has withheld antitrust immunity to 'pricing, inventory or yield management coordination or pooling of revenues, with respect to unrestricted coach-class fares or any business or first-class fares' in certain specified city-pair markets where the allied carriers dominate the traffic.[94] Early DOT issuances of antitrust immunity included 'carve-outs', whereby the dominant city-pairs at which the allied carriers maintained hub operations were exempted from antitrust immunity. As noted by Deputy Assistant Attorney General R. Hewitt Pate:

> [w]hen antitrust immunity has been sought, we have recommended that DOT 'carve out' certain unrestricted fares involving these city pairs from the order granting antitrust immunity. ... For example, the [Antitrust] Division recommended that seven city pairs be carved out of the Delta/Swissair/Sabena/Austrian alliance (Atlanta–Zurich, Atlanta–Brussels, Cincinnati–Zurich, New York–Brussels, New York–Geneva, New York–Vienna, and New York–Zurich); one for the American/Canadian Air alliance (New York–Toronto); two for the United/Lufthansa alliance (Washington–

92 DOT Order 99–8-14 (1999).

93 Ibid.

94 See, for example, *Application of American Airlines et al.*, DOT Order 2000–5-13 (2000) The DOJ has recommended that certain unrestricted fares to and from alliance-dominated city-pairs be 'carved out', and denied antitrust immunity. For example, Justice recommended DOT not confer antitrust immunity to the Delta–Swissair–Sabena–Austrian alliance between Atlanta–Zurich, Atlanta–Brussels, Cincinnati–Zurich, New York–Brussels, New York–Geneva, New York–Vienna and New York–Zurich; it recommended that New York–Toronto be carved out of the American–Canadian alliance; Justice recommended that Washington–Frankfurt and Chicago–Frankfurt be carved out of the United–Lufthansa alliance; and it recommended that Chicago–Toronto and San Francisco–Toronto be carved out of the United–Air Canada alliance. DOT accepted these recommendations except for the four New York–Europe routes for which antitrust immunity was sought by the Delta alliance. See *International Aviation Alliances: Market Turmoil and the Future of Airline Competition*, Statement of Deputy Assistant Attorney General R. Hewitt Pate before the Subcommittee on Antitrust, Competition, and Business Rights, Committee on the Judiciary, US Senate.

> Frankfurt and Chicago–Frankfurt); and two for the United/Air Canada alliance (Chicago–Toronto and San Francisco–Toronto).[95]

DOT also carved out Miami–Santiago and Miami–Lima from the American–LAN alliance, and carved Atlanta–Paris; Los Angeles–Auckland and Los Angeles–Sydney were removed from the United–Air New Zealand alliance, and Cincinnati–Paris from the Delta–Air France–KLM–Alitalia–Czech Airlines. However, concluding that they inhibit alliance efficiencies, the DOT no longer requires carve-outs, and many earlier carve-outs have since been removed.[96]

Exclusive dealing clauses in code-sharing agreements have been disapproved unless the country to and from which the carriers will operate has concluded an open skies bilateral air transport agreement with the US.[97] Nonetheless, immunity has been explicitly conferred on the determination of capacity (flight frequency and types of aircraft and their configuration), pricing, inventory and yield management, and pooling of revenue.

The DOT turned a sharp corner in 2005, when announced that antitrust immunity for alliances would no longer be granted unless the carriers created 'metal-neutral joint ventures',[98] arguably the least competitive alternative short of an outright merger. In other words, the DOT was insisting on further airline consolidation as a prerequisite for antitrust immunity.

What is metal neutrality? The DOT defines it as:

> an industry term meaning that the partners in an alliance are indifferent as to which operates the 'metal' (aircraft) when they jointly market services. Without a metal neutral sales environment, the partners have a strong economic incentive to book passengers on their own aircraft in order to retain a larger share of the revenue for themselves, which may not be in the best interest of the consumer or the alliance as a whole. Metal neutrality may be achieved through revenue and/or comprehensive benefit sharing arrangements.[99]

As the DOT noted:

> [w]e have emphasized the high standard necessary to justify a grant of immunity and the need for applicants to demonstrate that substantial public benefits are likely to be produced at the time the immunity is requested. For example, in the SkyTeam case in 2005, we tentatively denied a request for

95 Ibid.

96 www.transportation.gov/sites/dot.gov/files/docs/mission/office-policy/aviation-policy/9906/170104-all-immunized-alliances-05102017.pdf (visited 9.5.2018). See, for example, DOT Order 2009–7-10 (2009), at 20.

97 See, for example, *Application of American Airlines et al*, DOT Order 99–6-6 (1999).

98 DOT Show Cause Order 2005–12-12, at 2, 30, and 37.

99 DOT Show Cause Order 2010–2-13.

> antitrust immunity because there was both insufficient information in the record to make a complete assessment of public benefits and the competitive conditions were in flux. There ... the Department identified barriers to integration that we believed reduced the incentives of the airlines to integrate their operations and pass on the benefits of immunized cooperation to consumers.[100]

In negotiating the multilateral open skies agreement in 2007, the EU had urged the US to liberalise its foreign ownership restrictions to allow up to 49% foreign ownership, which is the rule on the European side of the Atlantic. Though the DOT was willing to proceed with a rulemaking to give the statute an elastic interpretation, the US Congress passed a funding bill for the DOT that explicitly prohibited such administrative activism. US regulators instead insisted on the creation of 'metal-neutral joint ventures' as the *quid pro quo* for antitrust immunity of airline alliances, which is the most anticompetitive alternative this side of an outright merger. DOT and alliance members allege that, although antitrust immunity allows competitors to fix prices and ration capacity, consumers benefit from such joint ventures in the form of lower prices. Normally, antitrust analysis assumes that reduced competition created market power in which service declines and/or prices increase. DOT analysis stands this presumption on its head.

DOT assumes that antitrust immunity is necessary for airlines to eliminate 'double–marginalisation.' Let us first explain the problem antitrust immunity seeks to remedy. Here is a simplified example. Assume carrier X operates from A to B, and carrier Y operates from B to C. Carrier X's nonstop fare between A and B is USD 50; carrier Y's nonstop fare between B and C is also USD 50. They may offer interline service between A and C as a combination of their two point-to-point fares, or USD 100. Assume they compete with Carrier Z, which operates nonstop from A to C but offers a nonstop fare between A and C of USD 90. Assume a passenger wants to fly from A to C. Carrier Z offers a nonstop fare USD 10 lower than the combined XY fare of USD 100, and offers a nonstop online flight as opposed to the XY interline connection. In this example, carriers X and Y will sell virtually no seats in the A to C market until carrier Z's planes are full and passengers are 'spilled' to the XY interline service. So, if they want to participate meaningfully as competitors on the A to C route, carriers X and Y will have to lower their respective point-to-point fares, usually in typical ticketing and baggage and joint-fare agreements whereby they will honour each other's tickets, provide through baggage handling from origin to destination, and offer a through combined fare. Assume they agree to lower their fares to USD 40 on interline customers; combining X's A to B USD 40 fare with Y's B to C USD 40 fare results in a through interline fare of USD 80. Now the customer wanting to fly from A to C has a choice: (1) an interline fare on carriers X and Y

100 DOT Show Cause Order 2005–12-12 at 2, 30 and 37.

with a connection in B of USD 80; or (2) a nonstop fare on carrier Z of USD 90. Some passengers will pay a premium for the nonstop fare;[101] others will opt for the less-convenient itinerary for a lower price. To add one more layer of intercarrier agreement, if carriers X and Y also want to mislead the customer into believing their interline flight is an online flight, they will code-share, so that both X and Y will falsely appear to fly between A and C.

No doubt, lowering the fare from A to C by 20% would enhance consumer welfare. However, the DOT seems to believe that prorating interline fares cannot be accomplished without antitrust immunity. But in fact, carriers have engaged in joint-fare agreements since the 1920s in international aviation under the auspices of IATA. Intercarrier agreements on fares on end-to-end city-pairs have never created the antitrust heartburn that have pricing discussions on parallel routes.

Further, in granting antitrust immunity, the DOT has repeatedly relied on a study produced by an airline industry consultant that alleged consumer savings of 15–25% resulting from double-marginalisation.[102] This theory is 'supported by a single study prepared by a paid advocate for one of the [antitrust immunity] applicants, and based solely … on pre-1999 data.'[103] Essentially, the DOT has adopted a presumption that prices fall whenever competition is circumscribed,[104] which is about as counterintuitive as any economic policy embraced by a government agency.

Industry expert Hubert Horan explained the fallacy of such specious reasoning:

> [u]nder this theory [of double-marginalization] the only ways to reduce the structurally higher costs of interline pricing are merger or full immunity to collude on prices. … This theory is completely indefensible. 'Double marginalization' does not exist, never existed, and has absolutely nothing to do with the actual legitimate benefits of immunized alliances. The 'double marginalization' theory was created out of whole cloth.[105]

Assuming, for the sake of argument, that double-marginalisation was an interline joint-fare problem that could only be remedied by antitrust immunity (which it is not), that is no justification to authorise airlines to collude on pricing, scheduling and capacity on parallel point-to-point routes.

By 2008, the DOJ had had enough. It issued a 55-page objection to the issuance additional antitrust immunity to the Star Alliance on grounds that the purported benefits alleged by the DOT had not been established. It found that the benefits alleged from immunised elimination of double-marginalisation did

101 In fact, 76% of passengers in the trans-Atlantic market fly non-stop even though prices are more than 8% higher than connecting fares. Gillespie and Richard 2012, p. 454.

102 Brueckner and Whalen 2000.

103 Horan 2010, pp. 261, 270.

104 Ibid. pp. 269, 276.

105 Ibid. pp. 273–274.

not exist, and that 'connecting fares offered by non-immunized alliances for transatlantic routes are no more expensive than fares offered by immunized alliances.'[106] Further, DOJ economists have studied the allegations of consumer benefits resulting from airline antitrust immunity and concluded that the data do not support such a claim. They deduce that 'grants of immunity to participants in international alliances ... have harmed consumers by raising prices on many routes and have not delivered the benefits that participants claimed at the DOT.'[107]

In response, two former senior DOT apologists published an article boasting that 'the emergence of alliances – and particularly immunized alliances – arguably has represented the most important development in the industry since the introduction of the jet aircraft.'[108] In other words, the emergence of a global aviation cartel is the most important development in the industry since the introduction of jet aircraft. That cartel consists of three immunised alliances, each of which has significantly reduced competition between its members, while taking traffic from non-aligned competitors. Why one speaks with such pride of creating a global cartel is perplexing. The *Economist* said it best:

> This lack of competition is partly the result of collusion sanctioned by regulators. On transatlantic routes members within each of the world's three big alliances – Star, oneworld and SkyTeam – share costs and agree on prices. ... [The DOT] has not only given its blessing to the rise of alliances, but actually requires airlines to collude fully within each of their groupings, and to share costs and agree on prices ... America's main antitrust regulator, the Department of Justice (DoJ), is rightly sceptical of the notion that collusion benefits consumers. It objected to the creation and expansion of the three transatlantic cartels, only to be ignored by the [DOT], which it cannot overrule on such matters. Earlier this year an unofficial study by two of the DoJ's economists crunched the most recent data available, and reached the opposite, and more plausible, conclusion: that fewer competitors means higher fares, as one would expect. The proponents of consumer-friendly cartels still find that the data support their theory. But if such drastically opposing conclusions can be drawn simply by shuffling the figures a different way, it is surely best to believe the outcome that most accords with common sense. A pity, then, that the [DOT] shows no sign of doing so. ... Blessing the cartels across the Atlantic and Pacific was a mistake, and should be reversed. Since the [DOT] seems unlikely to do

106 *Comments of the Department of Justice on the Show Cause Order: Joint Application of Air Canada, et al.*, DOJ, 26.6.2009, www.justice.gov/atr/comments-department-justice-show-cause-order-joint-application-air-canada-et-al.

107 Gillespie and Richard 2012, p. 467.

108 Dean and Shane 2010.

that, Congress should hand its remaining antitrust powers to the more pro-competition DoJ.[109]

By 2010, the highest levels of integration under antitrust immunity in 'metal-neutral' joint ventures had been achieved by the following airlines:

- Air Canada, Lufthansa, United-Continental.
- Air France–KLM, Alitalia, Delta.
- American, British Airways, Iberia.[110]

Table 4.6 lists the active intercarrier relationships that enjoy antitrust immunity as of 2017. Note that four global alliances were reduced to three after Air France's acquired KLM in 2004, then folded it into the SkyTeam alliance, leaving Northwest without a major European alliance partner, leading to Delta's acquisition of Northwest in 2008. The three alliances (SkyTeam, Star and Oneworld) collectively account for more than 80% of the passenger traffic flying between the US and EU.[111] Note also that the tentacles of immunised alliances have now extended beyond the transatlantic US–EU market and have spread to Asia and Australia.

Table 4.6 Active alliances immunised by DOT[112]

SkyTeam	*Star*	*Oneworld*	*Other*
Delta/Air France–KLM/Alitalia/ Czech/Korean Delta/Virgin Atlantic /Air France-KLM/ Alitalia	United/Air Canada /Brussels/ Lufthansa /Swiss/Austrian/ SAS /LOT/TAP United/Air New Zealand United/Asiana United/All Nippon Airways United/COPA	American/Lan Airlines/Lan Peru American/British Airways/Iberia/ Finnair/Royal Jordanian American/Japan Air Lines	SAS/Icelandair Delta/Virgin Australia

109 Open 2011. This view is also reflected by Schlangen 2000.

110 *Transatlantic Airline Alliances: Competitive Issues and Regulatory Approaches*, A report by the European Commission and the United States Department of Transportation, 16.10.2010.

111 Gillespie and Richard 2012.

112 As of 1.5.2017, source www.transportation.gov/sites/dot.gov/files/docs/170104%20-%20All%20Immunized%20Alliances_0.pdf (visited 9.5.2018).

Finally, at the end of the Obama Administration (in November 2016), the DOT issued two decisions that appeared to reflect some measure of newly discovered caution with respect to the Pandora's box it had opened. Delta Air Lines and Aeromexico sought antitrust immunity for a metal-neutral joint venture. Although Mexico had concluded an open skies bilateral air transport agreement with the US, the DOT expressed concern with the lack of transparency in slot allocations at the Mexico City's Benito Juarez International Airport (MEX), and the control by the two carriers of nearly 50% of the slots at that airport, which might enable them to exert market power at MEX and New York's John F. Kennedy Airport (JFK). DOT therefore conditioned the grant on surrendering 24 pairs of slots at MEX and six slots at JFK to US or Mexican LCCs, and limiting approval to a five-year term.[113]

Also in November 2016, the DOT denied the application of American Airlines and Qantas for antitrust immunity on grounds that the allied carriers would account for nearly 60% of US–Australia traffic, and the largest market share in nearly 200 city-pairs, thereby enabling the alliance to exert market power. Emphasis was placed on the unique geographic and demographic characteristics of the US–Australia market, with few passengers connecting via intermediate points, and limited flow within or beyond Australia. For the first time, the DOT concluded that 'many public benefits from customer service coordination could be obtained through traditional arms-length cooperation such as codesharing.'[114] The DOT also recognised that immunised alliances often have the 'effect of limiting access to their networks by competitors or independent airlines.'[115] The DOT concluded that the proposed alliance 'would substantially reduce or eliminate competition at the network, country-pair, and city-pair levels' and enable the applicants to unreasonably 'exclude present and future competitors from the market.'[116] The DOT found that the proposed benefits alleged by the applicants were 'likely to be limited, delayed, or ultimately not realized at all, due to the lack of adequate competition to discipline the alliance.'[117]

Whether this represents a long-overdue epiphany in public policy, or merely more restrictive decisions limited to the unique factual circumstances posed by these two applications, remains to be seen.

4.4 Analysis

The competitive landscape in international aviation has changed enormously during the last decade and a half. The regulators have insisted on 'metal-neutral

113 *Joint Application of Delta Air Lines and Aerovias de Mexico*, DOT Order 2016–11-2 (2016).
114 *Joint Application of American Airlines and Qantas Airways*, DOT Order 2016–11-16 (2016).
115 Ibid. at 17.
116 Ibid. at 18.
117 Ibid. at 19.

joint ventures' as the price of admission for antitrust immunity. Massive mergers have lessened competition as, in the US, seven major network airlines have been reduced to three, while in the EU, the British Airways, Lufthansa and Air France conglomerates have also reduced network competition. Three carriers on each side of the Atlantic now dominate transatlantic traffic in 'metal-neutral joint ventures' with antitrust immunity. In fact, DOT's insistence on metal-neutral joint ventures as the price for admission to antitrust immunity, coupled with consolidation of major airlines on both sides of the Atlantic, have created the global oligopoly of Star, SkyTeam and Oneworld. As DOJ's analysis has revealed, the market power that has emerged from antitrust abdication has resulted in consumer harm.

Meanwhile, many major US and EU alliance airlines complain about the alleged subsidies received by the Middle East airlines, which operate from countries without state aid prohibitions, and seek a roll back from the ubiquitous open skies bilateral air transport agreements with the UAE and Qatar.[118] Airlines are also immune from General Agreement on Trade and Services (GATS) antidumping prohibitions.[119] The result is a regulatory mess with no clear solutions.

The DOT has embraced a largely schizophrenic approach to airline competition. On the one hand, it has concluded liberalised open skies air transport agreements with more than 120 states.[120] On the other hand, it has enabled airline competitors to fix prices and limit capacity on common routes. The former enhances competition; the latter does the opposite. If open skies is the competitive Dr Jekyll, antitrust immunity is the anticompetitive Mr Hyde.

DOT appears to be using code-sharing and antitrust immunity to facilitate international megacarrier alliances because direct consolidation of airlines on a global scale is prohibited by statutory foreign ownership restrictions. While DOT has significantly liberalised those restrictions (allowing, e.g., up to 49% equity investment in US airlines so long as voting stock is limited to 25%), they stand as a barrier to outright mergers of airlines across national boundaries (as do the 'significant ownership and control' requirements in many bilateral air transport agreements). SAS, the multinational airline of Scandinavia, appears to be an example of the multinational airline DOT would like to see emerge on a *de facto* basis. In other words, DOT is using antitrust immunity to allow carriers to breach US antitrust laws; it is also using antitrust immunity to allow carriers effectively to breach the purpose behind explicit statutory foreign ownership and cabotage prohibitions.[121]

118 The US has an arsenal of regulatory, statutory and treaty countermeasures it could employ should it conclude that the competition provided by the Gulf carriers is unfair. See Dempsey 1987, pp. 121–164.

119 Dempsey 2017.

120 Reitzes and Moss 2008.

121 'Code-sharing does not violate the letter of U.S. law because the airplane actually carrying passengers within the United States is owned and operated by U.S. nationals. It does, however raise questions as to whether the spirit and intent of U.S. law is violated' (Kass 1994, p. 164).

Also worrisome is the competitive impact of code-sharing and antitrust immunity. After the Delta–Swissair–Sabena alliance was given antitrust immunity, American Airlines abandoned its long-standing New York–Zurich and New York–Brussels routes, and TWA exited from the New York–Zurich and New York–Geneva markets.[122] After the United–Lufthansa alliance was given antitrust immunity, American abandoned its Miami–Frankfurt route. Business fares rose 18%. By 1998, American had withdrawn from Chicago–Dusseldorf, as well.[123] Delta closed its Frankfurt hub, and TWA dropped its New York–Frankfurt flights.[124]

After British Airways took on American Airlines as an alliance partner, scorned US Airways was without a major alliance partner. TWA was never a member of a major alliance. Both carriers' financial positions worsened as their interline traffic softened. TWA issued a study entitled *The Anticompetitive Nature of Airline Alliances*,[125] but it was too little, too late, and TWA collapsed into bankruptcy and was acquired by American Airlines. After Delta jettisoned Swissair and Sabena in favour of an alliance with Air France, both Swissair and Sabena soon found themselves heading for bankruptcy. Whether these events are positively correlated or mere coincidence, it appears that carriers not allowed to join the three major global alliances may lose traffic to the cartel.[126] The telephone regulators insist on 'seamless interconnectivity'; the airline regulators allow 'preferential connectivity'.[127] Seamless connectivity enables more competitors to enter the market for network services; preferential connectivity chills the ability of new competitors from exchanging traffic with dominant providers.

Are alliances pro-competitive, or anticompetitive? Proponents point to the following consumer benefits:

- beyond-segment competition,
- one-stop travel purchase services,
- joint frequent flyer benefits,
- reciprocal airport lounge access,
- seamless connectivity of passengers and luggage, and
- coordinated arrival and departure scheduling.

One must remember that the statutory language involving the issuance of antitrust immunity to an anticompetitive agreement requires that it only be conferred where it

122 Goldberg 1999, p. 1.
123 Doganis 2001, p. 75.
124 McCartney 1997, p. B1.
125 Goldberg 1999, p. 1.
126 Of course, not all carriers need alliances to survive. In order to keep operations simple and costs low, Southwest Airlines shuns even interlining, and has been consistently profitable for more than 20 years. It is the network carriers that depend on marketing an array of city-pairs that are more vulnerable to traffic erosion.
127 Note that while the airline regulators embrace preferential connectivity with partner common carriers, the telephone regulators embrace nondiscriminatory connectivity with non-partner common carriers.

is necessary to meet a serious transportation need or important public benefits if there is no less-anticompetitive alternative. This author submits that all of the aforementioned public benefits can be achieved without serious threat of antitrust enforcement. It is collusion of airlines on pricing, entry, capacity, frequency and marketing in competitive markets that antitrust immunity has the most value to the carriers, and poses the most significant burden on consumers.

Alliances, particularly those involving code-sharing, price fixing and capacity rationalisation, can reduce competition[128] in ways that injure competitors[129] and consumers.[130] Code-sharing itself can be a predatory weapon,[131] resulting in higher fares or the foreclosure of competitors from markets,[132] while deceiving consumers into purchasing a product different from that actually being provided.[133] Awarding antitrust immunity to competing airlines results in the loss of independent competitors, resulting in higher fares.[134]

128 '[A]irline alliances result in fewer remaining competitors with less overlap and thus less inclination to compete on prices. ... As a result of the large airline alliances, competition has already diminished on some routes to gateway European cities dominated by alliances' (McShea 1997, p. 86).

129 'This form of systems competition, the hub-and-spoke model, creates serious anticompetitive concerns as alliances protect their respective hubs through predatory pricing or the threat of pricing below cost' (Hand 2011).

130 '[T]here can be little doubt that airline executives see alliances, especially when they involve code-sharing and capacity rationalization [sic], as a way of reducing or limiting competition' (Doganis 2006, p. 95).

131 Airlines 1998, p. 241.

132 US Deputy Assistant Attorney General Pate argued that code-sharing 'can result in market allocation, capacity limitations, higher fares, or foreclosure of rivals from markets, all to the injury of consumers' (See Truxal 2012, p. 136).

133 Edward Hasbrouck, author of 'The Practical Nomad':

> Code sharing is unnecessary for, indeed irrelevant to, any legitimate purpose or actual service. Code sharing doesn't enable an airline to fly to any more places. It just enables the airline to mislead travelers into thinking that they fly to places they don't. I call that fraud.
>
> (https://hasbrouck.org/articles/alliances.html (visited 9.5.2018))

134 'The evidence shows that a grant of antitrust immunity to two competing non-stop carriers in a trans-Atlantic route has a fare effect that is equivalent to the loss of an independent competitor, and fares are significantly higher in routes with fewer independent competitors. This finding supports the normal antitrust presumption that eliminating or substantially reducing competition through collaboration or merger enhances the market power of the remaining suppliers and leads to higher prices, harming consumers. ... The loss of competition in trans-Atlantic routes with non-stop service as a result of antitrust immunity grants adversely affects consumers' (Gillespie and Richard 2012). Alan Coles, chairman of the Guild of Business Travel Agents: 'Airlines say that alliances can reduce costs, but we have seen no evidence of prices coming down as a result' (Alliances 2000, p. 60).

5 Airline alliances

Permitted and prohibited practices in view of the EU law

Agnieszka Kunert-Diallo

5.1 Introduction

For decades inter-airline agreements were outside the scope of competition law. The Chicago Convention,[1] which established the principles of international air services, has introduced the privilege of non-scheduled flights (Article 5) and the prohibition of scheduled air services without proper permission or authorisation (Article 6). However, it has not regulated economic aspects associated with such services, including inter-airline agreements. Thus, these issues have usually been a matter of bilateral air services agreements (ASAs). Relationships between the air carriers entitled to exercise traffic rights under bilateral ASAs have been a crucial part of the mechanism that stimulates international air transport.

The most restrictive bilateral ASAs included provisions according to which designated airlines were even obliged to discuss aspects of their commercial activity to ensure equal opportunities for both airlines. Designated airlines were often the only competitors on routes agreed upon in bilateral ASAs and therefore they were subject of obligations and limitations imposed additionally through the inter-airline agreements. Until the 1970s, the framework of international air transport consisted of three pillars: bilateral ASAs, inter-airline pooling agreements and tariffs and pricing agreements negotiated through the International Air Transport Association (IATA).[2] For a very long time IATA played a quasi-regulatory role in international air transport and tariff consultations were widely accepted and even required by most bilateral agreements.[3]

Over time, the perception of airline cooperation has changed and some of the inter-airline agreements are no longer permitted from the competition law perspective. The role of IATA has been significantly reduced and its mechanism of tariff consultation has been denounced by nearly all countries. Although the market of international air transport has been extensively liberalised, it is not entirely free of economic regulations and many new restrictions have been

1 Convention on International Civil Aviation, signed in Chicago on 7 December 1944, entered into force 4 April 1947, ICAO Doc. 7300/9, 15 UNTS 295.

2 Doganis 2010, p. 26.

3 For the role of IATA in this period see also Chapter 2 of this book.

imposed on cooperation between airlines. This has been a response to airline alliances extending to all aspects of the airline business.

It has also been noticed that increased liberalisation and consequently increased market openness should be accompanied with effective implementation of competition rules. These rules should be applied in a way to ensure equal treatment of inter-airline agreements concluded under similar conditions. This enables market participants to cooperate effectively based on uniform criteria. However, the process of adopting competition rules to new market conditions has not been realised in the same way by all states.[4] The following analysis of inter-airline agreements will mainly focus on European law.

5.2 Diversity of airline alliances

There is no legal definition of inter-airline agreements and alliances. Most inter-airline agreements exist outside the scope of airline alliances. An alliance is the most advanced form of cooperation between airlines and may consist of various inter-airline agreements. According to M. Żylicz, the term inter-airline agreement may denote all types of possible agreements and practices, including decisions taken within airline associations, which do not necessarily have to take the form of documents, but are always concluded between airlines or their organisations.[5]

The term 'alliance' has evolved over the years. Initially, alliances were limited to only few airlines and covered a narrow scope of cooperation. The more advanced forms of alliances have been concluded in more competitive markets. Alliances may involve diverse types of inter-airline agreements. Most of these collaborations are commercial in nature, although typically technical arrangements are also not uncommon. Considering the complexity of inter-airline agreements, R. Doganis distinguishes two categories of alliances: strategic and marketing. Parties to the marketing alliances cooperate based on their individual commercial strategy and therefore marketing alliances ensure independency of airlines involved. Inter airline agreements within such alliances are by their nature commercial and include code-share agreements or joint frequent flyer programmes. More sensitive from the competition law perspective are the strategic alliances, which are the most advanced form of airline cooperation. Air carriers engaged in strategic alliances offer a common brand and uniform service. A strategic alliance may lead to a full merger.[6] Low level of coordination is involved in the case of simplest alliances created between two air carriers in respect to a limited number of routes. The goal of such cooperation is to address a specific deficiency in networks of the parties involved. These alliances most often cover

4 For perspectives of International harmonisation of competition rules in air transport see Chapter 3 of this book.

5 Żylicz 2011, p. 187. This includes airline alliances. Each alliance constitutes an inter-airline arrangement, but not every inter-airline agreement may be considered an alliance.

6 Doganis 2001, p. 81.

areas such as: ground handling, joint use of ground facilities, code-sharing, joint operations and coordination of flight schedules for directly related flights. Contrary to the simplest alliances, arms-length arrangements and the most advanced ones are designed to develop joint network and merger-like integration. They may also cover coordination of prices, routes, scheduling, facilities and so on. Revenue, cost and benefit sharing joint ventures and even capital engagement are also part of the most advanced alliances.[7]

The international aspect of airline alliances and the multiplicity of inter-airline agreements has drawn the attention of antimonopoly authorities. Increased competition between airlines and the predatory character of some agreements has caused change in the approach to airline cooperation. Some agreements, widely accepted for decades, are no longer permitted and some of them may only be accepted under certain conditions. However, despite limiting or eliminating competition, such agreements have mostly been accepted by the European Commission. Since Regulation 1/2003[8] came into force, no negative decision has been taken in this respect. The European Commission's decisions on alliance agreements indicate that the commitments offered by the parties involved in such deep cooperation give the opportunity to exempt alliances from prohibitions established in Article 101(1) of the TFEU.[9] The mentioned commitments offer concessions to non-allied competitors not being parties to an alliance and, thus, minimise barriers to market entry. However, this does not mean that alliances no longer adversely affect competition. They still infringe competition, but their negative impact is offset by their pro-competitive benefits, as defined in Article 101(3) TFEU.

The analysed issue is very problematic because of the multiplicity of inter-airline agreements included in an alliance and their unquestioned negative impact on competition. Regulation 1/2003 is based on a self-assessment principle. This means that there is no *ex ante* administrative review. In their cooperative undertakings, airlines must rely on their own judgement. Some hints may be found in previous European Commission's actions. The list of permitted inter-airline agreements has evolved strongly since the outset of liberalisation. However, mere increased access to the air transport market ceased to be an argument for lenient treatment. Consequently, airlines lost their privileges in the form of block exemptions from Article 101(1) TFEU.

7 *Transatlantic Airline Alliances: Competitive Issues and Regulatory Approaches. A report by the European Commission and the United States Department of Transportation.* 16 November 2010.

8 Regulation No. 1/2003/EC of the Council of 16 December 2002 on the implementation of the rules on competition laid down in Articles 81 and 82 of the Treaty, OJ L 1, 4.1.2003, pp. 1–25.

9 Treaty on the Functioning of the European Union (TFEU), signed on 25 March 1957 in Rome, entered into force on 1 January 1958 (then Treaty establishing the European Economic Community, later Treaty establishing the European Economic Community, consolidated version OJ C 202, 7.6.2016, pp. 47–199.

5.3 Airline alliances in view of the EU competition law

Article 101(1) TFEU prohibits all agreements between undertakings, decisions by associations of undertakings and concerned practices that may affect trade between member states and have as their objective or effect the prevention, restriction or distortion of competition. The evaluation of an agreement under Article 101(1) TFEU consists of two steps. The first one is to assess whether an agreement that can affect trade between member states has an anticompetitive objective or an actual or potential anticompetitive effect. The second step becomes relevant only if the agreement in question restricts competition. In such case, pursuant to Article 101(3) TFEU, the possible pro-competitive effects arising from the agreement will be weighed against its revealed anticompetitive impact. In this process it is necessary to demonstrate that all four conditions established by the Article 101(3) TFEU are met. These conditions are: efficiency gains, fair share for consumers, indispensability of the restrictions and no elimination of competition. The practice has shown, however, that in the case of some decisions regarding alliances these four conditions are difficult to identify. All restrictive agreements that fulfil the four conditions of Article 101(3) TFEU are covered by the exception rule.[10] However, some severe restrictions of competition, known as hard core restrictions, are unlikely to fulfil the conditions set forth in Article 101(3) TFEU. The most prominent examples of hard core restrictions are included in Article 101(1) TFEU. These are the following:

- fixing purchase or selling prices or any other trading conditions,
- limiting or controlling production, markets, technical development or investment,
- market sharing,
- applying dissimilar conditions to equivalent transactions with other commercial partners, and
- making the conclusion of contracts subject to acceptance by the other parties of supplementary obligations, which, by their nature or according to commercial usage, have no connection with the subject of such contracts.

The catalogue laid down in Article 101(1) TFEU is not exhaustive, therefore each inter-airline agreement should be assessed based on conditions specified in Article 101(1) TFEU.

Interestingly, the case of airline alliances shows that even the most restrictive agreements may obtain immunity from antitrust law. Only in a few cases has the European Commission banned inter-airline agreements. In principle, the prohibition applies to agreements that used to benefit from block exemptions, which

10 Some authors argue that Article 101 (3) TFEU adopts a function similar to the 'Rule of Reason' applicable in the US antitrust law that allows for validity of an anticompetitive agreement.

were granted by the Commission according to Regulation 1617/93 no longer in force.[11] In 1993 in this Regulation, the Commission allowed a block exemption from the competition rules for tariff conferences and for slots and scheduling conferences organised under the auspices of the IATA. Regulation 1617/93 was amended several times. The first revision brought about a substantial change to airline practices by removing consultations on cargo tariffs from the block exemption.[12] The European Commission considered that IATA cargo tariff conferences restricted price competition and that IATA had not succeeded in demonstrating that this restrictive system is indispensable for providing customers with efficient interlining services within the European Economic Area (EEA). When the next block exemption was adopted in 2006,[13] the European Commission made it clear that it would only be prolonged if air carriers prove that passenger tariff conferences continue to benefit consumers. IATA did not supply the data and the Commission decided not to renew the exemption for passenger tariff conferences concerning air routes between the EU and non-EU countries. The exemption has, thus, expired on 30 June 2007 for routes between the EU and the US and Australia, and on 3 October 2007 for routes between the EU and other third countries. Because of the concerns expressed by the Commission and shared also by other competition authorities around the world, IATA had to introduce a new system to set interline fares in replacement of its tariff conferences. At the same time, it was also determined that the consultations organised by IATA on airport slots and scheduling were clearly compatible with the competition rules.[14] This, however, was also a reason for discontinuing the exemption in so far as it appeared that these conferences did not need any special treatment in the form of a block exemption.

The European Commission took the same approach regarding revenue pooling. This type of inter-airline agreement was indicated in Regulation 2671/88, which

11 Regulation No. 1617/93/EEC of the Commission of 25 June 1993 on the application of Article 85 (3) of the Treaty to certain categories of agreements and concerted practices concerning joint planning and coordination of schedules, joint operations, consultations on passenger and cargo tariffs on scheduled air services and slot allocation at airports, OJ L 155, 26.6.1993, pp. 18–22.

12 Regulation No. 1523/96/EC of the Commission of 24 July 1996 amending Regulation (EEC) No 1617/93 on the application of Article 85 (3) of the Treaty to certain categories of agreements and concerted practices concerning joint planning and coordination of schedules, joint operations, consultations on passenger and cargo tariffs on scheduled air services and slot allocation at airports, OJ L 190, 31.7.1996, pp. 11–12.

13 Regulation No. 1459/2006/EC of the Commission of 28 September 2006 on the application of Article 81(3) of the Treaty to certain categories of agreements and concerted practices concerning consultations on passenger tariffs on scheduled air services and slot allocation at airports, OJ L 272, 3.10.2006, pp. 3–8.

14 *DG Competition Consultation Paper Concerning the revision and possible prorogation of Commission Regulation 1617/93 on the application of Article 81(3) to certain categories of agreements and concerted practices concerning consultations on passenger tariffs on scheduled air services and slot allocation at airports*, European Commission, 2004.

granted a block exemption during the first phase of EU liberalisation.[15] The exemption was dropped after implementation of the second liberalisation package. Pooling is a type of inter-airline cooperation that is sanctioned or even required in restrictive bilateral agreements, usually due to capacity considerations. It refers to flights operated by two carriers bearing designator codes of each other, that decide to share revenue and/or costs. In the past, under pooling agreements the revenue earned by different carriers operating on a particular route was shared between them according to a predetermined formula. In some cases, revenues were divided up in proportion to the capacity offered by each airline. Most pooling agreements were agreed between air carriers operating on the same route.[16]

As a result of the EU air transport liberalisation, block exemptions were also removed with regards to the following types of agreements:

- Agreements for the common purchase, development and operation of computerised reservation systems (CRS) – block exemption allowed airlines to set up and operate jointly-owned CRS under a number of conditions, essentially intended to make sure that all interested airlines have access to these systems and that there is no discrimination against any air carriers.
- Joint operations – block exemptions enabled smaller airlines to operate services with marketing and financial support from other airlines, thereby helping them to develop new routes or to continue service on less busy routes.
- Ground handling services agreements – block exemptions allowed airlines to enter into agreements regarding ground handling services and obliged suppliers of the ground handling services to deal in a non-discriminatory manner.

Despite the adoption of Regulation 487/2009 applying Article 101(3) TFEU to the air transport sector,[17] the European Commission has still not introduced any exemptions of specific airline behaviour from the discussed prohibition. This means that general rules established by the TFEU should apply to inter-airline agreements.

Mergers constitute an alternative for alliances. In the EU competition law mergers are governed by the general EU Merger Regulation[18] or by national rules depending on the aggregated turnover of the undertakings concerned.

15 Regulation No. 2671/88/EEC of the Commission of 26 July 1988 on the application of Article 85 (3) of the Treaty to certain categories of agreements between undertakings, decisions of associations of undertakings and concerted practices concerning joint planning and coordination of capacity, sharing of revenue and consultations on tariffs on scheduled air services and slot allocation at airports, OJ L 239, 30.8.1988, pp. 9–12.

16 Iatrou and Oretti 2007.

17 Regulation No. 487/2009/EC of the Council of 25 May 2009 on the application of Article 81(3) of the Treaty to certain categories of agreements and concerted practices in the air transport sector, OJ L 148, 11.6.2009, pp. 1–4.

18 Regulation No. 139/2004/EC of the Council of 20 January 2004 on the control of concentrations between undertakings, OJ L 24, 29.1.2004, pp. 1–22.

Contrary to alliances, mergers require prior notification to the European Commission or to national competition authorities. The assessment conducted by the European Commission in relation to mergers is very similar to that provided in the case of other alliances. It consists in an analysis of benefits that can be offered to consumers or other market players.

5.4 Airline alliances in view of market access regulations

The analysis of EU competition law in Section 5.3 does not give a clear answer as to permitted inter-airline agreements. With regard to air carrier alliances, some practices that are not permitted under Article 101(1) TFEU and fall within the catalogue of heaviest infringements can still be released from the ban subject to conditions specified in Article 101(3) TFEU. The European Commission's practice concerning some forms of cooperation in the aviation sector is very helpful in determining the scope of such permitted arrangements. Moreover, the admissibility of some inter-airline agreements arises directly form market access regulations.

5.4.1 Combining services and code-sharing

Regulation 1008/2008 is the basis for provision of air transport services within the EU.[19] It has removed all restrictions for the EU air carriers to operate intra-Community air services arising from bilateral agreements between the EU member states. It has also allowed combining services and code-share arrangements subject to compliance with the competition rules. The Regulation does not give a definition of combining services. It seems, however, that this notion can be understood very broadly and may refer to diverse options of flights/operations including passengers and cargo services of at least two air carriers.

EU carriers are free to conclude code-share agreements with any air carriers on air services to, from or via any airports of the member states or to any points in third countries. However, Regulation 1008/2008 allows member states to impose restrictions on code-share agreements between an EU carrier and a third-country air carrier, especially where a third country does not offer similar commercial opportunities to carriers from the EU operating in that third country. In liberalised ASAs concluded between the EU and third countries, such as the 2007 EU–US open skies agreement,[20] general restrictions regarding code-share

19 Regulation No. 1008/2008/EC of the European Parliament and of the Council of 24 September 2008 on common rules for the operation of air services in the Community, OJ L 293, 31.10.2008, pp. 3–20.

20 Air Transport Agreement between the United States of America and the Republic of Austria, the Kingdom of Belgium, the Republic of Bulgaria, the Republic of Cyprus, the Czech Republic, the Kingdom of Denmark, the Republic of Estonia, the Republic of Finland, the

agreements have been effectively abolished, while certain conditions for this kind of cooperation still apply.[21]

A code-share agreement is an arrangement between two carriers whereby one airline's designator code (marketing carrier) is shown on flights operated by its partner (operating carrier). Code-share agreements may go beyond mere sharing of the designator codes and be supplemented by other arrangements: for example, coordination of frequent flyer programmes, route and schedule planning, alignment of marketing, sales and distribution networks, joint pricing, sharing of facilities and services at airports, integration and development of information systems, and so on. They are also accompanied by key provisions of separate agreements, mainly Special Prorate Agreements (SPAs) and revenue settlement agreements. The SPAs determine how revenue from carriage of a passenger on flights operated by both carriers should be divided between them. A revenue settlement agreement contains provisions relating to the division of revenues, payment of code-share commission and revenue settlement procedures between the parties. The latter are potentially wider in scope than SPAs and may substitute for them. In practice, two types of code-share agreements have been developed between air carriers. The first one, called free flow (free sale) arrangement, gives the marketing carrier access to the operating carrier's inventory and allows it to market seats independently of the operating carrier, which solely determines seats availability. The second one, called blocked space agreement, allocates the marketing carrier a certain number or percentage of seats on flights provided by the operating carrier. Under the 'hard' blocked space arrangement commercial risk can be shared between both carriers. The marketing carrier is responsible for paying an agreed fee for the blocked seats to the operating carrier regardless of success in selling them. Within a 'soft' blocked space agreement, a marketing carrier may reimburse the space dedicated to it under the contractual conditions agreed with an operating carrier. Generally, code-share arrangements are concluded between carriers that have the traffic rights to operate routes covered by the agreement. Therefore, a marketing carrier cannot offer to sell

French Republic, the Federal Republic of Germany, the Hellenic Republic, the Republic of Hungary, Ireland, the Italian Republic, the Republic of Latvia, the Republic of Lithuania, the Grand Duchy of Luxembourg, Malta, the Kingdom of The Netherlands, the Republic of Poland, the Portuguese Republic, Romania, the Slovak Republic, the Republic of Slovenia, the Kingdom of Spain, the Kingdom of Sweden, the United Kingdom of Great Britain And Northern Ireland, and the European Community, done at Brussels on 25 April 2007 and at Washington on 30 April 2007, provisionally applied as from 30 March 2008, OJ L 134, 25.5.2007, pp. 4–41.

21 For example, parties to such agreements should hold appropriate authorities and their contractual arrangements must meet conditions prescribed under the laws and regulations normally applied by the state parties to the operation or holding out of international air transportation.

destinations to which it does not have an authorisation, although under some ASAs this may be partially possible.[22]

Code-share agreements are horizontal agreements that may have harmful effects on competition. The European Commission has never issued a decision concerning a code-share agreement as such. However, the competitive impact of code-share arrangements has been appraised in the context of other elements of airline alliances. Following an inquiry commenced in 2011, in December 2016 the Commission announced that it had sent a so-called statement of objections to TAP and Brussels Airlines setting out concerns that the code-share arrangement between the two airlines infringes Article 101(1) TFEU.[23] Another investigation related to a code-share arrangement between Lufthansa and Turkish Airlines, although this one has been discontinued. The Commission has confirmed that complementary code-share arrangements are common and often beneficial to passengers as they can help to extend network coverage and offer improved connections to passengers.[24] In principle, such agreements do not raise competition concerns. This is only on routes where the networks of the contracting airlines overlap. Generally, a code-share arrangement on an overlapping route would be considered as anticompetitive if no other airlines operate on that route.[25]

It seems from this discussion that the concept of code-sharing is itself neutral in terms of EU competition law. Possible infringement of this law may, however, depend on the combination of code-sharing with related arrangements and on the position of airlines on relevant markets. In particular, the European Commission believes that regardless of the form of their cooperation, air carriers engaged in code-sharing should act independently in a manner that is not detrimental to competition.

5.4.2 Aircraft leasing

Another type of inter-airline arrangement allowed under Regulation 1008/2008 is leasing. There are two types of leasing mentioned in the Regulation: wet leasing and dry leasing. A wet lease is an agreement between air carriers pursuant

22 This is usually subject to the condition that the code-share route is an extension of a service that is covered by the agreed market access rights. For example, LOT Polish Airlines owns traffic rights to Tokyo and has a code-share agreement with Japan Airlines on the Tokio–Sendai route, despite not having rights to the Tokyo–Sendai connection. However, LOT Polish Airlines cannot sell the Tokio–Sendai service alone, only the Warsaw–Tokyo–Sendai service.

23 European Commission 2016.

24 The Commission explained that it decided to close its inquiry in that case because Lufthansa and Turkish Airlines were not the only airlines competing on the routes involved, they did not have full marketing rights to each other's seats, they had different price strategies and the share of their sales on the relevant routes attributed to the code-share arrangement was only marginal. See European Commission 2016.

25 In the case of TAP–Brussels Airlines the Commission has alleged that these two airlines 'pursued an anti-competitive strategy' on the Brussels–Lisbon route due to capacity reduction, alignment of pricing policies and a mutual grant of unlimited rights to sell seats on each other's flights on that route. See ibid.

to which an aircraft is operated under an Air Operator Certificate (AOC) of the lessor. Within a dry lease agreement, an aircraft is operated under the AOC of the lessee. EU air carriers may freely operate wet-leased aircraft registered within the EU except where this would lead to endangering safety. Due to safety considerations, wet lease agreements under which the European Community (EC) air carrier is the lessee and all dry lease agreements require approval by national aviation authorities. Additional constraints have been imposed on wet lease of aircraft registered in third countries. In the latter case, a Community air carrier must obtain an approval from the competent licensing authority. The carrier must demonstrate that safety standards equivalent to those imposed by the EU or national law are met and that exceptional circumstances justifying leasing, as set forth in Regulation 1008/2008, have occurred. The consent is granted only for a limited period (seven + seven months) and the competent authority may introduce additional restrictions that should be included in the relevant agreement. Such time limits do not exist as regards wet leases between the EU carriers.

The EU regulations on code-share and wet lease are marked by unequal treatment of EU carriers and third-country carriers. The scope of freedoms granted to EU air carriers in respect of these arrangements indicates that the EU does not respect the provisions of existing bilateral agreements between its member states and third parties. This is because the application of EU rules on intra-Community air services has been extended by the European Commission to cover routes to third countries. Moreover, based on Regulation 1008/2008, an EU member state is authorised to impose restrictions on operators from a third country if this country does not provide for similar commercial opportunities to carriers from the member state concerned.

It is worth noting that the mentioned provisions have been questioned by the US authorities as being inconsistent with the 2007 open skies agreement. This agreement has established freedom in concluding wet lease arrangements provided that conditions and regulations applied by each interested state party are fulfilled. Under the agreement, it is not required for the lessor within a wet lease arrangement to hold relevant traffic rights. The US regulations also impose some extra requirements regarding wet lease arrangements, but they are not applicable to wet lease agreements concluded between two US carriers. According to 14 CFR part 212, foreign wet lessors are obliged to obtain a charter authorisation and a statement of authorisation from the Department of Transport (DOT) to operate in the US. This is regardless of the lessee, whether a US or a foreign carrier. In the past the US granted authorisations for an unlimited period to EU carriers that wet-leased aircraft from other EU carriers for their operations to and from the US. After the restrictions included in Regulation 1008/2008 were introduced, the DOT has started to impose time limitations similar to those established in the EU Regulation. This policy was driven by complaints from the US carriers, which recognised the EU time limitations as discriminatory and claimed that they prevent fair and equal opportunity to compete. The US counter-action became very problematic for EU air carriers since legal uncertainty has undermined their business planning. The EU has, therefore, decided to review Regulation 1008/2008 to ensure its compatibility with international obligations without the need to change the 2007 open skies agreement.[26]

The dispute between the US and EU shows that equal treatment of airlines is a very important indicator of market openness. The European Commission has yet not initiated any competition law proceedings regarding wet lease arrangements. However, Ryanair has asked the Commission[27] and the German Federal Cartel Office[28] to investigate the wet lease agreement between Air Berlin and Lufthansa (and its subsidiaries), which it found anticompetitive.

Both authorities stated that the deal raised no competition concerns, although they took different approaches in this respect. On the one hand, the German authority explained in its press release that the agreement did not raise competition concerns because the lease did not affect the re-allocation of slots. It has, though, left open the question of whether the wet lease concerned led to concentration. However, it has indicated that such an arrangement might constitute an acquisition of control. On the other hand, the European Commission did not believe that wet lease touches upon the problem of concentration at all. Importantly, the case is pending and may bring some new developments after Air Berlin insolvency filling and the grant of an emergency loan form the German government.

5.4.3 *Franchising and common branding*

Franchising and common branding have not been mentioned in Regulation 1008/2008, but references to such arrangements may be found in some ASAs concluded by the EU.[29] In ASAs, the regulation of franchising and common branding is similar to that concerning code-sharing. An airline may provide air services pursuant to a franchising or branding arrangement if it holds appropriate traffic rights to these services, meets the conditions prescribed under national laws and has received an approval form the relevant aeronautical authority. In most cases both the franchisor and the franchisee must possess traffic rights,

26 It is expected that some amendments will be introduced to Article 13 of the regulation soon. See *Proposal for a Regulation of the European Parliament and of the Council amending Regulation (EC) No 1008/2008 on common rules for the operation of air services in the Community*, COM(2016)818 final, 21.12.2016.

27 *Lufthansa/Certain Air Berlin* Assets, Commission decision of 27 October 2017, M.8633, C(2017) 7355 final.

28 Bundeskartellamt Entscheidung B9-190/16, *Lufthansa darf Flugzeuge von Air Berlin leasen*, 30.1.2017.

29 For example, 2007 UE–US, Euro–Mediterranean Aviation Agreement between the European Union and its Member States, of the one part, and the government of the State of Israel, of the other part, signed on 10 June 2013 in Luxembourg OJ L 208, 2.8.2013, pp. 3–67, applied provisionally, agreements on Common Aviation Area for example Common Aviation Area Agreement between the European Union and its Member States and the Republic of Moldova, signed on 26 June 2012 in Brussels, applied provisionally as of the date of signature, OJ L 292, 20.10.2012, pp. 3–37.

although this is not a rule. Franchising and branding arrangements are independent of code-share agreements, but they may coexist.[30]

Franchising is a very common practice and has become a crucial commercial strategy for EU airlines that seek to strengthen or enhance their position on the market.[31] Within this arrangement, the franchisee operates independently under its own AOC and according to its own commercial strategy but uses the brand of another airline (usually one with stronger market position) together with the associated intellectual property and know-how. Very often the arrangement is also accompanied by additional provisions, which prevent head-to-head competition. The services offered by the franchisor are charged upon an agreed price, but profits from the provided operations are allocated on the franchisee's account.

So far, franchise agreements have not been investigated by the European Commission. However, as in the case of code-sharing, it seems that as long as air carriers do not infringe Article 101(1) TFEU, such agreements would be admissible. Importantly, the very nature of a franchise agreement generally excludes competition between the contracting airlines, because the franchisee is an extension of the franchisor's brand. Therefore, if both airlines operate on the same market, competition law issues may result from the possible abuse of dominant position by the franchisor.

5.4.4 Other inter-airline agreements

There are also some unregulated inter-airline agreements that are backed up by antimonopoly authorities. IATA, which plays a major role in supporting inter-airline agreements, has developed an interline system that covers air transport services worldwide. Interlining occurs when a passenger uses a single ticket to travel on more than one airline. The system consists of two fundamental pillars: Multilateral Interline Traffic Agreement (MITA) and Multilateral Prorate Agreement (MPA). Based on MITAs, airlines accept (for passengers and cargo transportation) a standard traffic document to use various modes of transport involved in a route. The MPA determines how much an airline will receive for carrying an interlining passenger or cargo on any given journey segment. If these arrangements do not involve retail price coordination, they do not collide with Article 101(1) TFEU. The interlining system was very carefully investigated by the European Commission during its revision of the IATA passenger and cargo tariff conferences, that are an integral part of the system.[32] The European Commission has considered this process to be a technical improvement that is

30 Havel 2009, p. 647.

31 Denton and Dennis 2000, p. 180.

32 DG Competition Consultation Paper Concerning the revision and possible prorogation of Commission Regulation 1617/93 on the application of Article 81(3) to certain categories of agreements and concerted practices concerning consultations on passenger tariffs on scheduled air services and slot allocation at airports.

acceptable as long as the carrier cooperation does not involve prohibited practices listed in Article 101(1) TFEU. Moreover, in its airline alliance investigations, the European Commission has considered interlining as one of the crucial commitments that may help to justify an otherwise anticompetitive airline arrangement.[33] SPAs, whereby competitors sell tickets on interline flights, have received a similar treatment.[34] Airlines gain access to certain fares for other carriers' services and use them when marketing their own flights. The commitments offered by alliance partners also include: fare combinability agreements, frequent flyer programmes, ground handling agreements and agreements on joint sale organisation.[35] These kind of inter-airline agreements, that deal with products and activities that distinguish an airline from others, do not exist outside alliances.

5.5 Conclusions

There are many forms of cooperation between airlines. The most extensive and advanced are the airline alliances. Although the European Commission has removed block exemptions form the competition law restrictions, some of the inter-airline arrangements are still present in the advanced forms of airline alliance cooperation. Even though they infringe Article 101(1) TFEU, they are legalised subject to conditions specified in Article 101(3) TFEU based on commitments offered in exchange for an approval. It is interesting to note that these commitments are also considered by the European Commission as the only way for other competitors to gain access to the market, especially in the case of the most congested airports.

Only typically technical and complementary arrangements may benefit from the safe harbour as they are excluded from restrictions imposed by the competition law unless they involve some additional agreements caught by the Article 101(1) TFEU. Airlines must be very careful when entering into agreements even clearly permitted by the market access rules, such as Regulation 1008/2008 or ASAs, because their arrangements also constitute horizontal agreements from the competition law perspective and, therefore, almost in every case fall within the scope of Article 101(1) TFEU. Importantly, although Regulation 1008/2008 covers intra-Community routes, it also implies some restrictions on third-country air carriers by limiting their rights to conclude agreements with EU carriers. It also indicates that the same interline agreements may be treated differently depending on the nationality of the air carrier.

33 See *Air France/KLM*, Commission decision of 11 February 2004, COMP/M.3280, SG-Greffe(2004) D/200549; *Sociètè Air France/Alitalia Linee Aeree Italiane S.p.A.*, Commission decision of 7 April 2004, COMP/38.284/D2, C(2004) 1307 final.

34 See *Continental/United/Lufthansa/Air Canada*, Commission decision of 23 May 2013, COMP/AT.39595, C(2013) 2836 final; *US Airways/American Airlines*, Commission decision of 5 August 2013, COMP/M.6607, C(2013) 5232 final.

35 See European Commission Decisions: Case COMP/AT.39595; Case COMP/M.7021, *Swissport/Servisair, Commission decision of 18 December 2013, COMP/M.7021, C(2013) 9666 final.*

The European Commission has not always been consistent in its analysis of airline alliances. Therefore, the self-assessment conducted by airlines in relation to their possible cooperation is welcome in each case involving the mentioned forms of cooperation that are at risk of violating competition law. The practice indicates that very rarely airlines enter into only one type of inter-airline arrangement. Airlines are looking for new opportunities to enhance operational and marketing efficiencies to achieve better financial benefits. Thus, in most cases their cooperation involves several types of agreements. Additionally, the more airlines and arrangements involved, the more likely that the inter-airline cooperation will be approved by the European Commission. This is because such wide-scope arrangements have a greater potential to outweigh the negative effects of inter-airline agreements. Accordingly, in some sense, the alliances are the only premise for the European Commission's lenient approach.[36] Indeed, as long as airlines still have commitments to be offered to competitors, their agreements will be approved. However, once alliances themselves become the main obstacle to market entry the European Commission will be forced to revise the existing practice.

36 Cf. discussion of DOT policy in Chapter 4 of this book.

6 Competition in international air transport

An overview of EU policy developments

Paweł Zagrajek

6.1 Competition in air transport

There is a universal understanding of what competition means as a process or activity. The *Oxford English Dictionary* defines competition as 'the activity or condition of striving to gain or win something by defeating or establishing superiority over others'. More business-oriented definitions point to 'the effort of two or more parties acting independently to secure the business of a third party by offering the most favourable terms' (*Merriam-Webster Dictionary*). Accordingly, the ICAO has defined competition in air transport as 'the existent or potential rivalry between two or more operators, carriers or groups striving for advantage in the same market, including using price and quality of products or services to achieve the desired gains.'[1]

Taking into consideration the aforementioned definitions, competition must be viewed through the prism of market players (competitors), their offer (product and its price), place of rivalry (relevant market) and broadly understood end-users. Market structure should also be considered as it may vary significantly depending on competition intensity. It may range from fierce competition between many companies offering the same products, through less intense competition like in the case of oligopolies, to the markets dominated by monopolies where the competition does not exist.

From the perspective of competitors an important factor is the competitive advantage of an enterprise, that is, its ability to provide products or services at a lower price or with higher quality or more demanded features than its competitors. In the air transport industry, the competitive advantage is a result of a complex set of factors. Air carriers can build their advantages through the appropriate competitive strategy, including operations on specific markets, choosing suitable partners and offering adequate products. This strategy determines the airline business model. However, an airline can also gain competitive advantage through factors independent of the business model. Geographical advantage of the airline's operational base is one of the most prominent examples. For

1 *Competition in International Air Transport (Presented by the Secretariat)*, ICAO ATRP/13-IP/3, 17.8.2015, p. 3.

instance, Gulf hubs are favourably located with respect to European, North African, Indian Subcontinental and East Asian markets. Helsinki and London are European hubs located optimally to serve Far Asia and North American markets, respectively. Competitive advantage may also arise from the size of home market, both in terms of number of potential passengers and their purchase power. In addition, competitive advantage may result from the difference in the stage of development of the competing airlines. Incumbent airlines may have a competitive advantage over newcomers in terms of their position at certain airports, their size, range of their networks and their ability to exploit economies of scale and scope.

Any analysis of competition must refer to the concept of 'relevant market', which embraces geographical coverage of the market and the product offered. An air transport product is commonly defined as carriage of passengers, cargo or mail for remuneration. The geographic scope of the market is limited by itinerary, which may comprise either of a direct point to point route or a sequence of several direct routes – the so-called origin and destination approach (O&D).[2] Air transport product can be considered on its own or in combination with its attributes. Problematic issues include different itineraries serving the same city but different airport, and different itineraries serving the same O&D airports but differing in journey length, transfer time and block time due to different routes. The competition between itineraries is even more difficult to assess when taking into consideration differences in schedules (time of the day and week), service frequency and punctuality. The incorporation of qualitative travel attributes introduces even more complexity to the analysis of airline product. This is further complicated when services vary between legs of a journey operated by both one airline and multiple airlines on the basis of code-share or interline agreements.

6.2 International legal framework for competition in air transport

National or regional competition laws may differ as to their scope, regulatory solutions and so on, and may conflict with each other. According to research by the ICAO, this is the case regarding air transport competition regimes.[3] National competition laws typically regulate market behaviour of competitors in the private sector. This usually covers antitrust regulations, which address anticompetitive agreements and abuse of dominant position; and merger regulations, addressing any market concentration that leads to reduced competition. Additional state aid

2 According to the OECD, the definitions of relevant markets for airlines vary between competition authorities and only some of them apply O&D approach. See *Annex to the Summary Record of the 121st Meeting of the Competition Committee held on 18–19 June 2014 – Executive Summary of the Discussion on Airline Competition*, OECD DAF/COMP/M(2014)2/ANN4/FINAL, 28.10.2014, p. 5.

3 *Fair Competition in International Air Transport* (Presented by the Secretariat), ICAO ATConf/6-WP/4, 4.12.2012, p. 3.

regulation, which deals with unfair advantage gained through any kind of public support, is rather unique for the EU. It is therefore impossible to define and list all necessary elements of a national competition regime.

The concept of fair competition brings another layer of complexity to the analysis of the competition. It may be defined as 'competition reasonable in view of the interests of those competing and the public and not involving practices condemned by law as inimical to the public interest' (*Meriam-Webster Dictionary*). Fair competition is a conduct that adheres to and follows the legal framework in effect. Therefore, the actual meaning of this notion is inseparable from the legal framework in force and the applicable competition policy.

Some international treaties endeavour to build on the collective understanding of competition and introduce universal rules harmonising competition law in international relations. International trade relations, including to a limited extent competition issues, are regulated by the World Trade Organization (WTO) based on the principles of non-discrimination, transparency and most-favoured-nation treatment. More specifically trade in services is regulated by the General Agreement on Trade in Services (GATS).[4] Among others, the WTO regime addresses the issues of price dumping, subsidies, and dispute settlement procedure. However, the international air transport system is mostly based on bilateral, reciprocal exchange of market access rights which constitutes a complex system of agreements providing for different levels of market access. Its legal complexity and the principle of bilateral reciprocity makes the air transport system difficult to be implemented into the WTO/GATS regime, which is based on the most-favoured-nation treatment.

Consequently, international air transport services are not covered by this framework and it is unlikely that this will change in the foreseeable future. The GATS clearly states that the agreement, including its dispute settlement procedures, shall not apply to measures affecting traffic rights, however granted, and services directly related to the exercise of traffic rights. It applies only to measures affecting aircraft repair and maintenance services, selling and marketing of air transport services and computerised reservation system (CRS) services. Consequently, the current WTO/GATS framework neither supports nor promotes fair competition in global air transport.

As already mentioned, global air transport services operate primarily based on bilateral air service agreements (ASAs) developed under the Chicago Convention[5] system. ASAs cover in particular traffic rights, origin, destination and intermediate points, if applicable, capacity, frequency, designated airlines and other commercial arrangements such as pricing. In light of the state sovereignty principle

4 General Agreement on Trade in Services – Annex 1B of the Marrakesh Agreement Establishing the World Trade Organization, done in Marrakesh on 15 April 1994, entered into force on 1 January 1995, 1869 UNTS 183.

5 Convention on International Civil Aviation, signed in Chicago on 7 December 1944, entered into force on 4 April 1947, ICAO Doc. 7300/9, 15 UNTS 295.

imbedded in the Chicago Convention, international air transport operations are considered a privilege and an exception to the prohibition of international air transport services.[6] This system allowed governments to exercise full control over international air services, including competition between operating airlines, which was indeed very limited due to the specific nature of bilateral agreements. The Chicago system had, thus, introduced a framework in which issues of competition did not need to be addressed specifically. Although some traditional agreements made references to fair and equal opportunity to operate/ compete,[7] this statement is very general and leaves room for interpretations not necessarily referring to fair competition.

The Chicago system has gone through significant changes since the end of 1970s when the deregulation/liberalisation process was triggered by the Airline Deregulation Act of 1978[8] in the US. The US government has enabled unrestricted access to routes and free market pricing. A similar approach was taken at the international level and the US has since negotiated a number of so-called 'open skies' agreements aimed at opening international air transport markets. This strategy has been copied by many countries and multinational organisations leading to the current system of complex bilateral and multilateral agreements characterised by varied levels of market access and operational freedoms.

This process opens room for international free competition between air carriers. However, as mentioned before, air transport is not subject to a universal international regulatory framework to ensure 'fairness' of this competition.

In this case ASAs could serve as a natural instrument to regulate competition issues at least at bilateral or plurilateral level. A recent study completed by the ICAO shows, however, that reference to competition matters in ASAs is still an exception.[9] Analysis of competition clauses in ASAs is complicated by various levels of market opening provided in these agreements and the ambiguity of such clauses. Examples gathered in the ICAO study show that direct references to competition issues can be found only in more liberal types of agreements. Some of these ASAs call 'to eliminate all forms of discrimination and anti-competitive

6 Żylicz 1992, pp.61–62.

7 Cf. Cl. 4 of the preamble to the Agreement between the Government of the United Kingdom and the Government of the United States of America relating to Air Services between their Respective Territories (with Annex), signed in Bermuda on 11 February 1946, entered into force by signature, 3 UNTS 253, UKTS 3 (1946) Cm. 6747 ('Bermuda I Agreement'). This wording is derived directly from the Chicago Convention. Its preamble speaks of 'equality of opportunity' whereas article 44(f) refers to 'fair opportunity'.

8 The Airline Deregulation Act of 1978, Pub. L. 95–504 – 24 October 1978, 92 Stat. 1705.

9 ICAO noted that nearly 850 out of 2,600 of ASAs contained reference to the right of airlines to fair and equal opportunities to operate air services. Only 200 ASAs stated directly that air carriers possess the right to fair and equal opportunities to compete in providing air services. Around 190 of these agreements provided further details regarding unfair competition practices. See *Competition Provisions of Existing Air Services Agreements in Global or Regional Frameworks (presented by the Secretariat)*, ICAO ATRP/13-IP/2, 24.8.2015, pp. 1–2.

or predatory practices'[10] or contain provisions that request respecting internal competition regimes of each party as well as their application to international air carriage as well-set ground for cooperation of competition authorities. It should be noted, however, that among the examples presented by the ICAO only agreements signed by the EU contain references to subsidies.

Since neither the WTO regime nor ASAs provides for a comprehensive competition framework for international air transport, it might seem that the ICAO is a proper forum to address this issue. However, the preamble to the Chicago Convention, which states that international air transport services should be established on the basis of 'equality of opportunity', does not necessarily lead to pro-competitive interpretations.[11] Moreover, the ICAO regulatory system, which is based on Standards and Recommended Practices (SARPs) contained in Annexes to the Chicago Convention, is not designed to cover economic issues, including competition.[12] Adoption of SARPs in the field of economic regulation of air transport was discussed; however, no consensus has ever been achieved.[13] In general, ICAO position towards economic issues is only included in non-binding policies, recommendations and guidance materials. These materials refer to application of competition laws to air transport as well as state aids and subsidies. The ICAO gives a definition of subsidies and suggests a catalogue of state aids that may distort competition as well as those that may be justified under specific conditions.[14] The ICAO has also developed Template Air Services Agreements that contain fair competition clauses.[15] The templates offer three levels of approach to fair competition – from traditional to fully liberal. However even the most 'liberalised' clauses seem disappointing.[16] The templates also give a list of possible unfair competitive practices. Once again, this catalogue is limited in scope and addresses only the problem of predatory behaviour. It also does not provide any solutions for enforcement in this area, but only refers to the standard dispute resolution mechanisms. The templates also address the issue of cooperation in the area of competition laws.

10 *Competition Provisions of Existing* . . ., ICAO ATRP/13-IP/2, 24.8.2015, pp. 1–2.

11 Walulik 2017, p. 13.

12 These issues are not included in the catalogue of matters to be regulated in SARPs, set forth in Article 37 of the Chicago Convention.

13 The Arab Civil Aviation Commission (ACAC) has proposed to develop a new Annex to the Chicago Convention that would address air transport issues, reflecting guidelines and policies already developed by ICAO. This would make these regulations binding for member states. See *Issuance of Annex 20 to the Convention on International Civil Aviation (presented by Bahrain on behalf of Arab Civil Aviation Commission (ACAC))*, ICAO ATConf/6-WP/27, 1.2.2013.

14 These guidelines are patterned upon the state aid regime implemented in the EU. See *Manual on the Regulation of International Air Transport*, 2nd edition, ICAO Doc. 9626, pp. 2.3–6 – 2.3–8.

15 See *Policy and Guidance Material on the Economic Regulation of International Air Transport*, 3rd ed., ICAO Doc. 9587, Appendix 5.

16 This clause states only that 'each designated airline shall have a fair competitive environment under the competition laws of the Parties'.

To conclude, international air transport lacks suitable global regulations concerning competition issues.

6.3 Development of the EU competition policy in international air transport

In the late 1980s the EU decided to liberalise the European aviation market. This has led directly to formation of truly open internal airline operations. The EU carrier concept was introduced and has provided for a single airline legal framework across the entire EU. Carriers have been allowed to freely decide on routes, capacity, frequency and prices. The liberalisation of the European market has completely reshuffled the market. New airline business models have emerged. Competition between market players has intensified and has eventually brought significant benefits to the EU economy and citizens, including greater choice of routes and flight frequencies as well as lower ticket prices.

Importantly, since its formation the newly transformed market has become subject to European competition regulations. Moreover, the liberalisation process in Europe has been accompanied by the development of a legal framework encompassing areas such as licensing, slots, ground handling and airport charges. Some of the provisions included in these regulations refer either directly or indirectly to competition issues. Consequently, each European carrier is subject to a complex and rigid competition regulatory framework that is deeply rooted in both general competition rules and aviation specific regulations. However, third-country carriers operating air services to and from the EU are subject only to certain EU rules that do not address key areas of competition regulation.

In 2001 the European Commission issued a communication[17] in which it pointed to possible distortion of competition, in particular to the threat of predatory pricing, caused by state aid granted to the American airlines following the 11 September 2001 terrorist attacks. Regulation 868/2004[18] was then developed because of the EU airlines' concerns with pricing practices of the US carriers. It aimed to establish a defence mechanism against subsidisation and unfair pricing practices of third-country airlines.[19]

17 *The repercussions of the terrorist attacks in the United States on the air transport industry*, Communication from the Commission to the European Parliament and the Council, COM (2001)574 final, 10.10.2001.

18 Regulation No. 868/2004/EC of the European Parliament and of the Council of 21 April 2004 concerning protection against subsidisation and unfair pricing practices causing injury to Community air carriers in the supply of air services from countries not members of the European Community, OJ L 162, 30.4.2004, pp. 1–7.

19 See *Impact Assessment Accompanying the Document: Proposal for a Regulation of the European Parliament and of the Council on safeguarding competition in air transport, repealing Regulation (EC) No. 868/2004*, Commission Staff Working Document, SWD(2017)182 final, 8.6.2017, p. 34.

The development of a genuine EU aviation external policy was triggered by the Court of Justice of the EU (CJEU) 'Open Skies' judgments of 5 November 2002,[20] although they did not directly address the issue of competition at the international level. A communication issued by the European Commission in 2005 stated that a part of the new external aviation policy agenda would be:

> ensuring fair competition, i.e. promoting regulatory convergence, be it with regard to the economic conditions governing the operation of the markets (implementation of competition regulations, state subsidies or standards more specifically linked to aviation such as reservation systems, ground handling, etc.).

The Commission has envisaged the creation of a Common Aviation Area with the EU neighbouring countries that provides a high degree of regulatory convergence, including competition issues and negotiation of comprehensive ASAs with global partners that ensure provisions for fair competition.[21]

In a communication issued in 2012 the European Commission found that external aviation policy needed to be updated. Importantly, much attention was devoted to the issue of competition. The Commission stressed the need for a stronger European aviation legal framework with fair and open competition. It confirmed the requirement for relevant competition regulations to be included into aviation agreements and proposed to develop for this purpose a fair competition clause. It also recognised that Regulation 868/2004 appeared to be ineffective and proposed the introduction of new defence tools. Finally, it pointed to the ICAO framework as a potential tool to ensure, among other things, a global framework for fair competition.[22]

In the Aviation Strategy of 2015 the Commission identified 'tapping into growth markets, by improving services, market access and investment opportunities with third countries, whilst guaranteeing a level playing field' as three key priorities. The Commission reiterated the need to tackle the competition issue in external relations by further negotiations of the EU comprehensive air transport agreements. Furthermore, it declared to intensify

20 CJEU judgments of 5 November 2002: Case C-466/98 – *Commission v. United Kingdom of Great Britain and Northern Ireland*, Case C-467/98 – *Commission v. Kingdom of Denmark*, Case C-468/98 – *Commission v. Kingdom of Sweden*, Case C-469/98 – *Commission v. Republic of Finland*, Case C-471/98 – *Commission v. Kingdom of Belgium*, Case C-472/98 – *Commission v. Grand Duchy of Luxemburg*, Case C-475/98 – *Commission v. Republic of Austria*, Case C-476/98 – *Commission v. Federal Republic of Germany*, ('Open Skies').

21 See *Developing the agenda for the Community's external aviation policy*, Communication from the Commission, COM(2005)79 final, 11.3.2005.

22 See *The EU's External Aviation Policy – Addressing Future Challenges*, Communication from the Commission to the European Parliament, the Council, the European Economic and Social Committee and the Committee of the Regions, COM(2012)556 final, 27.9.2012.

competition policy action at the ICAO level as well as by amending Regulation 868/2004.[23]

In June 2017 Commission issued another communication,[24] which was part of a broader package consisting of documents proposed in the Aviation Strategy, including the draft amendment of Regulation 868/2004. Maintaining leadership in international aviation by safeguarding competition and by facilitating foreign investment into EU airlines has been pointed out as a major aim of the package. The communication stressed again the importance of fair competition in the functioning of the international European aviation market. This issue has been put in the context of connectivity and presented as an important condition to keep Europe well connected.[25] The communication also endorsed the EU policy areas described in previous communications, such as addressing fair competition at the ICAO level as well as safeguarding adequate provisions in aviation agreements. Moreover, for the first time the European Commission clearly indicated the WTO as being the right forum to develop multilateral rules governing issues of fair competition.

Expectations of the EU regarding the rules governing competition in international air transport were clarified in a working paper prepared for the ICAO Air Transport Conference held in Montreal in 2013.[26] The EU emphasised the need to create an adequate regulatory environment, which was defined as:

> the existence of efficient competition law at national or regional level covering the abuse of market power, merger control, anti-competitive agreements and concerted practices, which is applicable to international air transport, as well as clear, transparent and strict state aid rules applicable to undertakings under the jurisdiction of the state concerned and ensuring the achievement of the objectives associated with open and fair competition.

It also indicated the need for transparent and non-discriminatory minimum rules on aviation safety, security, air traffic management, ground handling, slots, air passenger rights, environmental protection, social rights of aviation personnel, taxes and user charges. Hence, the regulatory expectations of the EU were reaching far beyond competition itself and covered a broad spectrum of topics.

23 See *An Aviation Strategy for Europe*, Communication from the Commission to the European Parliament, the Council, the European Economic and Social Committee and the Committee of the Regions, COM(2015)598 final, 7.12.2015.

24 *Aviation: Open and Connected Europe*, Communication from the Commission to the European Parliament, the Council, the European Economic and Social Committee and the Committee of the Regions, COM(2017)286 final, 8.6.2017.

25 For connectivity matters see also Chapter 14 of this book.

26 *Basic Principles of Fair Competition (presented by Ireland on behalf of the European Union (EU) and its member states and other member states of the European Civil Aviation Conference)*, ICAO ATConf/6-WP/51, 14.2.2013.

Moreover, the EU did not limit the conditions for a fair competitive environment to the regulatory framework. It indicated the need for formulation and implementation of further institutional conditions, such as independence of national civil aviation authorities as well as independent competition authorities and judiciary that would review decisions on air transport matters. In addition, the EU proposed a set of economic conditions. First, that any support granted by a state to an air carrier should assume that the same decision would have been taken by a private investor, provided that this action would not have disturbed the competition on the market. The state aid can also be granted to fill a gap in services that serve public interest (e.g., remote areas), however, this must be subject to transparent and non-discriminatory rules. Second, that there should be transparency in relationships and structures between the state and other market players through the entire value chain. Finally, that the non-discriminatory and transparent treatment should be applied to foreign airlines.

6.4 Pillars of the EU competition policy in international air transport

6.4.1 Implementation of fair competition provisions in ASAs

As mentioned the European Commission has envisaged the conclusion by the EU and its member states of Common Aviation Area agreements and comprehensive ASAs with aviation partners. Within this framework fair competition has been secured by competition clauses negotiated by the EU and its partners. However, these agreements form only a part of the EU external aviation relations. Outside this framework, air transport between EU member states and third states is still ruled by bilateral ASAs. For this occasion, the European Commission has proposed in 2012 that analogous template competition clauses be included in ASAs.[27] Importantly, these standard clauses are not mandatory, and their application and enforcement is subject to member state decision.[28]

The EU template competition clause secures the application of competition laws of each contracting party to operations of air carriers. It requires cooperation of competent authorities and confirms their capacity to enforce competition laws. Three areas of distortive market behaviour are covered: any forms of discrimination or unfair practice, market concentration, subsidies and state support.

Public subsidies or support are not allowed if they significantly and adversely affect, in an unjustified way, the fair and equal opportunity of the airlines of other Contracting Party to compete in providing air transport services. In addition, the standard competition clause ensures transparency of public subsidies and support, by regulating accounting practices necessary to identify subsidies or support. It

27 *EU External Aviation Policy Package*, European Commission, MEMO/12/714, 27.10.2012.
28 See *Impact Assessment* . . ., SWD(2017)182 final, 8.6.2017, p. 41.

also gives a list of possible unfair practices in this area.[29] Contracting parties are obliged to provide on request financial reports and other related information that can assist in verifying the compliance with the regulations.

Antitrust provisions prohibit agreements, decisions or engagement in concerted practices which may affect air transport services to/from that Contracting Party and which have as their object or effect the prevention, restriction or distortion of competition. This prohibition, with certain caveats: may be declared inapplicable where such agreements, decisions or practices contribute to improving the production or distribution of services or to promoting technical or economic progress, while allowing consumers a fair share of the resulting benefit.

A consultation mechanism shall be implemented if allegations of unfair practices are substantiated. If the consultation mechanism is not initiated or fails, the clause allows for the introduction of restrictions on operations of an airline by refusing, withholding, revoking or suspending its authorisations and permits. It is also possible to 'impose duties or take other actions'.[30] The enforcement, however, should be appropriate, proportionate and restricted with regard to scope and duration to what is strictly necessary.

There are no data available regarding the success in implementation of the EU template competition clause. However, according to the European Commission, member states have effectively implemented the fair competition provisions into only a limited number of ASAs with third countries. The low level of implementation is caused primarily by the reluctance of third countries to accept fair competition rules. According to the European Commission, a better implementation of fair competition provisions has been achieved in comprehensive ASAs negotiated by the EU with the US, Canada, Israel, Jordan, Morocco, Moldova and Georgia. However, even here the implementation of fair competition rules varies between the agreements.

6.4.2 The defence instrument – Regulation 868/2004

Regulation 868/2004 was introduced because of the EU airlines' concerns about unfair practices of the US carriers following the 2001 terrorist attacks. It was inspired by the system of anti-dumping and anti-subsidy rules followed in trade of goods. The trade of goods defence logic is echoed throughout the regulation, from concepts and definitions to the scope of market practices addressed,

29 Cross-subsidisation; the setting-off of operational losses; the provision of capital; grants; guarantees; loans or insurance on privileged terms; protection from bankruptcy; foregoing the recovery of amounts due; foregoing a normal return on public funds invested; tax relief or tax exemptions; compensation for financial burdens imposed by public authorities; and access on a discriminatory or non-commercial basis to air navigation or airport facilities and services, fuel, ground handling, security, CRS, slot allocation or other related facilities and services necessary for the operation of air services.

30 This seems to be a reference to instruments included in Regulation 868/2004, although it is not explicitly stated in the standard clause.

procedural aspects and redressive measures. This approach, however, does not reflect the complexity and dynamics of the airline industry, which has led to dysfunctionality of this legal act.[31]

The competition problem in the regulation is based on the 'like air service' concept, which refers to routes that are the same or comparable to the air service under consideration. This very general idea does not take into consideration the complexity of airline networks and that competition takes place between airline itineraries rather than routes, which is of particular relevance to network carriers. An air journey from airport A to airport B may be direct, but also more complex via a set of routes with transfers at other airports. The lengths of the routes and transfer times may vary. What is more, the journey may originate and terminate at different airports serving the same city.

The concept of the like air service is an integral part of the definition of 'Community industry', which is used to determine Community representation that is required for the initiation of proceedings and the execution of redressive measures. According to the regulation, Community Industry means 'the Community air carriers supplying like air services'. Given the ambiguity of the definition of 'like air service' it is thus difficult to identify stakeholders in the proceedings. Moreover, the aforementioned concept demands that the proceeding may only be initiated by a unanimous decision of all stakeholders affected. Under regulation 868/2004, any subset of stakeholders, whether it is an individual airline or a group of airlines, is not permitted to initiate an investigation unless it constitutes a representation of all stakeholders affected.

The substantive requirements for an investigation create another challenge for the jeopardised air carriers. The launch of an investigation is conditional upon the existence of countervailable subsidies, unfair pricing practices, an injury and a causal link between the allegedly subsidised or unfairly priced air services and the alleged injury. Moreover, the determination of an injury shall be based on positive evidence and shall involve an objective examination of: (a) the level of fares of the air services under consideration and the effect of such air services on fares offered by Community air carriers; and (b) the impact of those air services on the Community industry, as indicated by trends in a number of economic indicators such as number of flights, utilisation of capacity, passenger bookings, market share, profits, return on capital, investment and employment. The regulation also requires identifying other possible factors independent of the analysed air services that could contribute to injury to make sure they are not attributable to the air services under consideration. Consequently, the initiation of proceedings must be preceded by a complex analysis and should cover a wide range of data, which are difficult if not impossible to collect, analyse, quantify and finally transpose into evidence material. The initiation of proceedings may appear even

31 The regulation has never been applied in practice. See *Impact Assesment* . . ., SWD(2017)182 final, 8.6.2017, p. 35.

more difficult if one takes into consideration the ambiguity of the definition of Community industry.

Another defect of Regulation 868/2004 are the provisions concerning unfair market practices. This act addresses two kinds of unfair market practices: subsidisation and unfair pricing practices. The definition of subsidy as set forth in the regulation concerns only financial contribution. Although this act proposes a vast list of financial aids including forgone revenues as well as transfer of goods and services, it lacks reference to non-financial support, for example, practices facilitating doing business, preferential treatment and so on. Moreover, there is a requirement for the existence of a benefit deriving from financial contribution. However, the regulation lacks the definition of 'benefit', which makes it even more difficult to apply. According to the regulation:

> unfair pricing practices shall be deemed to exist on a particular air service to or from the Community where non-Community air carriers benefit from a non-commercial advantage, and charge air fares which are sufficiently below those offered by competing Community air carriers to cause injury.[32]

The regulation also indicates many economic factors that must be considered when comparing air fares. However, determination of the final price level and its comparison with other fares are extremely difficult tasks. The final price is the outcome of a complex process of pricing and revenue management. Airlines, especially network carriers, offer a complex matrix of fares grouped into fare classes. These fares are subject to constant management, based on demand forecasting that aims to offer adequate prices to the market segments. The final price may differ depending on the route, itinerary (whether it is a round trip or a one-way journey), demand forecast, restrictions such as advance purchase, Saturday night rule, as well as service levels including service class, baggage allowance, ticket elasticity and so on. These restrictions, as well as product features, may differ between airlines. Importantly, the revenue management process is not linked with the cost of flights. It is aimed at generating a maximum level of revenue. This implies that some of the seats can be sold below costs. Currently, some air carriers use highly sophisticated O&D revenue management systems that maximise revenues from the network perspective irrespective of the individual route approach. The presence of code-share, interline agreements and consolidated fares add an extra dimension to the complexity of price setting. What is more, it is hard to determine how many seats are being offered at a given price. Basically, the availability of seats is structured into buckets of inventory defined by a sequence called nesting. The number of seats in these groups depends on complicated algorithms and a number of factors such as itinerary, forecasted demand and many other things. It would be also be difficult to determine the actual cost of operating on a given route. First of all, it would

32 Regulation 868/2004.

require access to detailed financial data, which is impossible in practice. Moreover, it is a normal practice that airlines keep operating unprofitable routes. If the route offers important feeding traffic it may be perceived as profitable from the perspective of the whole network. It is also normal that routes reach profitability after a certain initial period. This may be over a year in the case of long haul routes. Due to the listed reasons, it is extremely difficult if not impossible to identify and prove unfair pricing practices. This statement is further reinforced by the fact that a detailed methodology for determining the existence of unfair pricing practices required by the regulation has never been developed by the European Commission.

In addition to the deficiencies mentioned already, the proceedings under Regulation 868/2004 may last nearly a year, and many circumstances may even prolong this process. Although it is possible to take provisional measures in the meantime, they can be introduced only for a limited period. Taking into consideration the rapidly evolving airline business, these provisions are not adequate for meeting the real needs of the market.

According to the regulation, redressive measures, whether provisional or definitive, shall preferably take the form of duties imposed upon the non-Community carrier concerned. Although the catalogue is not limited to duties, the regulation clearly points to them as a preferred remedy. It should, however, be emphasised that duties are solutions provided for the trade in goods and are not adequate to deal with air transport services. At the same time, the regulation does not offer any other form of remedy better tailored to the needs of the air transport market.

Contrary to Regulation 868/2004, which has never been used, the US International Air Transportation Fair Competitive Practices Act of 1974 (IATFCPA)[33] has proved to be an efficient mechanism to defend US air carriers against unfair competition by foreign air carriers. The principles of the US instrument, however, differ greatly from the EU regulation. The IATFCPA addresses a wide scope of anticompetitive behaviour, including unjustifiable or unreasonable discriminatory, predatory or anticompetitive practice against an air carrier and unjustifiable or unreasonable restriction on access of an air carrier to a foreign market.

According to IATFCPA, the Secretary of Transportation may take actions upon a complaint lodged by a US airline or on their own initiative, provided that it is in in the public interest. There is no specific requirement for the complaint concerning evidence or industry representation. The US Department of Transport (DOT) has a maximum of 180 days to resolve or dismiss the case. The US Department of Transport (DOT) can choose from a wide spectrum of remedies to counter unfair competitive practices, not only within the scope of the IATFCPA procedure. That includes compensatory charges, restriction of the operations (denying, amending,

33 International Air Transportation Fair Competitive Practices Act of 1974, Pub. L. 93–623, 3 January 1975, 88 Stat. 2102, as amended, codified under 49 USC 41310.

modifying, suspending or revoking its operating permit) and restriction of schedules. Importantly, the affected air carriers have the right to reimbursement. The IATFCPA procedure requires diplomatic negotiations. The DOT claims that the intergovernmental process has been very successful in resolving complaints.[34] It has been reported that, in all but one case, diplomatic negotiations led to amicable resolutions and the removal of the unfair practices in question.[35] In conclusion, the IATFCPA presents a completely different approach to the defence mechanism in comparison to Regulation 868/2004. This general and simplified approach provides the US industry and administration with an effective tool to defend their interests. Consequently, this procedure was used quite frequently between 1986 and 1994.[36]

Although the European Commission's 2017 proposal to replace Regulation 868/2004[37] differs significantly from the IATFCPA, some of the projected provisions seem to be patterned upon the US instrument. The Commission proposal offers a different defence mechanism than Regulation 868/2004 and addresses a wider scope of anticompetitive practices. It still covers subsidies, however, in this respect instead of dumping practices it refers to discrimination. Contrary to current regulation, the proposal does not include a definition of benefit in the context of subsidies. The proposal also entitles the airlines to lodge a complaint in case of violation of applicable international obligations.[38]

It simplifies the process of initiating proceedings. The concepts of 'like air services' and 'community industry' have been dropped. Instead, proceedings may be initiated following a written complaint submitted by a member state, a EU air carrier or an association of EU air carriers or on the Commission's own initiative. This is aimed at facilitating the submission of complaints by EU air carriers and enables the initiative of member states, which is not possible under the regulation in force. The requirement for providing evidence as a condition for lodging a complaint is retained. There is also a requirement for proof of injury or threat of injury as well as a causal link between the alleged practice and the alleged injury or threat of injury. These requirements may still impede the effective implementation of the proceeding. However, the requirement of sufficient evidence has

34 DOT 2015.

35 *Impact Assessment* ..., SWD(2017)182 final, 8.6.2017, p. 34.

36 Ibid.

37 *Proposal for a Regulation of the European Parliament and of the Council on safeguarding competition in air transport, repealing Regulation (EC) No. 868/2004*, COM(2017)289 final, 8.6.2017.

38 Under the provisions of the proposed Regulation applicable international obligations shall mean:

> any obligations that are contained in an international air transport or air services agreement to which the Union is a party or any provision on air transport services included in a trade agreement to which the Union is a party, and which relates to practices that may affect competition or other conduct relevant to competition between air carriers.

been replaced by *prima facie* evidence. This should definitely facilitate the process of filing a complaint and defer the burden of collecting evidence to the investigation phase. Furthermore, the proposal offers the European Commission a right to carry out investigations in third countries; however, effectiveness of this proposed clause is doubtful. It also obliges member states to support the Commission in collecting evidence as well as to provide information on their own activity that could be relevant in the investigation.

In comparison to the regulation in force, the proposal offers more specific reference to redressive measures stating that they may take the form of either financial duties or any measures of equivalent or lesser value. However, this catalogue can still cause some interpretation difficulties. This is because any solutions introduced must be measured in monetary terms. Although the Preamble to the proposed new regulation offers some examples of redressive measures – suspension of concessions, of services owed or of other rights of the third country air carrier – this catalogue is still limited and does not give any guidance as to monetisation of anticompetitive practices and relevant redressive measures. According to the proposal, measures other than financial duties may be limited to a specific geographical area, which reflects the possibly divergent views on benefits accruing to third-country airlines on different European markets. Like the Regulation 868/2004, the proposed new regulation pays special attention to the EU interests and stipulates that the proceedings shall not be initiated, nor the redressive measures introduced, if it is against the EU interest.

Once introduced, the projected new regulation would increase the chance of launching proceedings. Major deficiencies of Regulation 868/2004 have been removed. Some doubts may, however, arise concerning, for example, the effectiveness of the Commission's investigations, the lack of definition of a 'benefit', the limited and unclear scope of redressive measures and the length of proceedings, which may take over a year and can be prolonged in specific cases.

6.4.3 Promoting regulation of competition at the ICAO

The EU has been actively promoting development of international rules concerning competition in aviation on several occasions. Importantly, the EU has always presented this issue as an inseparable part of the liberalisation process.

Liberalisation and fair competition were already discussed at the Fifth Worldwide Air Transport Conference in 2003. In its conclusions, the participants stated that liberalisation must be accompanied by appropriate safeguards to ensure fair competition.[39] The competition issue was once again deliberated at the Sixth Worldwide Air Transport Conference in 2013. The EU presented a separate

39 See *Report of the Worldwide Air Transport Conference: Challenges and Opportunities of Liberalization, Montréal 23–24 March 2003*, ICAO ATConf/5 2003, ICAO Doc. 9819, p. 36.

working paper devoted to these issues. It underscored the importance of fair competition in the functioning of air transport services and requested the ICAO to 'develop basic principles of fair competition in the international air transport sector at global level as well as instruments to establish and maintain it'.[40] In another working paper the EU postulated that the ICAO 'should adopt an ambitious, long-term "vision" for market access liberalization on a global scale'.[41] According to that EU paper, 'a relatively low-key, bottom up, incremental approach might provide the most widely palatable route to such a vision'.[42] Some of these postulates have been partially accepted in the conference conclusions and recommendations.[43]

In preparation for the ICAO Assembly in 2013, the EU recalled its key postulates.[44] The ICAO 38th Assembly in 2013 has endorsed the outcomes of Sixth Worldwide Air Transport Conference. Among others, it has confirmed that fair competition is an important general principle in the operation of international air services. The Assembly has requested the ICAO Council to 'develop tools such as an exchange forum to enhance cooperation, dialogue and exchange of information on fair competition between States with a view to promoting compatible regulatory approaches towards international air transport'.[45]

However, there was no agreement on the adoption of basic principles of fair competition. Although the EU initiative gained some support, a number of the ICAO member states opposed it. For instance, the US opted for regulatory cooperation instead of adoption of basic principles. The US has seen the ICAO role as being limited to facilitating cooperation by development of a database collecting knowledge on existing competition laws and practices.[46] The United Arab Emirates (UAE) stated that the competition clause included in ICAO Template Air Services Agreements is already an adequate recommendation concerning fair competition and requested that states should avoid unilateral actions in this respect.[47]

40 *Basic Principles of Fair Competition (presented by Ireland on behalf of the European Union (EU) and its member states and other member states of the European Civil Aviation Conference)*, ICAO ATConf/6-WP/51, 14.2.2013, p. 4.

41 *Liberalization of Market Access (presented by Ireland on behalf of the European Union (EU) and its member states and other member states of the European Civil Aviation Conference (ECAC))*, ICAO ATConf/6-WP/54, 14.2.2013, p. 3.

42 Ibid.

43 See *Sixth Worldwide Air Transport Conference: Sustainability of Air Transport*, Montréal, 18–22 March 2013, ICAO ATConf/6 2013, ICAO Doc. 10009, pp. 26–27.

44 See *European Priorities for the Economic Regulation of International Air Transport (presented by Lithuania on behalf of the European Union and its member states and the other member states of the European Civil Aviation Conference)*, ICAO A38-WP/63, 13.8.2013.

45 *Consolidated statement of continuing ICAO policies in the air transport field*, ICAO Assembly Resolution A38-14, Appendix A, Section II.

46 *Fair Competition and Regulatory Cooperation in the Aviation Sector (presented by the United States)*, ICAO ATConf/6-WP/62, 14.2.2013.

47 *Views of Arab States on Fair Competition (presented by the United Arab Emirates on behalf of a group of Arab States)*, ICAO ATConf/6-WP/32, 12.2.2013, p. 3.

6.5 Conclusions

The development of an international fair competition regime applicable to air transport seems distant. Fair competition is inherently difficult to analyse, monitor and address due to the extremely complex nature of the airline business. Moreover, individual states and national competition frameworks differ between states and are often contradictory. Consequently, it is difficult to develop global legal mechanisms governing competition problems applicable to this sector.

The EU has managed to submit its single air market to the broadest and the most complex international competition framework in the world. To secure a level playing field in third party relations the EU has undertaken an extremely challenging task of implementing fair competition rules into the international air transport industry. Importantly, the EU position is that open skies can only function well if this level playing field is secured. Thus, the EU insists that fair competition safeguards accompany any liberalisation measures in international air transport. This standpoint not only affects current air services but also influences the future opening of the market. This is because, in the absence of relevant rules on competition, the EU may be reluctant to further liberalise the market.

The EU has thus attempted to address the competition issue at various levels, including ASAs, the ICAO forum and by developing its own unilateral defence mechanisms. The future policy of the EU in this area may be influenced by the efficacy of the new instrument replacing Regulation 868/2004. Should this new tool be effective, the EU may be less determined to promote the fair competition issue at the multilateral forum as a prerequisite to further opening of the market within bilateral relations, especially as currently the implementation of fair competition clauses into comprehensive ASAs seems to be the most promising mechanism for the EU.

Part 3

Competition between air transport law and other regulatory regimes

The legal and economic development of the airline industry and the technical advancement of the aerospace sector has led to new regulatory problems concerning the relation of air law and other regimes. First, privatisation of space activities, emergence of commercial spaceflight, and soon-to-be air transport, leads to questions as to the adequate regulatory system for these activities, whether based on air or rather space law. These questions, which pertain to areas such as responsibility and liability, licensing and certification, traffic management and the application of criminal law, and are already partially dealt with by national regulators, will have to be rapidly responded by the international lawmaker. Second, the growing global consciousness of environmental problems and the long-awaited international mandate to tackle them, have brought about different regulatory schemes potentially conflicting with each other and also with the general principles of air law. They also evoke fears of potential revival of protectionism and unilateralism. Third, liberalisation in international aviation has not only introduced free market competition but also revealed the possible problem of non-commercial airline advantages deriving from more favourable non-aviation-specific labour legislations. These diverging labour regimes may stand in conflict with the purposes of airline economic regulation and competition policy in that they have the potential to unlevel the airline playing field.

7 Citius, Altius, Fortius

Regulating commercial spaceflight under air law or space law?

Frans G. von der Dunk

7.1 Private commercial human spaceflight – the context

Citius, Altius, Fortius – 'faster, higher, stronger': the famous motto of the Olympic Games could also serve as a one-liner capturing the development of aviation over time. From the Wright brothers' very first flight in 1903, achieving a speed of less than 11 km per hour and an altitude of some 3 m above the ground with a 12-horsepower propeller engine, to today's long-haul Airbus A380 with cruising speeds close to 900 km per hour at altitudes of over 12 km with four jet engines each capable of delivering a thrust close to 311 kN, aviation has to a large extent been about continuously extending the available power to push aircraft to higher speeds and higher altitudes.

Not always have such extensions been commercially successful, of course. Witness the fate of Concorde and its Soviet 'equivalent', the Tupolev Tu-144, achieving supersonic speeds at altitudes double that of 'normal' long-haul aircraft with engines themselves not as powerful as those of the Airbus A380: it was, among other things, the ability to fly higher that made them faster.

Current records of aircraft achievements in the realm of speed, altitude and engine thrust are listed as, respectively, some 7,297 km per hour achieved in October 1967, almost 108 km achieved in August 1963, both using the US X-15 vehicle, and the aforementioned Airbus A380's engines.[1]

From this background, it is not surprising that as soon as private commercial human spaceflight became feasible, with SpaceShipOne – launched from underneath WhiteKnightOne – winning the X-Prize in October 2004, especially among air lawyers the gut reaction was to simply propose extension, somehow, of air law to this about-to-happen exciting new sector.[2] Also known, though rather imprecisely, as 'space tourism', private human spaceflight concerns flights of humans intended to enter 'outer space' (a) at their own expense or that of another private person or entity, (b) conducted by private entities, or (c) both.[3]

1 See https://en.wikipedia.org/wiki/Aircraft_records (visited 9.5.2018).

2 See Abeyratne 2004; Hobe 2007; Von der Dunk 2007, pp. 403–420; Gerhard 2011, pp. 265–279.

3 See Von der Dunk, 2015a, p. 667.

Tellingly, the website listing the earlier-mentioned aircraft records actually indicates the current altitude record to be the 112 km reached by the SpaceShipOne in October 2004. However, as the name already indicates, there are serious questions as to whether this vehicle qualifies as an aircraft – and, as a consequence, more broadly speaking also whether air law is indeed the most logical and sensible existing legal regime to be applied.

It is this major question that the current chapter seeks to investigate. *Citius, Altius, Fortius* may be noble goals not only in the Olympics but in international transportation for the benefit of the global public as well. The law at least should focus on ensuring that such transportation does not risk also becoming *Pericolosius, Stultius, Inaestimabilis* ('more dangerous, more foolish, more unpredictable').

7.2 The basic tenets of air law

Summarising the basic tenets of air law with a view to possible application to commercial spaceflight, such application essentially hinges on two triggers: the area where a certain activity takes place, respectively the vehicle with which a certain activity is conducted, noting furthermore that many rules of air law somehow combine the two approaches in application.

As to the first generic trigger of application of air law, Article 1 of the Chicago Convention[4] confirms that individual states have absolute sovereignty over the airspace above their own respective territories as defined by Article 2 of the convention.[5] Conversely, the airspace above the high seas falls outside of the territorial sovereignty of any individual state. Characterised as 'international airspace', it is essentially regulated by common consensus of the state parties to the Chicago Convention involving ICAO.[6]

Within national airspace, however, it is by logical inference the sovereign state that is responsible, for instance, for the applicable rules of the air (Article 12 of the Chicago Convention), for the provision of relevant navigation aids and air traffic control operations (Article 28 of the Chicago Convention) and for accident investigation at a primary level (Article 26 of the Chicago Convention).[7]

As for the economic and commercial side of aviation, the major consequence of sovereignty over national airspace is the fundamental right of the state to keep out foreign aircraft unless it has one way or another consented to allow them in, by virtue of Article 3(c) of the Chicago Convention as far as state aircraft are

4 Convention on International Civil Aviation, signed in Chicago on 7 December 1944, entered into force 4 April 1947, ICAO Doc. 7300/9, 15 UNTS 295.

5 For air sovereignty see Wassenbergh, 1997, p. 22; Milde 2016, pp. 37–39.

6 Article 12 of the convention provides 'Over the high seas, the rules in force shall be those established under this Convention'. For air navigation over the high seas see also Grief, 1994, pp. 61–63; Milde, 2016, pp. 39–40.

7 For state responsibilities within its airspace see: Van Antwerpen 2007, pp. 25–42; Huang 2009, pp. 32–41; Schnitker and Van het Kaar 2010, pp. 7–11.

concerned, respectively Chapter II (especially Articles 5–11) of the Convention as far as other aircraft are concerned.[8] In the latter case, Articles 5–8 then effectively opened the door for the myriad bilateral air service agreements by which states agree on a reciprocal basis to open their national airspace for commercial aviation, as well as for the International Air Services Transit Agreement of 1944[9] and International Air Transport Agreement of 1944,[10] which aimed to do the same on a multilateral basis.[11]

The Chicago Convention is literally addressing its regime in this context to aircraft, which was, of course, back in 1944 the only kind of vehicle that mattered from this perspective. Further than that, territorial sovereignty, by inference and logical extension under principles of public international law, would in any event prohibit the entry of any foreign vehicle, whatever its legal nature, into national airspace except as permitted by the state at issue.

In a 'horizontal' sense, national airspace and the concurring territorial sovereignty of a state end at the national borders, either terrestrial or in terms of the outer limit to the territorial waters as per Article 2 of the United Nations Convention on the Law of the Sea.[12] Other than that, the 'geographic' dimensions of national sovereign airspace were not addressed, neither by the Chicago Convention itself nor by later aviation treaties. The issue of (maximum) 'vertical' extension of national sovereign airspace was irrelevant at the time of the Chicago Convention's conclusion. Ever since then, it has basically remained true from the 'aviation perspective' that for the purpose of regulating relevant aviation activities, there was no need to determine the precise altitude to which territorial sovereignty should, could or would extend. At all altitudes where aviation activities were normally conducted, there was no doubt that this concerned 'airspace' in the legal sense of the word.[13]

With regard to the second generic trigger of application of air law, the vehicle involved, following several Annexes to the Chicago Convention the definition of aircraft as any 'machine that can derive support in the atmosphere from the reactions of the air other than the reactions of the air against the earth's surface'[14] allowed for a rather clear understanding of what kind of vehicles air law generally deals with.[15]

8 See Milde, 2016, pp. 64 ff.

9 International Air Services Transit Agreement, signed in Chicago on 7 December 1944, entered into force on 30 January 1945, ICAO Doc. 9587, 84 UNTS 389.

10 International Air Transport Agreement, signed in Chicago on 7 December 1944, entered into force on 8 February 1945, ICAO Doc. 9587, 171 UNTS 387.

11 For these agreements see Wassenbergh 2000, pp. 11–20; Milde 2016, pp. 111–122.

12 United Nations Convention on the Law of the Sea, done in Montego Bay on 10 December 1982, entered into force on 16 November 1994, 1833 UNTS 3 and 1835 UNTS 261. Note that Article 3 determines the maximum breadth of the territorial seas as extending to 19.3 km offshore.

13 Milde 2016, pp. 38–39.

14 Annex 7 – Aircraft Nationality and Registration Marks, Annex 8 – Airworthiness of aircraft.

15 See Żylicz 1992, pp. 65–66; Vissepó 2005, pp. 185–189.

The Chicago Convention itself, for instance, explicitly addresses aircraft when it comes to the right of non-scheduled flight (Article 5), cabotage (Article 7) and the complete portfolio of safety regulations, emanating from such Articles as 11 (on applicability of air regulations), 12 (on the rules of the air), 31 (on certificates of airworthiness), 32 (on personnel licensing) and 37 (on Standards and Recommended Practices, as further elaborated by the various Annexes to the Chicago Convention).[16] Likewise, the application of criminal air law such as per the 1963 Convention on Offences and Certain Other Acts Committed on Board Aircraft[17] or private air law as per the 1999 Convention for the Unification of Certain Rules for International Carriage by Air[18] is fundamentally triggered by the involvement of an aircraft on board of which the criminal acts are conducted, respectively where the damage has occurred.[19]

The general approach is, on the one hand, harking back to the first trigger, that states carry general responsibility for all aircraft within their sovereign airspace (including foreign ones presumed to have been allowed to enter) but, on the other hand, that they do so for 'their' aircraft – read aircraft registered with them and hence endowed with their nationality pursuant to Article 17 of the Chicago Convention – wherever these are found to be operating.[20]

In sum, when tackling the question of whether private commercial spaceflight is perhaps already, or at least should preferably be, addressed by air law, space law or any combination of both, the underlying question now becomes: where do these activities take place and what vehicles are involved? Before turning to these analyses, however, we first have to address the space law side of the equation.

7.3 The basic tenets of space law

Following the same analytical approach as in Section 7.2 with respect to air law, the basic tenets of space law with a view to possible application to commercial spaceflight also essentially hinge on the same triggers: the area where a certain activity takes place, respectively the vehicle within which a certain activity is conducted, noting furthermore that in many details of the space law regime the application of the two approaches is again of an interconnected nature.

16 See Huang 2009, pp. 21–32; Milde 2016, pp. 71–73, 109–111.

17 Convention on Offences and Certain Other Acts Committed on Board Aircraft, done in Tokyo on 14 September 1963, entered into force on 4 December 1969, ICAO Doc. 8364, 704 UNTS 219.

18 Convention for the Unification of Certain Rules for International Carriage by Air, done at Montréal on 28 May 1999, entered into force on 4 November 2003, ICAO Doc. 9740.

19 See Milde, 2016, pp. 227–236, 305–308.

20 See Chapter 12 of this book. See also Żylicz 1992, pp. 66–67; Milde 2016, pp. 80–82.

As for the first generic trigger of application of space law, Article II of the Outer Space Treaty (OST)[21] provides for the generic status of outer space as, effectively, a 'global commons'.[22] Following this very fundamental baseline provision, the OST *inter alia* requires the use of the area of outer space to be in the interests of all countries on the premise of freedom of exploration and use of that area (Article I), prohibits certain military uses of outer space (Article IV), attributes international responsibility for activities conducted in outer space (Article VI) and requires states to abstain from harmful interference with other legitimate activities in that area (Article IX).

As with the fundamental aviation treaties, the OST does not in any way define outer space in a geographic sense. The closest that follow-on conventions on outer space came to such a definition was to use the concept of completing orbits around the earth as a loose way of determining what at least should be considered as included in that area (e.g., Article IV(1)(d) of the Registration Convention[23]). Much as this turns out to be rather more complicated upon closer view,[24] a still ongoing discussion arose on an appropriate virtual borderline separating the sovereign airspaces from the global commons of outer space.

States and experts generally disagreed as to what the most appropriate altitude for such a borderline would be, however; and some states (most notably the US) and experts even denied any need for establishing such a borderline, citing, for instance, the possibility of technical innovations allowing aircraft to fly higher and/or spacecraft to operate lower as reasons why it was premature to agree on such a borderline right now.[25]

Indeed, for the overwhelming part of history so far, the law of outer space could be applied without too many problems even in the absence of agreement on a particular borderline. Aircraft, as the main object of most air law, seldom reached higher than 50–60 km, whereas satellites, the major object of space law, seldom orbited lower than at approximately 120 km, so the exact borderline could be conveniently left undefined for the time being. Only on the issue of 'innocent passage' of spacecraft on their way to and/or back from outer space over the territories of other states did some discussion arise – at what altitude should such overflight be legally equated with flight through sovereign airspace, hence becoming subject to the underlying state's consent? Precisely

21 Treaty on Principles Governing the Activities of States in the Exploration and Use of Outer Space, including the Moon and Other Celestial Bodies (hereinafter Outer Space Treaty), done in London, Moscow and Washington on 27 January 1967, entered into force on 10 October 1967, 610 UNTS 205.

22 Freeland and Jakhu 2009, pp. 49 ff; Von der Dunk 2015a, pp. 55–60.

23 Convention on Registration of Objects Launched into Outer Space (hereinafter Registration Convention), done in New York on 14 January 1975, entered into force on 15 September 1976, 1023 UNTS 15.

24 See Von der Dunk 2013a.

25 See Hobe 2009, pp. 31–32; Von der Dunk 2015b, pp. 60–72.

the assumption that the borderline was an essentially academic issue, however, is now fundamentally challenged by the advent of the commercial spaceflight industry.

With regard to the second generic trigger of space law, both the OST and major follow-on conventions such as the Liability Convention[26] and the Registration Convention target many obligations to the involvement of a 'space object', the concept in space law closest to that of 'aircraft'.

Thus, the space law liability regime applies to damage caused by such a space object (Article VII of the OST and Articles II–V of the Liability Convention), obligations exist to return space objects to their original launching state (Article VIII of the OST and Article 5 of the Agreement on the Rescue of Astronauts, the Return of Astronauts and the Return of Objects Launched into Outer Space[27]) and space objects should be registered by the (or at least a) launching state (Article VIII of the OST and Articles II–IV of the Registration Convention).[28]

Space object, however, is not (really) defined by the space treaties. The OST just refers to objects launched into outer space, and while the Liability Convention (in Article I(d)) and the Registration Convention (in Article I(b)) contain identical text, the definition here is at best half-baked and semicircular: 'the term space object includes component parts of a space object as well as its launch vehicle and parts thereof'. Further, a more or less general consensus can now be discerned amongst the experts that a space object is a man-made object which is at least intended to be brought into outer space – by any means whatsoever.[29]

Interestingly, the reference to outer space in the context of defining a space object brings us back to the question of delimitation of outer space as discussed earlier: whether or not the altitude at which a particular vehicle is aimed at would be considered outer space or not would determine if it could be qualified as a space object or not.

Historically, this issue has not been considered to be of practical relevance, as most space objects at issue were unmanned and usually not destined to ever come back even close to the earth's atmosphere and/or any area feasibly defined as 'airspace'. The few manned spacecraft that have flown so far were all governmental in nature, launched from the national territory of a few large countries

26 Convention on International Liability for Damage Caused by Space Objects (hereinafter Liability Convention), done in London, Moscow and Washington on 29 March 1972, entered into force on 1 September 1972, 961 UNTS 187.

27 Agreement on the Rescue of Astronauts, the Return of Astronauts and the Return of Objects Launched into Outer Space, done in London, Moscow and Washington on 22 April 1968, entered into force on 3 December 1968, 672 UNTS 119.

28 See Marboe, Neumann and Schrogl 2013, pp. 63–70; Schmidt-Tedd 2013, pp. 249–304; Smith, Kerrest de Rozavel and Tronchetti 2013, pp. 116–147.

29 For a discussion of space object definition see Smith, Kerrest de Rozavel and Tronchetti 2013, pp. 109–110, 114–115; Von der Dunk 2015b, pp. 86–87.

and ultimately returning to them (or to the high seas, as in the case of US manned spaceflight). Again, however, this is fundamentally set to change with the advent of private commercial spaceflight.

7.4 Private manned spaceflight projects and the legal conundrum

The various impending projects for private commercial spaceflight raise fundamental issues with both existing legal regimes, of air law and space law respectively, and this in respect of both where the activities take place and what vehicles they intend to use for the purpose.[30]

To start with the 'spatialist' approach regarding the realms where relevant activities are conducted, private commercial spaceflight activities are generally subdivided into sub-orbital and orbital.[31] Sub-orbital flight plans of companies such as Virgin Galactic and Blue Origin are currently focused on space tourism, the intention being in particular to fly paying passengers in a hyperbolic trajectory peaking at altitudes of slightly over 100 km, essentially for the fun of it.[32] Orbital flight plans are currently being developed especially in the context of NASA-funded Commercial Orbital Transportation Services (COTS) and Commercial Crew Development (CCDev) projects. These are aimed at replacing the space shuttle capacity to carry astronauts and cargo to and back from the International Space Station (ISS), the shuttle having been retired in the course of 2011, with private capacity to serve the ISS, and currently involve companies such as Space-X, Boeing, Orbital and (again) Blue Origin.[33]

On the one hand, all such flights obviously cross over national airspace (unless, hypothetically at this stage, launched from the high seas) on their way to and back from outer space. This is not much of a problem of international law to the extent that the national airspace concerned normally is that of the state of departure and return of the flights at issue, and, so far, the problem has been solved almost routinely by creating under special aviation regulations time and airspace windows for space launches ever since these started being conducted. In that sense, all such flights by definition have to be accommodated by and through the relevant systems of air law. Problems, however, would arise once these flights do not remain confined to a single airspace, but start flying between various countries and their airspaces.

On the other hand, depending ultimately of course on what altitude is considered to present the lower boundary of outer space, all orbital flights are without any doubt intended to reach outer space and operate there, and all sub-orbital flights are supposed at least to top out in the lower areas of outer space.

30 See Vissepó 2005, pp. 169–178.

31 See Von der Dunk, 2007, pp. 403–408.

32 Although it must be said that future flights are also planned to serve astronaut training purposes and smaller, low-budget and low-altitude space experiments – which is precisely why the moniker 'space tourism' is somewhat inaccurate.

33 Hughes and Rosenberg 2005, pp. 1–11; Vissepó 2005, pp. 165 ff; Von der Dunk 2015a, pp. 663–708.

They would, legally speaking, find themselves outside the territorial sovereignty of any state, and only subject to its jurisdiction on the basis of the nationality of the company and/or the vehicle (Article VIII of the OST and Article II of the Registration Convention).

Here, the altitude issue is brought into sharp focus notably by these sub-orbital companies as they sell tickets claiming that they will provide the buyers with a spaceflight experience and astronaut status by reaching altitudes of above 100 km. Since that altitude has been quoted following other discussions as well, it may now perhaps be said that – in the absence of any formal 'legal' agreement on a demarcation of airspace and outer space (or even on the need for any demarcation as such) – at least a gradual convergence can be seen to emerge on the 100-km line as the most sensible informal line dividing air space from outer space.[34]

At this stage, already three national space laws have explicitly quoted the altitude for those purposes – the 2002-version of the Australian Act about space activities, and for related purposes[35] (section 8: 16th, 21st, 33rd and 35th bullets), the 2012 Kazakh Law on Space Activities[36] (Article 1(6)) and the Danish Law on activities in outer space of 2016[37] (section 4(4)) – and more countries are likely to follow. The 2008 Russian–Chinese proposal for a Draft Treaty on the Prevention of the Placement of Weapons in Outer Space, the Threat or Use of Force Against Outer Space Objects[38] contained a definition of outer space referring to the 100 km-altitude (see Article I(a)), although that reference has been deleted in a later version – presumably to try and make it slightly more palatable to some other countries.

Finally, both the EU and – surprisingly, in view of its formal resistance against any borderline – the US have in the context of security-sensitive technology export controls defined 'space-qualified technology' with reference to this altitude (see Annex I to Regulation 428/2009[39] at 134/28; respectively section 772.1 of the Export Administration Act[40] as updated in 2012 pursuant to the identical change in the context of the Wassenaar Arrangement).

As for the 'functionalist' approach regarding the technology used, the starting point is to realise that the definitions of aircraft and space object respectively are not complementary or even mutually exclusive. Vehicles can be and indeed have

34 See Gerhard 2011, pp. 280–282; Von der Dunk, 2015b, pp. 60–73.

35 An act about space activities, and for related purposes, No. 123 of 1998, assented to 21 December 1998; as amended by amending legislation up to No. 100 of 2002.

36 Law of the Republic of Kazakhstan on Space Activities, of 6 January 2012, 2012 No. 528-IV.

37 Law on activities in outer space (*Lov om aktiviteter i det ydre rum*), passed by Parliament with the third treatment, 3 May 2016, Parliament Gazette, 2015–17, No. L 128.

38 Draft Treaty on the Prevention of the Placement of Weapons in Outer Space, the Threat or Use of Force Against Outer Space Objects; presented 12 February 2008 to the Conference on Disarmament.

39 Regulation No. 428/2009/EC of the Council of 5 May 2009 setting up a Community regime for the control of exports, transfer, brokering and transit of dual-use items, OJ L 134, 29.5.2009, pp. 1–269.

40 Export Administration Act of 1979, Pub. L. 96–72 – 29 September 1979, 93 Stat. 503, as amended.

already been devised (witness the space shuttle) that are both able to make use of the upward lift of the air in order to qualify as an aircraft and intended to reach outer space so as to qualify as a space object. Even aircraft that merely serve to launch another vehicle into outer space without themselves ever aiming for that area, by dint of thus being 'launch vehicles', become space objects as well (Article I(d) of the Liability Convention). *Vice versa*, vehicles that neither use the upward lift of the air nor intend to go into outer space – such as early test prototypes of the ultimate space vehicle – would not qualify as either aircraft or space object.[41]

Looking at some of the actual projects being currently developed for the purpose of private commercial spaceflight, they include several with wings, which are able to use the upward lift of the air (this applies, e.g., to Virgin Galactic's SpaceShipTwo and its carrier aircraft the WhiteKnightTwo, but also to the Lynx vehicle of now-bankrupted XCOR and to Sierra Nevada Corporation's Dream Chaser), and some without wings, which can be flown without the ability to use the upward lift of the air (this applies for instance to Boeing's CST-100 Starliner and Space X's Falcon-9-plus-Dragon combination). All of them qualify as space objects – at least if the intended altitudes of a minimum 100 km for the sub-orbital vehicles among them are viewed as being in outer space.[42]

Hence, this is the major resulting conundrum: if many of the vehicles qualify as aircraft yet all of them qualify as space objects (on the assumption that the relevant altitudes are outer space), and if all of them cross airspace as well as (except early prototypes) intending to reach outer space and operate there, however shortly, how can we ensure that the potential application of both air law and space law to at least elements or aspects of private commercial spaceflight does not create dangerous gaps and complicating overlaps?

In the abstract, there would be two approaches. One would be to start addressing those activities as space activities covered by space law, and at a secondary level fill in gaps or remedy shortcomings by applying parts of air law or at least developing new rules coming from aviation, while ensuring these fit as much as possible and is necessary within a space law framework context. The second approach would essentially be the other way around.

7.5 The US approach – stressing the 'space' in 'spaceflight'

The one country that has not only seen most of the serious private commercial spaceflight projects developing within its borders but has also taken the most detailed steps so far to regulate them, is the US.[43] It has, essentially, taken a

41 See Vissepó 2005, pp. 164–184.

42 See Gerhard 2011, pp. 264–269, 282–283.

43 Note that, although Richard Branson's Virgin brand is originally British, Virgin Galactic after a few years (re)incorporated in the US; likewise, while the first initiative to use XCOR's Lynx vehicle came from a Dutch consortium called SXC (Space Experience Curacao), it was also legally relocated later on to the US.

space-law approach to the issue, and chosen to regulate all such flights – including sub-orbital ones – by adapting the existing law regulating private commercial space launches to include private commercial flights (read launches into and re-entries from outer space) carrying humans on board.

When in the 1980s the US government decided to stimulate private involvement in the launch service sector – exclusively targeting unmanned launches at the time, as private manned spaceflight did not yet constitute a viable proposition – it enunciated the Commercial Space Launch Act[44] in 1984, fine-tuning in particular the liability regime by way of amendments in 1988.[45] With a view to the later regulatory developments addressing private manned spaceflight, several key elements of the resulting regime should be noted.[46]

Most importantly, any private company with US nationality or launching from US territory was required to obtain a licence for each intended individual launch of an object into outer space from the licensing agency, the Office of the Associate Administrator for Commercial Space Transportation (now AST) within the Federal Aviation Administration (FAA) (51 USC 50904(a)). Conditions for the grant of a license related to safety, national security and compliance with international law, as well as an obligation to cover for third-party liability and liability for the use of governmental launch facilities resulting from accidents that could happen (51 USC 50905(a), 50914(a) and (b)). However, since no manned space launches had been foreseen at the time, neither was contractual liability *vis-à-vis* possible passengers provided for, nor requirements regarding certification of vehicles and/or licensing of crews – as is traditional for aviation.

Once, in the late 1990s, the advent of private manned space launches became a distinct possibility with the ongoing race for the X-Prize, it was the US launching regime that was adapted for the purpose – not US air law. A first step towards adapting the Commercial Space Launch Act to the possibility of private manned spaceflight operations was taken in 1998, when the Commercial Space Act[47] purportedly was 'amended ... to address liability and government indemnification concerns and to address licensing authority for RLVs [reusable launch vehicles]',[48] thus allowing the FAA to start licensing re-entry operations in addition to launches.

The next step was to kick-start a process of regulating such flights on an appropriate basis, even though legislation and regulation addressing this impending new activity were to remain confined to a minimum level required to protect key public interests, so as not to stifle this about-to-be-born industry. Consistent with the requirement to:

44 Commercial Space Launch Act, Pub. L. 98–575 – 30 October 1984, 98 Stat. 3055.

45 The Commercial Space Launch Act as repeatedly amended has meanwhile been codified as 51 USC.

46 See Vorwig 2010, pp. 404–415; Von der Dunk 2015a, pp. 683–687.

47 Commercial Space Act of 1998, Pub. L. 105–303 – 27 January 1998, 112 Stat. 2843.

48 Hughes and Rosenberg 2005, p. 4.

> encourage private sector launches, re-entries, and associated services and, only to the extent necessary, regulate those launches, re-entries, and services to ensure compliance with international obligations of the United States and to protect the public health and safety, safety of property, and national security and foreign policy interests of the United States
>
> (51 USC 50901(a)(7))

this overarching approach to private manned spaceflight also translated into limiting oversight with respect to the operator, with (for the time being) a ban on safety regulation and certification of the vehicle – so far 'the operator holds the ticket not the vehicle'.[49]

The result was the Commercial Space Launch Amendments Act of 2004[50] amending the 1984/1988 Act to achieve such goals, followed by further legal measures as part of the Code of Federal Regulations.[51]

Most fundamentally, the licensing obligation was now also applied to re-entry, whereas formerly it only applied to launches; the option of obtaining an experimental permit for test flights was created; the existing third-party and inter-party (*vis-à-vis* the US government) liability regimes continued to apply; and the (pre-existing) cross-waiver of liability was not extended to 'spaceflight participants', the new concept introduced to refer to what effectively would be passengers on these flights (51 USC 50904–50906, 50914).

As for the latter, instead operators were allowed to fly spaceflight participants without any statutory obligation to accept liability for damage caused to them, as long as all parties had signed an informed consent clause indicating that they are aware of probable accidents and 'that the US government has not certified the launch vehicle as safe for carrying crew or space flight participants' (51 USC 50905(b)). Resulting in some uncertainty still as to whether this would indeed amount to a waiver of contractual liability *vis-à-vis* spaceflight participants,[52] in 2015 the Commercial Space Launch Competitiveness Act[53] redressed this by amending the relevant section 50914(b)(1) of the Commercial Space Launch Act so that spaceflight participants are now included in the cross-waiver, meaning there is effectively no statutory obligation to accept contractual liability on the part of the spaceflight operators.

This regime is, obviously, targeted at allowing an infant industry to catch on, develop and mature; regulating it initially only as far as necessary 'to protect the

49 Ibid., p. 71.

50 Commercial Space Launch Amendments Act of 2004, Pub. L. 108–492 – 23 December 2004, 118 Stat. 3974.

51 Notably, 14 CFR Chapter III, Commercial Space Transportation, Federal Aviation Administration, Department of Transportation. See Hughes and Rosenberg 2005, pp. 11–24; Vorwig 2010, pp. 406 ff.

52 See Hughes and Rosenberg 2005, pp. 51–56; Yates 2012; Von der Dunk 2015a, pp. 691–696.

53 Commercial Space Launch Competitiveness Act; Pub. L. 114–190 – 25 November 2015, 129 Stat. 704.

public health and safety, safety of property, and national security and foreign policy interests of the United States' (51 USC 50901(a)(7)) and leaving it to the responsibility of spaceflight participants to decide whether they wish to fly or not, and – if the former – to what extent they wish to take out their own insurance in case of accidents.

This regime is, however, temporary in nature: section 107 of the Commercial Space Launch Competitiveness Act provides a sunset clause currently referring to 30 September 2025. Earlier versions of the Commercial Space Launch Act had referred to earlier dates, but extensions were granted as the commercial spaceflight industry did not take off as quickly as anticipated. Similarly, the ban on developing standards such as for certification of vehicles involved has, by means of section 111 of the Commercial Space Launch Competitiveness Act, been extended now to 1 October 2023.

This would also mean that if by 2023/2025 the spaceflight industry still has not taken off in any substantive manner, those sunset clauses might be expected to be once again extended. Only when private commercial spaceflight is considered a mature industry, would it be considered appropriate or even feasible to start developing statutory and mandatory approaches to passenger liability and safety certification along the lines of the aviation industry.

A final development of note concerns the possibility of government astronauts flying on such private vehicles.[54] The hybridisation of private flights carrying public employees into outer space gave rise to discussion on the extent to which NASA would allow its astronauts (and any foreign guest astronauts) to fly on vehicles 'not certified ... as safe for carrying crew or space flight participants' (51 USC 50905(b)(4)(B) and (5)(B)). Section 112 of the Commercial Space Launch Competitiveness Act, by creating a third category next to 'crew' and 'space flight participants' of 'government astronauts', has now opened the door to developing special procedures and rules for private commercial space flights with such astronauts on board.

7.6 The European approach – stressing the 'flight' in 'spaceflight'

Several of the initiatives regarding private commercial spaceflight were originally undertaken in Europe: Richard Branson and his Virgin Group, including initially Virgin Galactic, were British, whereas the first ideas to use XCOR's Lynx vehicle to undertake sub-orbital space tourism flights were formulated by a Dutch enterprise SXC aiming to fly from the Dutch-Caribbean island of Curacao. So far, with regards to Europe, in addition substantial interests in the possibilities of private spaceflight have arisen in particular in Sweden, the UK, and Spain (read Catalonia).

In view of all of this, it is not surprising that also in Europe discussions have arisen about to how to address such possibilities and interest has grown in the

54 See Von der Dunk 2015a, pp. 703–705.

legal and regulatory context. The initial approach was very much guided by the fact that ICAO already in the early 2000s started to investigate whether the sub-orbital flights in particular would not have to be addressed under the Chicago Convention and/or ICAO authority.[55] The investigation led to a report in 2005,[56] which, while pointing out that at least some of the sub-orbital vehicles on the drawing board fit within the definition of 'aircraft', desisted from urging the development of any Standards and Recommended Practices on the matter – which would have been the logical consequence otherwise of defining such vehicles as aircraft.[57]

Nevertheless, this approach of addressing private commercial spaceflight from the vantage point of aviation rather than space launches was initially further developed by the European Aviation Safety Agency (EASA), which investigated in greater detail the possibility of applying a special version of the international aircraft certification regime to such sub-orbital flights.[58] Around 2010, however, these efforts seem to have been silently put on hold.[59] Presumably there were two main reasons for this.

On the one hand, it was clear that the US, ever since the 2004 Commercial Space Launch Amendments Act, was not pursuing the 'aviation' approach but opting for the 'space' approach. Going the contrary route in Europe would at best stifle international agreement on the proper way to handle private spaceflight once it starts to morph into international transportation, and at worse preclude any initial development in Europe of what by all accounts was as of yet not even an infant industry but merely a 'cradle industry'. Indeed, the moves of the Virgin Galactic and XCOR/SXC initiatives to the US were already a foreboding of such scenarios.

The discussions within ICAO, which continued to monitor these developments, equally did not fail to notice that the US was developing national legislation and regulation following the space approach, and as late as 2015 it had still been merely decided 'to sensitise the Legal Committee on the legal aspects of commercial space flights',[60] without any specific call for action.

On the other hand, the jurisdictional situation in this respect within Europe was far from clear. Sweden, the first European country to show interest in becoming part of the private spaceflight sector as far back as the mid-2000s, initially was poised to regulate such flights under its rather brief and flexible Act

55 See Van Fenema 2005.

56 *Working Paper on Concept of Suborbital Flights*, ICAO Council, 175th Session, ICAO C-WP/12436, 30.5.2005.

57 For a discussion of the report see Hughes and Rosenberg 2005, pp. 76–77; Vissepó 2005, pp. 179–185.

58 See Marciacq et al. 2010a.

59 Cf. Marciacq et al. 2010b.

60 See *Commercial Space Flights (Presented by the Secretariat)*, ICAO Working Paper LC/36-WP/3-2, 20.10.2015.

on Outer Space Activities of 1982[61] and accompanying Decree.[62] After all, it was the Swedish Space Corporation operating the launch site of Kiruna that drove such interests.

Legislative developments at the level of the EU, however, then started to create confusion. Following the aborted Treaty establishing a Constitution for Europe of 2004,[63] the Treaty of Lisbon[64] drafted in 2007 and entering into force in 2009 provided for a measure of space competence for the EU institutions.[65] This included the possibility to 'establish the necessary measures' 'in accordance with the ordinary legislative procedure' (Article 189(2) of the Treaty on the Functioning of the European Union (TFEU),[66] in other words: to legislate on matters pertaining to outer space.[67]

There was one exception, however: such legislation was not allowed to result in 'any harmonisation of the laws and regulations of the Member States' (Article 189(2) of the TFEU), in other words: should not tread where member states individually had trodden before.[68]

At that point in time (2009, as the date of entry into force of the Treaty of Lisbon), there were already five EU member states that actually had a comprehensive national law addressing private space activities and their licensing in place. Apart from Sweden, chronologically speaking this concerned the UK with its Outer Space Act of 1986[69] (meanwhile in 2018 augmented by the Space Industry Act[70]), Belgium with its Law on the Activities of Launching, Flight Operations or Guidance of Space Objects of 2005,[71] the Netherlands with the

61 Act on Space Activities, 1982: 963, 18 November 1982; *National Space Legislation of the World*, Vol. I (2001), at 398; *Space Law – Basic Legal Documents*, E.II.1; 36 *Zeitschrift für Luft- und Weltraumrecht* (1987), 11.

62 Decree on Space Activities, 1982: 1069; *National Space Legislation of the World*, Vol. I (2001), at 399; *Space Law – Basic Legal Documents*, E.II.2; 36 *Zeitschrift für Luft- und Weltraumrecht* (1987), 11.

63 Treaty establishing a Constitution for Europe, done in Rome on 29 October 2004, never entered into force, OJ C 310, 16.12.2004, pp. 1–474.

64 Treaty of Lisbon amending the Treaty on European Union and the Treaty establishing the European Community, done in Lisbon on 13 December 2007, entered into force on 1 December 2009, OJ C 306, 17.122007, pp. 1–271.

65 Articles 4(3) and 189 of the Treaty establishing the European Community as amended by the Treaty of Lisbon.

66 Treaty on the Functioning of the European Union (TFEU), signed on 25 March 1957 in Rome, entered into force on 1 January 1958 (then Treaty establishing the European Economic Community, later Treaty establishing the European Economic Community, consolidated version OJ C 202, 7.6.2016, pp. 47–199.

67 For a discussion see Von der Dunk 2015c, pp. 255–258; Schmidt-Tedd 2011.

68 See Hobe et al. 2005; Gerhard 2011, pp. 287–288; Schmidt-Tedd 2011, pp. 302–306.

69 Outer Space Act, 18 July 1986, 1986 ch. 38; *National Space Legislation of the World*, Vol. I (2001), at 293; *Space Law – Basic Legal Documents*, E.I; 36 *Zeitschrift für Luft- und Weltraumrecht* (1987), 12.

70 Space Industry Act, 15 March 2018, 2018, Ch. 5.

71 Law on the Activities of Launching, Flight Operations or Guidance of Space Objects, 17 September 2005; *Nationales Weltraumrecht / National Space Law* (2008), at 183.

Law Incorporating Rules Concerning Space Activities and the Establishment of a Registry of Space Objects of 2007[72] and France with the Law on Space Operations of 2008.[73,74] Meanwhile Austria[75], Denmark[76] and Finland[77] have also enunciated such laws.

While it could be questioned whether an EU legislative initiative regarding private sub-orbital spaceflight could not be legitimately undertaken – after all, this concerned just one narrow and special category of private space activities, which none of the five existing national space laws had addressed in any detail, or even mentioned explicitly – the European Commission apparently chose the safer route of addressing private spaceflight as, primarily, 'flight', in order to bring its competences in the aviation sector, embodied and institutionalised by EASA, to bear.[78]

Even as the EASA initiative has been put on hold, the result is that a lot of confusion still reigns in the European 'environment' as to the proper legal and regulatory approach to private spaceflight. The UK has the aforementioned Space Industry Act on the table, which now addresses the sector in a national context very much mixing elements of space law with those of air law; Curacao – which is not subject to the EU's Transport Title – is trying to develop its 'regional' regulation, presumably following a US approach while nevertheless mixing in elements of air law; and other countries also seem at a loss as to what to do in this respect. Spain, for instance, does not even have a national space law.

While the fundamental thought originally behind the European approach – that not only third parties and the general public at large, but also any crew members and spaceflight participants should be entitled to a substantial level of protection by safety legislation – is to be applauded, the result threatens to become a worst-case scenario. If neither the public at large nor the operators or their possible clientele had any idea on how the law will develop in Europe, operators will (continue to) move to the US, which will consequently reap any benefits from the private investments and developments in the sector – as will spaceflight participants still interested in flying, obviously then under US law and regulations. Stifling an infant

72 Law Incorporating Rules Concerning Space Activities and the Establishment of a Registry of Space Objects, 24 January 2007; 80 *Staatsblad* (2007), at 1; *Nationales Weltraumrecht / National Space Law* (2008), at 201.

73 Law on Space Operations (*Loi relative aux opérations spatiales*); *Loi no. 2008–518 du 3 juin 2008*; unofficial English version 34 *Journal of Space Law* (2008), 453.

74 For a discussion of these acts see Gerhard 2011, pp. 283–286.

75 Federal Law on the Authorisation of Space Activities and the Establishment of a National Space Registry (*Bundesgesetz über die Genehmigung von Weltraumaktivitäten und die Einrichtung eines Weltraumregisters (Weltraumgesetz)*), 6 December 2011, Federal Law Gazette of 27 December 2011; 61 *Zeitschrift für Luft- und Weltraumrecht* (2012), 37–42, 56–61.

76 Law on activities in outer space (*Lov om aktiviteter i det ydre rum*), passed by Parliament with the third treatment, 3 May 2016, Parliament Gazette, 2015–17, No. L 128.

77 Act on space activities, 63/2018, of 23 January 2018.

78 See Gerhard 2011, pp. 269–277.

industry in the cradle in Europe will not create a safe spaceflight sector there – it will preclude any development thereof in the first place.

7.7 Finding the best mix

In sum, the baseline approach to addressing private commercial spaceflight seems increasingly to be developed on the basis of space law, in spite of the fact that at least some of the vehicles being developed would qualify as aircraft. The consequences of following such a qualification for the sake of a seemingly straightforward application of air law would raise a host of complicated issues, which in the end would neither allow the industry to appropriately develop nor do much about enhancing safety in view of the fact that all technologies currently developed are novel as well as different from current aviation technology, and until actual flight data have been collected it would be very difficult to recognise specific risks and address those by way of regulation.

Thus, at the national level, in many cases the application of elaborate and specially crafted sets of rules is made contingent upon an aircraft belonging to a specific category of aircraft, referring to such criteria as size, use and operational characteristics, or to specific types of operations regardless of the craft used. The new category of private spaceflight vehicle flights may fit ill into any of those.

As the author was involved in a relevant analysis for the purpose of developing a legal framework for space tourism in Curacao, the specific example of that regime may serve as an illustration here. Would, should or could private spaceflight vehicles for the purpose of airworthiness certification, qualify as 'utility aircraft', 'aerobatic aircraft', 'light aircraft' or 'experimental aircraft' – all of which require airworthiness certificates in conformity with detailed yet varying sets of rules – or would, in any event, a new category have to be devised? Differences are also highlighted under the regulations between aircraft of less than 5,700 kg – where, for example, XCOR's Lynx vehicle would have fit into the latter category – and operations. The regulations, in addition, fundamentally differentiate between various activities such as 'commercial air traffic', 'round trips', 'aerial work' flights and 'special aviation activities'.[79]

The starting point of any regulatory regime for private commercial spaceflight being that of space law, both internationally and nationally, however, does not mean air law should be completely ignored or any application of elements thereof should be ruled out.

First, it is evident that any spaceflight would have to cross air space in order to arrive at relevant altitudes – even if merely sub-orbital trajectories topping out at a little over a 100 km are at issue. National air legislation generally allows for options to close a certain section of airspace for a limited amount of

79 See Von der Dunk 2013b, pp. 24–29.

time (or even permanently) for special reasons, and of course it would make most sense to continue to apply those special regimes for commercial spaceflight operations launching and/or re-entering through national airspaces, at least initially.

Once, moreover, private commercial spaceflight becomes a regular occurrence, it would make sense not to use such exceptional regimes on a more or less *ad hoc* basis, but to fundamentally integrate such flights into the prevalent system for air navigation, air space management and air traffic management services. Currently it seems far too early for that, if only because it is as yet uncertain which of the various technologies being developed and tested in this context will ultimately make it to commercial maturity. For example, the level of manoeuvrability of a classical rocket launched vertically is considerably different from that of a spaceplane taking off horizontally, which should obviously direct relevant regulation trying to enhance safety.

In the same vein, once commercial space traffic become a more regular, perhaps even routine, feature a version of traffic management for the higher echelons of airspace (so far usually not covered by concepts such as 'controlled (national) airspace') and the lower areas of outer space would also become necessary.[80] It would be rather unwise not to build such a system at least partially upon the existing air traffic management regimes, all the while being careful to include the specifics of operating in outer space and/or in the context of space law properly in the equation.

Likewise, at such a level of maturity not only could certification and other standard-oriented safety legislation be introduced – such as already currently foreseen by the US legal regime, provisionally beyond 2023/2025 – but also other elements of air law could be either extended to relevant space vehicles or used as guidance for the development of specific space law documents on the issue.

At least for the time being, however, this should not encompass third-party liability. On the one hand, the Liability Convention has the rather victim-oriented approach of holding states, still generally the entities with the deepest pockets, liable without limit (Articles I(c), II–V, XII of the Liability Convention), thus strongly urging them to use their legal, regulatory and enforcement powers to ensure the highest possible level of safety – and it is widely ratified, by currently 95 states including all major spacefaring nations.[81] On the other hand, the 'latest' international treaty on third-party aviation liability in force, the Rome Convention of 1952,[82] as applicable in combination with

80 See Von der Dunk 2016.

81 As of 1.1.2017, See www.unoosa.org/res/oosadoc/data/documents/2018/aac_105c_22018crp/aac_105c_22018crp_3_0_html/AC105_C2_2018_CRP03E.pdf (visited 9.5.2018).

82 Convention on Damage Caused by Foreign Aircraft to Third Parties on the Surface, signed at Rome on 7 October 1952, entered into force on 4 February 1958, ICAO Doc. 7364, 310 UNTS 181.

the 1978 Protocol to amend Rome Convention of 1952,[83] by contrast provides for limits to liability and is relatively poorly ratified – in particular with reference to the major aviation countries.[84]

The legal regime to be developed for private commercial spaceflight, however, at some point in the future may come to encompass passenger liability (where currently no such liability applies under space law, either internationally or in the US) along the lines of the Montreal Convention of 1999 or criminal liability along the lines of the Tokyo Convention of 1963. The essential equality of registration of aircraft pursuant to Article 17 of the Registration Convention and registration of space objects pursuant to Article VIII of the OST and the Registration Convention, both offering the registering state quasi-territorial jurisdiction over such aircraft respectively space objects, could make this into a fairly straightforward exercise.

At the end of the day, legislation and regulation that should ensure that private manned spaceflight will become *Citius, Altius, Fortius* while avoiding becoming *Pericolosius, Stultius, Ineastimabilis*, should recognise that its own baseline must be knowledge of and experience with the actual technologies that will come to be used, not misguided or blind copying of rules developed in a different age targeting a different kind of technology and operations.

83 Protocol to Amend the Convention on Damage Caused by Foreign Aircraft to Third Parties on the Surface signed at Rome on 7 October 1952, done in Montréal on 23 September 1978, entered into force on 25 July 2002, ICAO Doc. 9257, 2195 UNTS 370.

84 See www.icao.int/secretariat/legal/Lists/Current%20lists%20of%20parties/AllItems.aspx.

8 Between global climate governance and unilateral action

The establishment of the Carbon Offsetting and Reduction Scheme for International Aviation (CORSIA)

Elena Carpanelli

8.1 Introduction

The adoption of Resolution A39-3 during the 39th Assembly of the International Civil Aviation Organization (ICAO) on 6 October 2016[1] has been generally welcomed as a historical breakthrough.[2] Through this resolution ICAO member states have ultimately agreed to implement, as part of a basket of measures, a global market-based measure scheme – the Carbon Offsetting and Reduction Scheme for International Aviation (CORSIA) – designed to address any annual increase in total CO_2 emissions deriving from international civil aviation above the 2020 level.[3] The envisaged mechanism relies on offsetting, thus requiring airlines to purchase carbon credits from other sectors.

Resolution A39-3 foresees a phased implementation of CORSIA: after a pilot phase (from 2021 to 2023) and a first phase (from 2023 to 2026), both open to voluntary participation of states, a second mandatory phase will follow (from 2027 to 2035), during which the scheme will apply to all ICAO member states except for some least developed countries. As of 11 January 2018, 73 states have expressed their willingness to voluntarily participate in CORSIA from its outset.[4] A number of fast-growing states have, however, filed reservations with respect to specific paragraphs of the resolution.[5]

The adoption of CORSIA has not occurred in a 'vacuum'. To the contrary, it comes as the ultimate step of protracted negotiations within ICAO and as a

1 *Consolidated statement of continuing ICAO policies and practices related to environmental protection – Global Market-Based Measures (MBM) Scheme*, ICAO Assembly Resolution A39-3.

2 For an early comment see Ashby 2017; Erling 2017.

3 On the topic of designing a global market-based measure scheme for international civil aviation see: Abeyratne 2015; Symposium 2016.

4 See www.icao.int/environmental-protection/Pages/market-based-measures.aspx (visited 9.5.2018).

5 See, for instance, reservations of China and Russian Federation concerning ICAO Assembly Resolution A39-3. All reservations are available at: www.icao.int/Meetings/a39/Pages/resolutions.aspx.

'follow-up' to the European Union (EU) resort to 'contingent unilateralism' as a pressure tool to speed up multilateral efforts to tackle climate change concerns deriving from international aviation.[6] Moreover, Resolution A39-3 was adopted less than a year after the conclusion of the Paris Agreement, by which state parties have agreed to hold the increase in the global average temperature below 2°C compared to pre-industrial levels.[7]

The new measure agreed upon in the framework of ICAO thus primarily questions its impact in the context of multi-level climate governance, and, more generally, its intersections with other environmental measures existing at both the regional and universal level. In this respect, the caution (and scepticism) by which the EU has seemingly reacted to CORSIA[8] deserves particular attention, for it raises serious doubts as to the capability of this measure to put an end to the long-standing saga concerning aviation emissions reduction and, conversely, paves the way to multiple possible scenarios.

What is more, environmental policies may, at times, also distort competition.[9] Thus, any evolution in this field also requires an assessment of the interplay between measures aimed at addressing climate change, on the one hand, and fair competition concerns, on the other hand. Consequently, this chapter will examine possible impacts of CORSIA on the dynamics of 'climate governance' in relation to the aviation sector and will indicate consequences of the evolution in the said dynamics for fair competition.

8.2 A tale of two stories: the ICAO–EU 'dialogue' on the reduction of aviation emissions

Whilst aviation emissions currently account only for a minor percentage of global CO_2 emissions, they are growing at an exponential rate.[10] According to some projections, without appropriate action, aviation emissions could in fact increase to the extent that they will account for 22 per cent of global CO_2 emissions by 2050.[11]

Despite growing concerns, international aviation emissions are not directly regulated by climate change international instruments. Article 2.2 of the Kyoto

6 The expression 'contingent unilateralism' is used, inter alia, in Scott and Rajamani 2013, pp. 209–223. See also Buenger 2013, p. 421; Prum and Kisska-Schulze 2015, pp. 1–47.

7 Paris Agreement, signed in Paris on 12 December 2015, entered into force on 4 November 2016.

8 Regulation 2017/2392/EU of the European Parliament and of the Council of 13 December 2017 amending Directive 2003/87/EC to continue current limitations of scope for aviation activities and to prepare to implement a global-market based measure from 2021, OJ L 350, 29.12.2017, pp. 7–14.

9 See Bodansky, Brunnée and Rajamani 2017, p. 328.

10 See *Emission Reduction Targets for International Aviation and Shipping*, European Parliament, Directorate General for Internal Policies, November 2015, Doc. IP/A/ENVI/2015-11, pp. 9 ff.

11 Ibid.

Protocol[12] merely states that developed countries shall pursue a reduction of international aviation emissions through the ICAO.[13] Disagreement among states has, however, undermined any significant progress in multilateral negotiations for more than two decades.

It is against this backdrop that, in 2008, through the adoption of Directive 2008/101, the EU decided to include the aviation sector within its Emission Trading Scheme (ETS).[14] Pursuant to this directive, starting from 1 January 2012, operators of aircraft departing or landing at an airport located in the territories of EU member states have been obliged to surrender allowances for CO_2 emissions. With limited exceptions, the measure applied to all aircraft, regardless of the state of registry, and also to emissions released outside EU airspace.

The EU decision raised much criticism and protest. Several states contested it for allegedly being a unilateral trade measure impinging on third states' sovereignty and threatened economic retaliation.[15] The US even passed a bill whereby US air carriers were prohibited from participating in the EU ETS.[16]

From the perspective of public international law, the measure raised several concerns, the majority of which related to its extra-territorial application.[17] The doubtful consistency of the EU ETS's extension to emissions produced outside EU member state territories with the customary principle of state complete and exclusive sovereignty over airspace (recognised in Article 1 and 6 of the Chicago Convention[18]) and with the freedom to fly over the airspace on the high seas (recognised in Article 12 of the same convention) has been stressed in several academic works.[19] Attempts to reconcile the EU move – and, in particular, the exercise of extra-territorial jurisdiction underpinning it – with international law on the ground of the 'effects doctrine' or the 'protective

12 Kyoto Protocol to the United Nations Framework Convention on Climate Change (UNFCCC), signed in Kyoto on 11 December 1997, entered into force on 16 February 2005, 2303 UNTS 162.

13 Note that, at the same time, the Paris Agreement does not include any explicit reference to international aviation emissions.

14 Directive No. 2008/101/EC of the European Parliament and of the Council of 19 November 2008 amending Directive 2003/87/EC so to include aviation activities in the scheme for greenhouse gas emissions allowances trading within the Community, OJ L 8, 13.1.2009, pp. 3–21. The EU ETS is a cap-and-trade scheme that has operated in the EU since 2005.

15 See Joint Declaration urging the EU to refrain from including flights by non-EU air carriers in its ETS scheme in ***Inclusion of international civil aviation in the European Union emissions trading scheme (EU ETS) and its impact ICAO***, ICAO C-WP/13790, 17.10.2011, Annex. See also Manzini and Masutti 2012, pp. 307–324.

16 European Emissions Trading Scheme Prohibition Act of 2011. Pub. Law 112–200, 27 November 2012, 126 Stat. 1477. For a discussion on this issue see Jančić 2015, pp. 185 ff.

17 See Giemulla and Van Schyndel 2011; Kulovesi 2015; Ryngaert 2015.

18 Convention on International Civil Aviation, signed in Chicago on 7 December 1944, entered into force on 4 April 1947, 15 UNTS 295. All EU Member States have ratified the Chicago Convention.

19 See Mullen 2013, pp. 783–801; Quirico 2014.

principle' have similarly been the object of careful scrutiny, although failing to meet an overall consensus.[20]

Extra-territorial effects apart, additional concerns about the inclusion of the aviation sector in the EU ETS related to the compatibility of this measure with Articles 15 and 24 of the Chicago Convention, which indirectly govern the admissibility of environmental charges or taxes,[21] and with the environmental principle of common but differentiated responsibilities (CBDR) and respective capabilities, which entrusts developed countries with primary responsibility for tackling climate change concerns.[22]

On top of that, a further complex key issue lays in the EU controversial resort to unilateral actions *vis-à-vis* the 'multilateral solution' target enshrined in Article 2.2 of the Kyoto Protocol and the duty of cooperation in environmental matters.[23] Strictly linked to it, further grounds of debate included: the role that 'inaction' may allegedly play in 'triggering' countermeasures; the relevance of environmental principles such as the precautionary principle, the principle of inter-generational equity and the principle of sustainable development as grounds to justify the resort to unilateral measures and their application to environmental problems beyond national jurisdiction; and, finally, the normative weight to be attributed to multilateral commitments embodied in ICAO Assembly resolutions.[24]

The dismay originating from the EU's decision to include the aviation sector in the EU ETS eventually turned into a legal battle. Three US airlines and their trade association challenged the inclusion of aviation within the scope of the EU ETS before the High Court of Justice of England and Wales, which, in turn, decided to refer the matter to the Court of Justice of the European Union (CJEU). The High Court posed the following question for a preliminary ruling:

> [a]re any or all of the following rules of international law capable of being relied upon in this case to challenge the validity of Directive 2003/87 as amended by Directive 2008/101 so as to include aviation activities within the EU Emissions Trading Scheme: (a) the principle of customary international law that each State has complete and exclusive sovereignty over its airspace; (b) the principle of customary international law that no State may validly purport to subject any part of the high seas to its sovereignty; (c) the

20 See Voigt 2011–2012, pp. 497 ff.; Hartmann, pp. 206–209. The expression 'effects doctrine' refers to a particular understanding of the territoriality principle, pursuant to which state jurisdiction should be based on the location of the effects produced by a certain conduct.

21 See Martínez-García 2012, pp. 103–130.

22 See Scott and Rajamani 2013, pp. 219–222. See also Scott and Rajamani 2012, pp. 469–494.

23 See, for instance, Principle 4 of the *Stockholm Declaration on the Human Environment,* UN Conference on the Human Environment, Stockholm, 16.6.1972 and Principles 7, 14 and 27 of the *Rio Declaration on Environment and Development*, UN Conference on Environment and Development, Rio De Janeiro, 14.6.1992.

24 For a detailed overview of these issues see Carpanelli 2015, pp. 695–738.

> principle of customary international law of freedom to fly over the high seas; (d) the principle of customary international law ... that aircraft overflying the high seas are subject to the exclusive jurisdiction of the country in which they are registered, save as expressly provided for by international treaty; (e) the Chicago Convention (in particular Articles 1, 11, 12, 15 and 24); (f) the 2007 EU-US open skies agreement[25] (in particular Articles 7, 11(2)(c) and 15(3)); (g) the Kyoto Protocol (in particular, Article 2(2))?[26]

In its much-awaited judgement issued on 21 December 2011, the CJEU upheld the legitimacy of the inclusion of the aviation sector within the EU ETS, thus upholding the validity of the contested directive.[27] The Court's ruling, however, answered only partially the question submitted to it. At the outset, in fact, the CJEU excluded the possibility that it could assess the validity of the directive in the light of the Chicago Convention and the Kyoto Protocol. As for the former instrument, the Court based its decision on the fact that the EU was not party to the convention and was not bound by it, given that the powers exercised by EU member states in the relevant field of application had not been fully transferred to the EU.[28] With respect to the Kyoto Protocol, the CJEU held instead that its provisions were not unconditional and sufficiently precise to confer to individuals the right to rely on them in order to challenge the validity of the directive.[29] Accordingly, the Court only ascertained whether the directive was consistent with international customary law and with the US-EU Open Skies agreement. Concerning the first aspect, according to the CJEU, the fact that the EU ETS – as amended in 2008 – also covered emissions produced outside the EU territory was 'not such as to call into question, in the light of the principles of customary international law capable of being relied on in the main proceedings, the full

25 Air Transport Agreement between the United States of America and the Republic of Austria, the Kingdom of Belgium, the Republic of Bulgaria, the Republic of Cyprus, the Czech Republic, the Kingdom of Denmark, the Republic of Estonia, the Republic of Finland, the French Republic, the Federal Republic of Germany, the Hellenic Republic, the Republic of Hungary, Ireland, the Italian Republic, the Republic of Latvia, the Republic of Lithuania, the Grand Duchy of Luxembourg, Malta, the Kingdom of The Netherlands, the Republic of Poland, the Portuguese Republic, Romania, the Slovak Republic, the Republic of Slovenia, the Kingdom of Spain, the Kingdom of Sweden, the United Kingdom of Great Britain And Northern Ireland, and the European Community, done at Brussels on 25 April 2007 and at Washington on 30 April 2007, provisionally applied as from 30 March 2008, OJ L 134, 25.5.2007, pp. 4–41.

26 *Reference for a preliminary ruling submitted by the High Court of Justice of England and Wales*, Queen's Bench Division (Administrative Court), 22.7.2010.

27 *The Air Transport Association of America, American Airlines Inc., Continental Airlines, Inc., United Airlines Inc. v. The Secretary of State for Energy and Climate Change*, CJEU (Grand Chamber) judgment of 21 December 2011, Case C-366/10. For comments on this judgment see Bogejević 2012, pp. 345–356; Gattini 2012, pp. 977–991; Hartmann 2012; Havel and Mulligan 2012, pp. 3–33.

28 Case C-366/10, §§57–72.

29 Ibid., §§73–78.

applicability of the European Union law in that territory'.[30] This finding stemmed from the assumption that the EU had not acted extra-territorially, as clearly made evident by another part of the decision, where the Court held that the application of the scheme to foreign aircraft:

> d[id] not infringe the principle of territoriality or the sovereignty which the third States from or to which such flights are performed have over the airspace above their territory, since those aircraft are physically in the territory of one of the Member States of the EU and are thus subject on that basis to the unlimited jurisdiction of the European Union.[31]

As it has been noted:

> the CJEU ... reflect[ed] the view that the exercise of EU jurisdiction in regulating aviation emissions [wa]s based on territorial connection between the aircraft being regulated and the EU. ... Thus, the <trigger> for the EU to exercise its jurisdiction [wa]s the fact that an aircraft land[ed] at, or t[ook] off from an EU airport.[32]

The Court further concluded that the Directive did not impinge on the obligations laid down in the US–EU Open Skies agreement and, in particular, on Articles 7 (subjecting only aircraft located in EU member state territories to the EU laws and regulations), 11 (exempting fuel load from taxes or other charges) and 15 (requiring environmental measures to be applied in a non-discriminatory manner).[33]

However, the CJEU's reasoning is hardly convincing in several respects. As it has been noted, it indeed seems to reflect once again the 'love–hate' relationship existing between the EU and international law[34] and, more specifically, the controversial reluctance of the EU to recognise the primacy of international norms any time they establish a lower standard of protection than EU norms.[35] In this context, it is significant that the CJEU referred expressly to the high level of environmental protection provided for in Article 191.2 of the Treaty on the Functioning of the European Union (TFEU)[36] as a ground to justify its

30 Ibid., §106.
31 Ibid., §125.
32 See Kulovesi 2015, p. 14.
33 See Case C-366/10, §§131–157.
34 Mayer 2012, p. 1114.
35 See CJEU (Grand Chamber) judgments: *Yassin Abdullah Kadi and Al Barakaat International Foundation v. Council and Commission* of 3 September 2008, Cases C-402/05 and C-415/P; *European Commission and others v. Yassin Abdullah Kadi* of 18 July 2013, Cases C-548/10 P, C-539/10 and C-595/10. See also Mayer 2012, p. 1115.
36 Treaty on the Functioning of the European Union (TFEU), signed on 25 March 1957 in Rome, entered into force on 1 January 1958 (then Treaty establishing the European Economic

regulatory authority over activities taking place beyond the EU territory.[37] It has been noted that, in doing so, the CJEU implicitly (and contestably) founded such authority on a sort of 'transnational extension of the aspirational guarantees contained in the TFEU'.[38] Accordingly, in the CJEU's judgment, political goals related to environmental protection would have ended up trumping international law.[39]

Furthermore, quite disappointingly, the Court only briefly addressed the core questions of jurisdiction and sovereignty and refrained from undertaking an in-depth analysis of some of the complex legal questions at stake, such as, for instance, the problem of EU member states' conflicting obligations potentially arising out of the TFEU and the Chicago Convention. Likewise, by ruling out the possibility of assessing the consistency of the directive with treaty provisions, the Court avoided dealing specifically with legal arguments that, although not being expressly referred to in the reference for a preliminary ruling, could still have been weighed in deciding the case. These include arguments based on environmental law principles and the interplay between unilateral action and multilateral commitments.[40]

Despite the CJEU's 'green light', in April 2013 the EU decided to suspend the implementation of Directive 2008/101 with respect to flights operating to and from non-EU countries, pending negotiations on a global solution to be reached in the framework of ICAO's (then) upcoming 38th Assembly. This was probably due to the constant threat of retaliatory measures.[41] As a consequence of this decision, the scope of application of the EU ETS has been limited to flights within the European Economic Area (EEA) ('intra-EEA flights').

Notably, however, whereas the 'stop of the clock' on the implementation of the EU ETS to extra-EU flights has removed (at least temporarily) the spotlight from the normative hurdles underpinning its extra-territorial application, it has not affected in any way the other legal issues, previously underlined, which characterise the discussed EU measure even in its application to intra-EEA flights, first and foremost those arising from the 'unilateral' character of this measure.

Following the decision reached at the ICAO's 38th Assembly to develop a global market-based measure mechanism for international aviation emissions by

Community, later Treaty establishing the European Economic Community, consolidated version OJ C 202, 7.6.2016, pp. 47–199.

37 See Case C-366/10, §128.

38 See Buenger 2013, p. 454.

39 See Havel and Mulligan 2012, p. 32.

40 The latter issue has been expressly considered by Advocate General Kokott. See *Opinion of Advocate General Kokott*, Cases C-403/08 and C-429/08, 6.10.2011, §175 et seq.

41 Decision No. 377/2013/EU of the European Parliament and of the Council of 24 April 2013 derogating temporarily from Directive 2003/87/EC establishing a scheme for greenhouse gas emission allowances trading within the Community, OJ L 113, 25.4.2013, pp. 1–4 ('stop the clock' decision).

2016,[42] on 14 April 2014 the EU adopted Regulation 421/2014, whereby it extended the temporary suspension of the application of the EU ETS with respect to flights to and from non-EU countries.[43] The 'exemption' provided therein was made, however, fully dependent on the outcome of negotiations within the ICAO. According to preamble to the Regulation 421/2014, in fact:

> [t]he derogations provided for in this Regulation take into account the results of bilateral and multilateral contacts with third countries, which the Commission will continue to pursue on behalf of the Union, in order to promote the use of market-based mechanisms to reduce emissions from aviation.

Moreover, the Regulation provides that:

> following the 2016 ICAO Assembly, the Commission shall report to the European Parliament and to the Council on actions to implement an international agreement on a global market-based measure from 2020, that will reduce greenhouse gas emissions from aviation in a non-discriminatory manner ... In its report, the Commission shall consider, and, if appropriate, include proposals in reaction to, those developments on the appropriate scope for coverage of emissions from activity to and from aerodromes located in countries outside the EEA from 1 January 2017 onwards.

8.3 After CORSIA: unilateralism reloaded or the end of the game?

The agreement reached within the framework of ICAO on a global offsetting mechanism inevitably calls into question some contextualised reflections. In fact, the ability of the newly adopted scheme to represent a historical breakthrough much depends on its effectiveness, as well as, indirectly, on its capability to successfully tackle unilateral drifts and interact with the existing international legal regime.

8.3.1 Effectiveness of CORSIA

There is little doubt that the consensus reached within the ICAO on a first multilateral move to tackle aviation emissions is an appraisable result and

42 See *Consolidated statement of continuing ICAO policies and practices related to environmental protection – Climate change*, ICAO Assembly Resolution A38-18.

43 Regulation No. 421/2014/EU of the European Parliament and of the Council of 16 April 2014 amending Directive 2003/87/EC establishing a scheme for greenhouse gas emission allowance trading within the Community, in view of the implementation by 2020 of an international agreement applying a single global market-based measure to international aviation emissions, OJ L 129, 30.4.2014, pp. 1–4.

important achievement in line with Article 2.2 of the Kyoto Protocol. That notwithstanding, whilst several aspects are still to be negotiated, the scheme already presents features that hinder its very capability to serve the purpose for which it has been agreed upon. These include, in particular, the lack of enforcement mechanisms and the absence of a cap for permitted emissions. As far as this last aspect is concerned, the agreed mechanism requires, in fact, operators to surrender off-set units to be bought by other sectors in order to compensate for the emissions produced whilst on route between states participating in the scheme, but does not set a maximum threshold of emissions.

The outsourcing of environmental protection to other sectors also raises concerns as to the positive impact that CORSIA could eventually have.[44] Moreover, the voluntary nature of the scheme, at least in the initial phases of its implementation, and the reservations filed by some states representing important aviation markets, further weaken the ability of CORSIA to act as an effective instrument to reduce international aviation emissions. This is because international flights on route to or from states that do not participate in the scheme are exempt from it.

The discretion left to participating states in implementing CORSIA in their domestic legal orders and the lack of a dispute settlement mechanism at the international level additionally hinder the effectiveness of the recently adopted global solution.[45]

Another important issue is how specific aspects of CORSIA – such as, *inter alia*, the establishment of a monitoring and reporting programme and the definition of emissions unit criteria – will be defined within the framework of ICAO. It seems that the very text of Resolution A39-3 already precludes any amendment to the Chicago Convention in this respect. The scheme and its technicalities will, in fact, take the form of international Standards and Recommended Practices (SARPs).[46] This, however, brings into the picture additional uncertainty. Pursuant to Article 38 of the Chicago Convention, states can, in fact, file differences with SARPs any time they find it impracticable to comply in all respects or to bring their own regulations and practice in line with international standards. As a result, states will be entrusted with a high degree of discretion in the implementation of CORSIA.

8.3.2 Intersection between 'legal orders' and the risk of a resurgence of unilateral drifts

The EU 'wait and see' reaction to the adoption of Resolution A39-3 seemingly upheld all concerns underlined in Section 8.3.1, leaving the door open to the

44 See Korber Gonçalves 2017, p. 453.

45 On the importance of dispute settlement mechanisms in preventing unilateral actions in the environmental domain see Boisson de Chazournes 2000, p. 332. The Author resorts to the example of the fisheries regime and the role that the introduction of a dispute settlement mechanism provided for in treaty law has had on the assessment of the lawfulness of unilateral measures.

46 See Ahmad 2014, pp. 123 ff.

possible resurgence of the extension of the EU ETS to its full scope. In addition, it does not seem to eliminate the controversial legal questions raised by the application of the EU ETS to intra-EEA flights. The EU has indeed adopted in December 2017 Regulation 2017/2392, which extends the suspension of the application of the EU ETS to flights to and from non-EU states until 31 December 2023, pending further negotiations within ICAO, and makes the adoption of further steps dependent on a more in-depth assessment of CORSIA.[47] According to the regulation, any review of the EU ETS should, in fact, be postponed to a time in which more clarity will exist as to the content and nature of CORSIA's operational measures, as well as to domestic measures adopted by third countries and the level of participation to the scheme.[48] Moreover, any such review should take into account the EU's own environmental policies and commitments.[49]

As has been underlined, the EU's stance raises political tensions and compatibility issues between the two schemes.[50] Arguably, it also potentially raises both old and new legal issues. It can be questioned, for instance, whether unilateral moves by the EU – either in re-expanding the EU ETS to its full scope or, as it has already done with the adoption of Regulation 2017/2392, by confirming its application to intra-EEA flights – could possibly be rooted in (and legitimised by) the scarce effectiveness of the multilateral measure agreed upon in the framework of ICAO or in the reluctance by states to eventually abide by it.

According to Principle 12 of the Rio Declaration on Environment and Development 'environmental measures addressing transboundary or global environmental problems should, as far as possible, be avoided'. Whilst this principle has been relied on to suggest a mere preference for multilateral solutions,[51] one may wonder whether it may further act as general 'authorisation' for unilateral actions even where a multilateral solution – although existent – is not effective. In principle, this argument could find support in the emerging notion of 'common concern' with respect to environmental issues, which arguably gives rise to states' shared responsibility in dealing with climate change concerns and legitimises states to assert an interest in the protection of resources outside their jurisdiction.[52] This would thus legitimise, *inter alia*, state *uti universi* actions to protect the environment.[53] Moreover, against the alleged inefficiency of a solution agreed at the multilateral level, unilateral actions could also be tentatively grounded on general principles of

47 Regulation 2017/2392.

48 Ibid., Article 1.

49 Ibid.

50 See Dobson 2017.

51 For example, *United States – import prohibition of certain shrimps and shrimps products. Recourse to Article 21.5 of the DSU by Malaysia*, Report of the Appellate Body, AB-2001-4, WTO Doc. WT/DS58/AB/RW, 22.10.2001, §124.

52 See Pineschi 2014, p. 141. For the concept of common concern of humankind see Hey 2016, pp. 62–64.

53 Ibid.

international environmental law, such as, in particular, the precautionary principle (pursuant to which the lack of scientific certainty concerning potential harm cannot act as a justification for inaction),[54] and the principle of intergeneration equity (pursuant to which the climate system should be protected in the interests of present and future generations).[55] However, the vague content and little normative weight of these principles raise doubts as to the possibility to ground on them unilateral acts, especially when they concern problems beyond national jurisdictions.[56] Moreover, one could also question the very applicability of the aforementioned principles in the case at hand: can we really talk, for instance, of scientific uncertainty with respect to the environmental problems raised by the exponential growth of international civil aviation? In addition, a positive answer to the underlined question seems hardly consistent with a strict textual reading of the multilateral commitment upheld in Article 2.2 of the Kyoto Protocol.

On top of this, the very arguments used to support the admissibility of unilateral actions in dealing with international civil aviation emissions seem to have ruled out the option to act unilaterally once a multilateral solution has been agreed upon. By way of example, one could recall the statement of Advocate General Kokott:

> the Contracting Parties' preference for a multilateral solution within the framework of the ICAO is only translated by Article 2.2 of the Kyoto Protocol into a very general obligation of conduct. If no agreement is reached within the framework of the ICAO within a reasonable period the Parties to the Kyoto Protocol must be at liberty to take the measures necessary to achieve the Kyoto objectives at national or regional level.[57]

Accordingly, one could draw the conclusion that unilateral actions would be permissible only if no agreement is reached at the multilateral level, as instead has occurred in the case at stake.

The reiteration of the fact that the ICAO is 'the appropriate forum to address emissions from international aviation' contained in the Preamble to Resolution A39-3 may be seen as an additional bar to unilateral drifts. Although these kind of ICAO Assembly resolutions have no binding effect, one could still argue that states that have concurred to their adoption cannot, in the light of the principles of good faith and cooperation,[58] infringe on the underpinning commitments or,

54 Cf.: Principle 15 of the Rio Declaration, Article 3.3 of the United Nations Framework Convention on Climate Change (UNFCCC), signed in New York on 9 May 1992, entered into force on 21 March 1994, 1771 UNTS 107; Article 191.2 of the TFEU.

55 Cf.: Principle 3 of the Rio Declaration; Article 3.1 of the UNFCCC.

56 On the vagueness and inconsistency of application of the precautionary principle see Fitzmaurice 2017, pp. 355 ff.

57 See Opinion of Advocate General Kokott . . ., §184.

58 As recognised by the ICJ, the good faith principle is one of the main principles governing the creation and existence of international norms, regardless of their source. See *Nuclear Tests (New Zealand v. France)*, ICJ judgment of 20 December 1974, ICJ Reports 1974, p. 457,

at least, if they do so, should explain the reasons behind their conduct.[59] On the other hand, however, pro-environment arguments at the core of the adoption of unilateral initiatives should also pass the test of the good faith principle in order to ascertain whether they are indeed meant to support (even implicitly) the interests of the international community.[60]

Furthermore, the possible resort to the state of necessity argument – according to which unilateral acts in breach of international norms would not trigger responsibility when intended to protect an essential interest of the state or the international community from a serious and imminent risk[61] – would hardly be applicable to the case of aviation emissions, especially in light of the restrictive interpretation that the International Court of Justice (ICJ) has given of the 'sufficiently imminent' character of the risk.[62]

A difference could in addition be drawn between unilateral measures that potentially affect the rights of other states and unilateral actions that do not. As has been noted, in general the legitimacy of unilateral actions depends on several circumstances, including state reactions.[63] Accordingly, unilateral measures that do not impinge on other states' rights (such as in the case of the application of the EU ETS in its reduced scope) would almost always be legitimate, contrary to what occurs when unilateral acts interfere with other states' rights (such as in the case of the application of the EU ETS in its full scope).[64]

Clearly, the re-establishment of the full scope of application of the EU ETS would also revive the more general legal debate over the admissibility, under international law, of legislative extra-territorial jurisdiction. Regardless of the CJEU's pronouncement, it is indeed questionable whether any decision to re-extend the EU ETS to flights to and from non-EU countries would be compatible with international law and, more specifically, with the principle of territorial jurisdiction.[65] In addition, from a policy perspective, such an action could be interpreted as a further attempt to rely on the threat of imposing economic costs on non-EU carriers in order to influence and exercise coercive pressure towards strongest regulatory actions within the ICAO. In this respect, however, the 'wait

§49. The key role of the good faith principle in international relations is also recognized in the Vienna Convention on the law of treaties, concluded at Vienna on 23 May 1969, entered into force on 27 January 1980, 1155 UNTS 331 (i.e. the Preamble and Articles: 26, 31).

59 See Conforti and Focarelli 2015, pp. 476–477.

60 On this topic, although from a partially different perspective, see Morgera 2014, pp. 109–142.

61 See Article 25.1 of the International Law Commission (ILC) 2001 Draft Articles on the Responsibility of States for Internationally Wrongful Acts and Article 25.1 of the ILC 2011 Draft Articles on Responsibility of International Organizations.

62 *Gabčikovo-Nagymaros Project (Hungary v. Slovakia)*, ICJ judgment of 25 September 1997, ICJ Reports 1997, p. 7, §51.

63 See Hartmann 2015, p. 31.

64 Ibid.

65 Some Authors have argued, however, that, at least under certain circumstances, inclusion of extra-territorial emissions within the scope of state domestic laws would be legitimate. For example, Scott 2016, pp. 167–177.

and see' approach already advanced at the EU level may be arguably seen as an attempt by the EU to exercise 'coercion with kid gloves'[66] with respect to the pending negotiations aimed at clarifying the operational implementation of CORSIA.

Another pressing issue underpinning the most recent developments is how CORSIA can interplay with the EU ETS, either in its full or reduced scope of application. In both cases, the main problem lies in the circumstance that CORSIA applies to international flights, defined as 'civil aviation flights that depart in one country and arrive in a different country',[67] thus including intra-EEA flights. As a consequence, the same flight may end up being 'covered' by both schemes.

Finally, as stated in the previous paragraph, the way in which CORSIA's technicalities are defined will inevitably have an impact on the interplay between 'international' and 'domestic' legal orders. This should clarify in fact the states' margin of discretion in implementing this scheme at the national level. In this respect, the situation of EU member states is somewhat peculiar: if, in the future, CORSIA is made an integral part of EU secondary law, member states will be obliged to abide by the relevant provisions as defined in the EU law.

8.3.3 Interplay with other international norms

The recent developments within the framework of the ICAO also question the consistency of implementing acts of the envisaged global market-based scheme with international law and, more specifically, with the Paris Agreement, international environmental principles and the Chicago Convention.

Regardless of the several acknowledgements of the Paris Agreement in the Preamble and text of Resolution A39-3, it has been argued, for instance, that the offsetting model agreed upon within the framework of the ICAO – coupled with the other weaknesses of the scheme – would be inconsistent with the overall target of CO_2 reduction to which states parties to the Paris Agreement have committed themselves.[68] In assessing the European Commission's proposal for a new regulation on EU ETS, the European Economic and Social Committee has, in fact, expressed some reservations, due to the fact that the environmental ambitions linked to the implementation of CORSIA 'would be lower than the full scope of the EU ETS and such scheme could be somehow detrimental to the EU's domestic climate targets and international commitments'.[69]

Moreover, regardless of the opposite statements contained in Resolution A39-3, double claiming issues could potentially arise from the intersection between

66 This expression is used in Birchfield 2015.
67 See ICAO Assembly Resolution A39-3, §5.
68 See Korber Gonçalves 2017, p. 454. Note that the EU has ratified the Paris Agreement.
69 See *Opinion of the European Economic and Social Committee*, European Economic and Social Committee Doc. NAT/710-EESC-2017–1228, 31.5.2017, §1.2.

CORSIA and other mitigation schemes adopted in abidance to the Paris Agreement. This may happen, for instance, when emission units generated under CORSIA are already relied on by the host country of a CO_2 reduction project to assert compliance to mitigations commitments undertaken under the Paris Agreement.[70]

Initiatives aimed at dealing with aviation emissions should also be tested against international environmental law principles. One example is state obligation to conduct an Environmental Impact Assessment (EIA) at the stage of planning an industrial activity that may have a significant adverse impact in a transboundary context, whose customary law nature has been recognised by the ICJ.[71] Whereas this obligation leaves it up to domestic law to determine the specific content of EIA in each case, one could still wonder whether the absence of some sort of 'authoritative imposition' coming from 'international' organs[72] may prejudice the overall compliance.

Another issue is the consistency of the scheme with the principle of CBDR. The Preamble to Resolution A39-3 acknowledges this principle, which led to the inclusion of a special facultative exemption for least developed countries from the second phase of application of CORSIA. However, it is questionable whether such exemption in the aviation sector does indeed abide by the main international instruments on climate change, given that some air carriers based in developing countries are today among the most fast-growing undertakings.[73] Apart from that, the principle of CBDR raises more general issues with regard to international civil aviation in the context of the Chicago Convention principles of non-discrimination and equality of opportunity. In light of the practice embodied in bilateral air service agreements,[74] the latter principle may, in fact, be interpreted as underpinning the idea of a level playing field that provides for fair competitive opportunities (rather than equality of benefits).[75] In this respect, it has been argued, however, that:

> it will not be prudent to embrace an archaic, tough established, principle, namely the principle of non discrimination and equality of opportunity, enshrined in a treaty, namely the Chicago Convention, that does not address a very recent global problem, namely climate change and global warming, and to simultaneously discard a new principle, namely the CBDR principle, that deals with that global problem and can ensure widespread participation by developing countries.[76]

70 See Erling 2017, p. 8.
71 See *Pulp Mills on the River Uruguay (Argentina v. Uruguay)*, ICJ judgment of 20 April 2010, ICJ Reports 2010, p. 14, §204. See also *Certain Activities Carried Out by Nicaragua in the Border Area (Costa Rica v. Nicaragua)* and *Constitution of a Road in Costa Rica along the San Juan River (Nicaragua v. Costa Rica)*, ICJ judgment of 16 December 2015, ICJ Reports 2015, p. 665, §104.
72 See Fitzmaurice 2017, pp. 366 ff.
73 See Ahmad 2014, p. 108.
74 In line with Article 31.3(c) of the Vienna Convention on the Law of Treaties.
75 Cf. Walulik 2017, p. 179.
76 Ahmad 2014, p. 111.

This statement solidly relies on the ICJ's findings in its judgment in the *Gabcikovo-Nagymaros project* case, whereby it has recognised that:

> new norms and standards have been developed. Such new norms have to be taken into consideration, and such new standards given proper weight, not only when States contemplate new activities but also when continuing with activities began in the past.[77]

In this respect, however, negotiations leading to CORSIA appear to have been successful in reconciling the two opposing principles at stake. As has been noted, in fact, this goal has been achieved by envisaging a route-based approach, which subjects to the scheme all air carriers operating on the same route between countries participating in it, and by a phased implementation of the mechanism based on voluntary participation.[78] This result is well embodied in the upholding of the principle of specific circumstances and respective capabilities, contained in Resolution A39-3, which opens up to an undifferentiated treatment for developed and developing countries.[79]

The number of countries that will effectively implement CORSIA will shed light on whether this principle has indeed met the aspirations of both developed and developing countries and, as a consequence, will prove effectively operational.

Whether the new regime would abide by other environmental operational principles, such as integrity and transparency,[80] will instead mainly depend on the future determination of implementation techniques, especially those concerning monitoring and verification systems.

8.4 CORSIA and market distortions

The adoption of Resolution A39-3, as well as the multifaceted scenarios possibly originating from it, also pose questions as to the resulting market distortions. Both CORSIA and the EU ETS (whose application strictly relates to the effectiveness of CORSIA itself) do not make any distinction among air carriers based on their nationality or other characteristics. Even if this circumstance excludes from the outset any direct market distortions, the risk still exists, however, of indirect effects.

As far as CORSIA is concerned, the application of the principle of CBDR recognised therein may lead, in principle, to market distortions. This, however, is

77 *Gabčikovo-Nagymaros Project* . . ., ICJ Reports 1997, p. 7, §140.

78 See Erling 2017, p. 7.

79 For more on this topic see Piera 2015.

80 On these principles see Hey 2016, pp. 75–76 and pp. 83–84. For an overview on transparency in environmental matters see also Ebbesson 2013. For some remarks on the alleged lack of transparency of ICAO's negotiations on CORSIA see O'Leary 2017.

mitigated by the fact that CORSIA simultaneously upholds the principle of special circumstances and respective capabilities and relies on a route-based approach. By way of example, the exclusion from the scope of application of CORSIA of flights en route to or from states not participating in the scheme may lead passengers to favour one route via a non-participating state over a route via a participating state to the benefit of airlines from the former.

Although the aviation industry is not free from market distortions, one could wonder whether a global market-based measure should contribute to their existence and whether this is in line with the general principles underpinning the Chicago Convention regime.[81]

As noted by the European Commission in its impact assessment related to the proposal of a new EU ETS regulation, differences in the implementation of CORSIA may also lead to market distortions. This may affect the market, at least in the case of operations of carriers originating from third states that do not implement CORSIA.[82]

Competition issues could also arise from the EU decision to maintain aviation within the EU ETS, either in its full or in its reduced scope. For example, the subjection of air carriers to both CORSIA and the EU ETS, at least for intra-EEA flights, may lead them to prefer routes via airports just outside the EEA.[83] Moreover, the reduced scope of application of the EU ETS may raise *per se* concerns related to the different treatment between EU and non-EU air carriers, potentially bringing unjustified competition advantages to the latter.

Lastly, the inclusion of aviation in the EU ETS brings about concerns in relation to both fair competition among different transport sectors and state aid. With respect to the latter issue, potential free allocation of emission allowances may be deemed state aid distorting the market, and as such be prohibited under Article 107 of the TFEU.

That notwithstanding, whereas the current uncertainties surrounding the implementation and application of CORSIA and the EU normative developments do not allow for any decisive conclusions to be drawn as far as market distortions are concerned, the very low operational costs that the offsetting system seems to impose on air carriers are likely to mitigate possible competition issues.

8.5 Conclusions

The adoption of Resolution A39-3 undoubtedly represents an important turning point in international climate change governance and, more specifically, in the fight to reduce international civil aviation CO_2 emissions.

81 Piera 2014, p. 354.

82 *Impact Assessment accompanying the document Proposal for a Regulation of the European Parliament and of the Council amending Directive 2003/87/EC*, Commission Staff Working Document, SWD(2017)31 final, 3.2.2017, p. 37.

83 Ibid., p. 38.

However, whereas any in-depth assessment of CORSIA much depends on the pending definition of its operative and technical elements, the analysis in this chapter indicates the complexities that may arise from CORSIA interplay with other universal and regional normative regimes, either in relation to the protection of the environment or to fair competition. Moreover, the cautious approach adopted by the EU leaves the door open to manifold options, thus making the future scenario extremely uncertain.

In this respect, the EU attitude towards CORSIA arguably confirms once again its willingness to exercise pressure for multilateral actions in order to facilitate the adoption of stringent environmental measures at the global level and, more generally, to vindicate its primary role in climate change global governance.

Hopefully, the underlined difficulties will be considered by states when defining CORSIA implementation and operational technicalities so as to avoid, or at least minimise, the possible tensions between legal frameworks and to maximise the effectiveness of the envisaged measure in reaching its declared environmental goals. Conversely, the inability of CORSIA to fully halt unilateral manoeuvres would revive the question of the compatibility of this measure with international law and represent a partial defeat of the multilateral efforts undertaken within the ICAO.[84]

84 This chapter was concluded and sent to the press before the ICAO Council adopted, on 27 June 2018, a set of Standards and Recommended Practices (SARPs), which define, inter alia, monitoring, reporting and verification mechanisms and offsetting requirements for CORSIA implementation (First edition of Annex 16, Volume IV, to the Chicago Convention). Contracting states have time until 22 October 2018 to disapprove the amendments and, unless more than a half of contracting states does so, the SARPs will become applicable from 1 January 2019. Notably, these last developments represent an important step in ensuring effectiveness to the scheme and in avoiding the revival of unilateral actions. The endorsement of implementing rules prompted, in fact, a positive reaction from the EU (see, e.g., Statement by Commissioners Bulc and Arias Canete on the rules of the first-ever global scheme on aviation emissions, Brussels, 28 June 2018). That notwithstanding, state discretion underpinning SARPs, the non-global reach of the scheme, and the uncertainties that continue surrounding some implementing technicalities in the context of a 'in progress' process, as well as the fact that most of the highlighted critical aspects do not find a solution in the endorsed standards, make the issues underlined in the present chapter still timely.

9 Airline non-commercial advantages and fair competition

The issue of labour conditions

Andrea Trimarchi

9.1 Introduction

Civil aviation is a strategically crucial sector of the global economy. It performs a cardinal role in facilitating globalisation, trade and tourism, as well as promoting economic growth, in particular in developing countries. Although air transport is among the most technologically advanced and fastest growing industries, fierce competition between air carriers is a relatively recent phenomenon. It has been exponentially rising only since the adoption of national and regional policies aimed at deregulating international air transport services in the 1980s.[1]

Still, the global legal scheme appears significantly fragmented. Absent a universal competition law regime, individual states and regional organisations, such as the EU, have dictated the terms of domestic or regional policies in this respect. Importantly, these laws and policies may also apply 'extraterritorially' to cross-border air services.[2] Therefore, the International Civil Aviation Organization (ICAO) is placing emphasis on the dogma of 'fair competition' in air transport. This means promoting harmonisation of legal regimes and cooperation between competition authorities as well as attempting to establish clear principles governing competition between airlines.[3]

In this context, the highly international nature of the aviation industry leads to some peculiarities. The uneven position of international air carriers is not only a product of discrepancies in airline regulatory regimes. It also arises from other circumstances, which are not connected with sector-specific regulatory or commercial grounds, such as peculiar geographic location, differences in tax regimes, as well as unequal labour standards and conditions.

1 Giemulla and Weber 2011, pp. 130–137. The two key examples of this process come from the US and the EU. In 1978, the US adopted its Airline Deregulation Act aimed at deregulating the aviation sector. In the late 1980s, the EU started a long process of liberalisation, which led to the establishment of a single air market.

2 See Mendes de Leon 2017, p. 68. See also Burghouwt and De Wit 2015a, p. 32.

3 Mendes de Leon 2017, p. 70.

This chapter will discuss if, and to what extent, divergent labour conditions and corresponding different labour regulations may affect fair competition in the airline industry. The analysis will focus on assessing whether labour conditions may be considered a part of the wider category of non-commercial advantages. This notion has yet not been fully defined in doctrine or in jurisprudence. The chapter will, however, consider legal sources that, in a way, make use of that terminology – namely the World Trade Organization (WTO) Agreement on Subsidies and Countervailing Measures (ASCM)[4] and the EU Regulation 868/2004 dealing with third country unfair subsidisation to national carriers.[5]

9.2 Fair competition in aviation

The issue of fair competition is currently one of the key points of interest in international aviation relations. Many countries and the ICAO have acknowledged this problem, which has led to inclusion of specific clauses in air services agreements (ASAs) and in domestic laws. However, the term 'fair competition' is not formally envisaged in the Chicago Convention, which is the constitution of international civil aviation. Indeed, Article 44 of this convention only refers to 'preventing economic waste caused by unreasonable competition' when listing the ICAO economic objectives.

The adjectives 'unfair' and 'unreasonable' seem to overlap to a certain extent and both imply some degree of governmental control. However, it is the contraposition between the terms 'fair' and 'free' that should be brought to the attention of the reader. These terms are usually associated with the term 'competition', both in legal and economic aspects. Whereas the notion of 'free competition', which has dominated in the last century, presumes a free interaction of competitive forces on the market, the more recent concept of 'fair competition' elaborates further upon the free competition doctrine and foresees more regulatory intervention.

9.2.1 A patchwork of regulatory regimes

On a regional level, the European Commission has recognised in 2012 that EU carriers are fighting to survive in a rigid international market that is characterised by diverse regulatory frameworks and cultures, by bilateral ASAs that restrict

4 Agreement on Subsidies and Countervailing Measures, part of the Multilateral Agreements on Trade in Goods – Annex 1A of the Marrakesh Agreement Establishing the World Trade Organization, done in Marrakesh on 15 April 1994, entered into force on 1 January 1995, UNTS, 1869 UNTS 14.

5 Regulation No. 868/2004/EC of the European Parliament and of the Council of 21 April 2004 concerning protection against subsidisation and unfair pricing practices causing injury to Community air carriers in the supply of air services from countries not members of the European Community, OJ L 162, 30.4.2004, pp. 1–7.

market access and by competition 'that is often distorted in third countries by unfair subsidies or practices such as over-flight restrictions'.[6]

Competition and antitrust laws are far from being internationally harmonised and significant differences exist between the most important competition regimes across the globe.[7] With respect to international aviation, efforts have been made by the ICAO to promote the adoption of a common 'fair competition' policy and to foster harmonisation of existing domestic regulations. However, the current legal scenario in this respect is still an outcome of a patchwork of national and regional policies. For instance, the EU has established a unified regime of competition law at the treaty level. Provisions aimed at preventing distortion of competition and anticompetitive behaviour in the EU market have been incorporated in the Treaty on the Functioning of the EU (TFEU).[8]

9.2.2 The role of bilateralism

The commercial regulation of international air transport has been traditionally conditioned by long-standing and rigid national protectionism.[9] The Chicago Convention clearly confers a primary position to state sovereignty, which in accordance to Article 1 is absolute and complete.[10] The intuitive corollary of Article 1 is that national airspace is *de jure* closed to foreign aircraft and operators.[11] However, the convention succeeded in establishing a concessionary regime[12] through which states may negotiate and confer traffic rights to other states on a case-by-case basis. This allows for the provision of international air services.[13]

Thus, the aviation relations between states have been carried out by means of conclusion of so-called ASAs, which have been negotiated on a bilateral or, rarely, multilateral basis. ASAs are described as international agreements in

6 *Impact Assessment Accompanying the Document: Proposal for a Regulation of the European Parliament and of the Council on safeguarding competition in air transport, repealing Regulation (EC) No. 868/2004*, Commission Staff Working Document, SWD(2017)182 final, 8.6.2017, p. 5.

7 For a short overview of competition policies and practices applicable to air transport see *Fair Competition in International Air Transport*, ICAO ATConf/6-WP/4, 4.12.2012.

8 Treaty on the Functioning of the European Union (TFEU), signed on 25 March 1957 in Rome, entered into force on 1 January 1958 (then Treaty establishing the European Economic Community, later Treaty establishing the European Economic Community, consolidated version OJ C 202, 7.6.2016, pp. 47–199.

9 Haanappel 2001, p. 90.

10 Abeyratne 2014, p. 62

11 Mendes de Leon 2017, p. 47.

12 Article 6 of the Chicago Convention prescribes that 'no scheduled international air service may be operated over or into the territory of a contracting State, except with the special authorization of that State, and in accordance with the terms of such permission or authorization'.

13 Wassenbergh 1998, p. 18.

which the governmental aviation authorities of two or more nations establish *inter se* a valid and binding regulatory spectrum for the performance of commercial air services between their respective territories.[14] Originally, bilateral ASAs represented a forum for the exchange of traffic rights and the regulation of certain basic technical, safety-related and commercial elements. However, today liberal open skies ASAs also govern a number of corresponding economic issues in air transport, including competition and labour.

The ICAO has developed and drafted a so-called 'fair competition' template clause and has succeeded in encouraging many states to incorporate it in their bilateral ASAs. The global fragmentation of competition laws and the flexibility of air services suggest that bilateral forum may currently be a proper one for regulating competition issues. Indeed, ASAs have demonstrated their ability to rapidly adapt to different priorities. However, this strategy may not work in a long-term perspective. This is because bilateral agreements are anchored to individual political concessions, and thus cannot provide for a harmonized international regime.

9.3 The notion of 'non-commercial advantages'

The aim of this section is to explain and define the idea of 'non-commercial advantage'. This notion has not been clearly defined in doctrine or jurisprudence. The *Oxford English Dictionary* defines 'advantage' as 'a condition or circumstance that puts one in a favourable or superior position'. This term alone seems clear. It is the adjective 'commercial' that may complicate the discussed matter. In legal terms, according to the *Black's Law Dictionary*, the word 'commercial' means 'relating to or connected with trade and traffic or commerce in general'.

Consequently, a non-commercial advantage will mean a condition or circumstance that places the carrier in a favourable position and which by nature is extraneous to trade or commerce. This means that the advantage cannot stem from usual commercial practices, not that it is absolutely unrelated to trade.[15] The discussed advantage may result from a variety of reasons or events, for example, legislation, geographical conditions, natural resources, as well as social or political circumstances. Implicit in the neo-liberal theory is that national policies – such as labour standards – are a legitimate source of comparative advantages, no more and no less than natural resources and the skills and attributes of citizens.[16] Should this theory be strictly followed, it would be evident that each national law, or regulation, has the potential of somehow

14 Dempsey 2008b, p. 517.

15 It may well be argued that any advantage or benefit has a commercial component and impact on a given market. See McGonigle 2013, 10.

16 Such conception far extends the notion of comparative advantages that, in economics, had been envisioned by Smith, Ricardo and Mill. Critically though, this theory can only possibly be justified on the basis that such policy expresses the 'aggregated preferences' of the individuals that make up the nation undertaking such policy. See Turnell 2002, p. 111.

introducing a comparative advantage. However, it is not clear whether such economic advantage will in legal terms always translate into a 'non-commercial advantage', which negatively affects competition. This issue should be subject to a careful case-by-case analysis.

9.3.1 Trade law and WTO

International trade law and the WTO are responsible for establishing a normative framework concerning subsidies and financial aid. This framework does not expressly identify 'non-commercial advantages'. However, according to the ASCM,[17] a subsidy may consist of two elements: (i) a financial contribution by a government (given in any form of income or price support) and (ii) a benefit.[18]

For the sake of completeness, it must be noted that the operation of air transport services is covered only in small part by the WTO regime under the General Agreement on Trade in Services (GATS).[19] GATS basic principles, namely 'most-favoured nation', 'transparency', 'market access' and 'national treatment' were seen to potentially cause problems in specific and peculiar sectors, such as air transport. The 'most-favoured nation' concept, for instance, is in total contrast with the existing legal regime governing air transport, which is based on reciprocity, concessions and benefits/opportunities between countries.[20]

The ASCM specifically applies to product trade; GATS applies to trade in services. Whereas GATS does not provide any definition of subsidies, the ASCM could give valuable guidance. The definition of subsidy contained in the ASCM, which does not apply to aviation *per se*, may be an inspiration for lawmakers in air transport. Although the ASCM does not explicitly include references to

17 Agreement on Subsidies and Countervailing Measures, part of the Multilateral Agreements on Trade in Goods – Annex 1A of the Marrakesh Agreement Establishing the World Trade Organization, done in Marrakesh on 15 April 1994, entered into force on 1 January 1995, 1869 UNTS 14.

18 Article 1 of the ASCM reads as follows:

> For the purpose of this Agreement, a subsidy shall be deemed to exist if: (a) there is a financial contribution by a Government or any public body within the territory of a Member, i.e. where (i) a Government practice involves a direct transfer of funds (e.g. grants, loans, and equity infusion), potential direct transfer of funds or liabilities (e.g. loan guarantees); (ii) Government revenue that is otherwise due is foregone or not collected (e.g. fiscal incentives such as tax credits); (iii) a Government provides goods and services other than general infrastructure, or purchase goods; (iv) a Government makes payments to a funding mechanism, or entrusts or directs a private body to carry out one or more of the type of functions illustrated in (i) to (iii) above which would normally be vested in the Government and the practice, in no real sense, differs from practices normally followed by governments; and (b) a benefit is thereby conferred.

19 General Agreement on Trade in Services – Annex 1B of the Marrakesh Agreement Establishing the World Trade Organization, done in Marrakesh on 15 April 1994, entered into force on 1 January 1995, 1869 UNTS 183.

20 Baruah 2016, p. 75.

'non-commercial advantages', the inclusion of the term 'a benefit' in the definition of subsidy shall be given special attention. This wording means that subsidies include all those activities that may confer an advantage to a certain undertaking, including fuel subsidies, transactions with governmental parties or governmental entities and public investment in airport infrastructure.

9.3.2 EU Regulation 868/2004

The provisions of Regulation 868/2004 have been partly shaped on the aforementioned ASCM.[21] EU law, however, expressly refers to 'non-commercial advantages' when regulating subsidies conferred to non-EU carriers by non-EU countries. Regulation 868/2004 was adopted with the intent of preventing anti-competitive effects resulting from subsidies granted by non-EU countries to their domestic carriers, as well as from unfair pricing practices put in place by non-EU airlines. The regulation, which was patterned upon an earlier Regulation 4057/86 dealing with unfair pricing practices in maritime transport,[22] was primarily adopted in response to a scheme of aid provided by the US government to support US airlines after tremendous financial losses following the terrorist attacks of 11 September 2001.[23] Although it has little relevance in practice, the regulation constitutes an important act in the context of aero-political relations insofar as its primary aim is to level the intrinsic differences between the strictly regulated European market and the fragmented and not harmonised international aviation arena.[24] Therefore, Regulation 868/2004 is believed to be one of most ambitious pieces of EU legislation in the field of aviation external relations.[25]

The preamble to the regulation seems to adopt a negative definition of 'non-commercial advantages' for it tends to associate this category with any advantages that cannot be clearly identified as subsidies.[26] The scope of 'non-commercial

21 For this issue see Chapter 6 of this book.

22 Regulation No. 4057/86/EEC of the Council of 22 December 1986 on unfair pricing practices in maritime transport, OJ L 378, 31.12.1986, pp. 14–20. This regulation covers only 'unfair pricing practices' by 'third-country ship-owners' engaged in international cargo liner shipping (as opposed to bulk shipping) on routes to from or within the EU.

23 Balfour 2002, p. 399.

24 Trimarchi 2017, p. 74. This is confirmed in the Explanatory Memorandum that accompanied the proposal of Regulation 868/2004 according to which:

> the airline industry in the Community is facing a critical challenge: the need for it to compete with third country airlines which benefit from generous subsidies, while the Community industry is subject to strict rules on Government aid. ... This instrument is designed to restore the <equality of arms> with some of our competitors in providing protection against unfair pricing practices in air transport.

25 Balfour 2002, p. 398.

26 See Cl. 9 of the Preamble to the Regulation.

advantages' in aviation has not been considered in jurisprudence since no complaints have been brought before the European Commission under Regulation 868/2004. The regulation has even been described by the EU carriers as a 'toothless tiger' and the European Commission has already considered its formal and comprehensive revision.[27] However, the European Commission has expressed its views with respect to the notion of 'non-commercial advantage' under the aforementioned Regulation 4057/86.[28] The Commission held that the exclusive right to carry certain kinds of strategic commodities, tax benefits and write-offs constituted 'non-commercial advantages'.[29]

Following this interpretation, many authors have come to envision similar advantages with regard to the aviation sector. For instance, a specific part of the US legislation (the Fly America Act), has been claimed to confer 'non-commercial advantages' by *de jure* providing that any travel funded by the US government must take place on a US flag airline.[30] Discussions have also arisen with respect to the peculiar status of some Gulf carriers, which are said to benefit from certain 'non-commercial advantages'.[31] The first is a geographical one. These carriers are able to benefit from a unique geographical location allowing them to structure their business on a long-haul hub-and-spoke scheme resulting in significant reduction of average operational costs.[32] The second pertains to the peculiar nature of these countries' fiscal regimes.[33]

9.4 Labour standards as non-commercial advantages

David Ricardo was the first economist to distinguish international trade from domestic trade, showing that international trade follows different rules than domestic trade, and advocating evident and automatic benefits due to country specialisation in light of comparative advantages.[34] Although such assumption makes sense in economic terms, it may be partially challenged from a fair

27 See *Proposal for a Regulation of the European Parliament and of the Council on safeguarding competition in air transport, repealing Regulation (EC) No 868/2004*, COM(2017)289 final, 8.6.2017. See also Chapter 6 of this book.

28 *Hyundai Merchant Marine Co., Ltd.*, Commission Decision of 21 December 2015, AT/39.850.

29 Bergamasco 2015, p. 35.

30 See McGonigle 2013, p. 8.

31 See De Wit 2013, p. 24.

32 Doganis 2002, p. 104. In case of long-haul hourglass hubs, such as Dubai, Abu Dhabi and Doha, both the distance advantages and the economies of scale of the aircraft act to depress the unit costs. Moreover, the use of wide-body aircraft, such as Boeing 777–300 and Airbus 380–800, and the increase of stage lengths imply a reduced cost per seat kilometre'.

33 It is generally affirmed that tax discrepancies constitute indirect subsidies. See: O'Connell 2011, p. 339; Gaines, Olsen and Sørensen 2012, p. 140; Burghouwt and De Wit 2015a, p. 11. This issue exceeds the scope of this chapter.

34 See Ricardo 1817.

competition perspective. Especially with respect to global industries such as aviation, comparative, or non-commercial, advantages may unlevel the playing field in which air carriers compete.

Air transport activity is very international in nature. However, labour relations in this industry are regulated on domestic basis. Examples of international (regional) harmonisation are very limited. Employment in the aviation sector is characterised by a number of peculiar features. Airline employees may be based in countries other than the country where their employment contract is concluded and may be subject to different (and in certain instances to several) national laws. Moreover, aircrew is generally required to work long hours, do night work and operate from multiple bases.

Consequently, heterogeneous working conditions and conflicting domestic labour regimes may raise compelling issues. A recent study by the European Transport Workers' Federation has indeed pointed out that, in the name of 'competitiveness', the aviation industry is witnessing:

> a downgrading of working conditions, training, health, safety and wages. Each company cites unfair competition to justify tougher working condition and impose more flexibility, wage cuts or a weakening of the welfare of its workers, such as the use of unsafe working practices, which increase the risks of industrial accidents.[35]

On the one hand, the European Commission has expressly identified divergences in labour-related conditions and standards between EU carriers and their third-country competitors as the main reason for the lack of EU airline competitiveness. The European Commission has pointed out that the levels of taxes and social charges applicable to airline worker salaries vary drastically across different regions. While in some parts of the world, including the Gulf area, carriers may not pay any tax or social security contribution, in the EU the impact of such taxes and charges accounts for 10–45% of workers' gross salaries.[36]

On the other hand, the Middle-East carrier Etihad has claimed that since labour laws may vary from country to country based on their level of development, one state cannot impose a mandate on another state to have stronger labour laws.[37] This argument, however, goes against the International Labour Organization

35 ETF 2014, p. 4.

36 See *The EU's External Aviation Policy – Addressing Future Challenges*, Communication from the Commission to the European Parliament, the Council, the European Economic and Social Committee and the Committee of the Regions, COM(2012)556 final, 27.9.2012, §2.

37 *Etihad Airways Response to Claims raised about State-owned Airlines in Qatar and the United Arab Emirates*, before the United States Department of Commerce, Transportation and State, Washington DC, 31.5.2015, Docket Nos. DOC-2015–0001, DOS-2015–0016; and DOT-OST-2015–0082.

(ILO) *Declaration on Social Justice for a Fair Globalisation*,[38] which states that labour standards shall neither be used as legitimate comparative advantage in international trade nor as protectionist trade instruments.

9.5 The regulation of labour in the aviation industry

The evolution of air transport increased market competition in the aviation industry, which brought about significant benefits to consumers in terms of air transport prices and accessibility. Nonetheless, strong competition and prevalence of new business models have contributed to the emergence of a number of atypical and specific contractual forms including, *inter alia*, self-employment, fixed-term work, work via temporary work agencies, zero-hour contracts and pay-to-fly schemes.[39] Therefore, it seems that the international air transport market has reached a point where some harmonisation of labour issues is required to ensure free, fair and undisturbed competition.

9.5.1 *The choice of international forum*

Labour relations in the aviation sector are not specifically regulated on the international level. Neither the ICAO nor the ILO have thus far adopted international legal instruments aiming at maintaining and enhancing labour standards. The regulation of labour still appears as a national matter, which leads to legal fragmentation. From a regulatory perspective, it would be beneficial if an international body took the lead to promote comprehensive harmonisation of domestic legal labour regimes. Moreover, given the sensitivity and topicality of the issue, such international body could work to establish an *ad hoc* legal framework to delineate basic rules concerning employees of airlines and workers involved in the aviation industry.

The question arises as to which international body is best equipped to pursue the above objectives. One perspective is that high technical competence of the ICAO would make this institution the best promoter of a global aviation labour regime and the most suitable monitoring body in this respect. The other view is that the ILO, despite not dealing specifically with aviation matters, may make better use of its expertise on labour matters. In particular, the ILO may draft an aviation labour convention (or standards) developing on the principles already gathered in the Maritime Labour Convention governing employment relations in the maritime field, concluded under the auspices of the ILO in 2006.[40] This position is supported by the fact that the aviation and maritime industries share

38 *ILO Declaration on Social Justice for a Fair Globalisation*, International Labour Conference 97th Session, Geneva, 10.6.2008.

39 See Jorens et al. 2015, p. 24.

40 Maritime Labour Convention done in Geneva on 23 February 2006, entered into force on 20 August 2013, UNTS, Vol. 2952, No. 51299.

some fundamental elements, for example, cross-borders operations and multiple base employment contracts.

9.5.2 The choice of legal instrument

The second question to be answered is which type of legal instrument would be most suitable in the discussed area. It may be argued that both ILO standards and ICAO Standards and Recommended Practices (SARPs) have limited binding legal force. Especially, unless properly implemented in national law, they are not directly binding upon air transport enterprises and their employees. Some scholars even call them soft law, which cannot be easily enforced.[41] However, introduction of a fully binding international regulation would indeed require conclusion of a new convention under the ILO or the ICAO auspices. This option is promising for it could introduce universally binding and self-executing norms of international law. However, it looks like a long process. It must be based on consensus of a considerable number of countries, which may not be easy to achieve. Therefore, it seems that an appropriate solution should consist of an international hard-law regulatory framework combined with the inclusion of specific clauses in ASAs.

ASAs have historically played a crucial role in the evolution and development of commercial air transport. They implicitly find their roots in the Chicago Convention, although the convention itself never expressly refers to ASAs or bilateralism.[42] The reason why bilateral ASAs became a legal fundament in aviation is their flexibility and adaptability. Over the years, bilateral agreements have changed their main focus from technical aspects of overflight to regulation of certain commercial elements of air transport, such as competition and, eventually, labour conditions.[43] In fact, the current open skies agreements are devoted to providing a comprehensive legal framework for the operation of international air services whereby countries negotiate their traffic rights and corollary concessions.[44]

For the aforementioned reasons, ASAs can be an appropriate instrument for individual countries to discuss, negotiate and regulate potential discrepancies in terms of domestic labour laws. ASAs may be renegotiated to include provisions to acknowledge or establish basic principles for the treatment of employees in aviation. Although the inclusion of a 'labour standards clause' could have a beneficial impact, this effect would always be limited to the two or more state parties to an agreement. Being kind of pacts between contracting states, ASAs are binding upon these countries. However, these kinds of agreements have no effect for other states than signatories.

41 Milde 2008, p. 35.
42 Havel and Sanchez 2014, p. 167.
43 Ibid. p. 178.
44 Havel 2009, p. 122.

Therefore, ASAs would not fully eliminate the need for a global aviation labour law framework. It seems that this framework should concentrate on crystallising the main legal principles and policy objectives of aviation labour regime. This may include, among other things, flight hours schemes, minimum wages and the identification of certain types of pilot contracts, having regard to both pilots and training pilots. Furthermore, a crucial key element would concern the regulation of employees' contracts with regard to governing law and jurisdiction especially in cases of employees operating in a country other than the one where the contract has been signed or in the case of multiple bases operations.

To achieve worldwide consensus the convention should, however, refrain from regulating consequences of non-compliance or other politically vulnerable issues. These matters should be left to ASAs which would support and supplement the existing universal standards.

International harmonisation of standards may not always be sufficient to eliminate illegitimate comparative advantages arising from domestic labour legislation or enforcement policy. Thus, just as in case of fair competition clauses, ASAs may address the issue of non-commercial advantages deriving from different employment and labour legislations. In this respect, labour clauses in ASAs should provide for international enforcement instruments. In particular a party could have the right (after consultations) to revoke or suspend the authorisation of another party's air carrier if the latter party or its carrier doesn't comply with international labour standards, which results in a non-commercial advantage to its carriers. Importantly, before the mentioned international convention comes into force, ASAs shall also regulate relevant labour standards.

9.6 Concluding remarks

The analysis in this chapter has revealed that air carrier advantages may derive from differences in national legislations concerning employment and work in the aviation industry. These legal discrepancies may result in comparative advantages having a direct impact on competition between airlines. The examples of carriers that benefit from labour costs-related advantages exhibit that the lack of uniformity in labour law may upset the so-called 'level playing field'.

In such instances these comparative advantages may be illegitimate and thus fall within the category of 'non-commercial advantages'. This notion derives from the ASCM and EU Regulation 868/2004. Although these acts do not directly apply to the discussed problem, the idea of 'non-commercial advantages' may be a useful theoretic instrument. Labour conditions have been found to belong to this category insofar as they provide a certain advantage to airlines that implicitly benefit from regulatory differences.

The identification of such labour-driven 'non-commercial advantages' leads to the need for harmonisation of relevant domestic legal regimes. A global policy aimed at maintaining high standards and protection of airline employees could represent an important item on the agenda of the two specialised UN agencies, namely the ICAO and the ILO, which both seem well equipped to deal with this issue. These bodies should promote the implementation of global labour standards, which should translate into adoption of a new convention including provisions that are directly binding upon state parties and in state party national regimes. Furthermore, the ICAO could play a crucial role in promoting standard clauses concerning labour issues for ASAs. These agreements could supplement the prospective convention especially in terms of enforcement instruments.

Part 4

Regulation, deregulation or non-regulation of aerospace activities

The final part of the book deals with specific questions concerning various topical problems in aviation and aerospace activity and the adequate regulatory responses thereto, whether this be regulation, deregulation or non-regulation. This starts with a warning against possibly counterproductive and harmful means of economic liberalisation in aviation and a call for priority of long-term policy goals over current political availability of certain liberalisation measures. It is explained how some 'cheaper' paths of liberalisation can compromise aviation safety and also hamper future economic liberalisation in other areas, namely in airline investment. The latter issue is also examined in detail in respect of the EU air carrier licensing system and the embedded criteria of substantial ownership and effective control. The issue of space commercialisation returns in the context of sector-specific regulations concerning sub-orbital traffic. It is discussed whether new legal measures shall be developed, on what principles the possible instruments should be based and when they need to be introduced in order to facilitate safe and balanced development of the nascent industry. Further, this part includes an ever-valid call for regional liberalisation. This voice comes from the Middle East and is backed with an outline of the economic role of air transport in the Arab world. Included is a detailed analysis of the very rarely discussed 2004 Damascus Agreement, the reasons for the little practical interest in this 'open skies' instrument and the need for its revival. Finally, air connectivity gaps are considered. This embraces a debate over the sources of this problem and the effectiveness of regulatory solutions and leads to conclusions as to further areas of research.

10 Cheap liberalisation

Cutting regulatory corners in air transport or cutting one's own throat?

Jan Walulik

10.1 Introduction

Airline liberalisation has been the leading trend in air law for over 30 years. Restrictions in air carrier activities have been lifted in national regimes as well as in bilateral air services agreements (ASAs) and within regional economic groupings. This shift is widely perceived as successful. However, international airline liberalisation is far from being complete. Aviation institutions and commentators usually recommend further liberalisation, in particular, in terms of traffic rights (7th and 9th freedoms of the air), operational rights, as well as airline ownership and control.

Generally, this call for liberalisation seems sound. However, the actual choice of deregulatory actions should be based on the long-term goals of aviation policy, rather than on current political availability of certain legal measures. What is more if liberalisation is to proceed smoothly, it must not be treated as an end itself. Indeed, application of some liberalisation measures may be ineffective or inefficient in serving the goals of the airline regulatory reform. Consequently, this chapter will attempt to indicate potentially counterproductive directions of liberalisation.

The discussion will start with recalling the principles of air policy and the theory of regulatory reform. Given these guidelines, the effectiveness and efficiency of some liberalisation proposals will be debated. The chapter will concentrate on 7th and 9th freedoms of the air. It will be presented how liberalisation in these areas may bring needless social cost or hamper liberalisation awaited in other fields of air law. In conclusion, a balanced solution will be proposed.

10.2 Air policy and regulation

Before the instances of dubious liberalisation are examined it will be useful to recall some basics of air policy and theory of economic regulation. Air policy is the sum of state actions to maintain and develop legal and material foundations of air transport activity and to use it for certain ends.[1] These actions embrace

1 Wassenbergh 1962, p. 15.

both national and international sphere and submit to two key aims of air policy: (1) the optimisation of air services and (2) the optimisation of national share in international air transport. The former goal requires provision of adequate air transport service at a reasonable cost to meet the requirements of society, other sectors of the economy and travelling public. The latter calls for maximisation of national share. Both policy aims are subject to general economic rationality tests.[2]

In this chapter the discussed instruments of air policy are regulation of air transport. Selected liberalisation measures will be examined in this field. Importantly, this study will transcend the national perspectives and will refer to the international air transport market as a whole. Accordingly, this chapter will concentrate rather on the goal of optimising air services globally, than on national shares in the discussed sector. This approach will be supported with normative theory of regulation. Within this concept regulation should be aimed at optimising market effectiveness both in financial and social aspects.[3] The theory of regulation suggests that legal measures should be assessed in terms of their efficiency and effectiveness in achieving the goal of market optimisation.[4]

Consequently, the task in this chapter will be to disclose and discuss some suggested regulatory directions, which in the longer perspective will lead to sub-optimal performance of air services globally. This will include liberalisation proposals which may hamper international competition in air transport (ineffective regulation) or bring needless social cost, in particular, compromise aviation safety (inefficient regulations). The same tests will be applied in the search for regulatory alternatives to the counterproductive liberalisation measures.

10.3 Liberalisation trends and drivers

The participants of the 1944 Chicago Conference could not reach consensus on economic matters in air transport. As a result, there has never been universal freedom in performing international air services. The current system of economic regulation in air services relies on particular national statutes and on bilateral, regional or multilateral international ASAs whereby states exchange rights applicable to their air carriers, that is, to carriers that are substantially owned and effectively controlled by the nationals of those states or those states themselves. This provides for a structure of thousands of closed air markets, which are accessible only to the airlines of the contracting states. Within these arrangement states traditionally exchange traffic, operational and ancillary rights concerning their air carriers.[5]

2 Żylicz 1992, pp. 5–7.
3 See Majone 2005, pp. 28–29.
4 Labory and Malgarini 2000, p. 97.
5 For a classification of these rights see *Manual on the Regulation of International Air Transport*, 2nd edition, ICAO Doc. 9626.

The boundaries of these closed markets are defined by route rights or traffic rights (freedoms of the air). States have regularly exchanged technical freedoms, that is, the privileges to fly across their territories without landing (1st freedom) and to land in their territories for non-traffic purposes (2nd freedom).[6] In times of restrictive regulation commercial traffic was predefined by route rights, which confined services to particular eligible points within the territories of the contracting states. Some ASAs allowed carriers designated by one state party to perform services between points located in the territory of another state party or between points within this territory and destinations in a third state.

The process of liberalisation, which started 40 years ago, has opened aviation markets in terms of previously restrictively regulated operational rights (designation, capacity, tariffs). States learned to share market access by means of traffic rights that refer to a defined type of traffic between respective territories, irrespective of particular points or routes.[7] This included commercial freedoms related to scheduled international air services consisting in the rights to put down passengers, mail and cargo taken on in the territory of the state whose nationality the aircraft possesses (3rd freedom) and to take on passengers, mail and cargo destined for the territory of the state whose nationality the aircraft possesses (4th freedom). Some liberal agreements have gone further to allow airlines of the state parties to take on passengers, mail and cargo destined for the territories of any other states or to put down passengers, mail and cargo coming from such territories (5th freedom).[8] However, these privileges, are still subject to the condition that the services in question originate or terminate in the designating state. From the market access perspective, the aforementioned system means that international traffic between the territories of two countries and beyond is limited to airlines of those countries. At the same time traffic within the territory of a state (cabotage) is reserved for its own airlines.

Therefore, at this stage the potential for further liberalisation in air transport concerns services performed by airlines entirely outside their designating states. This would require grants of 7th freedom of the air and cabotage. The former refers to services performed between the granting state and third countries that do not include any point in the territory of the designating state. The latter concerns serving points within the territory of the granting state, either directly (9th freedom or stand-alone cabotage) or on a service that originates or

6 These freedoms have been exchanged multilaterally by 130 states in the International Air Services Transit Agreement of 1944, ICAO Doc. 9587, 84 UNTS 389. Grants of 1st and 2nd freedoms have also been a regular element of bilateral ASAs.

7 Although traffic rights have been already exchanged by some states in the International Air Transport Agreement of 1944, ICAO Doc. 9587, 171 UNTS 387.

8 As of 2006 5th freedom traffic rights were granted in two-thirds of all ASAs included in ICAO World Air Services Agreements (WASA) database. Most these agreements did not include other features of open skies agreements. See *Second Review of the Air Transport Annex Developments in the Air Transport Sector (Part Two) Quantitative Air Services Agreements Review (QUASAR)*, WTO Doc. S/C/W/270/Add.1, 30.11.2006, p. I. 42.

terminates in the designating state or, in connection with 7th freedom, in a third state (8th freedom, consecutive cabotage). Cabotage may be allowed by means of national laws or ASAs, either reciprocally or as a matter of unilateral liberalisation, provided that cabotage rights are not granted on an exclusive basis (Article 7 of the Chicago Convention).[9] The situation with 7th freedom is more complicated. To make use of it and to perform services between state 'B' and 'C', a state 'A' carrier must bloc 7th freedom rights granted to state 'A' airlines by both state 'B' and state 'C'. This requires a combination of bilateral ASAs or a multilateral agreement.

The 7th freedom rights have been granted in some open skies agreements. States tend to be more eager to exchange these privileges in all-cargo services. Outstandingly, the US support 7th freedom rights for cargo services in their Model Open Skies Agreement and this idea is already present in some US and non-US open skies agreements.[10] A number of countries have also been open to 7th freedom passenger operations.[11] Presence of cabotage rights in typical bilateral ASAs has been less frequent and these incidental grants have sometimes not been a matter of liberal air policies.[12] The 7th–9th freedom traffic rights are an important part of some regional liberalisation arrangements. They are key elements of common aviation markets in the EU[13] and West African Economic

9 Convention on International Civil Aviation, signed in Chicago on 7 December 1944, entered into force 4 April 1947, ICAO Doc. 7300/9, 15 UNTS 295.

10 For example, Air Transport Agreement between the United States of America and the Republic of Austria, the Kingdom of Belgium, the Republic of Bulgaria, the Republic of Cyprus, the Czech Republic, the Kingdom of Denmark, the Republic of Estonia, the Republic of Finland, the French Republic, the Federal Republic of Germany, the Hellenic Republic, the Republic of Hungary, Ireland, the Italian Republic, the Republic of Latvia, the Republic of Lithuania, the Grand Duchy of Luxembourg, Malta, the Kingdom of The Netherlands, the Republic of Poland, the Portuguese Republic, Romania, the Slovak Republic, the Republic of Slovenia, the Kingdom of Spain, the Kingdom of Sweden, the United Kingdom of Great Britain And Northern Ireland, and the European Community, done at Brussels on 25 April 2007 and at Washington on 30 April 2007, provisionally applied as from 30 March 2008, OJ L 134, 25 May 2007, pp. 4–41; Multilateral Agreement on the Liberalization of International Air Transportation (MALIAT), done at Wellington on 1 May 2001, entered into force on 21 December 2001, 2215 UNTS 33; Agreement between the Government of New Zealand and the Government of Australia relating to Air Services, done at Auckland on 8 August 2002, entered into force on 25 August 2003, 2003 ATS 18; 2003 NZTS 13; 2258 UNTS 177.

11 Chile has proposed this in its model air transport agreement and reported that it has offered this privilege to more than 20 states, see *Proposals for Market Access Liberalisation (Presented by Chile)*, ICAO ATConf/6-WP/28, 13 February 2013. 7th freedom traffic has also been accepted in the 2007 ASA between the UK and Singapore.

12 It has been reported that cabotage grants have appeared in the China–Albania, New Zealand–Brunei Darussalam and the UK–Singapore ASAs, see *Second Review of the Air Transport Annex Developments*… (S/C/W/270/Add.1), p. I. 43. Chile reported it has granted cabotage rights to 10 states, see *Proposals for Market Access Liberalisation* … (ATConf/6-WP/28).

13 See Regulation No. 1008/2008/EC of the European Parliament and of the Council of 24 September 2008 on common rules for the operation of air services in the Community, OJ L 293, 31 October 2008, pp. 3–20.

and Monetary Union.[14] The 2002 Australia and New Zeeland open skies agreement provides for a Single Air Market including cabotage services. The 7th freedom has been partially adopted in the Latin American Civil Aviation Commission open skies agreement.[15] At least one non-regional multilateral arrangement includes grant of the discussed rights. The Multilateral Agreement on the Liberalisation of International Air Transportation of 2001 (MALIAT)[16] exchanges 7th freedom rights in all-cargo services whereas an additional protocol[17] offers 7th–9th freedoms of the air to all carriers of the state parties. Still being rare instruments, the 7th–9th freedoms are, however, a matter of fact in modern civil aviation.[18]

What is more, granting of the 7th freedom has been recommended as a bilateral or multilateral instrument of liberalisation on several occasions. This has been suggested as a direction for the evolution of air cargo market.[19] New Zeeland and the US have been promoting MALIAT, with its 7th freedom clause, as a universal and convenient liberalisation measure at the International Civil Aviation Organization (ICAO) 6th Air Transport Conference.[20] The Agenda for Freedom working papers have gone even further to advise reciprocal exchange of all traffic rights, including 7th–9th freedoms, by means of unilateral state declarations.[21]

From the economic perspective, restrictions on 7th–9th freedoms traffic are one of the main reasons why a global air transport market with global airline

14 See Regulation No. 24/2002/CM/WAEMU of 18 November 2002 establishing the conditions of access by air carriers to the WAEMU community air routes.

15 Multilateral Open Skies Agreement for the Member States of the Latin American Civil Aviation Commission (*Acuerdo Multilateral de Cielos Abiertos*), done at Punta Cana, Dominican Republic, on 5 November 2010, LACAC Assembly Resolution No. A19-03.

16 It has been signed or acceded to by Brunei Darussalam, Chile, Cook Islands, Mongolia (cargo services only), New Zealand, Samoa, Singapore, Tonga and the US.

17 Protocol to the Multilateral Agreement on the Liberalization of International Air Transportation, done at Wellington on 1 May 2001, entered into force on 21 December 2001, 2215 UNTS 402. It has been signed by Brunei, Chile, Cook Islands, New Zealand and Singapore.

18 In 2006 WTO reported that 7th freedom traffic rights of any kind (cargo, passenger, conditional unconditional) were included in only 2 per cent of all bilateral agreements in ICAO WASA database, see *Second Review of the Air Transport Annex Developments* ... (S/C/W/270/Add.1), p. I. 42.

19 See OECD 2002, pp. 13–14; *Proposals for Market Access Liberalisation* ... (ATConf/6-WP/28); *Air Transport Regulation Panel Twelfth Meeting (ATRP/12), Montréal, 26–30 May 2014*, ICAO ATRP/12, §2.2.1.4.

20 See *The Multilateral Agreement on the Liberalisation of International Air Transportation: A Basis for the Future Economic Regulation of Air Services (Presented by New Zealand)*, ICAO ATConf/6-WP/34, 12 February 2013; *Liberalisation of Market Access (Presented by the United States of America)*, ICAO ATConf/6-WP/60, 14 February 2013. These views have even penetrated to the conference final conclusions, see *Sixth Worldwide Air Transport Conference: Sustainability of Air Transport*, Montréal, 18–22 March 2013, ICAO ATConf/6 2013, ICAO Doc. 10,009, p. 13.

21 *A Short Path to Greater Commercial Freedom for Airlines*, Agenda for Freedom Summit, Istanbul, Turkey, 25–26 October 2008, p. 4.

competition cannot emerge. Even within current open skies agreements, the market is usually confined to routes including points in the territories of the state parties (3rd–5th freedoms traffic) and is reserved purely for the carriers of those states (ownership and control requirements). This prevents true international competition, which exists in other product or service markets. In P. Forsyth's words, it is not possible for the world's airlines best suited to serve a route (most competitive) to do so.[22] Regulation limits the competition mechanism and there is no doubt that in many cases this may contribute to sub-optimal market efficiency, in particular, to higher costs and lower gains from international air transport. Hence the discussed restrictive regulation may be ineffective in realising the mentioned air policy goal of optimising air services, at least in terms of competition mechanism.

The main source of state reluctance to 7th–9th freedom liberalisation is the other air policy goal, that is, the market share optimisation. States traditionally perceive the routes between points in their territories and other countries as their own market and would trade their 'legitimate share' only for some other privilege.[23] Indeed, the bilateral exchange of rights is problematic when applied to 7th–9th freedoms. First, the potentials of the partners' cabotage and beyond markets may differ significantly. Second, a state seeking these rights often has no reciprocal benefits to trade with. Third, in case of 7th freedom, the state in question must exchange privileges with at least two partners for this traffic right to be operative.[24] Finally, in some extreme configurations of bilateral agreements, the grants of 7th freedom rights could give foreign carriers wider scope of market access than that enjoyed by own airlines.[25]

However, if wider economic context is considered, the service optimisation aim may in some situations prevail over simple market share argument and thus act in favour of opening to 7th–9th freedoms. From the outset, such liberalisation would strengthen the threat of new entry. It may also bring more airlines to the market and thus increase competitive rivalry in the industry. These forces should facilitate competition mechanism, which is expected to translate into consumer benefits. The wider economic benefits of such liberalisation may also concern growth in inbound tourism and overall improvement of connectivity.[26]

International practice indicates that, given the above policy determinants, diverse groups of states may decide to liberalise 7th–9th freedom traffic. First

22 Forsyth 2011, p. 211.
23 Walulik 2017, pp. 12–15.
24 Cf. Forsyth 2011, pp. 217–218.
25 This may theoretically happen when state 'A' designated airline aggregates 7th freedom rights from state 'A' – state 'B' and state 'A' state 'C' bilateral agreements to serve routes between state 'B' and state 'C', whereas carriers form state 'B' and state 'C' are precluded from serving the same routes because there is no ASA between state 'B' and state 'C' or such agreement does not provide for 3rd and 4th freedom services or limits such traffic by route rights or operational rights.
26 See Forsyth 2011, pp. 220–222. For connectivity issues see also Chapter 14 of this book.

are states which institute liberalisation on a regional basis. In this case exchange of 1st–9th freedoms within the group is essential for the establishment of a true common aviation market.[27] These countries merge their national shares in search of joint optimisation of air services. Second are states that exchange 7th freedom all-cargo rights. This is a deal for those who look for new markets for their air cargo services and those who have no market share or potential in air cargo and seek benefits purely from enhanced air traffic. The third group comprises of states that sponsor any kind of liberalisation in air services, including grants of unconditional 7th–9th freedom rights, and even unilaterally, to improve their air connectivity.

The aforementioned arguments, however, concentrate overly on impact on the competition mechanism and disregard wider effects of liberalising 7th–9th freedom rights. In this respect, in some instances liberal instruments may prove to be an inefficient regulatory option. Although, they may bring benefits associated with opening the market to international competition, at the same time they may produce costs that should be considered in the regulatory impact assessment. The grants of 7th and 9th freedoms of the air lead directly to 'offshore' operations, that is, flight operations away from the designating state, state of registry or state of the operator.[28] This may easily translate into emergence of flags of convenience where air carriers originating from countries with lower taxes, less stringent safety oversight or more favourable employment laws would make use of their 7th and 9th freedom rights serving air traffic in countries with more rigorous regulations.[29] One result is that there would be no level playing field for 'offshore' and local carriers and the competition mechanism would be jeopardised by safety, social[30] and tax dumping.[31] The other outcome could be that 'offshore' operations cause social costs by compromising safety or labour protection. In some cases, it may also complicate processing compensation claims due to jurisdiction issues.

From the regulatory efficiency perspective, the labour and tax dumping arguments can probably be easily dismissed by the fact that this adverse impact is

27 In such arrangements 7th freedom traffic rights may either be limited to the territories of the state parties or serve also in third-party relations.

28 ICAO State letter EC 2/93, AN 11/41–05/83, 12 August 2005, p. A-4. In the case of consecutive cabotage, this problem exists only in combination with 7th freedom.

29 It is argued that the exchange of traffic rights is the characteristic that prevents the emergence of flags of convenience in the airline industry, contrary to the maritime sector where the concept of traffic rights does not exist. See Böhmann 2001, p. 727; Lelieur 2002, pp. 80–81. This is true. However, as will be explained, this mechanism will cease to exist when all traffic rights (3rd–9th freedoms) are exchanged.

30 For social dumping in aviation see Chapter 9 of this book.

31 With regard to 7th freedom operations, note that according to ICAO guidelines income from international air transport activity should be taxed in the place where enterprise has its fiscal domicile not in the place where the services are actually performed, see *Consolidated statement of continuing ICAO policies in the air transport field*, ICAO Assembly Resolution A39-15. Cf. *Model Tax Convention on Income and on Capital*, OECD, 2014.

pecuniary by nature and, at least in some cases, may be offset by other economic benefits connected with opening the market (e.g., new workplaces, tax income from inbound tourism). More complicated is the issue of safety, where 'offshore' operations lead to a negative externality. As will be presented, the framework for safety oversight in civil aviation as set forth in the Chicago Convention and ICAO Standards and Recommended Practices (SARPs) does not provide ready instruments concerning 'remote' air operations and seems to be dysfunctional in this case.

10.4 Safety oversight challenges

Most duties concerning safety oversight present in the Chicago Convention are incumbent upon the state of aircraft registry. This includes the obligation to confirm airworthiness of registered aircraft engaged in international navigation and to approve competency of the members of their operating crews (Articles 31–32). The state of registry is also responsible for issuing licences to install and operate radio transmitters on board aircraft (Article 30). Finally, the Convention requires that this state must ensure that every aircraft carrying its nationality mark, wherever such aircraft may be, shall comply with the rules and regulations relating to the flight and manoeuvre of aircraft there in force (Article 12). These duties are further specified in ICAO SARPs, particularly in Annex 1 to the Chicago Convention – Personnel Licensing; Annex 6 to the Convention – Operation of Aircraft; and Annex 8 to the Convention – Airworthiness of Aircraft. None of the mentioned convention's provisions refer directly to airlines. However, distinct responsibilities of the state of the operator (airline) arise from ICAO SARPs and are generally associated with the certification of air operators laid down in Annex 6 to the Convention. The aforementioned obligations of the state of registry and the state of the operator extend to continued control and supervision in respect of the mentioned matters.

Consequently, within this system regulatory tasks are split between the state of registry and the state of the operator. Some uncertainties concerning distribution of these responsibilities and application of national regulations may arise if it happens that these duties are not concentrated in one country.[32] In such instances it is more practical for the state of the operator not the state of registry to supervise aircraft safety. At least this is the case with domestic and 3rd–5th freedom international operations where the engaged foreign registered aircraft is based in the territory of the state of the operator. For this occasion, in 1997

32 For example, the operator may use foreign-registered aircraft subject to lease charter or interchange agreement or it may register its own fleet in a state where aircraft registry is open to foreigners (open registry). Relations between the state of the operator and the state of registry responsibilities are outlined in Annex 6 to the Convention. For specific guidance material see ICAO State letter EC 2/93, AN 11/41–05/83; *Manual of Procedures for Operations Inspection, Certification and Continued Surveillance*, 5th edition, ICAO Doc. 8335; *Safety Oversight Manual*, 2nd ed., ICAO Doc. 9734.

Article 83*bis* has been added to the Chicago Convention. This provision enables the state of registry to transfer all or part of its functions and duties arising from Articles 12, 30, 31 and 32(a) of the Convention to the state of the operator, which takes over these responsibilities subject to an agreement concluded between both states.

With this division of responsibilities, discharging safety oversight duties is already problematic when the air operator uses foreign registered aircraft. First, several states have yet not accepted Article 83*bis*.[33] Second, the transfer of responsibilities under Article 83*bis* is voluntary. Third, the scale of implementation of this provision and the level of its practical application is far from satisfactory.[34] Although, absent Article 83*bis* transfer, there may be no proper oversight at all. The state of registry actual safety oversight may be impossible if its aircraft and its licensed air crews permanently base in distant locations outside this state. Some states of registry may also be unwilling to do their overseas surveillance duties. Nevertheless, according to Annex 6 the state of the operator should ensure that its actions are consistent with the approvals and acceptances of the state of registry and that the air operator follows state of registry requirements (Part I, Attachment C, section 2.5.1 and Part III, Attachment E, section 2.5.1). This at best leads to some duplication of effort. In many cases, however, the state of the operator may be incapable of fulfilling the above-mentioned obligations due to limited resources.[35] These circumstances have already contributed to some flag of convenience operations, where airlines have reflagged their aircraft and leased them back.[36]

The introduction of 7th and 9th freedom operations may even exacerbate the current difficulties concerning fulfilment of the state of registry obligations. If the state of registry is different than the state of the operator and the aircraft is permanently engaged in remote operations in third states, the state of the registry will hardly be able to properly discharge its responsibilities. The third states where the operations take place would be theoretically best suited to take over the state of registry duties, but Article 83*bis* does not provide for such transfer. The transfer to the state of the operator will still be possible. However, given the above circumstances, the regulatory oversight abilities of the latter state may be unsatisfactory.[37]

33 That is, the Protocol Relating to an Amendment to the Convention on International Civil Aviation (Article 83*bis*), signed at Montréal on 6 October 1980, ICAO Doc. 9318, 2122 UNTS 321.

34 See *Safety Aspects of Economic Liberalisation and Article 83bis (Presented by the Secretariat)*, ICAO LC/35-WP/3–2, Rev. 30.4.2013.

35 For example, the state of the operator may have no experience with a particular type of foreign registered aircraft.

36 See: Fitzgerald 2011, pp. 115–116, 124–125; *Air Carrier Ownership and Control (Presented by the International Transport Workers' Federation)*, ICAO ATConf/5-WP/75, 26 February 2003.

37 Analogous problems arise with cascading subleases when an aircraft registered in one state is dry leased to the operator in another state and later wet leased under this operators AOC to another operator in a third state. See *Manual of Procedures for Operations Inspection* . . . (ICAO Doc. 8335), p. V-3–2.

What is more, with the 7th and 9th freedom operations, the safety problems will have an even wider dimension. The state of the operator will face difficulties similar to those already suffered by the state of registry. Under Annex 6 to the Chicago Convention the state of the operator is obliged to establish a system for certification and continued surveillance of the operator (Part I, section 4.1.2.8 and Part III, section 2.2.1.8). During the process of air operator certification, the state of the operator must ascertain that facilities located in other states, which are to be utilised by the operator, are adequate and that crew licences are acceptable to other states where operations will take place. Later, within its surveillance activity, the state of the operator should conduct headquarters, station facility, aerodrome, apron and en-route inspections.[38] If a significant part of the operator's activity is performed entirely outside the territory of the state of the operator, the fulfilment of these obligations may be illusory.[39]

Whereas the state of registry may always seek a transfer of its responsibilities (Article 83*bis*) in the case of 'offshore' operations, the state of the operator has no analogous instrument to assign its duties internationally. The state of the operator may, however, delegate some of its responsibilities upon an *ad hoc* agreement with the state where the air operations are performed.[40] Unfortunately, such a solution would be far from perfect. This arrangement would neither officially relieve the state of the operator of its Chicago system obligations nor would it be practical. First, as a matter of expedience, the delegation of responsibilities would need to involve all states where the operator activities take place[41] and would be confined only to distinct elements of safety oversight related to the overseas activities. Second, even if the state of the operator succeeded in concluding these many agreements, the resulting safety oversight system would become fragmented and barely manageable.[42]

38 Ibid. p. IV-1–1.

39 Also wet leasing may result in the mentioned problems. Consequently, leasing of foreign supplied aircraft with their own foreign crews and operating under foreign AOC is traditionally prohibited, see Fitzgerald 2011, p. 89.

40 Before Article 83*bis* entered into force, a similar arrangement was recommended by ICAO for the state of registry – state of the operator relations, see *Lease, Charter and Interchange of Aircraft in International Operations*, ICAO Assembly Resolution A23-13. Also, where the transfer under article 83*bis* was absent (e.g., interchange and short-term lease), coordination agreements have been practiced between state of registry and state of the operator to improve supervision of aircraft. See, e.g., Latin American model discussed in *The Dual Oversight Model for the Interchange of Aircraft from Different States (Presented by 22 Member States, Members of the Latin American Civil Aviation Commission (LACAC))*, ICAO ATConf/6-WP/57, 19 February 2013.

41 As already mentioned, some of the accepting states, although involved in a 7th freedom operation, may not be bound by any ASA.

42 Note that whereas particular state of registry obligations transferable under Article 83*bis* are distinct and relatively independent, the duties of the state of the operator pertaining to operational certification and supervision are complex and interdependent (Annex 6 speaks of a system of certification and continued surveillance).

While the state of the operator has limited practical abilities to supervise carriers engaged in advanced 7th and 9th freedom services, the legal instruments available to states where these operations take place are not sufficient to guarantee safety. On the one hand, Article 12 of the Chicago Convention requires that states undertake to adopt measures to ensure that every aircraft flying over or manoeuvring within their territories shall comply with the rules and regulations relating to the flight and manoeuvre of aircraft there in force. Since 2008 this has been further specified in Annex 6, which now requires that states shall establish programmes with procedures for the surveillance of operations in their territories by foreign operators and for taking appropriate action when necessary to preserve safety (Part I, section 4.2.2.2 and Part III, section 2.2.2.2).[43] On the other hand, Article 16 of the Convention gives contracting states only the right to search, without unreasonable delay, aircraft of the other contracting states on landing or departure, and to inspect the certificates and other documents prescribed by the Convention. The ICAO model safety clause to be included in ASAs specifies that the purpose of this search is to verify the validity of the relevant aircraft documentation, the licensing of its crew and that the aircraft equipment and the condition of the aircraft conform to the standards established pursuant to the Convention.[44]

By law and by necessity, such investigations are limited in scope and duration. Ramp inspections under Article 16 cover only selected aspects of aircraft airworthiness, while document reviews verify the completeness and formal correctness of aircraft, crew and operator credentials.

By no means does the scrutiny of foreign operators resemble the complex system of certification and continued surveillance prescribed in Annex 6, nor can it substitute for this system. Whereas the function of the latter is to provide aviation safety by ensuring permanent compliance with standards and regulations, the role of the former is to verify safety levels at random and to react to revealed concerns.[45] This is a logical consequence of the above-mentioned model, where the responsibility for safety issues has been distributed between the state of the operator and the state of registry.

43 This was in line with the 2007 Assembly resolution, which reminded that states need to assure themselves that foreign operators flying in their territory receive adequate oversight from their own state and need to take appropriate action when necessary to preserve safety, see *State Recognition of the Air Operator Certificate of Foreign Operators and Surveillance of their Operations*, ICAO Assembly Resolution A36-6.

44 The model clause on aviation safety was adopted in ICAO Council resolution of 13 June 2001. Current versions of the clauses are included in ICAO Template Air Services Agreements, which are published in *Policy and Guidance Material on the Economic Regulation of International Air Transport*, 3rd ed., ICAO Doc. 9587, Appendix 5. A similar solution was proposed by the ECAC in 1998. Analogous clauses have also been adopted in 2002 by the OECD in its draft Multilateral Agreement for the Liberalisation of Air Cargo Services, see *Liberalisation of Air Cargo Transport*, DSTI/DOT(2002)1/REV1, OECD, 2002, Part IV.

45 For detailed differences see *Manual of Procedures for Operations Inspection* . . . (ICAO Doc. 8335).

The other consequence of this arrangement is that approvals granted by one state party to the Chicago Convention should be recognised by other state parties. The admission of a foreign carrier to services in national airspace takes the form of an operating authorisation (or separate technical permission) and is conditioned upon the airline being qualified to meet conditions prescribed under the laws and regulations normally applied to the operation of international air transport services by the state considering the application[46] as well as upon the state party designating the airline (the state of the operator) being in compliance with ICAO standards.[47] These prerequisites will be verified in accordance with ICAO procedures for the recognition of aviation standards. Article 33 of the Chicago Convention demands that certificates of airworthiness, certificates of competency and licences issued (or rendered valid) by the state in which an aircraft is registered, be recognised by other states.[48] This is extended to the Air Operator Certificates (AOCs) in Annex 6 (Part I, section 4.2.2.1 and Part III, section 2.2.2.1). The premise for the recognition of these certificates or licences is merely formal and refers to the general safety oversight level represented by the state granting these admissions. Such a test will be positive if the requirements under which the approvals in question were issued are at least equal to the minimum standards, which may be established pursuant to the Convention (in case of AOCs, standards specified in Annex 6 and Annex 19).

This system works semi-automatically. The ICAO recommends that when an ASA exists and provides for the aforementioned mutual recognition of approvals, the foreign operator shall be authorised by the accepting state if the mentioned formal conditions are fulfilled. Absent a recognition clause, the accepting state shall examine the safety oversight capabilities and record of the state of the operator and the state of registry, as well as the operational procedures and practices of the operator.[49] In each case the state of registry and the state of the operator compliance with safety standards may be confirmed by Universal Safety Oversight Audit Programme (USOAP) reports or additionally verified in audits conducted by national aviation authorities. The operator skills may be tested by means of ramp check-ups and reviews of operator documentation, and may be supplemented by audits led by third-state authorities or independent aviation audit organisations.[50] Once approved by the accepting state, the operator will be subject to analogous oversight instruments. Deficiencies on the part of the operator may lead to suspension or revocation of its authorisation. The same may be a result of

46 This is a traditional requirement present in ASAs that was proposed already in the ICAO Standard Form of Agreement for Provisional Air Routes.

47 This requirement is introduced in ASAs by the safety clause as proposed in ICAO Template Air Services Agreements, see in *Policy and Guidance Material*... (ICAO Doc. 9587).

48 This provision is also replicated in recognition of certificates clauses in ASAs, see Ibid.

49 See *Manual of Procedures for Operations Inspection*... (ICAO Doc. 8335), Attachment B.

50 For example, IATA Operational Safety Audit (IOSA).

the designating state shortcomings in maintaining ICAO safety standards, should the ASA include a separate safety clause.[51]

The described distribution of rights and responsibilities within the Chicago-bilateral system was designed for typical situations when at least the state of the operator is fit, willing and able to ensure safety of the operations of its designated airlines. The role of the accepting state is to confirm that this basic task was executed properly, in line with ICAO SARPs. This model of surveillance is practical only when the operations involve the state of the operator. However, in case of fully developed 7th and 9th freedom services it may be dysfunctional and could thus threaten aviation safety. With its carriers regularly operating 'offshore' the state of the operator has less power and less incentive to exert regulatory control. There might even be some temptation to export more air services and expand the national share in air transport markets at the expense of the aviation partners safety. In extreme cases this may lead to no continued surveillance from the state of the operator at all.

At the same time the oversight of the accepting state, which relies on formal documents, safety ratings and random selective checks, may be ineffective. If the state of the operator formal implementation of respective SARPs is irreproachable and its safety record is still good (particularly because overseas operations constitute a relatively small part of its operators' activities), it will be insufficient for the accepting state to simply invoke the mentioned suspicious characteristics of the offshore operations, especially as this feature is a regular consequence of the already agreed 7th or 9th freedoms traffic. However, it is doubtful whether in such a case the accepting state would endeavour to seek and prove the possible negligence on the part of the state of the operator. This is because the incentive for the former state to debate the latter state's performance may be suppressed by one of the main drivers of 7th and 9th freedoms liberalisation – the pursuit of connectivity. In this case, the accepting state would rather put on a brave face and try to unilaterally take over some of the state of registry and the state of the operator duties. Yet such intensification of foreign carrier supervision may be challenged by airlines owing to the above-mentioned principles ingrained in the Chicago-bilateral framework.

10.5 Risks and safeguards

Given these legal and economic considerations, the offshore traffic will likely become a regulatory orphan in terms of safety supervision. Does this scenario sound like a theoretical consideration? Not exactly. On the one hand, it may be argued that, because available consecutive cabotage and beyond market is of little significance for air carriers and 5th freedom traffic represents a small part of their operations (mainly due to codeshare alliances), the possible 7th and 9th freedom

51 Before suspension or revocation consultations between states will be required. See ICAO Template Air Services Agreements in *Policy and Guidance Material*... (ICAO Doc. 9587).

services will remain marginal phenomena too. On the other hand, business characteristics of the airline sector speak against such extrapolation. First, economics of 7th and 9th freedom operations and those of 5th and 8th freedom services are different. The non-stop character of the former set of operations makes them more convenient for airlines. Second, the mentioned group of states that may be supportive of offshore operations will probably grow in number due to the development trends in the industry. Progressive erosion of flag carriers and consolidation between air transport enterprises will lead to more states falling within two categories: those seeking larger stakes for their air carriers in international aviation and those looking for more connectivity. This stratification is already visible in the air cargo segment and, as already mentioned, propels the 7th freedom liberalisation there.

However, the risks associated with offshore traffic are neither equally probable nor equally dangerous across different types of international arrangements. First, given the nature of bilateral and multilateral traffic rights exchange, it is more likely that fully developed 'remote' operations will emerge within a framework of a multilateral (regional or plurilateral) ASA.[52] Second, the scale of hazards concerning 7th and 9th freedoms liberalisation depends on the manner in which this liberalisation is instituted. Should this be on an exclusive (in particular regional) basis, there is still a reasonable chance that this process will be supplemented with effective safeguards addressing the aforementioned issues. Within a common air market, where the exchange of 7th and 9th freedoms is required, the implementation of ICAO standards or even stricter safety rules may be protected by a centralised approach. This might include adopting common aviation requirements. Such a system could include legal measures directly binding upon airlines as well as penalties for non-compliance. Additionally, state parties may set up a Regional Safety Oversight Organisation (RSOO) and might delegate some of their regulatory oversight to it or at least coordinate their aviation authorities' activities within such an organisation.[53]

The 7th and 9th freedoms liberalisation becomes much more challenging in terms of flag of convenience when it is introduced as a non-exclusive arrangement, either incrementally through bilateral ASAs or by means of a multilateral

52 The balance of rights argument makes the bilateral exchange less encouraging in terms of 7th freedom exchange. This is because 7th freedom rights are operational if exchanged in at least two agreements. Therefore, there is a concern that the bilateral partner with whom such freedoms are exchanged will gain advantage by combining these freedoms with more third-party 7th freedom grants or with grants that allow for more valuable connections. This balance of rights argument vanishes if the discussed rights are exchanged reciprocally between a larger number of states within one agreement.

53 This type of regional cooperation has been recommended by ICAO, see *Regional Cooperation and Assistance to Resolve Safety-Related Deficiencies*, ICAO Assembly Resolution A37-8. Many regional groupings have established different types of RSOOs. An advanced model of regional aviation safety oversight harmonisation has been consequently advanced in the EU. For a digest of possible solutions concerning regional aviation safety oversight see *Safety Oversight Manual*... (ICAO Doc. 9734), Part B.

agreement of inclusive nature. First, in such cases there is no chance for a RSOO and the corresponding harmonisation of standards. As already mentioned, other types of cooperative arrangements between states concerning safety surveillance could be ineffective. This is due to the indivisible nature of air operator oversight as well as to the number and dispersion of engaged states. Second, the Chicago framework, even if supplemented by safety clauses as proposed by the ICAO, is no comprehensive solution to cope with remote operations. Third, the outcomes of multilateral 7th and 9th freedoms liberalisation may be unpredictable in terms of possible acceding state parties and their carriers that could be admitted to numerous configurations of offshore routes.[54]

Therefore, where no harmonised safety oversight is implemented, the 7th and 9th freedoms liberalisation should be subject to some conditions. Currently, 7th freedom operations are usually limited to all-cargo services.[55] Although inspired by economic rather than safety reasons, this solution is also uncontroversial in respect of the latter issue because of the relatively little exposure of human life and health to the aviation safety hazards in air cargo transport. Another limitation would be to perform multilateral liberalisation of 7th and 9th freedom rights selectively. For instance, a multilateral ASA may allow state parties to express reservations concerning application of these rights to selected state parties. However, this instrument could also be used for protectionist reasons and undermine the effectiveness of traffic rights liberalisation.

To prevent risks associated with pure offshore passenger operations, 7th freedom and cabotage privileges could be granted subject to the condition that the exercise of such rights by an aircraft of the contracting party be interrupted with particular frequency (e.g., no more than three subsequent 7th or 9th freedom operations) by 1st–5th freedom operations or ferry flights that involve the state of the operator. Alternatively, 7th and 9th freedoms traffic could be limited to a particular number or proportion of operations in a traffic season executed by an air carrier within the air transport agreement (e.g., a maximum of 100 or no more than 1/3 of operations). Such limits may well be combined. Until more comprehensive international solutions become available, this would give the state of the operator more practical ability to supervise its carriers. At the same time, despite operational limitations, the liberalisation should partially facilitate competition mechanism by actual or even possible new entry (potential competition).

10.6 Regulatory alternatives

The liberalisation of 7th and 9th freedoms, which is limited to air cargo or to regional groupings, generally does not pose an important threat to aviation safety

54 This may happen with MALIAT and its protocol exchanging 7th freedom rights, which are open to accession by third parties.

55 For example, MALIAT, the US Model Open Skies Agreement.

or may be supplemented by economically neutral safeguards (regional safety harmonisation). However, in other instances the exchange of these privileges requires special limitations. Application of these precautions means that the traffic rights in question would only be partially available to air carriers. Such half-solutions will never be fully effective and the economic benefits of this kind of liberalisation will be moderate. Thus, a comprehensive instrument would be welcome instead.

Perhaps the safety problem could be best resolved if states pooled their duties concerning enforcement of aviation safety rules within one international system. However, this kind of cooperation has only recently paved its way within regional organisations. Global governance in this respect is currently politically unthinkable. Yet, this does not mean that the risky 7th and 9th freedoms liberalisation cannot be substituted worldwide with other better balanced and readily available instruments.

The discussed freedoms of the air consist in privileges for an airline of the designating state to perform services within the territory of the accepting state (cabotage) or between the territories of two accepting states (7th freedom). The cabotage market is always open to carriers of the accepting state whereas the 7th freedom traffic is open to airlines of the two accepting states provided that these states have exchanged 3rd–4th freedoms of the air. Hence, from the market access standpoint, in most situations 7th and 9th freedom operations could be substituted by 3rd–4th freedom and domestic operations performed by a subsidiary air carrier established in the territory of another state. This, however, is precluded by most national regulations and ASAs, which require that the carriers are substantially owned and effectively controlled by the nationals of the designating state (state of the operator).[56] Consequently, liberalisation of the airline ownership and control rules could bring about economic results comparable to the exchange of 7th and 9th freedoms. Just as in the case of these freedoms, such liberalisation would require a single bilateral agreement, a set of two or more bilateral agreements or a multilateral arrangement allowing for the designation of foreign-owned or controlled airlines. Additionally, national airline establishment regimes would have to be changed in line with the liberalised ASAs.[57]

The advantage of the airline nationality liberalisation is that the new air services it enables, which substitute for 7th and 9th freedoms traffic, do not constitute non-supervised offshore operations. These domestic, 3rd and 4th freedom services always involve the state of the operator, which eliminates all the mentioned problems concerning practical safety oversight abilities. In this configuration a foreign-owned or controlled carrier is required to have a substantial commercial and legal presence in the state of the operator, where

56 For a digest of current national and international regulations see Walulik 2016, 2017, pp. 25–53.

57 There are several legal techniques of liberalising airline ownership and control requirements, see Walulik 2017, pp. 135–166.

it is established, certified and licensed.[58] Accordingly, this state should be able to exert regulatory control over the carriers activity.[59] This can be further reinforced by liberalised designation clauses in ASAs, which require the airline to have a principal place of business in the state of the operator that designates it and to be under effective regulatory control of that state.[60] What is more, the foreign-owned or controlled airline is subject to labour, safety, security, environmental, tax and other rules of the state where it is established and, depending on the laws of that state, it may also be obliged to use aircraft registered in that state and locally certified crews. Finally, contrary to 7th and 9th freedoms exchange, the liberalisation of airline establishment regimes facilitates antitrust enforcement and allows the limitation of the role of foreign government sponsored airlines, which are now an important concern in terms of fair competition.[61]

Consequently, airline ownership and control liberalisation offers more instruments for protection against the flag of convenience problem than does the exchange of equivalent traffic rights (7th and 9th freedoms). Provided that these safeguards are in place, air carrier nationality liberalisation enables the avoidance of unnecessary social cost associated with jeopardising aviation safety and hence makes a more efficient regulatory solution than the one it substitutes for. This unfortunately is not reflected in current discussions, where the flag of convenience problem in the airline sector is usually unduly associated with airline nationality liberalisation and is rarely raised in the context of 7th and 9th freedoms exchange. This is probably because the critique of airline liberalisation in the developed markets has been captured by high-wage countries' trade unions, which struggle for *status quo* in respect of employment issues. Indeed, from their perspective the establishment of foreign-owned subsidiaries in less developed markets may likely lead to labour substitution, which is not the case if these markets were served directly based on 7th and 9th freedom rights.

This is not to say that ownership and control liberalisation will be a perfectly effective instrument in all situations. As already mentioned, where 3rd and 4th freedom rights are not present, the right of establishment will not be a substitute for 7th freedom exchange. It will also be no substitute in case of those regional groupings, where 7th and 9th freedoms are crucial elements of the single aviation market. The requirement for a local establishment may also raise questions concerning regulatory efficiency. This is because airlines would be weighed

58 Annex 6 to the Chicago Convention defines the state of the operator as the state in which the operator's principal place of business is located or, if there is no such place of business, the operator's permanent residence.

59 Cf. Böhmann 2001, pp. 713–714; Havel and Sanchez 2014, pp. 85–86; Von den Steinen 2006, pp. 216–217.

60 See ICAO Template Air Services Agreements in *Policy and Guidance Material*... (ICAO Doc. 9587).

61 For more on safeguards that may be combined with airline ownership and control liberalisation see Walulik 2017, pp. 167–195.

down by the overhead associated with maintaining subsidiary companies and be deprived of some elasticity in network planning as compared to 7th and 9th freedom operations. However, the above-mentioned inconvenience could be mitigated by extra grants of operational rights, including interchange or leasing, whereas Article 83*bis* of the Chicago Convention should then be used to ensure due regulatory oversight of the aircraft. The experience of existing joint venture airline groups in Latin America and Southeast Asia proves that business organisation based on subsidiary companies may be perfectly operative.[62] Hence, such a system, although more complex, need not be prohibitively expensive. When its possible limits are measured against the lack of proper safety oversight in the case of pure offshore operations, it becomes clear that regulatory efficiency analysis speaks for grants of the right of establishment, not for the 7th and 9th freedoms of the air, at least as regards passenger air services.

What is equally important is that deregulation of airline nationality requirements should be effective in pursuing liberalisation goals in a long-term perspective. Conversely, grants of 7th and 9th freedom rights, which offer instant market access, may put a drag on future economic liberalisation initiatives. As mentioned, in most cases traffic rights and right of establishment are economic substitutes. It is agreed that the relaxation of ownership and control rules would make the current restrictions in 7th and 9th freedom rights largely obsolete and, consequently, should foster the exchange of these rights or even work as an alternative for them.[63] Some authors believe also in an opposite relation, that is, that common exchange of all traffic rights would simplify future airline nationality deregulation, which is explained by the nature of aviation negotiations.[64] However, this argument is not convincing.

Indeed, it is more likely that the exchange of 7th and 9th freedom rights will hinder future liberalisation of airline ownership and control rules. On the one hand, for some carriers the widespread liberalisation of 7th freedom and cabotage may diminish the interest in ownership and control deregulation because airlines would already possess a more convenient tool for an offshore market entry. For the same reason, in many situations the right of establishment would be unused if available in parallel with 7th and 9th freedom rights. On the other hand, for some other carriers the abolishment of ownership and control requirements would be a trigger for relocation of their businesses and for serving their markets from the outside based on 7th and 9th freedom rights.[65] To prevent such flag of

62 Cf. Fitzgerald 2011, p. 129; Hocking 2011, p. 64.

63 See Forsyth 2011, p. 216; Doganis 2001, p. 47, 2002, p. 72; Havel 2009, p. 171; Lelieur 2002, p. 73; Patel 2008, pp. 511–512.

64 I. Lelieur claims that after such deregulation there would be less risk that airlines would lose traffic rights and because substantial ownership and effective control restrictions would become useless as a bargaining chip in the negotiations over ASAs. See Lelieur 2002, pp. 78, 100–101.

65 Serving the home market from the outside is a practice that has long been limited, see Dempsey 1987, pp. 179–183.

convenience operations sates would have no option but to refrain from airline nationality liberalisation.

Additionally, political motives may lead liberalisation to stop at the exchange of 7th freedom rights. This is because, searching for a reciprocal profit, some states will choose to trade many rights but not the right of establishment, which they still prefer to reserve for their citizens due to national security reasons or mentioned labour interests.[66] What is more, the goal of market share optimisation suggests that in some instances aviation powers may actively seek the exchange of 7th freedom rights with states representing less developed aviation markets, provided that airline establishment rules remain unchanged. This is because, in such configuration, ownership and control requirements prevent business relocations and flight of capital and guarantee the advantage of these powers.[67] From the perspective of their weaker aviation partners, such process may in the short term bring desirable connectivity or competition on air routes. However, in the long term it will undermine local industries by preventing access to international capital and airline investors.

10.7 Summary

Despite four decades of liberalisation the current international regulatory framework for civil aviation is still fragmented and prohibits emergence of truly global enterprises, market and competition known from other sectors. This structure clashes with the international nature of the airline business and is a bottleneck that hinders development of this industry. Great potential for further liberalisation lies therefore within services performed by airlines entirely outside their home states. This potential may be unlocked by means of different legal tools. However, these various instruments are not perfectly equivalent, and their application should not be treated as an end itself. Completing regulatory reform internationally requires a choice of sustainable measures that are based on the common goal of national aviation policies, rather than on short term national gains or political affordability of particular actions. Obviously, what seems simpler or more easily available now may be costly or prove unproductive later.

Particular attention should be payed to the exchange of 7th and 9th freedoms of the air. This chapter shows that in many situations this kind of liberalisation will lead to market access but not to optimisation of air services. First, this

66 It is widely believed that the US have been consistently reluctant towards airline ownership and control liberalisation for national security reasons. See Walulik 2017, pp. 211–216.

67 Once again MALIAT gives a good example of such policy. The agreement exchanges 7th freedom rights for air cargo. In this treaty the nationality requirement in the designation/authorisation clause is confined to effective control being held by nationals (as opposed to traditional requirement for both substantial ownership and effective control). However, in line with the US proposal, the agreement includes an extra clause whereby the authorisation may be refused or revoked if the party receiving the designation determines that substantial ownership is vested in its own nationals.

solution will often be inefficient because it brings social costs associated with threatening aviation safety. The 7th and 9th freedoms are home to pure offshore airline services. These operations not only break out from the ICAO safety oversight model but also offer some apparent incentives for non-compliance in respect of safety. Second, the exchange of 7th and 9th freedoms may be an ineffective regulatory measure in the long-term perspective. It is likely that it will thwart future airline ownership and control liberalisation – a reform that could give much more than market access. In effect, it will deprive the industry from benefits associated with international investment and capital injections, to the greatest detriment of the less developed airline markets that could be easily captured by offshore operating foreign carriers.

It seems from the discussion here that states should be very cautious with regards to 7th and 9th freedoms exchange. Generally, any unconditional liberalisation in this respect should be confined to certain uncontroversial fields. The safety argument itself does not speak against opening 7th and 9th freedoms traffic in air cargo services and within those regional groupings that are able to enforce common safety standards. In other areas, however, market access liberalisation should rather be secured by the alternative airline nationality deregulation and its accompanying regulatory safeguards. Furthermore, to prevent flag of convenience operations, ownership and control liberalisation should be combined with 7th freedom grants only subject to operational conditions that would facilitate proper safety oversight. This system, although legally more complicated, should be much better balanced in terms of safety and economic issues than the 'cheaper' liberalisation based on straightforward 7th and 9th freedoms exchange.

11 Airline nationality

A reconstruction of the EU ownership and control rules

Elmar M. Giemulla

11.1 Introduction

European aviation law requires in Regulation 1008/2008[1] that an EU member state issues an air carrier operating licence only if – among other things – the carrier is owned and effectively controlled by EU member states or nationals of EU member states. This rule stems from the times of bilateral air services agreements (ASAs) and is related to the ownership clauses contained therein.

In the age of liberalised air transport and new air operator business models it must be increasingly questioned whether this requirement is still up-to-date, if the aviation industry can afford to observe it and how aviation authorities can effectively control it. These issues have become increasingly relevant due to cross-border cooperation and investments in airlines. Especially the financial interdependencies and the need for cooperation and modern financing instruments (e.g., alliances and aircraft leasing) clash with the discussed requirement.

Nonetheless, as the rule still exists, the national aviation authorities need to verify compliance with it. Since there is no legal definition of effective control in the EU regulation, it rests with the national aviation authorities to determine their own examination scale. Therefore, relevant information is required to understand the functioning of an airline's governance and to find out who effectively controls it.

The future perspective of the ownership and control requirement is not foreseeable yet. Since cross-border cooperation and investments are still growing, the industry needs the restrictions to be loosened. However, protectionism seems to become a more and more popular instrument in general politics.

11.2 Ownership and control as legal requirements

The relevant pre-condition for issuing an operating licence under Article 4(f) of the Regulation 1008/2008 reads:

1 Regulation No. 1008/2008/EC of the European Parliament and of the Council of 24 September 2008 on common rules for the operation of air services in the Community, OJ L 293, 31 October 2008, pp. 3–20.

> Member States and/or nationals of Member States own more than 50% of the undertaking and effectively control it, whether directly or indirectly through one or more intermediate undertakings, except as provided for in an agreement with a third country to which the Community is a party.

Therefore, the two statutory requirements for issuing an operating licence (Article 2 (1)) are, firstly, majority ownership of EU citizens or governments and, secondly, effective control of the majority shareholders over the company. The tests of ownership and control are cumulative, and both have to be met. In case an EU carrier becomes 'majority owned' or effectively controlled by a third country or a national or nationals of third countries, the competent licensing authority would have to revoke the operating licence and the carrier could no longer be considered a 'community air carrier' (Article 2(11)). Consequently, it could not take advantage of the liberalised EU aviation market any more.

National ownership and control requirements for obtaining or maintaining an operating licence are a common feature in international aviation that can be found in legislations outside the EU as well. Requirements of that kind are usually included in national aviation laws[2] and in bilateral ASAs as a condition for granting traffic rights.[3] Nowadays, such requirements primarily serve the purpose of ensuring that such traffic rights are exercised exclusively by the participating parties and not, either directly or through subsidiaries or by means of code-sharing, by companies from third countries. Moreover, they prevent the latter companies from operating services within a state or group of states through subsidiaries established in that state or group of states.

This issue has become more and more relevant due to cross-border cooperation and investments in airlines. According to the EU Aviation Strategy of 2015,[4] the European Commission intends to carefully examine the relevance and importance of ownership and control requirements, bearing in mind the commercial and financial relevance of many airlines and the financial needs of airlines to efficiently operate in a highly competitive environment.

According to Regulation 1008/2008 foreign investors are able to invest in EU airlines but cannot hold more than 49% of ownership, while control over the company must remain in EU hands. However, the 2007 EU–US open skies agreement[5] even provides for a substantially worse position of EU investments in

2 For a digest of national regulations on ownership and control see Walulik 2016.

3 For a digest of ownership and control clauses in ASAs and their evolution see Walulik 2017.

4 *An Aviation Strategy for Europe*, Communication from the Commission to the European Parliament, the Council, the European Economic and Social Committee and the Committee of the Regions, COM(2015)598 final, 7 December 2015.

5 Air Transport Agreement between the United States of America and the Republic of Austria, the Kingdom of Belgium, the Republic of Bulgaria, the Republic of Cyprus, the Czech Republic, the Kingdom of Denmark, the Republic of Estonia, the Republic of Finland, the French Republic, the Federal Republic of Germany, the Hellenic Republic, the Republic of Hungary, Ireland, the Italian Republic, the Republic of Latvia, the Republic of Lithuania, the Grand

US airlines (Annex 4a, Article 1). The permission is subject to two limitations. Firstly, foreign ownership of more than 25% of a corporation's voting equity is excluded. Secondly, actual control of a US airline by foreign nationals is also not possible.

11.3 Review of airline ownership and control

With regard to EU carriers, the relevant passages of Regulation 1008/2008 have to be reviewed under two aspects: firstly, regarding the property situation of shares and, secondly, regarding the exercise of effective control.

As to ownership, Article 4 of the Regulation states very clearly, that the majority of an undertaking has to be held by member states and/or EU nationals. There is no further legal definition. The concept of ownership is based on the notion of equity capital. Hence, either more than 50% of stock or shares in business (50% plus at least one share) have to be owned by EU nationals or member states.

The concept of effective control is less clearly defined than ownership. Article 2(9) of Regulation 1008/2008 defines effective control as:

> a relationship constituted by rights, contracts or any other means which, either separately or jointly and having regard to the considerations of fact or law involved, confer the possibility of directly or indirectly exercising a decisive influence on an undertaking, in particular by:
>
> (a) the right to use all or part of the assets of an undertaking;
> (b) rights or contracts which confer a decisive influence on the composition, voting or decisions of the bodies of an undertaking or otherwise confer a decisive influence on the running of the business of the undertaking;

Apart from Articles 2 and 4(f) of the Regulation there are no further explanations or interpreting guidelines – neither in legislation ('hard law') nor in administrative interpretative material ('soft law').

The responsibility for reviewing and assessing whether the requirements concerning ownership and control are met rests with the competent national licensing authority. The national authority is obliged to verify these requirements before granting an operating licence as well as to monitor whether the provisions are continuously observed (this results from the monitoring requirements under Article 8 of Regulation 1008/2008).

Duchy of Luxembourg, Malta, the Kingdom of The Netherlands, the Republic of Poland, the Portuguese Republic, Romania, the Slovak Republic, the Republic of Slovenia, the Kingdom of Spain, the Kingdom of Sweden, the United Kingdom of Great Britain and Northern Ireland, and the European Community, done at Brussels on 25 April 2007 and at Washington on 30 April 2007, provisionally applied as from 30 March 2008, OJ L 134, 25 May 2007, pp. 4–41.

The European Commission has the right to request all necessary information on airline ownership and control from its member states (Article 26 of Regulation 1008/2008). This right may be exercised by the European Commission to ensure uniform application of European rules. Furthermore, the European Commission has the right to make its own assessment based on the information obtained and may take a decision to request a national licensing authority to take appropriate corrective measures or to suspend or revoke the operating licence where necessary (Articles 25–26 and Article 15(3) of Regulation 1008/2008).

An enterprise applying for a licence needs to prove that it complies with the requirements set forth in Regulation 1008/2008. The same applies where, at a later stage, there are reasonable doubts as to whether these requirements continue to be met. It is the role of the carrier to make sure that sufficient proof is made available to the competent national licensing authority. Any assessment in this respect should be done on a case-by-case basis, looking not only at the legal but also at the factual position in each individual case. The competent national authority has to verify the presence of the prerequisites with due discretion based on the documents submitted by the carrier and in line with Articles 2(9) and 4(f) of the Regulation.

11.4 Interpretative guidelines

Apart from the EU law, the ownership and control requirements also form an integral part of international aviation law. However, none of the international treaties related to air activity (Chicago Convention,[6] International Air Services Transit Agreement of 1944[7] and International Air Transport Agreement of 1944[8]) defines the terms 'ownership' and 'effective control'. Consequently, there are no universally accepted definitions of these terms.

Importantly, in contrast to the ownership criterion, the question of effective control requires a deep analysis, because it is not a matter of figures (which are obvious at first glance) but rather of the question as to who actually controls the airline. Control over a corporation is commonly considered as the power to direct its internal and external policy.

There is also a difference between the US approach to 'substantial ownership' and the concept of ownership in the EU. While in the US the substantial ownership standard is less clear, there is a legal definition of 'majority ownership' in the EU. In contrast to the US air law, the EU air law also legally defines the

6 Convention on International Civil Aviation, signed in Chicago on 7 December 1944, entered into force 4 April 1947, ICAO Doc. 7300/9, 15 UNTS 295.

7 International Air Services Transit Agreement, signed in Chicago on 7 December 1944, entered into force on 30 January 1945, ICAO Doc. 9587, 84 UNTS 389.

8 International Air Transport Agreement, signed in Chicago on 7 December 1944, entered into force on 8 February 1945, ICAO Doc. 9587, 171 UNTS 387.

term effective control. In the US the term 'control' is only defined in the Securities Exchange Act of 1934.[9]

As already mentioned, there are no interpretative guidelines on ownership and control that could be binding for the national licensing authorities. Consequently, the competent licensing authorities need to adopt their own standards applicable to assessment of ownership and control. In this respect, the following EU legal documents might be taken into consideration:

- EU regulations with regard to ownership and control in general,
- relevant former decisions in the EU where such rules have been applied,
- national rules regarding ownership and control in aviation, especially those of other EU member states, and
- any other adequate rules.

This uncertainty significantly changed on 8 June 2017, when the European Commission adopted the *Interpretative guidelines on Regulation (EC) 1008/2008 – Rules on Ownership and Control of EU air carriers.*[10] The Commission itself describes the character of these guidelines as an explanation of 'how the Commission understands the Regulation on this point and how it considers it should be applied'. Furthermore, the Commission declares that these guidelines 'are not intended to create new legal obligations and are without prejudice to the competence of the Court of Justice of the European Union (CJEU)' to interpret ownership and control rules.[11]

These interpretative guidelines are not a legal act of the EU according to Article 288 of the Treaty on the Functioning of the European Union (TFEU).[12] The Commission's notice is an opinion with no binding legal force. Nevertheless, these guidelines could be enforceable when it comes to a dispute before the CJEU. It is likely that the European Commission would proceed against a member state that does not observe the relevant rules as interpreted by the Commission.

11.4.1 The notion of 'nationality'

At this stage, as it affects all kind of interpretative guidelines and other material, it has to be stated that 'nationality' means 'citizenship'. The EU member states determine the conditions and procedures for obtaining and forfeiting citizenship. Persons concerned having more than one citizenship usually are considered EU citizens, if at least one citizenship is the citizenship of an EU member state.

9 Securities Exchange Act of 1934, Pub.L. 73–291, 6 June 1934, 48 Stat. 881.

10 *Interpretative guidelines on Regulation (EC)1008/2008 – Rules on Ownership and Control of EU air carriers*, Commission Notice, C(2017)3711 final, 8 June 2017.

11 Idem p. 5

12 Treaty on the Functioning of the European Union (TFEU), signed on 25 March 1957 in Rome, entered into force on 1 January 1958 (then Treaty establishing the European Economic Community, later Treaty establishing the European Economic Community, consolidated version OJ C 202, 7 June 2016, pp. 47–199.

To verify nationality of an airline, usually copies of passports for individual shareholders and and/or organisational charts for corporate structures are required. Such charts must show all companies and all relationships within the corporate structure and include ownership percentages to demonstrate any interest that other entities have in the licence holder/applicant.

11.4.2 EU regulations on control

Ownership and control are a matter of economic and corporate law. There is a legal definition of concentration in the EU Merger Regulation[13] that also deals with the issue of control. In this regulation the legal requirements for control are laid down as follows:

1. Control shall be constituted by rights, contracts or any other means which, either separately or in combination and having regard to the considerations of fact or law involved, confer the possibility of exercising decisive influence on an undertaking, in particular by:
   (a) ownership or the right to use all or part of the assets of an undertaking;
   (b) rights or contracts which confer decisive influence on the composition, voting or decisions of the organs of an undertaking.
2. Control is acquired by persons or undertakings which:
   (a) are holders of the rights or entitled to rights under the contracts concerned; or
   (b) while not being holders of such rights or entitled to rights under such contracts, have the power to exercise the rights deriving therefrom.

These rules apply in all economic areas and, therefore, also in the aviation sector. The applicability of the Merger Regulation depends on an aggregate turnover. Although these rules are designed for mergers, they are not limited exclusively to such transactions. The standards included in the Merger Regulation can therefore be evoked in comparable situations in other areas of EU law where the question of control is present. Nevertheless, the existing differences between the legal regimes should be kept in mind when applying the merger rules to the airline licensing requirements.

11.4.3 Former cases in the EU

The national licensing authorities and the European Commission had to assess several cases regarding ownership and control in the aviation industry. The backlogs were cooperation and mergers and acquisitions between EU airlines

13 Regulation No. 139/2004/EC of the Council of 20 January 2004 on the control of concentrations between undertakings, OJ L 24, 29 January 2004, pp. 1–22.

and airlines from third countries. Over the past three years, the European Commission investigated certain non-EU investments in European airlines. This included Delta Air Lines' 49% stake in Virgin Atlantic; Etihad Airways' 29% stake in Air Berlin, 33% stake in the Swiss undertaking Darwin Airlines (now renamed Etihad Regional) and 49% stake in Alitalia; Korean Air's 44% stake in CSA Czech Airlines; and HNCA's 35% stake in Cargolux. None of the above-mentioned investments has been questioned.

The European Commission has adopted only one formal decision concerning compliance with the ownership and control provisions following the investment of Swissair in Sabena (the so-called Swissair–Sabena decision[14]). The Commission had to verify, among other things, whether Sabena complied with the requirements of being majority owned and effectively controlled by member states and/or nationals of member states as provided for in Article 4(2) of Regulation 2407/92[15] (the predecessor of the current Regulation 1008/2008). The Commission has considered the definition of ownership and control and has determined the standards of its assessment for the first time. The issues reviewed by the Commission were (1) voting arrangements between the Belgian shareholders, (2) Sabena's corporate governance, (3) draft cooperation agreement and (4) general considerations about the case.

In the Swissair–Sabena case the European Commission has stated that ownership and effective control must be interpreted and applied in the overall context of the licensing regulation. Firstly, the requirements for majority ownership and effective control have to be examined separately.[16] Secondly, the concept of ownership of an undertaking is essentially based on the notion of equity capital. Holders of such capital usually have the right to participate in decisions affecting the management of the undertaking as well as to share its residual profits or, in the event of liquidation, its residual assets after all other obligations have been satisfied. The question of whether a particular type of capital qualifies as equity capital (and must therefore be considered within the ownership concept) can be answered only on a case-by-case basis in light of all relevant circumstances.[17] Thirdly, each individual case must be assessed in view of the objective of safeguarding the interests of the EU air transport industry. This implies, in particular, that companies from third countries must not be allowed to take full advantage, on a unilateral basis, of the EU liberalised internal air transport market. Hence, the ultimate decision-making power in the management of the air carrier concerned must rest in the hands of EU member states or their nationals. They must be able, either directly or indirectly through appointments to the decisive corporate bodies of the carrier, to have the final say on such key questions as, for example, the carrier's

14 Decision No. 95/404/EC of the Commission of 19 July 1995 on a procedure relating to the application of Council Regulation (EEC) No. 2407/92 (Swissair/Sabena), OJ L 239, 7 October 1995, pp. 19–28.

15 Regulation No. 2407/92/EEC of the Council of 23 July 1992 on licensing of air carriers, OJ L 240, 24 August 1992, pp. 1–7.

16 See point IX of Decision No. 95/404/EC.

17 See point X of Decision No. 95/404/EC.

business plan, its annual budget or any major investment or cooperation projects. What is more, such ability must not be substantially dependent upon the support of natural or legal persons from third countries.[18]

11.4.4 National guidelines on ownership and control

In May 2011, the Commission for Aviation Regulation of the Republic of Ireland published a guidance note on ownership and control criteria.[19] This document serves as direction for the assessment of standards included in Article 4(f) of Regulation 1008/2008 for the Irish licensing authority. In addition to the discussion of the concepts of ownership and control, this document also contains some relevant remarks on the assessment process and the ongoing compliance.

According to the guidance note, the concept of 50% plus one share is a general rule. When evaluating ownership, the Irish authority does not take ownership structures at face value and will analyse complex structures in detail. Licence holders or applicants must explain the rights attaching to different classes of shares and the authority needs to know the real owners of the shares. It is important to distinguish between legal ownership and beneficial ownership when evaluating compliance with this requirement. In this regard, the authority 'looks through' the structure to evaluate who the ultimate beneficiaries are.

In this context, the assessment of effective control does not only include direct control, which normally follows share ownership, but extends to situations where control might not be a direct function of ownership. This may happen if some shares have more voting powers than others, or if conditions included in certain agreements or contracts confer on a lender, lessor or other entity powers to directly or indirectly exercise decisive influence on the licence holder. The guidance note gives the example of a large single shareholder who may have particular influence due to the sheer size of its shareholding, especially if other shareholders are thinly spread, are financial or small investors or if there is no device to ensure that they exercise their voting powers in concert. Of course, other factors such as the right to appoint directors are considered. However, this is not always clear. If an investor is entitled to appoint only a minority of the directors, it does not necessarily mean that the influence of that minority is always lower than that of the majority of directors. The focus of the Irish authority is to examine the level of control that the majority shareholder exercises over the company. The majority shareholder has to be independent of the support of the minority shareholders to operate the business and make decisions. It must always be in a position to exercise control. Especially key decisions related to the business model, operations, financial issues and key personnel have to stay with the majority shareholder.

18 See point XI of Decision No. 95/404/EC.

19 *Guidance note on ownership and control criteria applicable to applicants/holders of an Operating Licence issued under Regulation (EC) No 1008/2008 on common rules for the operation of air services in the Community*, Commission for Aviation Regulation, 2011, www.aviationreg.ie/_fileupload/ocguidance_note_22_11_12.pdf.

Therefore, for the assessment of effective control at least the following aspects should be taken into consideration:

- the composition of a company's board and the management structure,
- internal control systems and lines of reporting,
- rights of respective shareholders,
- key legal documents (e.g., articles of association, lease agreements, business plan),
- debt/loan agreements, and
- consultancy/adviser agreements.

11.4.5 EU guidelines on ownership and control

The mentioned EU Aviation Strategy of 2015 included, among other measures, the adoption by the European Commission of interpretative guidelines on ownership and control of EU carriers. A relevant document was announced as the *Draft Interpretative Guidelines on EC Reg. 1008/2008 – Rules on Ownership and Control of EU air carriers* in 2016. The purpose of the draft guidelines was to provide guidance for the assessment of ownership and control based on the Commission's past cases (including the Swissair–Sabena decision) and the best practices developed by national licensing authorities. They were meant to bring more legal certainty for investors and airlines alike as to how the European Commission interprets the ownership and control requirements. These interpretative guidelines were discussed as draft guidelines with no binding legal force.

On 8 June 2017 the mentioned official interpretative guidelines were published. In the view of the European Commission, they are still not binding. However, these guidelines outline the current legal opinion of the Commission that can be enforced when ownership and control come into question. Any non-compliance would probably result in infringement proceedings launched by the Commission. A ruling of the CJEU would then lead to a binding interpretation of the legal requirement of ownership and control. Anyhow, for the time being these interpretative guidelines can be taken as a point of reference by national licensing authorities.

It is not always possible to express in figures the level of influence the investor has on the management of an airline. The European Commission considers that, in order to qualify for the requirement laid down in Article 4(f) of Regulation 1008/2008, holders of equity capital should normally have the right to:

- participate in decisions affecting the operations of the air carrier, and
- obtain a share in the residual profits or, in the event of liquidation, in the residual assets of the undertaking after all other obligations have been met.[20]

20 In other words, the shares must reflect the risk and rewards of normal business.

Whereas the competent national licensing authority should analyse all complex structures, the Commission considers that a detailed analysis is required in particular when the following issues arise:

- existence of different classes of shares with different values and characteristics, and
- existence of warrants or options that will risk rendering ineffective the 'equity capital' attributes of a class of shares.

The assessment criteria shall include corporate governance, shareholder rights (such as the right to veto a transfer of shares, pre-emption rights, right of the non-EU shareholder to sell its shares, right to purchase additional shares, conditions of the investment), financial links between the EU carrier and the non-EU shareholder, and commercial cooperation. The analysis of corporate governance should cover both legal and factual elements. It should identify the decision-making bodies, their competences, their composition, nomination, election, remuneration and dismissal, the nature of the decisions they take, their decision-making procedures, including quorum requirements and voting rules (majorities, consensus) and any prerogatives accorded to other bodies (regarding e.g., proposals, nominations, consultation, binding or non-binding opinions, recommendations, consent).

There are still no binding pan-EU interpretative rules for the ownership and effective control requirement set forth in Regulation 1008/2008. A possible solution for the EU member states who do not have their own rules in this respect is to adopt the Commission guidelines as best practice. Other countries with binding national regulations on this issue do not have a similar problem. However, the latter countries must keep in mind that the European Commission guidelines outline the current legal opinion of the Commission on Regulation 1008/2008. Only an amendment of this regulation or a ruling of the CJEU could have the effect of a binding interpretation of the legal requirement of ownership and control. However, for the time being, the guidelines of the Commission shall ensure uniform application of EU law, which is highly desirable. They should delete differences in the application of law and, therefore, create an equal situation for airlines within the EU internal market.

11.5 Ownership and control assessment process

The national licensing authority should observe the relevant rules on ownership and control both within the initial licensing process and within the permanent overview over the air operators.

11.5.1 German two step approach for licensing

In Germany the first stage examination focuses on the ownership structure. The applicant (or the undertaking, when it comes to continuous monitoring) must unveil and describe its ownership structure. Majority ownership by nationals of EU member states can usually be proved by presenting the articles of association (e.g., in the case of a company with limited liability) or an excerpt from the share register (in the case of a stock corporation). To ensure that ownership requirements are also observed by stock corporations, the German legislator has introduced a special regulation.[21] A stock corporation must track the nationality structure of its shareholders, which means that all shares must be registered and their transferability needs to be restricted. To ensure or even re-establish the majority of EU nationals, the corporation may squeeze out third-country nationals if their stake becomes too large.

It is assumed that if EU member states or their nationals own an undertaking, the owners exercise the effective control and therefore fulfil the requirements of Article 4(f) of Regulation 1008/2008. Further investigation is done only if special concerns regarding effective control arise. As already described, there can be different reasons for such concerns. In such cases, the national authority can enter a deeper examination. Without a certain suspicion (e.g., questionable parts of the articles of association, stakes held by third country nationals) such additional examination process is not likely to be performed. If an in-depth examination is deemed necessary, the verification of effective control can be done by all existing means. Submission of additional documents (e.g., contracts or protocols of shareholders' meetings) by the applicant may be necessary. Based on the gathered evidence, the national authority will test if the majority owners really execute effective control in the relevant organs of the undertaking. This is the point where the interpretative guidelines need to be used by the national licensing authorities.

11.5.2 Ongoing compliance

Once an undertaking receives a licence, it is obligated to maintain the ownership and control standards set forth in Regulation 1008/2008. The economic freedom of action is limited by this requirement. In order to guarantee compliance with this rule, the undertaking has to notify the national authority in advance of actions mentioned in Article 8(4)–(7) of Regulation 1008/2008. *Inter alia*, planned changes in the ownership structure (direct or indirect) are subject to notification and, under the circumstances mentioned in Article 8(7), are also subject to approval. Mergers and takeovers also belong to changes that require notification.

21 Law to Ensure Proof of Ownership and Control of Air Carriers for the Maintenance of Air Transport Management and Air Transport Rights' (*Gesetz zur Sicherung des Nachweises der Eigentümerstellung und der Kontrolle von Luftfahrtunternehmen für die Aufrechterhaltung der Luftverkehrsbetriebsgenehmigung und der Luftverkehrsrechte – Luftverkehrsnachweissicherungsgesetz*), 5 June 1997, Bundesgesetzblatt I S. 1322. Its role is to ensure proof of ownership and control of air carriers that are stock corporations domiciled in Germany.

11.6 Conclusions

Under the EU law, European air carriers have to be owned and effectively controlled by EU nationals (and/or governments). This requirement must be considered when it comes to cross-border cooperation, new business models and strategic investments in airlines. Investments by third-country nationals into EU air carriers are therefore limited. The new interpretative guidelines of the European Commission do not directly affect the ownership and control rule, but rather harmonise the application of this rule by the national licensing authorities. As regards complex structures, a thorough analysis of the requirement of effective control is necessary. Assessment criteria shall include corporate governance, shareholder rights, financial links between the EU carrier and the non-EU shareholders, and commercial cooperation.

The reason for establishing the ownership and control requirement was primarily to ensure the reciprocity of bilateral ASAs. The market between two countries traditionally was (and in many cases still is) shared by the airlines of these two countries. The grant of traffic rights creates an economic value for an airline designated by its government. However, this view takes into consideration only the bilateral demand for air transport and disregards the globalised air transport streams. Today there are many hubs in the airline networks where passengers and cargo transfer. Aviation does not work bilaterally anymore. In many cases, third countries are involved in the air transport streams between two countries. The discussed restrictions are not favourable from an open market perspective. In most other businesses it does not matter anymore where goods and services are produced. A shirt may come from India, a phone may come from China. However, the air transport sector is not part of the World Trade Organization (WTO) and most aviation related services are excluded from this framework.

Therefore, the question arises whether a nationality clause is still adequate in a liberalised air transport environment. Traditional airline nationality solutions may be replaced gradually by other modern concepts.[22] Consequently, the European Commission aims to create a level playing field for EU carriers and some third-country carriers by modifying the nationality requirements. This will allow cross-border cooperation and investments, which are more than just alliances. The future will show whether this will result in final implementation of global open skies.

22 For a digest of such concepts see Walulik 2017. See also Chapters 2 and 10 of this book.

12 Sub-orbital traffic

A new regulatory or non-regulatory discipline

Małgorzata Polkowska

12.1 Introduction

Some observers have noticed that the private sector was already active in outer space in the 1960s. However, only during the last decade has there been a rapidly growing interest in private space tourism. This interest in private space operations concentrates also in private space transport and sub-orbital flights – activities that are in many ways analogous to air transport.[1]

The space tourism is not the future any more. It is the present. Private sub-orbital flight activity was born over a decade ago. The successful launch of White Knight in October 2004 and its journey at an altitude over 100 km has started a new era of short sub-orbital flights with passengers on board.[2] Since 2008 thousands of passengers have booked such flights. One of the space industry pioneer companies – Virgin Galactic – after a number of tests (including a fatal accident during a test flight of its first vehicle), announced recently that it is on track to begin commercial passenger spaceflights by the end of 2018. About 500 people have signed up to take a ride on SpaceShipTwo and tickets are currently being sold for USD 250,000.[3] It is predicted that by 2030 space traffic will achieve a level of 5 million passengers. It is also expected that this will be accompanied by the creation of adequate infrastructure for tourists with hotels and orbital sport centres.

Richard Branson, the founder of Virgin Galactic, has even predicted that a sub-orbital flight from Singapore to London can take 30 minutes. However, the very high cost of such flights is still a barrier for regular traffic.[4] Some have observed that, thanks to the development of technology, safety of regular transport of passengers and cargo from point A to point B on Earth through airspace and outer space may be guaranteed in less than 15 years. It is suggested that this form of travel will become routine for the public and that ticket prices will fall to

1 See Skaar 2007, pp. 5–31; Farand 2010; Mirmina 2010.
2 Walker 2007, pp. 375–404; Sgobba 2010.
3 Carrington 2016.
4 Skaar 2007, pp. 16–17.

approximately USD 100,000–20,000 per person.[5] However, the idea of sub-orbital transport is not free from criticism.[6]

As activity in the space private sector increase, the governmental activities go down. The global space activity and private entities grew to USD 314 billion in 2013. Between 2012 and 2013 revenue from commercial space products and services grew 7%; commercial infrastructure and support industries increased by nearly 5%; while government spending decreased by almost 2%.[7]

This observation does not change the fact that states are still responsible for non-governmental activities in outer space. The outer space commercialization (its use for commercial purposes) will definitely be a test for the regulators. Outer space is now seen as 'a high potential' private sector. Transporting passengers and freight through outer space is a very appealing business for many. However, the following questions arise: does the private space sector need any kind of specific regulations yet? Are they necessary? Or, conversely, can they be an obstacle to undertaking space activities? These issues already became vital to the industry ***in statu nascendi*** and its leaders even addressed them at the International Civil Aviation Organization (ICAO) Legal Committee during a hearing on reducing regulatory barriers in the space industry.[8] One thing is certain, it will be crucial for the regulators to design and introduce a legal regime that will work to support the rising private sector.[9]

12.2 Regulatory challenges in outer space commercialization

There are several legal issues that may interfere with the development of commercial use of outer space. These include limitations concerning the definitions of airspace and outer space, the definition of space objects and their legal status, the need for exchange of transit rights and the rules of air navigation.[10] This section will present key regulatory problems related to sub-orbital flights.

12.2.1 Status of sub-orbital flights

Presently, the lack of a proper international legal framework prevents undisturbed development of the space business. To overcome this problem, the legal status of space transport needs to be determined first. The notion of 'sub-orbital flights' itself has not been wider defined by law. In the US they are covered by the law of 2004.[11] Some authors have tried to form their own

5 See Wassenbergh 1996, p. 28.
6 See O'Donnell and Hurtak 2011, p. 212.
7 Dempsey 2016, p. 3.
8 Klotz 2017.
9 Łukaszuk 2006, p. 23.
10 Hobe, Goh and Neumann 2007, pp. 359–373.
11 Commercial Space Launch Amendments Act of 2004, Pub. L. 108–492 – 23 December 2004, 118 Stat. 3974.

definitions.[12] Other commentators believe that future regulation for sub-orbital flights should be based on the Chicago Convention.[13] Yet, the existing international legal framework does not provide for any effective regime securing private use of outer space. A group of states, including the US, have signed a memorandum of understanding concerning commercial activities in outer space. However, such an approach may be harmful for the developing states and even for commercial space activities in general.[14]

The use of airspace and outer space are covered by two entirely different legal regimes – the Chicago Convention[15] and the Outer Space Treaty (OST)[16] respectively. Whereas the former act is grounded on the principle of sovereignty of the states in their airspace, the latter treaty is based on the principle of non-appropriation of outer space. The question is whether sub-orbital flights fall (or should fall) within the scope of either or both regimes.

Notably, there is still no consensus as to where the border between airspace and outer space lies, which delimits the application of those two regimes, although the need for strict delimitation has been suggested already in 1956. The Karman Line (100 km above the Earth) can work for such a limit, but it has never been accepted in a binding multilateral treaty.[17] What is more, some space faring nations do not consider this lack of regulation to be a problem. It is sometimes believed that the matter of strict legal delimitation is more of a political issue than a practical one.[18] Indeed, it has important practical implications in various areas, which will be discussed later. Therefore, this matter probably will need to be solved internationally.

12.2.2 Transit issues

Notwithstanding the discussion on the boundary of the outer space, any sub-orbital transport operation will always demand transit through the airspace. Transit rights will not be necessary only in space transport operations within the national airspace of the operator, over the high seas or in outer space. In many situations operations will involve passage through airspace of other states. This space is, however, subject to state sovereignty according to the Chicago Convention. Consequently, national regimes may impose restrictions on foreign

12 For example, Nase 2012, p. 747.

13 See Jakhu and Bhattacharya 2002, pp. 112–131.

14 See Zhao 2004, p. 282.

15 Convention on International Civil Aviation, signed in Chicago on 7 December 1944, entered into force 4 April 1947, ICAO Doc. 7300/9, 15 UNTS 295.

16 Treaty on Principles Governing the Activities of States in the Exploration and Use of Outer Space, including the Moon and Other Celestial Bodies, done in London, Moscow and Washington on 27 January 1967, entered into force on 10 October 1967, 610 UNTS 205.

17 National legislation concerning space border exists in Australia and South Africa. See Goodman 2010, pp. 37, 112.

18 See Su 2013, p. 377.

sub-orbital transport devices crossing their territorial airspace. Thus, consent from states will be required, each time their airspace is crossed. Due to the fact that sub-orbital transport (or space tourism) will generally be a commercial activity, some states may not agree to issue such consent or may try to impose legal or financial barriers.

There is no clear and universally accepted rule of innocent passage for spaceships crossing the airspace of foreign states. A survey prepared by the UN Committee on the Peaceful Uses of Outer Space (UNCOPUOS) has shown that only six states recognized that satellites should enjoy innocent passage rights in foreign airspace. Over 20 states declined such a right. However, the discussed passage is inevitable, and there are important reasons for states to agree to the innocent passage rule for space objects within their territorial airspace.[19] It seems some actions should be undertaken by UNCOPUOS. One solution may be to prepare a draft bilateral agreement for launching and return operations. A bilateral agreement for transit of commercial operations could follow. Such agreements, however, would not rule out globally the questions of borders, innocent passage and sovereignty.[20]

12.2.3 Registration of objects and operations

The issue of status of sub-orbital flights also implicates the question of whether ships engaged in such flights shall be registered as space objects and if their operations shall be notified to the United Nations Office for Outer Space Affairs (UNOOSA). The application of the Registration Convention[21] to sub-orbital operations becomes even more problematic as regards international corporations launching their ships from the high seas.

This situation needs international consideration. It should be clear which state is responsible for a particular commercial flight, which state is the registration state and which state is the licensing state of the operator. Some commentators have therefore pointed out that the existing system of national registration of space flights with the UN will not be practical for commercial activities. They propose to submit private space operations to the rules applicable to air carriers,[22] especially that these rules provide for a liability and insurance regime.[23] However, the discussed registration shall also be related to space law, namely to state responsibility and liability for space operations – an issue that is crucial in the context of environmental protection of outer space (space debris).[24]

19 See Su 2014, pp. 327–342.
20 Langston 2011, p. 317.
21 Convention on Registration of Objects Launched into Outer Space, done in New York on 14 January 1975, entered into force on 15 September 1976, 1023 UNTS 15.
22 See Gorove 1991, p. 359.
23 See O'Brien 2004.
24 See Nase 2012, pp. 77–100

12.2.4 Safety and security

Commercialization of space activities and emergence of sub-orbital transport will lead to significant new traffic in airspace and outer space. This will bring about problems concerning safety and security of operations. The first group of issues are related to navigation in airspace and outer space. High speeds and altitudes plus relatively low manoeuvrability of sub-orbital ships will cause greater risk to passengers and third parties than in the case of traditional aircraft. Space objects returning to ground may require priority landing ('go around' option may be impossible). Second, presently the launching infrastructures across the world (e.g., in Russia, Switzerland, the UK or the US) have their own corresponding safety procedures. There is no unification of regulations as to spaceports, launches, radiation, space debris or radio spectrum frequencies. Sub-orbital operations are complex issues that will require cooperation between governments, space agencies and space enterprises.[25] At some stage sub-orbital flights will require the establishment of an international mechanism for outer space traffic management.

Some kind of international governance in this respect will be welcome. The US observers proposed to establish a new institution – International Space Flight Organization (ISFO), by analogy to the ICAO, and Space Transition Corridors (STC), which should effectively take care of industrial use of both air and outer space. Opponents of that idea believe that the establishment of one international organization would be more efficient. Given the many analogies of air navigation it is often believed that sub-orbital traffic should be handled within the ICAO system along with air traffic. States can give their mandate to that institution to regulate space issues concerning safety and security. However, the question arises of how these new ICAO competences should be reflected in treaty law. Shall air treaties be supplemented by space issues or are new space conventions necessary?

Even if sub-orbital traffic itself was not incorporated into the ICAO system, during its re-entry to airspace the sub-orbital space object[26] may be deemed aircraft and therefore be subject to two different international legal regimes (space law and air law). This will have implications for such issues as registration, airworthiness, certification, licensing and operational requirements. Consequently, there may be a need to change Annex 7 to the Chicago Convention – Aircraft Nationality and Registration Marks. In particular, the definition of aircraft may require some revision. For instance, under current the ICAO definition some space objects (e.g., White Knight Two) would qualify as aircraft when crossing airspace and some (e.g., SpaceShipTwo) would not. For instance, in the US and Canadian legislation the definition of aircraft extends to some space objects ('any machine capable of deriving support in the atmosphere from reactions of the air, and includes a rocket').

25 Pelton 2014, p. 80.

26 The term 'space object' is not defined in international conventions, but from practical point of view the space object must be equipped with all components which facilitate its launching into outer space.

There are also other safety and security aspects of private space activity. First, there are potential environmental threats related to the commercial use of outer space. Second, there is a concern regarding national security issues. This is because outer space is widely used for military purposes and some militarization and weaponization problems influence the commercial use of outer space.[27]

12.2.5 Passenger status

Space activities also bring about questions concerning the legal status of space passengers (or tourists). For instance, space travel requires the travelling public to be well prepared for flights. Thus, procedures such as medical examinations for psychophysical requirements may be obligatory. However international law lacks provisions on space passengers, their training or medical fitness necessary for sub-orbital flights.[28]

The Astronauts Rescue Agreement[29] includes only definitions of 'astronauts' and 'personnel'. According to the OST every astronaut is treated as 'envoi of mankind'[30] in outer space. In case of emergency, all contracting states shall help the astronauts in landing on the ground or on the high seas. Space tourism may require amendments to the Rescue Agreement to cover 'passengers'. Another idea is to include space flight rules in Annex 2 to the Chicago Convention – Rules of the Air.[31]

Some legal acts already include provisions concerning space passengers. The US Commercial Space Launch Amendments Act of 2004 establishes a definition of 'crew' and 'participants of a space flight'. Very similar clauses are included in the International Space Station Agreement. Anyway, it seems that the role of 'passenger' or 'tourist' in space is very different from the one of an 'astronaut' and thus their status should be regulated differently.

12.2.6 Civil liability and insurance

The liability issue is among the most important legal concerns related to sub-orbital transport and space tourism.[32] Whereas international air law conventions protect passenger (Warsaw–Montreal system[33]) and third-party (Rome–Montreal

27 See Jakhu 2007; Robinson 2002, pp. 527–534.

28 Langston 2011, p. 314.

29 Agreement on the Rescue of Astronauts, the Return of Astronauts and the Return of Objects Launched into Outer Space, done in London, Moscow and Washington on 22 April 1968, entered into force on 3 December 1968, 672 UNTS 119.

30 OST refers to terms such as 'envoi of mankind', 'astronaut' and 'personnel'.

31 Yan 2011, p. 192.

32 See Yun 2009, p. 960.

33 Convention for the Unification of Certain Rules Relating to International Carriage by Air, signed at Warsaw on 12 October 1929, entered into force on 13 February 1933, 137 LTNS 11, with amending conventions and protocols; Convention for the Unification of Certain Rules for International Carriage by Air, done at Montréal on 28 May 1999, entered into force on 4 November 2003, ICAO Doc. 9740, 2242 UNTS 350 (Montréal Convention 1999).

system[34]) claims, space law touches upon third-party liability only (OST and Liability Convention 1972[35]). According to these acts, the launching state is responsible for damages caused by its space objects or its parts on Earth, in airspace or in outer space. Loss of life and damages to property or other physical damages are compensable.[36] However, these conventions were designed for state not private space activity. Space passengers or tourists cannot bring individual legal actions against launching states and be compensated individually based on these international conventions because states enjoy sovereign immunity.

In this situation, private claims must be placed against the operators and need to be grounded on national laws.[37] Not all states have introduced provisions in this respect. Private compensation of damages related to space activity is a subject of statutes in several states (Australia,[38] Japan,[39] Russia,[40] South Africa,[41] Sweden,[42] the UK[43] and the US).[44] This, however, does not necessarily mean that compensation is guaranteed. For example, in the US the passenger is informed about liability conditions by the operator and must agree to them in writing, which may lead to no practical liability ('informed consent').[45] In many European jurisdictions second-party and third-party liability are obligatory. However, there is no harmonized EU legislation in this area.[46]

What contributes to uncertainty regarding private claims concerning space flights is that some commentators believe that the Montreal Convention of 1999 (including its liability, insurance and protection of passenger rights provisions) applies also to space passengers.[47] Critics of this concept point out that the

34 Convention on Damage Caused by Foreign Aircraft to Third Parties on the Surface, done in Rome on 7 October 1952, entered into force on 4 February 1958, ICAO Doc. 7364, 310 UNTS 181; Convention on Compensation for Damage Caused by Aircraft to Third Parties, done at Montréal on 2 May 2009, not in force, ICAO Doc. 9919; Convention on Compensation for Damage to Third Parties, Resulting from Acts of Unlawful Interference Involving Aircraft, done at Montréal on 2 May 2009, not in force, ICAO Doc. 9920.

35 Convention on International Liability for Damage Caused by Space Objects, done in London, Moscow and Washington on 29 March 1972, entered into force on 1 September 19729, 61 UNTS 187.

36 See Polkowska 2016a, p. 93.

37 Bourély 1991, p. 266; Wereszczetin 1997, pp. 59–68.

38 An act about space activities, and for related purposes, No. 123 of 1998, assented to 21 December 1998. See Lee 2000, pp. 57–61; Trepczynski 2007, p. 221.

39 Law Concerning the National Space Development Agency of Japan, No. 50 of 23 June 1969, as amended in 1998.

40 Law About Space Activities (*Закон о космической деятельности*) of 20 August 1993, No. 5663-I.

41 Space Affairs Act No. 84 of 1993, assented to 23 June 1993.

42 Act on Space Activities, 1982: 963 and Decree on Space Activities, 1982: 1069.

43 Outer Space Act, 18 July 1986, 1986 Ch. 38.

44 Commercial Space Launch Act, Pub. L. 98–575 – 30 October 1984, 98 Stat. 3055.

45 The main target of this approach is to support the new-born business on the one hand and to protect the passenger rights on the other hand. See Dasgupta 2013, p. 278.

46 Some authors believe the European Commission should have the mandate to regulate this issue. See Masson-Zwaan 2015.

47 See Ordyna 2010, pp. 231–250.

Montreal Convention of 1999 cannot be applied, at least when space flights start and end at the same point on Earth.[48] It seems that, in the longer perspective, the lack of clarity and international unification of liability rules will eventually become a barrier for the development of the space industry. Therefore, some authors openly call for creating adequate international provisions on civil liability.[49] However, others believe that the national forum is a better place to deal with this issue.[50]

Lack of uniformity of rules in the discussed matter also contributes to problems with travel insurance, product liability insurance and third-party insurance in space transport. Currently, conditions of such insurance are not regulated internationally. Some provisions on space insurance are included in statutes (e.g., in the US Commercial Space Launch Amendments Act of 2004). However, insurance agreements are generally negotiated on a case-by-case basis.

Due to very high risks associated with providing space activities and possible compensations, the insurers are generally reluctant to insure such activities.[51] Therefore, there is a need for governments to support this kind of space activity.[52] For instance, additional governmental guarantees may be essential to reinsure private space operators. However, the lack of legal clarity concerning liability rules also contributes to high insurance costs. For this reason, cooperation among states is very welcome.[53] Once the space tourism and sub-orbital transport business grows larger, regulators will need to establish clear liability limits for owners and operators using outer space. In doing so they will have to consider such factors as the length of the flight, the type of space object and the experience of the astronauts. Liability limits shall make space insurance affordable for users and will open up a competitive space insurance market (just as in the airline sector).

12.2.7 Ownership in space

Private space operations also raise a couple of questions regarding ownership rights of objects in space and their status as space objects (e.g., Moon hotels). Importantly, these operations may also pose a threat to the Common Heritage of Mankind concept. Thus, it seems there is a need to update the existing space treaties in order to accommodate ownership problems. However, according to many observers, international law should not overregulate these issues. Importantly, it shall also be feasible to implement future regulations in different local legal regimes. The role of national law should be to supplement international rules.[54]

48 See Langston 2011, pp. 307–311.
49 For example, Chatzipanagiotis 2011, p. 52.
50 For example, Kazemi, Mahmoudi and Golroo 2011, pp. 272–273.
51 See Ryabinkin 2004, pp. 135–136.
52 See Kayser 1991, pp. 341–379; Nesgos 1991, p. 421; Polkowska 2008, pp. 56–61.
53 Masson-Zwaan 2015.
54 See Jasentuliyana 1997, pp. 191–202, 205–217; Nyman-Metcalf 1999, pp. 373 and 387.

12.2.8 Criminal jurisdiction

Space tourism also raises questions related to criminal jurisdiction. No international space treaty provides for any regulations in this respect. Aviation law, by contrast, covers these issues in a couple of conventions: the Tokyo Convention of 1963,[55] the Hague Convention of 1970[56] and the Montreal Convention of 1971.[57] Private space activity will need analogous international rules, at least as regards establishment of state jurisdiction.

12.3 Results of the debate on space transport regulation

The legal problems related to private space activity have been discussed on many occasions. This section will present the current results of this debate regarding matters relevant for the regulation of space transport activities.

In May 2013 the Institute of Air and Space Law at McGill University and the International Association for the Advancement of Space Safety held an expert conference on the perspectives of aerospace transport. The conference not only analysed the current situation, but assessed legislative and operational challenges and suggested policy and mechanisms facilitating sub-orbital transport. During the conference much attention was paid to the need to standardize safety in space transport to facilitate business development. Some issues raised concerned liability of space carriers, especially the question of whether there is a need to regulate this matter now. Many authors believe this is not a priority.[58] The problem of transit of sub-orbital flights was also discussed. It was concluded that the ICAO and the UNOOSA should be encouraged to undertake collaboration in the discussed matters. The main target of this conference was to exchange the information and experiences in space operations between those two UN organizations.[59] Conference participants suggested establishing a study group and organizing common symposia.

55 Convention on Offences and Certain Other Acts Committed on Board Aircraft, done in Tokyo on 14 September 1963, entered into force on 4 December 1969, ICAO Doc. 8364, 704 UNTS 219. This convention will be amended by the Protocol to Amend the Convention on Offences and Certain Other Acts Committed on Board Aircraft, done at Montréal on 4 April 2014, not in force, ICAO Doc. 10034.

56 Convention for the Suppression of Unlawful Seizure of Aircraft, signed at The Hague on 16 December 1970, entered into force on 14 October 1971, ICAO Doc. 8920, 860 UNTS 105. This convention has been amended by the Protocol Supplementary to the Convention for the Suppression of Unlawful Seizure of Aircraft, done at Beijing on 10 September 2010, entered into force on 1 January 2018, ICAO Doc. 9959.

57 Convention for the Suppression of Unlawful Acts against the Safety of Civil Aviation, signed at Montréal on 23 September 1971, entered into force on 26 January 1973, ICAO Doc. 8966, 974 UNTS 177. This convention will be superseded by the Convention on the Suppression of Unlawful Acts Relating to International Civil Aviation, done at Beijing on 10 September 2010, not in force, ICAO Doc. 9960.

58 For example, Haanappel 2014, pp. 118–120.

59 See Graham 2014, p. 3.

The space issue was introduced to the ICAO in 2015 by its Legal Committee and presented at the ICAO Council 174th session.[60] The discussion concentrated on sub-orbital flight and related air navigation safety issues. During formal and informal meetings, the delegates to the Council shared their views about the necessity of regulating such flights under the aviation safety regime. The discussions touched upon the need for adequate changes to the ICAO Standards and Recommended Practices (SARPs). Some questions referred to space debris hazards, safety management in air navigation and the ICAO Global Air Navigation Plan (GANP).[61] It was argued that the broad provisions of the Preamble to the Chicago Convention, which enable the ICAO to take care of safety and security in airspace, should also work for sub-orbital flights crossing this airspace. The opponents, however, did not find space regulations to be a priority for the ICAO.

These debates have not lead to clear conclusions, but – thanks to the ICAO initiative and its cooperation with the UNOOSA – more aerospace meetings were organized and the discussed issues were put on the agenda of the ICAO Space Learning Group. The ICAO and its Legal Committee are also very interested in the safety of air navigation and sub-orbital flights. Close cooperation with the UNOOSA in this area is very promising. Under the ICAO auspices a working space group was established to cooperate with governments, the UNOOSA, academia, space industry and business.

The ICAO and the UNOOSA have organized a series of Aerospace Symposia gathering distinguished worldwide experts and representatives of the industry and administration. The first one was held on 18–20 March 2015 in Montreal, the second one on 15–17 March 2016 in Abu Dhabi and the last one took place in Vienna on 29–31 August 2017. Aviation safety and space sustainability were the key areas of consideration at these meetings. Discussed were also some challenges and hazards such as space weather and space debris. Other areas of concern included data gathering, analysis and protection, spectrum protection, harmful interference between radio communication services, protection of critical ground infrastructures, protection of space systems and aviation systems. It was acknowledged that cyber security poses a serious challenge that requires further exploration and collaboration between aviation, space and telecommunication sectors. The delegates noticed, in respect of sub-orbital traffic, that there is high and increasing demand for launching of revenue-generating operations.

60 See Polkowska 2017, p. 165.

61 ICAO Space Learning Group made a proposal to add into GANP provisions referring to sub-orbital operations. ICAO will need to consider formal integration of the commercial space initiatives into the Global Aviation Safety (GASP) and the GANP and to any associated modules within the Aviation System Block Upgrades (ASBUs). The ICAO Space Learning Group will focus on integration of sub-orbital space transportation with aviation, and avoid duplicating efforts on initiatives underway with UN COPUOS activity such as orbital debris and delimitation of space. The outcome of its works is planned to be presented at the ICAO General Assembly in 2019.

The Aerospace Symposia recognized that the emerging commercial space transportation sector is evolving rapidly and demands better coordination at the intergovernmental level, especially in the context of differences in international legal regimes for aviation and for space activities. The ICAO, the UNCOPUOS, the International Telecommunication Union (ITU) and the International Maritime Organisation (IMO) shall play a significant role here. Also, the European Aviation Safety Agency (EASA), which is responsible for air safety in Europe, recently expressed its interest in the emerging space issues. The Civil Air Navigation Services Organisation (CANSO) and the EUROCONTROL representatives pointed out that there is a need to further explore possible future establishment of an international space traffic management system that would be interoperable with the global air traffic management system and supporting infrastructure, into which aerospace activities must be safely integrated.

At the symposia some delegates raised the issue of complexity of activities and legal regimes in near space. It was concluded that this matter needs to be further studied to eliminate uncertainties that may restrict the industry. In particular, international harmonization of certain requirements such as licensing, authorization, supervision of orbital and sub-orbital activities may help the governments in establishing their internal regulations. During the symposia representatives of the following national space agencies presented their home legislations as samples: France-CNES, Germany-DLR, the US-FAA and the UK (latest law of 2017 entering into force in March 2018). It was declared that national authorities work closely with the industry, the private sector, non-governmental organizations and academia to define the best requirements for stability, consistency and predictability in developing and applying a national regulatory framework for commercial space transportation. The representatives of the space sector underlined the need for legislation stability, which is key for business predictability. It was specified that governments must consider the emerging aerospace activities, including human space transportation, the different nature of orbital and sub-orbital environments, the inherently different requirements under international air law and international space law, and the established mandates of the intergovernmental bodies involved. This also requires clarifying the scope of aerospace activities that should be studied, conducting gap analysis and determining further work programmes. Performance-based standards that look at associated risks also need to be considered to allow for flexibility of future technological development, an increase in predictability and transparency and augment implementation.

The symposia proved that the ICAO–UNOOSA Space Learning Group works are productive in fostering dialogue between the aviation and space communities. The group plays an important role in bringing together governmental authorities, international intergovernmental and non-governmental organizations, as well as industry and private sector actors, which helps in sharing experience and raising awareness of different realities and requirements in aviation and space activities. At the last ICAO–UNOOSA Aerospace Symposium held in Vienna the Space

Learning Group established the Terms of Reference for the next steps to be taken within the common ICAO–UNOOSA approach. The idea of creating a legal subgroup was also discussed. The Vienna symposium report[62] concluded that the series of ICAO–UNOOSA Aerospace Symposia succeeded in bringing aviation and space communities closer, which has contributed to mutual understanding and to recognition of common areas of interest and concern for current and future aerospace activities.

On 20–21 June 2018 the international community gathered in Vienna once again at the UNISPACE+50 – a special segment of the 61st session of the UNCOPUOS. The UNISPACE +50 commemorated the 50th anniversary of the first UN Conference on the Exploration and Peaceful Uses of Outer Space in 1968. The aim of this forum was to consolidate the international efforts undertaken at ICAO and UNOOSA level and build upon existing sustainable developments goals to create a closer cooperation concerning further air and space activities.

12.4 Summary

It seems that sub-orbital traffic is a regulatory discipline with regard to large areas of this activity. There is a need to provide a unified legal regime for future space transport; otherwise the emerging market would be lost. Expenditures in space business are relatively high and very risky. Therefore, the prospective legal regime should provide stability and facilitate investment. There are, however, several regulatory scenarios. First, sub-orbital traffic may be internationally unregulated, and regulations will be introduced on a case-by-case basis in bilateral or regional agreements. Second, a new organization will be created and charged with responsibility for space issues. Third, the ICAO may take care of safety of sub-orbital flights and regulate them in new technical annexes (the new definition of aircraft would be expanded to sub-orbital flights as well). This last solution seems to be the simplest and quickest. The scope of ICAO competence may be expanded to space activities to ensure stable and predictable regulatory conditions. This will not require amending the Chicago Convention. However, there may be a need to delimit airspace and outer space in a protocol to this convention.

A new system for space traffic management should probably follow. It looks as if a new convention referring to sub-orbital traffic is not necessary. Nonetheless, to achieve the goals of safety and security in sub-orbital traffic, the UNCOPUOS shall start deliberating on the space standards and recommended practices patterned upon the ICAO SARP's.[63] Although some observers strongly support it, the creation of a new space organization does not appear to be necessary at this stage. The ICAO and the UNOOSA can fulfil their functions in cooperation

62 It yet has not been published and will be submitted to the next UNCOPUOS regular meeting.
63 Dempsey and Mineiro 2010, pp. 250–252; Polkowska 2016b.

with industry players and non-governmental organizations and serve as a forum for facilitating collaboration according to the established models and practices. The cooperation within a UN system of compliance and supervision of sub-orbital operations seems to be essential. With an increasing number of states getting involved, proactive harmonization will be required in this area in the common interest of all space stakeholders.

13 The need for regional liberalisation

The issue of Damascus Agreement of 2004

Shadi A. Alshdaifat and Bashar H. Malkawi

13.1 Introduction

Regional liberalisation[1] has been successful in a range of socioeconomic and geographical environments as a channel and catalyst for increased economic growth and employment. The most prominent example of such a successful policy is the common market in the EU. At the same time the experience of many other states, proves that the alternatives to liberalisation are likely be much costlier.[2]

In air transport it generally was not until the 1970s–1980s that countries began to deregulate the national aviation regimes and liberalise their international aviation relations. This progress has been even less rapid for Arab states and, yet, they have not removed their own barriers in order to liberalise airline markets. The reasons for the fear of liberalisation are complex, including deep-seated structural problems, weak policy frameworks and institutions, and protection of their absolute sovereignty. Within the Arab world, the benefits of liberalisation to the economy could have been dramatic.

However, as regards aviation, liberalisation of market access between Arab states and investments by other Arab states in Arab airlines are usually still restricted. The aviation relations between Arab states have been dominated by bilateral air services agreements (ASAs). On the one hand, some Arab states unilaterally apply open skies policy, that is, Oman, Kuwait, Bahrain, Lebanon and the United Arab Emirates (UAE).[3] On the other hand, there are states that are reluctant towards airline liberalisation. Currently there are not many agreements creating open skies between Arab states.[4] Most agreements impose limits on the number of flights, the capacity or other restrictions that supress the growth of the air transport sector in these states.

1 For the idea of regional liberalisation see Blackwell 2011, p. 725.

2 See *ICAO Global Symposium on Air Transport Liberalisation. The Economic Benefits of Liberalising Regional Air Transport. A Review of Global Experience*, ICAO Symposium Paper, No. 3, 2006, p. 7.

3 Arab Air Carriers Organization 2009, p. 28.

4 See Cristea, Hillberry and Mattoo 2014, p. 10.

However, a starting tool has been developed over a decade ago for airline liberalisation in the Arab world – the Damascus Agreement of 2004.[5] This multilateral agreement is a product of cooperation between the Arab states at the forum of Arab Civil Aviation Commission (ACAC). It was adopted by the Council of Arab Transport Ministers in 2004. The agreement provides for fundaments of liberalisation that include market access, ownership and control of airlines, and fair competition (harmonisation of competition, non-discrimination rules, antidumping policies, antitrust rules).

The overall intention of the agreement is to liberalise air transport regulations. Unfortunately, to date, little progress has resulted from this agreement and it is notable that most of the Arab states are not parties to the agreement. To date 13 Arab states have signed the agreement,[6] and only eight have ratified it.[7] The key countries that still have not accepted the agreement include Egypt and Saudi Arabia.[8]

In the last decade, however, the Arab world has seen a significant leap in aeronautics. Today, several Arab airlines are on top of the world aviation sector, such as Qatar Airways, Emirates, Etihad and Air Arabia. The Arab and Middle East markets provide substantial contributions to the world economy. Most of these carriers originate from the UAE, which has developed the second largest economy in the Arab world (after the economy of Saudi Arabia) with a gross domestic product (GDP) of USD 693 billion (AED 2.5 trillion) in 2017. Importantly the UAE has been successfully diversifying its economy, which is strictly related to the development of its aviation sector. It is interesting how this expansion of Arab air markets could influence the development of the Damascus Agreement framework.

13.2 Economic impact of aviation in Arab states

Over the course of a century civil aviation has become a major industry. Today, without air travel, mass international tourism would not exist, nor could global supply chains function. Some 40% of high-tech sales depend on good quality air transport, and there is no alternative mode of transport for perishable commodities such as fresh food or cut flowers. Air transport systems are interdependent, involving airlines, all service providers and authorities on the ground.[9] Air transport in total directly supported nearly 8.4 million jobs in 2010.[10]

5 Agreement on Liberalisation of Air Transport between the Arab states done in Damascus on 19 December 2004, entered into force on 18 February 2007.

6 Bahrain, Egypt, Iraq, Jordan, Lebanon, Oman, Palestine (West Bank and Gaza, not party to the Chicago Convention), Somalia, Sudan, Syria, Tunisia, Saudi Arabia and Yemen.

7 Jordan, Lebanon, Morocco, Oman, Palestine, Syria, Yemen, and the UAE.

8 See also Tan 2016, pp. 278–279.

9 Bamber et al. 2009, p. 640.

10 Vasigh, Tacker and Fleming 2008, p. 79.

The International Civil Aviation Organization (ICAO) confirmed that 3.8 billion passengers made use of the global air transport network for their business and tourism needs in 2016. The annual total passenger number was up by approximately 6.8% compared to 2015 and is expected to reach over 6.4 billion by 2030.[11] Historically, air travel growth has been doubling GDP growth. In 2017, passenger kilometres globally increased by 5.7% compared to world GDP average growth of 5.5%.[12]

Despite a more convenient legal environment and economic climate in Europe and North America, the traffic of the European and North American airlines increased less than the world average. The Asia-Pacific has thus become the world's largest air transport market,[13] and the Arab states remain the fastest growing air transport market globally.

The first Arab airline was Egypt Air, which was established in 1931. Over the last nine decades airlines based in the Middle East have grown significantly. Now Egypt Air, along with Saudia, Qatar Airways, flydubai, Gulf Air and Oman Air are among the top airlines in the Middle East market.[14] Emirates airline of Dubai was established in 1985 and today it is one of the world's largest. Huge public investments in airports have been an important driver in attracting flights. Dubai airport allows traffic at any time of the day or night, which enables Emirates to use its planes 24 hours a day. Qatar Airways and Etihad Airways are two other fast-growing airlines from the region.[15]

The three big Middle Eastern airlines long remained outside the three alliances (Star Alliance, SkyTeam and Oneworld). However, their integration with global airline networks is moving forward. In September 2012 a global partnership between Emirates and Qantas was announced, followed by the announcement of Qatar joining Oneworld and Etihad Airways implementing a commercial partnership with the Air France–KLM Group and Air Berlin.[16]

In the Arab states aviation plays a progressive economic and social role, embodied by such carriers as Emirates, Royal Jordanian Airlines, Egypt Air and Etihad Airways. Major focus in Arab states is traditionally on the fields of cooperation, tourism, providing employment opportunities and having a positive effect on other sectors of the economy. The direct contribution of aviation to the economies of Arab states is, however, rapidly growing and so is the interest of Arab policymakers in aviation as an independent sector of the industry and a standalone source of GDP.

In the UAE, a leading state in the Arab region, aviation has contributed approximately AED 61.3 billion (6.2%) to the GDP. This total comprises of:

11 *Annual Report of the Council*, ICAO, 2016, p. 5.
12 Oxley 2017.
13 The Asia-Pacific is responsible for 40% of international air traffic in 2014. See IATA 2017.
14 Maslen 2015.
15 Bamber et al. 2009, p. 641.
16 Air Transport News 2014.

AED 35.2 billion directly contributed through the output of the aviation sector (airlines, airports and ground services), AED 14.5 billion indirectly contributed through the aviation sector supply chain and AED 11.6 billion contributed by the spending by employees of the aviation sector and its supply chain.[17]

In addition, there is AED 84.5 billion in 'catalytic' benefits through tourism, which raises the overall contribution to AED 145.8 billion or 14.7% of GDP.[18] The aviation sector supports 224,000 jobs in the UAE. This total comprises of 141,000 jobs directly supported by the aviation sector, 46,000 jobs indirectly supported through the aviation sector supply chain and 37,000 jobs supported through the spending by the employees of the aviation sector and its supply chain.[19]

Royal Jordanian Airlines has been an essential contributor to the national economy of Jordan, bringing in hard currency and playing a key role in attracting tourists from all over the world. It contributes to 3% of the country's GDP.[20] The aviation sector supports 33,300 jobs in Jordan. This is made up of 12,200 jobs directly supported by the aviation sector, 11,000 jobs indirectly supported through the aviation sector supply chain and 10,100 jobs supported through the spending by the employees of the aviation sector and its supply chain. In addition, there are a further 46,000 people employed through the catalytic (tourism) effects of aviation.[21]

In Egypt, the aviation sector contributes EGP 15.0 billion (1.2%) to the GDP. This comprises of EGP 7.7 billion directly contributed through the output of the aviation sector (airlines, airports and ground services), EGP 4.9 billion indirectly contributed through the aviation sector supply chain, and EGP 2.3 billion contributed through the spending by the employees of the aviation sector and its supply chain. In addition, there is EGP 81.1 billion in 'catalytic' benefits through tourism, which raises the overall contribution to EGP 96.1 billion or 8.0% of GDP.[22]

13.3 Arab civil aviation liberalisation potential

It seems that the rapid growth of the Arab air industry has not been accompanied by corresponding shift in aviation policies and regulations in the region. Many Arab states desperately need to re-regulate their aviation sectors and, in particular, to liberalise their skies.

As mentioned in the introduction, the open skies idea has been introduced only partially and fragmentary across the Arab world. Notably, ASAs between

17 Kader 2011.
18 Oxford Economics 2011a, p. 4.
19 Ibid.
20 www.rj.com/en/meet-rj/our-standards/profile (visited 9.5.2018).
21 Oxford Economics 2011b, p. 4.
22 Oxford Economics 2011c, p. 4.

Arab states and with the US or the EU are more open than those between Arab states themselves. Not surprisingly, the benefits of the rapidly increasing Arab air traffic concentrate in a few airlines and airports.

Progressing liberalisation in the Arab region could help to expand the aviation boom from the Arabian Peninsula to the whole region, and this should be to the benefit of both the fast-growing Gulf carriers and the currently underserved Arab air markets. This win-win strategy is possible because liberalisation generally leads to increased air service levels and to lower fares, which in turn stimulates additional traffic volumes and brings about increased economic growth and employment.

Further liberalisation of Arab skies can provide substantial benefits for air passengers and the wider economy directly and indirectly in a number of ways. Additional economic activity in the local aviation sectors could be generated by the growth in maintenance and auxiliary services. Air services facilitate arrival of larger numbers of business and leisure passengers to a region or country. Travellers' spending can support a wide range of tourism related businesses such as hotels, restaurants, theatres and car rentals. Finally, the 'catalytic impacts' of air transportation are responsible for facilitating growth and productivity in the general economy by increased trade, business activity and greater personal productivity.

For instance, in the UAE liberalisation of market access was forecast to generate 70,000 full-time equivalent (FTE) jobs, while ownership and control liberalisation was expected to generate a total of 55,100 FTE jobs. The two forms of liberalisation in combination were forecast to generate 125,100 FTE jobs in total. In addition to employment, liberalisation was also forecast generate incremental GDP of between AED 3.3 billion and AED 6.0 billion.[23]

Obviously, increase in air traffic requires extra resources to handle the additional passengers and aircraft. Employment growth in the aviation sector is, however, not confined to the airlines and their operational bases. It is also related to the servicing, management and maintenance of additional air traffic wherever it occurs. This includes activities at airlines, airports, air navigation and other aviation-related businesses. Furthermore, additional aviation activity has 'spin-off' impacts into the wider economy known as indirect or multiplier impact.

These concern, for example, food wholesalers that supply catering on flights, trucking companies that move goods to and from the airports, refineries processing and oil for jet fuel. These indirect impacts generate additional employment in a range of industries.[24]

Additionally, availability of air transport facilitates mobility of workforce. This improves overall cohesion of regions and contributes to economic opportunities and social equity. The air traffic in the Arab states has attracted migrant employees, and their numbers have increased substantially in recent years. The Arab

23 InterVISTAS-EU 2009, p. iv.
24 Ibid.

states hosted 17.8 million migrant workers in 2013, and the majority are from Asia, with a sizeable number also coming from Africa, especially Egypt. Migrants in the six Gulf states account for over 10% of all migrants globally, while Saudi Arabia and the UAE host respectively the fourth and fifth largest migrant populations in the world. Migrant workers make up the majority of the population in Bahrain, Oman, Qatar and the UAE (and more than 80% of the population in Qatar and the UAE); while in construction and domestic work in Gulf states, migrant workers make up over 95% of the work force.[25]

In 2015, there were already 32 million international migrants in the Arab states region sharing employment with Arab nationals. Migrants in the Arab states remitted over USD 109 billion in 2014, with Saudi Arabia and the UAE ranking second and third globally in terms of remittance outflow after the USA.[26]

From a long-term perspective, liberalisation of the skies is desirable and even necessary to enhance economic efficiency, political legitimacy and stability in the Arab states. In particular, this process should unleash substantial investment in infrastructure between the rich and the poor Arab states. Importantly, for some Arab national aviation industries liberalisation will mean more than concluding open skies agreements. It will require a shift from the centralised and outdated airline model towards an open and competitive model where business decisions of Arab airlines will be determined by supply and demand rather than by political considerations.[27] However, the examples of states that have already liberalised their air transport prove that setting aside politics and bridging economies offers great benefits to all.

13.4 The Damascus Agreement of 2004

Despite current relatively little interest among Arab states, the Damascus Agreement is potentially the best-suited legal instrument to address the needs of aviation liberalisation in the Arab world. The agreement was sponsored by the ACAC – a specialised organisation of the League of Arab States.[28] Over the last few decades, this institution (and its predecessor – the Civil Aviation Council of Arab States) has continuously pushed for cooperation and for liberalisation of the civil aviation sector in the Arab world.

The conclusion of the Damascus Agreement is a continuation of an earlier policy adopted by the Council of Arab Transport Ministers in an agreement of

25 www.ilo.org/beirut/areasofwork/labour-migration/lang–en/index.htm (visited 9.5.2018).

26 Ibid.

27 For a discussion of such processes in the international airline industry see Walulik 2017.

28 The League of Arab States, or the Arab League, was founded in Cairo on 22 March 1945. Current members of the league are: Egypt (1945), Iraq (1945), Jordan (1945), Lebanon (1945), Saudi Arabia (1945), Syria (1945), Yemen (1945), Libya (1953), Sudan (1956), Morocco (1958), Tunisia (1958), Kuwait (1961), Algeria (1962), Bahrain (1971), Oman (1971), Qatar (1971), United Arab Emirates (1971), Mauritania (1973), Somalia (1974), Palestine (West Bank and Gaza) (1976), Djibouti (1977), and the Comoros (1993).

1999, which intended to liberalise intra-Arab air services over a period of five years by gradually reducing restrictions for carriers of the ACAC member states. This programme resulted in the signing of 17 open skies agreements among ACAC member states including Bahrain, Jordan, Lebanon, Morocco, Oman, Qatar, Syria, and the UAE.[29]

The Damascus Agreement itself is grounded on the principles of the agreement for facilitating and promoting inter-Arab trade adopted by Arab Economic and Social Council in 1981,[30] which provides for cooperation of the parties in facilitating multimodal transport and communications on preferential terms among them. It is also based on the provisions of Article 5 of the ACAC Agreement,[31] which states that it is among the objectives and aims of the commission to endeavour to increase and develop Arab air transport in such a manner that meets the needs of the Arab nations for a safe, regular, efficient and sound Arab transport.

The preamble of the Damascus Agreement specifically declares the intent to achieve greater liberalisation of air transport services between the Arab states by 'coordinating Arab air transport policies in order to eliminate any obstacles to the development of Arab air transport'. It seeks effective participation of Arab air carriers in offering services inside the Arab air transport market on the basis of fair competition.

The Damascus Agreement generally applies to scheduled air transport. However, it also includes an annex concerning performance of non-scheduled air transport services.[32] With regard to applicable regular air services it introduces wide scale liberalisation in terms of market access, operational and ancillary rights.

This exchange of rights is, however, not free from some imprecision. The main doubts concern the grant of traffic rights. What is out of the question is that Damascus Agreement supports unlimited 1st–4th freedom air traffic,[33] and that it precludes cabotage services (Article 4.3).

The rights granted to the parties designated airlines include the following: the right to over fly any territories of the territories of states-parties; the right to land in any of the territories of the state-parties for non-commercial purposes; and the right to embark and disembark passengers, cargo and mail, whether separately or in combination, from and to any of the territories of the state parties (Article 4.2).

29 For the ACAC liberalisation program see: Schlumberger and Weisskopf 2012, p. 253; Tan 2010, pp. 5–6.

30 Agreement for Facilitation and Promotion of Trade among Arab States, signed in Tunis on 22 February 1981, entered into force on 1 January 1998.

31 Agreement for the Creation of Arab Civil Aviation Commission, signed in Cairo on 15 September 1994, entered into force on 7 February 1996.

32 Non-scheduled Arab air services are also ruled by Agreement for Non-Scheduled Air Transport between Arab States, signed in Tunis on 15 December 1978.

33 Cf. Schlumberger 2010, p. 69; Walulik 2017, p. 150. Note that 1st and 2nd freedom among Arab states is also secured by Agreement on First and Second Freedoms of the Air for Arab Civil Aircraft signed in Cairo on 25 March 1963 and by International Air Services Transit Agreement, signed in Chicago on 7 December 1944, entered into force on 30 January 1945, ICAO Doc. 9587, 84 UNTS 389.

The above-mentioned wording could, however, suggest that the agreement allows also for some 'beyond' traffic (5th and 7th freedom services). On the one hand, such interpretation could be supported by Article 14 on operational flexibility, which allows any airline of the state party to, *inter alia*, operate flights in one direction or both directions, to operate flights to points in the territories of the state parties, and also to intermediate points as well as to points beyond the states parties and vice versa, to eliminate stop points on any point or points and also to operate flights to any points lying beyond any point within the territory of the state party.

On the other hand, it seems that these 'beyond' rights should be limited. There is no doubt that the agreement does not provide for 5th and 7th freedom services including those beyond points that are located outside the territories of the state parties to the Damascus Agreements. This is because the agreement explicitly specifies that it grants rights with the purpose of operating regional air services among states parties (Article 4.1)[34] and that these rights apply to scheduled services operated from any territory of state party territories to the territory of another state party (Article 4.2). It seems, thus, that 5th and 7th freedom traffic is limited to points within the territories of the contracting states. However, the wording of the agreement is not precise, and some commentators question the existence of 7th freedom rights within the Damascus Agreement framework.[35]

To operate the agreed services airlines must be designated by state parties but the agreement does not include any restrictions on the number of operating airlines (Article 5.1). It also does not restrict capacity and frequency of flights. Any limitation in this respect must be non-discriminatory and be justified by environmental, technical, safety or security reasons (Article 7). Although no reservations should be made to the agreement (Article 42.2), state parties may, upon prior notification, limit traffic rights capacity and frequencies, but only for a limited period of 12 months (Article 41).

Airline schedules require prior acceptance of the state parties (Article 6). Pricing regulations are semi-liberal. There is no obligatory up-front government tariff approval. Nonetheless tariffs for air carriage of passengers, cargo and mail must be determined by airlines in conformity with an annex to the agreement and have to be filed with the authorities, which may suspend them each time they find they are non-compliant with the agreement (Article 8).

The exercise of rights by a designated airline is subject to its authorisation by the accepting state. In this respect, the Damascus Agreement introduces the nationality pooling concept.[36]

The authorisation of a designated carrier is subject to substantial ownership and effective control of that airline being vested either in the designating state

34 The 'regional air services' mean air carriage of passenger, cargo and mail where the originating point and the end point are located in the territories of the state parties (Article 1).

35 Cf. Tan 2010, p. 6; Schlumberger 2010, pp. 67–71, p. 69; Schlumberger and Weisskopf 2012, p. 254.

36 For more on that concept see Walulik 2017, pp. 139–152.

party and its nationals or in any state parties and their nationals. It also requires that the main headquarters of the airline is in the territory of one of the state parties (Article 5.2). This liberal provision is of great significance because it allows for cross-border airline investment between the contracting states and for establishment of multinational Arab airlines.

The Damascus Agreement grants to the air carriers of the state parties a wide range of rights for doing business. These concern transferring revenues, employing personnel, sale and marketing of services, establishment of offices and ground handling (Article 12). It also facilitates cooperative arrangements between airlines such as joint enterprises, blocked space or code-sharing (Article 13), and within intermodal services (Article 16).[37]

The agreement also includes extensive provisions concerning safety, security, tax and air charges (Articles 20–24). As regards environment protection it requires compliance with ICAO Standards and Recommended Practices (SARPs) (Article 27).

To protect the level playing field within the liberalised air transport market the Damascus Agreement includes wide fair competition and non-discrimination provisions. It declares that state parties shall have equal and fair opportunity to exercise the rights arising from the agreement (Article 9). Annex 2 to the agreement specifies state obligations concerning competition issues. It requires the ban of agreements that can negatively affect competition between airlines.

Adoption of national competition rules and dispute resolution in competition issues is subject to international comity. Consultations are obligatory before any unilateral legal action is taken. Additionally, to guarantee a minimum participation of the designated airlines of a state party in the agreed market and to prevent unfair competition, Annex 3 to the agreement defines possible misconduct and specifies allowed countermeasures. Notwithstanding, Article 19 of the agreement requires state parties to refrain from granting governmental support to the designated airlines, which may upset the negotiated trade and constitute unfair competition. Resolution of arguments in this respect is based on comity procedures. However, in special or exceptional circumstances unilateral countervailing measures are also possible.

The Damascus Agreement also strives to protect consumers. First, a general consumer protection clause is included. It requires that state parties undertake to cooperate to protect consumer rights (Article 28). Second, the agreement demands that airline cooperative arrangements do not cause passenger bias (Article 13.3).

Finally, it obliges airlines to apply the Arab Code of Conduct for regulating and operating computerised reservation systems (CRS) (Article 17).

The agreement extensively regulates consultation and dispute resolution procedures (Articles 29–30). Consultations are obligatory before revocation of an authorisation of a designated airline (Article 11.2).

37 Multimodal transport in the League of Arab States is also ruled by the Agreement on Multimodal Transport of Goods between the Arab States, signed in Cairo on 9 September 2009.

The Damascus Agreement is open to accession by all 22 members of the League of Arab States. Importantly, it does not entirely rule out the existing bilateral ASAs between state parties. Provisions of the Damascus Agreements supersede relevant clauses in bilaterals.

However, bilateral provisions concerning issues not included in the Damascus Agreement still remain applicable (Article 2.3). The agreement precludes contracting parties from granting or even negotiating any rights to third parties that would affect the rights granted to state parties to the Damascus Agreement. Any such rights shall be negotiated and settled collectively by the state parties to the Damascus Agreement (Article 31).

However, on the basis of reciprocity, each state party may exchange the transport rights set forth in the Damascus Agreement with any group of non-party states that are gathered in an economic integration organisation. This is to accommodate state-party obligations arising from participation in other regional groupings, in particular in the African Economic Community with its 1999 Yamoussoukro Decision concerning gradual liberalisation of scheduled and non-scheduled intra-Africa air transport services.[38] The Damascus Agreement does not impede further-reaching bilateral or sub-regional liberalisation among its contracting states, that is, within the prospective Gulf states common aviation programme.

13.5 Conclusions

Aviation liberalisation initiatives throughout the world give many examples of success stories. These stories could and should become part of the Arab world. The significant effort undertaken at the ACAC level has already produced a ready instrument for air market development in this region – the discussed Damascus Agreement. Striking is the discrepancy between the economic significance of air transport to the Arab states and the rapid growth of this sector in the Arab region on the one hand, and the outdated regulatory framework for international air services on the other hand. The Arab region is probably the only so well-developed aviation market that is still based predominantly on bilateral restrictive regulations.

While the Damascus Agreement provides for a comprehensive framework for the liberalisation of air transport among Arab states, political instability in the region has plotted against its full ratification and implementation.[39] What is more, the eight state parties that have ratified the agreement still rely on bilateral agreements to govern their air services, rendering the agreement *de facto*

38 Decision Relating to the Implementation of the Yamoussoukro Declaration concerning the Liberalisation of Access to Air Transport Markets in Africa of 14 November 1999, United Nations Economic and Social Council, Economic Commission of Africa, ECA/RCID/CM. CIVAC/99/RPT, Annex 1. The Yamoussoukro Decision, entered into force on 12 August 2000. For the Yamoussoukro Declaration see also Schlumberger 2010.

39 Salazar and Fenema 2017, p. 290.

inapplicable.[40] It seems Arab League member states still have strong traditional convictions on their absolute sovereignty.

What theoretically may contribute to the low popularity of the Damascus Agreement among Arab states is that the African Arab states are engaged in two liberalisation agendas, the ACAC programme including the discussed Damascus Agreement and the mentioned Yamoussoukro Decision of the African Economic Community. However, as has been indicated, nothing precludes combining both regimes. The Damascus Agreement even includes an explicit provision that allows for such arrangement. Additionally, ACAC is well prepared for such a solution and also has a separate instrument to negotiate agreements with other regional and sub-regional groupings.[41]

It is probably more likely that the reluctance towards liberalisation within the Damascus Agreement is driven by the fact that the rapid growth of the Gulf 'Big Three' airlines (Emirates, Qatar Airways and Etihad Airways) is based on long-haul traffic to destinations outside the territories of ACAC member states.[42] This growth, although an unquestionable success, has at the same time become a trap for the intra-Arab air market development. Importantly, whereas the Damascus Agreement concerns regional Arab traffic, the key Arab market players have their fleets and strategies oriented at transcontinental international traffic. Therefore, probably, there has yet been little interest in the Damascus Agreement framework for those governments that could lead the Arab aviation liberalisation process.

This, however, may change with the development of the Arab aviation market. First, in the long term, sustainable growth of the Big Three air carriers will probably require diversified strategies that would rely less on the long-haul intercontinental traffic. These carriers have been developing a vast hub and spoke network in the Arab world to feed their trunk operations. Second, the Arab aviation boom has produced a second generation of air carriers, such as Air Arabia of Sharjah. These carriers concentrate on the regional Arab and neighbouring markets. As far as the current state of airline liberalisation allows, Air Arabia opens joint-venture subsidiaries to operate from bases in other Arab states.

With the advancement of this business model we should probably observe more interest in regional aviation liberalisation in ACAC from the Arab aviation powers. There is a fair chance that this interest will lead to international pressure that will end up in the revival of the 2004 Damascus Agreement, especially since this is a comprehensive instrument that already provides for a system of necessary economic safeguards and balances to ensure a level playing field between states of different air transport potential and development level.

40 Ibid.

41 Agreement for Collective Negotiations with Regional and Sub-Regional Groups, signed in Damascus on 19 December 2004.

42 Cf. Salazar and Fenema 2017, p. 290.

14 Air transport connectivity gap

Is regulation the answer?

Piotr P. Dziubak[*]

14.1 Air transport connectivity

Aviation is an essential element of today's global economy. It supports other sectors of the economy such as trade and tourism, creates new opportunities for business, education and culture, fosters innovation and increases labour productivity. Some studies estimate that in 2014 aviation contributed USD 2.7 trillion to the global gross domestic product (GDP). Direct benefits (i.e., employment and economic activity generated by the air transport industry) are estimated at USD 664 billion, whereas indirect benefits (generated by employment and economic activity of suppliers of the air transport industry) amount to USD 761 billion. The induced effects of aviation add up to USD 355 billion and are also related to tourism catalytic effects of USD 892 billion.[1]

The role that aviation plays in each country can be measured in numerous ways. Statistics show the number of flights, number of passengers, tonnes of cargo or mobility indicators. However, many recent studies focus on the importance of air transport connectivity. This idea refers to the level at which each country, as well as its regions and cities, is connected to other destinations around the world.[2]

The term 'connectivity' is used in other network industries, in particular in telecommunications, where adding new subscribers to the network creates opportunities for the entire network. Connectivity has implications for the flow of information and contributes to the concept of 'World City Network'.[3] The connectivity concept has also been applied to the transport sector,[4] which also has important network characteristics. In aviation connectivity reflects range, frequency of service, the economic importance of destinations and the number of onward connections available through the aviation network.

* All views expressed in this chapter should be attributed solely to the author.

1 See Air Transport Action Group 2016.

2 *Aviation: Open and Connected Europe*, Communication from the Commission to the European Parliament, the Council, the European Economic and Social Committee and the Committee of the Regions, COM(2017)286 final, 8.6.2017, p. 2.

3 See Rutherford 2005.

4 See Xie and Levinson 2007.

The studies show that connectivity is important for countries. It has implications for the growth of economy and also for regions and cities. It brings about new opportunities for the aviation industry and business in general. This is the reason why connectivity is included in national policies of many states around the world. For instance, Gulf states, in particular the United Arab Emirates (UAE), have a long tradition of supporting development of their air network,[5] which brings now tangible benefits for the economy. In Europe the connectivity issue is more often considered from a local perspective of a region or city.[6]

14.2 Measuring connectivity

Although interest in air connectivity has grown recently, this issue has already been analysed for many years by many institutions, including World Bank, International Air Transport Association (IATA) and Airport Council International. World Bank has developed the Air Connectivity Index (ACI), based on the gravity model[7] that weights value of a route based on the number of onward connections available, reflecting the benefits of hubs. IATA Connectivity Index captures the importance of destinations based on the size of the final destination airport.[8] Airport Council International has used the SEO NetScan connectivity model. It produces direct, indirect and hub connectivity indices, based on quantitative (number of weekly connections) as well as qualitative metrics.[9] According to these studies, the connectivity is correlated with GDP and there is a strong relation between the overall air connectivity of a region to other regions and the overall value of trade between those parts of the world. There is also the evidence of a relation between connectivity and labour productivity, as well as competitiveness of travel and tourism sectors.

Air connectivity has also been measured from the European perspective. Connectivity growth in Europe is not as fast as in the Middle East, Asia-Pacific region and Africa. ACI Europe statistics show that despite total connectivity growth in the EU, which can be mainly attributed to indirect connectivity, the direct connectivity in the EU decreased between 2008 and 2014. This is explained by the growing role of Middle East, Turkey and Russia and their increase of connectivity, despite the crisis of 2011. The importance of air connectivity is well recognised in the EU. The European Commission has mandated the Network Manager, which has considerable experience in preparing Air Traffic Management statistics, to conduct a regular assessment of connectivity of EU airports and regions. This exercise should provide a better understanding of EU connectivity and network effects.

5 See Hooper et al. 2011.
6 For example, Di Francesco and Pagliari 2012.
7 See Arvis and Shepherd 2016.
8 See IATA 2000.
9 See Airport Council International Europe 2016.

14.3 The connectivity gap

The term that illustrates the low level of connectivity is known as the 'connectivity gap'. Some studies define the connectivity gap as a deficiency of a region or particular country to ensure high level of connections. This section will describe the issue of air connectivity gap based on the example of Central, Eastern and Southeastern Europe. The problem has been identified by some member states of the EU, who requested the European Commission to provide the data that will illustrate it.

A respective study was prepared for the Commission by the consulting company PricewaterhouseCoopers (PwC).[10] This was to assess the social and economic effects following the bankruptcy of Malev Hungarian Airlines in February 2012. The case of Malev served as an example for the entire region, where airlines had been in fragile financial condition. The study analyses the impact of bankruptcy on connectivity and consumer welfare. The collapse of Malev was capitalised by low cost carriers (LCCs), in particular by Wizz Air, which had been already present in Hungary, and Ryanair that has drastically increased the offering on the Hungarian market.[11] The rapid change in LCC share at Budapest Liszt Ferenc International Airport affected connectivity, customer choice, service quality and fares. LCCs operated higher capacity aircrafts, offering point-to-point connections with lower frequency. Passengers lost the possibility to use long-haul direct connections to the US and China, as airlines operating on those routes lost their traffic feeder – Malev. Several European routes were no longer operated by any network carriers, which became inconvenient for business passengers who could not make a one-day trip. The level of connectivity also declined as available destinations became smaller, less connected and were usually secondary airports. The connections offered to European non-EU countries had for a period of time been limited to services operated by third-country carriers or there was no service at all. This was because some non-EU countries did not recognise the EU-designation principle and, in the absence of a Hungarian flag carrier, did not accept EU carrier services originating from Budapest.

The PwC study was supposed to provide information on the consequences of Malev collapse. However, it has also identified five key connectivity enablers that were found to be unsatisfactory for the whole Central, Eastern and Southeast Europe region: poor connections to major and secondary hubs, lack of strong flag carriers, low presence of key alliances in the region and poor intermodal connectivity. The airline consolidation process present in Western Europe has also caused some shift in the traffic and changes in connectivity levels.[12]

The described connectivity gap was largely attributable to the difference in business models between network carriers and LCCs. Network carriers organise

10 PwC 2014.
11 The LCC capacity has doubled over the period from July 2011 to July 2012.
12 Burghouwt and De Wit 2015b, pp. 104–111.

their business in line with the hub and spoke concept and achieve benefits from economies of density, by feeding the traffic from local airports in order to establish profitable long-haul routes. Their networks are characterised by geographical concentration around the hub and temporal concentration to ensure short transfer times. The design of their network structure makes the product and process very complex. LCCs offer direct connections (point-to-point), gain from aircraft utilisation economies and focus on less congested secondary airports, but generally do not offer frequent services and the possibility to transfer for other destinations.[13] Recently some convergence between these models may be observed.

14.4 Solutions to address connectivity gaps

Air connectivity is not equally spread around the world. The EU has recognised the need to address cases where, on certain routes and due to specific conditions, insufficient demand or market failure prevented provision of flights with the frequencies and capacity required to serve the needs of local communities. In such cases PSO can guarantee that peripheral or developing regions are well-connected to the rest of Europe.[14] As of April 2017 PSO was used in 12 countries in Europe[15] to mandate a minimum level of commercial air transport service in isolated regions and on thin routes, that is, with low traffic, generally in domestic traffic.

The European Commission does not provide any detailed information on how the service is organised, as it lies within the competence of EU member states or local communities. However, it has estimated the amount spent on PSO in 2014 to be EUR 330 million.[16] In 2010 PSO service was used in 11 EU countries. The detailed analysis shows that in 2010 there were 352,000 registered PSO movements in Europe, providing 36.4 million seats with total public spending of USD 747.6 million.[17] The high number of PSO services in this study is due to the Spanish discount scheme (discount for services provided between mainland and the Canary Islands and Balearic Islands and within these islands).

The EU member states use PSO to improve access to certain territories, either to expand incoming trade and tourism or to provide lifeline services for local

13 See Gillen and Morrison 2005; Pels 2008.

14 *Aviation: Open and Connected Europe*, Communication from the Commission to the European Parliament, the Council, the European Economic and Social Committee and the Committee of the Regions, COM(2017)286 final, 8.6.2017, p. 5.

15 *List of Routes (178) with Public Service Obligations*, European Commisssion, April 2017.

16 Commission Staff Working Document, SWD(2015)261 final, 7.12.2015, Accompanying the document Communication from the Commission to the European Parliament, the Council, the European Economic and Social Committee and the Committee of the Regions, *An aviation Strategy for Europe*, p. 41.

17 Allroggen, Malina and Wittman 2016, p. 120. These figures do not cover subsidies in Italy and only part of the subsidies in Greece and France.

communities. The PSO can establish a point-to-point connection or access to a wider aviation network, if the service covers a hub. The Global Connectivity Index has been used to measure how the PSO improves connectivity of a city or region. The results are mixed. Some countries, in particular Germany and France, were able to establish PSO routes to hub airports that resulted in high connectivity gains, while many others (Sweden, Norway and Greece) despite spending similar funds on PSO per movement or per seat, have not achieved such results.[18]

PSO in the EU is only allowed under very specific conditions set out in Article 16 of Regulation 1008/2008.[19] However, experience shows that the existing rules are not always implemented in a consistent manner, which may undermine the objective of safeguarding both connectivity and competition on the routes where PSO has been applied. The European Commission has, therefore, prepared interpretative guidelines to bring clarity on the questions raised by member states and local authorities in the conception, design and implementation of their PSO regimes.[20] These guidelines explain the methodology used by the European Commission to assess PSO. The aim of the guidelines was to help member states to properly apply PSO rules to address connectivity gaps. As a next step, the Commission plans to review the existing PSO rules and, if needed, to propose some changes for greater effectiveness and clarity.

In the US a measure corresponding to PSO is the Essential Air Service (EAS) programme, which addresses connectivity issues concerning a group of predefined small and rural communities. The US Department of Transportation (DOT) organises a tender procedure to establish routes that will provide eligible EAS communities with access to the National Air Transport System. The EAS contracts are awarded, after consultation and evaluation processes, to airlines that submit proposals to the DOT. EAS generally consists in subsidising two round trips a day with 30–50 seat aircraft, or additional frequencies with aircraft of nine seats or less. EAS is financed from federal budget and is initiated by the airline, not a local community, as opposed to the European PSO system.[21] In 2010 there were 164,000 EAS movements in the US that provided 3.1 million seats with total public spending of USD 155.6 million. What distinguishes EAS form PSO in Europe is the requirement to link a remote city with a major hub airport. As a result of this rule, the connectivity gains to spending ratio is much higher in the US than in Europe.[22]

18 Ibid., pp. 119–121.

19 Regulation No. 1008/2008/EC of the European Parliament and of the Council of 24 September 2008 on common rules for the operation of air services in the Community, OJ L 293, 31.10.2008, pp. 3–20.

20 *Interpretative Guidelines on Regulation (EC) No 1008/2008 – Public Service Obligations (PSO)*, Commission Notice, C(2017)3712 final, 8.6.2017.

21 PSO might be financed from the state budget or the local budget. For an overview of EAS see DOT 2017.

22 Allroggen, Malina and Wittman 2016, pp. 117–118.

Programmes like PSO or EAS play a very important role for isolated, especially islanding regions. It is worth noticing that they are not only typical for Europe or the US.[23] Australia has its Remote Air Service Subsidy. Some Caribbean countries, highly dependent on tourism, are known to subsidise airlines and airport facilities in order to maintain the aerial bridges connecting their territories to major tourism markets.[24] The International Civil Aviation Organization (ICAO), together with the World Tourism Organization, have even developed a scheme for subsidised international air services called Essential Service and Tourism Development Route.[25] It should be noted, however, that PSO, EAS and similar programmes are sometimes questioned as distorting the level playing field in aviation. The carriers in Europe and their employees often see PSO as a tool to defend local jobs.[26]

Direct regulatory contributions to connectivity consist in the above-mentioned support programmes. Other relevant regulatory factors include Air Services Agreements (ASAs) that define the level of liberalisation of the market, fiscal regimes, environmental constraints and even consumer and employee protection level. However, not only regulatory measures play their part. The connectivity is also dependent on geography that might be characterised by location of airports, demographics and size of the population, strength of economy described by GDP levels and condition of infrastructure (airport and air navigation services capacity). Connectivity is also influenced by intermodal connections, as well as the historic, cultural and trading links of a country. Finally, the connectivity is highly related to the level of airline industry development, including the existence of the network air carriers and the presence of the airline alliances.

Whereas some of the aforementioned factors to enhance connectivity are determined by geography, demography or economic development, most of them can be controlled by proper aviation policies. This might take a form of infrastructure improvements that will be contributing to greater air transport capacity. Equally significant may be the development of network carriers that would add destinations to the network and ensure further connections to long-haul service.[27] Development of fast and reliable rail and road connections to the airports would also be beneficial. Such actions should be taken with careful planning and good monitoring.[28]

23 Similar programmes exist in Australia (Remote Air Service Subsidy – RASS) or in Canada (where the support is different for National Airport System – biggest airports and regional/local airports).

24 See Holder 2010.

25 See Walulik 2017, p. 186.

26 Tretheway and Andriulaitis 2015, pp. 100–101.

27 It should be noted that not only network carriers, but also LCCs can bring important possibilities for connectivity, as self-hubbing is becoming more popular.

28 Importantly, in the EU the European Commission is currently developing a connectivity index to better identify connectivity gaps and to benchmark different levels of air services between EU regions.

These solutions belong to national economic policies and go hand-in-hand with taxation and administration efficiency. However, they may constitute an important alternative to direct regulation. The European Commission's recent plans to review PSO rules within the framework of Regulation 1008/2008 offer a good opportunity to rethink the role of market regulation in ensuring connectivity. As has been indicated, reinforcing air networks in today's forms such as PSO has limited potential to improve connectivity and can also undermine fair competition. This issue has to be analysed together with the antitrust policy, merger and state aid control functions of the European Commission.

14.5 Conclusions

This chapter has described the role aviation plays in today's global economy and presented measures that describe the importance of this sector for each country. It has focused on the air transport connectivity and has referred to the metrics that are used to capture this phenomenon. It has further developed on the connectivity gap and explored possible measures to reduce it. The chapter has presented a literature review on the subject and pointed to key findings in the light of the Malev collapse in 2012, which had consequences for the entire Central, Eastern and Southeastern Europe region. Some measures have been discussed that are used to limit the connectivity gap in Europe and elsewhere, namely PSO, EASs and similar programmes. This has led to the conclusion that according to the recent studies, these measures were not always efficient and were even questioned for distorting level playing field in aviation. Finally, some other factors that may influence the level of connectivity have been discussed. It is recommended that further studies are undertaken on these non-regulatory solutions to improve connectivity and facilitate air policy development.

Bibliography

Abeyratne R. (2004), *Space Tourism – Parallel Synergies between Air and Space Law?* Zeitschrift für Luft- und Weltraumrecht, 53, 184–202.

Abeyratne R. (2014), *Convention on International Civil Aviation. A Commentary*, Cham: Springer International Publishing.

Abeyratne R. (2015), *Global Market-Based Measures for Aviation Emissions*, Environmental Policy and Law, 45, 102–127.

Ahmad T. (2014), *Environment Effectiveness of ICAO's Basket of Mitigation Measures to Arrest Emissions from International Civil Aviation*, Annals of Air and Space Law, 39, 75–128.

Air Transport Action Group. (2016), *Aviation Benefits Beyond Borders.* https://aviationbenefits.org/media/149668/abbb2016_full_a4_web.pdf.

Air Transport News. (2014), *Gulf Carriers Compete for World Dominance*, 1.7.2014.

Airline. (1992), *Airline Official Gave $100,000 to GOP*, Washington Post, 6.12.1992.

Airlines. (1998), *Airlines Behaving Badly: The Code-Sharing Threat*, Consumer Reports Travel Letter, 14.

Airport Council International Europe. (2016), *Airport Industry Connectivity Report.* Retrieved from www.aci-europe.org/policy/connectivity.html.

All. (2009), *All Hail, Bob Crandall*, dallasnews.com, 17.4.2009, www.dallasnews.com/business/airlines/2009/04/17/all-hail-bob-crandall.

Alliances. (2000), *Alliances Fail to Convince Agents*, Travel Trade Gazette UK and Ireland, 25.9.2000.

Allroggen F., Malina R., Wittman M.D. (2016), *Public Service Obligations for Air Transport in the United States and Europe: Connectivity Effects and Value for Money*, Transportation Research Part A: Policy and Practice, 94, 112–128.

Arab Air Carriers Organization. (2009), *Annual Report*, 42nd General Assembly, Jeddah.

Armantier O., Richard O. (2006), *Evidence on Pricing from the Continental Airlines and Northwest Airlines Code-Share Agreement* [in:] D. Lee (ed.), *Advances in Airline Economics 1*, Boston: Elsevier, 91–109.

Arvis J.F., Shepherd B. (2016), *Measuring Connectivity in a Globally Networked Industry: The Case of Air Transport*, The World Economy, 39, 369–385.

ASEAN. (2017), *ASEAN Nations Meet to Discuss Formation of Single Aviation Market*, malasiandigest.com, 5.9.2017, www.malaysiandigest.com/world/695924-asean-members-work-together-to-build-up-single-aviation-market.html.

Ashby E. (2017), *International Aviation and Climate Change*, Michigan Journal of Environmental and Administrative Law Blog, 11. 4.2017, www.mjeal-online.org/international-aviation-and-climate-change/.

Balfour J. (2002), *EC Policy on State Aid to Airlines Following 11 September 2001*, Air and Space Law, 27, 398–405.

Balfour J., Bisset M. (eds.) (2016), *Getting the Deal through – Air Transport 2017*, London: Law Business Research Ltd.

Bamber G.J., Hoffer Gittell J., Kochan T.A., Von Nordenflycht A. (2009), *Contrasting Management and Employment-Relations Strategies in European Airlines*, Journal of Industrial Relations, 50, 635–652.

Baruah R. (2016), *A Legal Discourse on Subsidies in Air Transport. Trade War, Fair Competition and WTO* (LLM thesis), Institute of Air and Space Law, Leiden University.

Bergamasco F. (2015), *State Subsidies and Fair Competition in International Air Services: The European Perspective*, Issues in Aviation Law and Policy, 15, 29–76.

Birchfield V.L. (2015), *Coercion with Kid Gloves? The European Union's Role in Shaping a Global Regulatory Framework for Aviation Emissions*, Journal of European Public Policy, 22, 1276–1294.

Blackwell W. (2011), *Regional Liberalisation of Trade in Services. The World Economy*, Journal of World Trade, 34, 725–740.

Bodansky D., Brunnée J., Rajamani L. (2017), *International Climate Change Law*, Oxford: Oxford University Press.

Bogejević S. (2012), *Legalising Environmental Leadership: A Comment on the CJEU's Ruling in C-366/10 of Inclusion of Aviation in the EU Emission Trading Scheme*, Journal of Environmental Law, 24, 345–356.

Böhmann K. (2001), *The Ownership and Control Requirement in U.S. and European Union Air Law and U.S. Maritime Law – Policy; Consideration; Comparison*, Journal of Air Law and Commerce, 66, 689–738.

Boisson de Chazournes L. (2000), *Unilateralism and Environmental Protection: Issues of Perception and Reality of Issues*, European Journal of International Law, 11, 315–338.

Bourély M. (1991), *Quelques réflexions au sujet des législations spatiales nationales*, Annals of Air and Space Law, 16, 245–266.

Brenner M., Leet J., Schott E. (1985), *Airline Deregulation*, Washington, DC: ENO Foundation.

Brueckner J.K., Whalen W.T. (2000), *The Price Effects of International Airline Alliances*, Journal of Law and Economics, 43, 503–545.

Buenger M.L. (2013), *The EU's ETS and Global Aviation: Why 'Local Rules' Still Matter and May Matter Even More in the Future*, Denver Journal of International Law and Policy, 41, 417–465.

Burghouwt G., De Wit J. (2015a), *EU Air Transport Liberalisation: Process, Impacts and Future Considerations*, OECD International Transport Forum, Discussion Paper No. 2015/04. Paris: OECD.

Burghouwt G., De Wit J. (2015b), *In the Wake of Liberalisation: Long-Term Developments in the EU Air Transport Market*, Transport Policy, 43, 104–113.

Byerly J. (2004), *US–EU Aviation Relations – Charting the Course for Success. Remarks before the International Aviation Club*, Washington, DC, 13.7.2004.

Carpanelli E. (2015), *Il difficile dialogo tra dimensione universale e dimensione regionale sulle emissioni di gas a effetto serra derivanti dall'aviazione civile internazionale*, Diritto dei Trasporti, 28, 695–738.

Carrington D. (2016), *What Does a $250, 000 Ticket to Space with Virgin Galactic Actually Buy You?* CNN, 16.8.2013, https://edition.cnn.com/travel/article/virgin-galactic-250000-ticket-to-space/index.html.

Chatzipanagiotis M. (2011), *The Impact of Liability Rules on the Development of Private Commercial Human Spaceflight*, 54th Colloquium on the Law of Outer Space, Prague.

Clyde & Co. (2003), *Aviation Bulletin*, 2–3 February 2003.

Conforti B., Focarelli C. (2015), *Le Nazioni Unite*, Padova: CEDAM.

Cosmas A, Belobaba P., Swelbar W. (2011), *Framing the Discussion on Regulatory Liberalisation: A Stakeholder Analysis of Open Skies, Ownership and Control*, International Journal of Aviation Management, 1, 17–39.

Cristea A., Hillberry R., Mattoo A. (2014), *Open Skies over the Middle East*, World Bank Policy Research Working Paper, No. 6937.

Dasgupta U. (2013), *Legal Issues on Sub-Orbital Space Tourism: International and National Law Perspectives*, Annals of Air and Space Law, 38.

Dean W., Shane J.N. (2010), *Alliances, Immunity and the Future of Aviation*, Air and Space Lawyer, 22(1), 17–22.

Dempsey P.S. (1978), *The International Rate & Route Revolution in North Atlantic Passenger Transportation*, Columbia Journal of Transnational Law, 17, 393–449.

Dempsey P.S. (1979), *The Rise and Fall of the Civil Aeronautics Board – Opening Wide the Floodgates of Entry*, Transportation Law Journal, 11, 91–185.

Dempsey P.S. (1987), *Law and Foreign Policy in International Aviation*, Dobbs Ferry, NY: Transnational Publishers.

Dempsey P.S. (1989), *America's Grand Experiment in Airline Deregulation: Good Intentions and Bad Results*, Annals Air and Space Law, 14, 21–34.

Dempsey P.S. (1990), *Airline Deregulation and Laissez Faire Mythology: Economic Theory in Turbulence*, Journal of Air Law and Commerce, 56, 305–412.

Dempsey P.S. (1991), *The Disintegration of the U.S. Airline Industry*, Transportation Law Journal, 20, 9–46.

Dempsey P.S. (1992), *European Aviation Regulation: Flying through the Liberalization Labyrinth*, Boston College International and Competition Law Review, 15, 311–374.

Dempsey P.S. (1994a), *The Prospectus for Survival and Growth in Commercial Aviation*, Annals Air and Space Law, 19, 163–219.

Dempsey P.S. (1994b), *Must the Airline Industry Collapse?* Jurisconsultus, 59–78.

Dempsey P.S. (1995), *Airlines in Turbulence: Strategies for Survival*, Transportation Law Journal, 23, 15–98.

Dempsey P.S. (2001), *Competition in the Air: European Union Regulation of Commercial Aviation*, Journal of Air Law and Commerce, 66, 979–1153.

Dempsey P.S. (2002a), *Predatory Pricing & Monopolization in the Airline Industry: A Case Study of Minneapolis/St. Paul*, Transportation Law Journal, 29, 129–187.

Dempsey P.S. (2002b), *Predation, Competition & Antitrust Law: Turbulence in the Airline Industry*, Journal of Air Law and Commerce, 67, 685–840.

Dempsey P.S. (2003), *The Cyclical Crisis in Commercial Aviation: Causes and Potential Cures*, Annals Air and Space Law, 28, 1–17.

Dempsey P.S. (2004), *European Aviation Law*, The Hague; London; Boston, MA: Kluwer Law International.

Dempsey P.S. (2006), *Nationality Requirements and Cabotage Restrictions in International Aviation: Sovereignty Won and Sovereignty Lost*, Studies in Air and Space Law, 20, 129–151.

Dempsey P.S. (2008a), *The Financial Performance of the Airline Industry Post-Deregulation*, Houston Law Review, 45, 422–485.

Dempsey P.S. (2008b), *Public International Air Law*, Montréal: McGill University, Institute and Centre for Research in Air and Space Law.

Dempsey P.S. (2016), *National Laws Governing Commercial Space Activities: Legislation, Regulation, & Enforcement*, Northwestern Journal of International Law and Business, 36, 1–44.

Dempsey P.S. (2017), *Public International Air Law*, 2nd ed., Montréal: McGill University, Institute and Centre for Research in Air and Space.

Dempsey P.S., Mineiro M. (2010), *The ICAO's Legal Authority to Regulate Aerospace Vehicles* [in:] J.N. Pelton, R. Jakhu (eds.), *Introduction to Space Safety Regulations and Standards*, Oxford, UK; Burlington, MA: Elsevier, 245–256.

Denton N., Dennis N. (2000) *Airline Franchising in Europe: Benefits and Disbenefits to Airlines and Consumers*, Journal of Air Transport Management, 6, 179–190.

De Wit J. (2013), *Unlevel Playing Field? Ah Yes You Mean Protectionism*, Journal of Air Transport Management, 41, 22–29.

Di Francesco A., Pagliari R. (2012), *The Potential Impact of Removing Public Service Obligation Regulations on Air Fares between the Italian Mainland and the Island of Sardinia*, Journal of Transport Geography, 24, 332–339.

Dobson N. (2017), *Maintaining the Pressure: The EU Leaves ICAO Hanging Despite 'Historic' Emissions Agreement for Civil Aviation*, Renforce Blog, 19. 3.2017, http://blog.renforce.eu/index.php/en/2017/03/19/maintaining-the-pressure-the-eu-leaves-icao-hanging-despite-historic-emissions-agreement-for-civil-aviation/.

Doganis R. (2001), *The Airline Business in the Twenty-First Century*, London; New York: Routledge.

Doganis R. (2002), *Flying off Course: The Economics of International Airlines*, London; New York: Routledge.

Doganis R. (2006), *The Airline Business in the Twenty-first Century*, 2nd ed., London; New York: Routledge.

Doganis R. (2010), *Flying off Course: Airline Economics and Marketing*, Abingdon, UK; New York, NY: Routledge.

DOT. (2015), *IATFCPA Complaints*, Press release, www.transportation.gov/policy/aviation-policy/iatfcpa-complaints.

DOT. (2017), *Essential Air Service: Overview*, Press release, www.transportation.gov/policy/aviation-policy/small-community-rural-air-service/essential-air-service.

easyJet. (1996), *easyJet threatens KLM*, Flight International, 7. 8.1996, www.flightglobal.com/news/articles/easyjet-threatens-klm-12225/.

Ebbesson J. (2013), *Global or European Only? International Law on Transparency in Environmental Matters for Members of the Public* [in:] A. Bianchi, A. Peters (eds.), *Transparency in International Law*, Cambridge, New York: Cambridge University Press, 49–75.

Erling U.M. (2017), *International Aviation Emissions under International Civil Aviation Organization's Global Market Based Measure: Ready for Offsetting?* Air and Space Law, 42, 1–12.

ETF. (2014), *Social Dumping in Civil Aviation*, Brussels: European Transport Workers' Federation.

European Commission. (2002), *Commission Closes Probe into KLM/NorthWest and Lufthansa/SAS/United Airlines Transatlantic Air Alliances*, Press release, Brussels, 29.10.2002.

European Commission. (2016), *Antitrust: Commission sends Statement of Objections to Brussels Airlines and TAP Portugal on Code-Sharing on Brussels-Lisbon Route*, Press release, Brussels, 27.10.2016.

European Commission. (2017), *Antitrust: Commission Re-Adopts Decision and Fines Air Cargo Carriers €776 Million for Price-Fixing Cartel*, Press release, Brussels, 17.3.2017.

Farand A. (2010), *The Influence of Space Tourism on Space Activities in General*, paper presented at Conference The Regulation of Suborbital Flights in the European Context, Leiden, 16.10.2010.

Fitzgerald P.P. (2011), *In Defense of the Nationality of Aircraft*, Annals of Air and Space Law, 36, 81–132.

Fitzmaurice M. (2017), *Legitimacy of International Environmental Law. The Sovereign States Overwhelmed by Obligations: Responsibility to React to Problems Beyond National Jurisdiction?* Heidelberg Journal of International Law, 77, 339–370.

Foerster D. (2001), *Caged Birds in Open Skies: Comments on the Emergence of a Dominant Carrier*, Asper Review of International Business and Trade Law, 1, 171–184.

Fones R.W. (2015), *Airline Consolidations and Competition Law–What Next?* FIU Law Review, 10, 447–465.

Forsyth P. (2011), *The Economics of 7th Freedom* [in:] J.F. O'Connell, G. Williams (eds.), *Air Transport in the 21st Century: Key Strategic Developments*, Farnham, UK; Burlington, VT: Ashgate, 211–234.

Fox E.M., Ordover J.A. (1994), *Antitrust – Harmonization, Accommodation and Coordination of Law*, paper presented at the Tokyo meeting of the project on Competition Policy in a Global Economy.

Freeland S., Jakhu R.S. (2009), *Article II* [in:] S. Hobe, B. Schmidt-Tedd, K.U. Schrogl (eds.), *Outer Space Treaty (Vol. I, Cologne Commentary on Space Law)*, Köln: Carl Heymanns Verlag, 44–63.

Gaines S.E., Olsen B.E., Sørensen K.E. (eds.) (2012), *Liberalising Trade in the EU and the WTO: A Legal Comparison*, Cambridge: Cambridge University Press.

Gattini A. (2012), *Between Splendid Isolation and Tentative Imperialism: The EU's Extension of Its Emission Trading Scheme to International Aviation and the ECJ's Judgment in the ATA Case*, International and Comparative Law Quarterly, 61, 977–991.

Gayle P. (2008), *An Empirical Analysis of the Competitive Effects of the Delta/Continental/Northwest Codeshare Alliance*, Journal of Law and Economics, 51, 743–766.

General Court of the European Union. (2015), *The General Court Annuls the Decision by Which the Commission Imposed Fines Amounting to Approximately €790 Million on Several Airlines for their Participation in a Cartel on the Airfreight Market*, Press Release No. 147/15, Luxembourg, 16.12.2015.

Gerhard M. (2011), *Space Tourism – The Authorisation of Suborbital Space Transportation* [in:] F.G. von der Dunk (ed.), *National Space Legislation in Europe*, Leiden: Martinus Nijhoff Publishers, 263–296.

Ghoshal S., Bush D. (2008), *Predatory Conduct and Predatory Legislation: Exclusionary Tactics in Airline Markets*, Houston Law Review, 45, 344–394.

Giemulla E., Van Schyndel H. (2011), *Aviation and the European Emissions Trading Scheme* [in:] E. Giemulla, L. Weber (eds.), *International and EU Aviation Law. Selected Issues*, Alphen aan den Rijn: Kluwer Law International, 377–393.

Giemulla E., Weber L. (2011), *International and EU Aviation Law: Selected Issues*, Alphen Den Rijn: Kluwer Law International.

Gillen D., Morrison W. (2005), *Regulation, Competition and Network Evolution in Aviation*, Journal of Air Transport Management, 11, 161–174.

Gillespie W., Richard O.M. (2012), *Antitrust Immunity Grants to Joint Venture Agreements: Evidence from International Airline Alliances*, Antitrust Law Journal, 78, 443–469.

Goldberg L. (1999), *International Airline Partnerships Are Drawing Praise – And Some Flak*, Houston Chronicle, 10.1.1999.

Goodman T.W. (2010), *To the End of the Earth: A Study of a Boundary between Earth and Space*, Journal of Space Law, 36, 87–114.

Gorove S. (1991), *Developments in Space Law: Issues and Policies*, Dordrecht: Springer Netherlands.

Graham N. (2014), *Message from the ICAO* [in:] R. Jakhu, K.W. Chen (eds.), *Regulation of Emerging Modes of Aerospace Transportation*, Montréal: McGill University, 1–3.

Gray R.R. (1978), *The Impact of Bermuda II on Future Bilateral Agreements*, Air Law, 3, 17–22.

Gremminger M. (2003), *The Commission's Approach Towards Global Airline Alliances – Some Evolving Assessment Principles*, EC Competition Policy Newsletter, 1, 75–79.

Grief N. (1994), *International law in the Airspace of the High Seas*, Dordrecht; Boston; London: Martinus Nijhoff Publishers.

Haanappel P.P.C. (1980), *Bilateral Air Transport Agreements – 1913–1980*, Maryland Journal of International Law, 5, 241–267.

Haanappel P.P.C. (1984a), *Pricing and Capacity Determination in International Air Transport. A Legal Analysis*, Deventer: Kluwer.

Haanappel P.P.C. (1984b), *An Analysis of U.S. Deregulation of Air Transport and Its Inferences for a More Liberal Air Transport Policy in Europe*, Council of Europe Parliamentary Assembly, Committee on Economic Affairs and Development, AS/Ec (36) 3, 21.5.1984.

Haanappel P.P.C. (2001), *Airline Ownership and Control and Some Related Matters*, Air and Space Law, 26, 90–103.

Haanappel P.P.C. (2003), *The Law and Policy of Air Space and Outer Space. A Comparative Approach*, The Hague; London; New York: Kluwer Law International.

Hand R.W. (2011), *Continental Joins the (All) Star Alliance: Antitrust Concerns With Airline Alliances and Open-Skies Treaties*, Houston Journal of International Law, 33, 641–678.

Hardin G. (1968), *The Tragedy of the Commons*, Science, 162, 1243–1248.

Hartmann J. (2012), *The European Emissions Trading System and Extraterritorial Jurisdiction*, EJILTalk!, 23. 4.2012, www.ejiltalk.org/the-european-emissions-trading-system-and-extraterritorial-jurisdiction/.

Hartmann J. (2014), *A Battle for the Skies: Applying the European Emissions Trading System to International Aviation*, Nordic Journal of International Law, 82, 187–220.

Hartmann J. (2015), *Unilateralism in International Law: Implications of the Inclusion of Emissions from Aviation in the EU ETS*, Questions of International Law, Zoom-In, 11, 19–32, www.qil-qdi.org/wp-content/uploads/2015/01/03_Aviation_Hartmann.pdf.

Havel B.F. (2009), *Beyond Open Skies: A New Regime for International Aviation*, Alphen aan den Rijn: Kluwer Law International.

Havel B.F., Mulligan J.Q. (2012), *The Triumph of Politics: Reflections on the Judgment of the Court of Justice of the European Union Validating the Inclusion of Non-EU Airlines in the Emission Trading Scheme*, Air and Space Law, 37, 3–33.

Havel B.F., Sanchez G.S. (2014), *The Principles and Practice of International Aviation Law*, New York: Cambridge University Press.

Hey E. (2016), *Advanced Introduction to International Environmental Law*, Cheltenham; Northampton: Edward Elgar.

Hobe S. (2007), *Legal Aspects of Space Tourism*, Nebraska Law Review, 86, 439–458.

Hobe S. (2009), *Article I* [in:] S. Hobe, B. Schmidt-Tedd, K.U. Schrogl (eds.), *Outer Space Treaty (Vol. I, Cologne Commentary on Space Law)*, Köln: Carl Heymanns Verlag, 25–43.

Hobe S. et al. (2005), *A New Chapter for Europe in Space*, Zeitschrift für luft- und Weltraumrecht, 54, 336–356.

Hobe S., Goh G.M., Neumann J. (2007), *Space Tourism Activities – Emerging Challenges to Air and Space Law?* Journal of Space Law, 33, 359–374.

Hocking A.J. (2011), *Ownership and Control in Australia's Air Services Agreements: Further Reform Needed for Genuine Commercial Freedom?* Annals of Air and Space Law, 36, 29–80.

Holder J.S. (2010), *Don't Burn our Bridges: The Case for Owning Airlines*, Kingston, Jamaica: University of the West Indies Press.

Hooper P., Walker S., Moore C., Al Zubaidi Z. (2011), *The Development of the Gulf's Air Transport Networks – The First Century*, Journal of Air Transport Management, 17, 325–332.

Horan H. (2010), *'Double Marginalization' and the Counter-Revolution against Liberal Airline Competition*, Transportation Law Journal 37, 251–291.

Huang J. (2009), *Aviation Safety and ICAO*, Alpen aan den Rijn: Kluwer Law International.

Hughes T.R., Rosenberg E. (2005), *Space Travel Law (and Politics): The Evolution of the Commercial Space Launch Amendments Act of 2004*, Journal of Space Law, 31, 1–79.

Hylton K.N. (2011), *'Brown Shoe' Versus the Horizontal Merger Guidelines*, Boston University School of Law Working Paper No. 11-05, www.bu.edu/law/workingpapers-archive/documents/hyltonk020311.pdf.

IATA. (2000), *Global Airport Connectivity Monitor.*

IATA. (2016), *Collaboration Needed to Stem Unruly Passenger Incidents*, Press Release No. 53, 28. 9.2016, www.iata.org/pressroom/pr/Pages/2016-09-28-01.aspx.

IATA. (2017), *2036 Forecast Reveals Air Passengers Will Nearly Double to 7.8 Billion*, Press Release No. 55, 24.10.2017, www.iata.org/pressroom/pr/Pages/2017-10-24-01.aspx.

Iatrou K., Oretti M. (2007), *Airline Choices for the Future: From Alliances to Mergers*, Aldershot, UK; Burlington, VT: Ashgate.

ICAO (2012) *Consumer Protection and Definition of Passenger Rights in Different* Contexts *(Presented by the Secretariat)*, ICAO ATConf/6-WP/5, 7. 12.2012.

InterVISTAS-EU. (2009), *The Impact of International Air Service Liberalisation on the United Arab Emirates.*

Ito H., Lee D. (2007), *Domestic Code Sharing, Alliances, and Airfares in the U.S. Airline Industry*, Journal of Law and Economics, 50, 355–380.

Jakhu R.S. (2007), *Some Legal Aspects of Commercial Development of Space*, paper presented at McGill University Institute of Air and Space Law Conference in Macau, 16-21.4.2007.

Jakhu R.S., Bhattacharya R. (2002), *Legal Aspects of Space Tourism*, Proceedings of the Forty Fifth Colloquium on the Law of Outer Space, International Institute of Space Law of the International Astronautical Federation, Houston, TX, 10-19.10.2002.

James R., Michaels D. (2013), *Etihad Airways Builds Global Reach*, Wall Street Journal, 24.12.2013.

Jančić D. (2015), *The Transatlantic Connection. Democratizing Euro-American Relations through Parliamentary Liason* [in:] S. Stavridis, D. Irrera (eds.), *The European Parliament and its International Relations*, Abingdon, UK; New York, NY: Routledge, 178–196.

Jasentuliyana N. (1997), *Space Law: The Newest Branch of International Law*, Annals of Air and Space Law, 22, 343–362.

Jorens Y., Gillis D., Valcke L., De Coninck J. (2015), *Atypical Forms of Employment in the Aviation Sector*, European Social Dialogue, European Commission.

Kader B.A. (2011), *Diversification Raises Non-Oil Share of UAE's GDP to 71%*, Gulf News Economy, 18.4.2011, http://gulfnews.com/business/economy/diversification-raises-non-oil-share-of-uae-s-gdp-to-71-1.795268.

Kass H. (1994), *Cabotage and Control: Bringing 1938 U.S. Aviation Policy into the Jet Age*, Case Western Reserve Journal of International Law, 26, 143–181.

Kayser V. (1991), *An Achievement of Domestic Space Law: U.S. Regulation of Private Commercial Launch Services*, Annals of Air and Space Law, 16, 341–379.

Kazemi H., Mahmoudi H., Golroo A.A. (2011), *Towards a New International Space Liability Regime Alongside the Liability Convention 1971*, 55th Colloquium on the Law of Outer Space, Naples.

Klem R.H., Leister D.V. (1979), *The Struggle for a Competitive Market Structure in International Aviation: The Benelux Protocols Take United States Policies a Step Forward*, Law and Policy in International Business, 11, 557–592.

Klotz I. (2017), *Spaceflight. Virgin Galactic Aims to Fly Space Tourists in 2018, CEO Says*, space.com, 28.4.2017, www.space.com/36654-virgin-galactic-fly-space-tourists-2018.html.

Korber Gonçalves V. (2017), *Climate Change and International Civil Aviation Negotiations*, Contexto Internacional, 39, 443–458.

Kulovesi K. (2015), *Unilateral Extraterritorial Action or 'Minilateralism' within Territorial Jurisdiction? The EU Emission Trading Scheme for Aviation Emissions and International Law*, Questions of International Law, Zoom-In, 11, 3–17, www.qil-qdi.org/wp-content/uploads/2015/01/02_Aviation_Kulovesi.pdf.

Labory S., Malgarini M. (2000), *Regulation in Europe: Justified Burden or Costly Failure?* [in:] G. Galli, J. Pelkmans (eds.), *Regulatory Reform and Competitiveness in Europe. Vol. 1: Horizontal Issues*, Cheltenham, UK; Northampton, MA: Edward Elgar, 81–126.

Langston S.M. (2011), *Suborbital Flights: A Comparative Analysis of National and International Law*, Journal of Space Law, 37, 299–325.

Lee R.J. (2000), *The Australia Space Activities Act: Creating a Regulatory Regime for Space Activities*, Air and Space Law, 25, 57–61.

Lelieur I. (2002), *Law and Policy of Substantial Ownership and Effective Control of Airlines: Prospects for Change* (PhD thesis), Institute of Air and Space Law, McGill University.

Levine M. (2006), *Why Weren't the Airlines Reregulated?* Yale Journal on Regulation, 23, 269–297.

Light A. (1998), *European Airline Industry Review*, Salomon Smith Barney, 5.3.1998.

Loy F.E. (1968), *Bilateral Air Transport Agreements: Some Problems of Finding a Fair Route Exchange* [in:] E. McWhinney, M. Bradley (eds.), *The Freedom of the Air*, Leyden; Dobbs Ferry, NY: Sijthoff, Oceana Publications.

Łukaszuk L. (2006), *Rola ONZ w kształtowaniu prawa kosmicznego*, Stosunki międzynarodowe, 33, 9–27.

Majid A.A. (1983), *Impact of Current US Policy on International Civil Aviation*, Zeitschrift für Luft-und Weltraumrecht, 32, 295–325.

Majone G. (2005), *The Political Economy of Regulation* [in:] G. Majone (ed.), *Regulating Europe*, London; New York: Routledge.

Manzini P., Masutti A. (2012), *The Application of the EU ETS System to the Aviation Sector: From Legal Disputes to International Retaliations?* Air and Space Law, 37, 307–324.

Marboe I., Neumann J., Schrogl K.U. (2013), *The 1968 Agreement on the Rescue of Astronauts, the Return of Astronauts and the Return of Objects Launched into Outer Space* [in:] S. Hobe, B. Schmidt-Tedd, K.U. Schrogl (eds.), *Rescue Agreement/ Liability Convention/Registration Convention/Moon Agreement (Vol. II, Cologne Commentary on Space Law)*, Köln: Carl Heymanns Verlag, 1–82.

Marciacq J.-B., Morier Y., Tomasello F., Erdélyi Z., Gerhard M. (2010a), *Accommodating Sub-Orbital Flights into the EASA Regulatory System* [in:] J.N. Pelton, R.S. Jakhu (eds.), *Space Safety Regulations and Standards*, Oxford, UK; Burlington, MA: Butterworth-Heinemann, 187–212.

Marciacq J.-B., Morier Y., Tomasello F., Erdélyi Z., Gerhard M. (2010b), *Towards Regulating Suborbital Flights: An Updated EASA Approach*, 61st International Astronautical Congress, Prague, 2010, Paper IAC-10-D2.9.5.

Markhvida K. (2017), *Antitrust and Competition Law* [in:] P.S. Dempsey, R. Jakhu (eds.), *Routledge Handbook of Public Aviation Law*, Abingdon, UK; New York, NY: Routledge, 308–389.

Martínez-García J.D. (2012), *The EC Decision to Include the Aviation Activities in the European Emissions Trading System (EU ETS): A Breach of International Law?* Revista Colombiana de Derecho Internacional, 20, 103–130.

Maslen R. (2015), *Analysis: Airlines in the Middle East – The Biggest and Fastest Growing Operators*, routesonline.com, 17.9.2015, www.routesonline.com/news/29/breaking-news/250952/analysis-airlines-in-the-middle-east-the-biggest-and-fastest-growing-operators/.

Masson-Zwaan T. (2015), *Liability and Insurance in Air and Space Law; Regulation of Suborbital Flights in Europe*, ICAO/UNOOSA Aerospace Symposium, 18-20.3.2015.

Mayer B. (2012), *Case C-366/10, Air Transport Association of American Airlines and Others v. Secretary of State for Energy and Climate Change, Judgment of the Court of Justice (Grand Chamber) of 21 December 2012*, Common Market Law Review, 49, 1113–1139.

McCartney S. (1997), *Are Airline Alliances Bad News for Consumers?* Wall Street Journal, 17.6.1997.

McGonigle S. (2013), *Past its Use-by Date: Regulation 868 Concerning Subsidy and State Aid in International Air Services*, Air and Space Law, 38, 1–20.

McShea S. (1997), *The 'Dominant Position' Doctrine and the European Union's Response to the British Airways/American Airlines Alliance*, Boston College International and Comparative Law Review, 23, 71–90.

Mendes de Leon P. (2012), *Enforcement of the EU ETS: The EU's Convulsive Efforts to Export Its Environmental Values*, Air and Space Law, 37, 287–306.

Mendes de Leon P. (2017), *An Introduction to Air Law*, Alphen Den Rijn: Kluwer Law International.

Meneghetti A., Perrotta P. (eds.) (2017), *The International Comparative Legal Guide to Aviation Law 2017*, London: Global Legal Group Ltd.

Milde M. (2008), *International Air Law and ICAO*, Utrecht: Eleven International Publishing.

Milde M. (2016), *International Air Law and ICAO*, 3rd ed., The Hague: Eleven International Publishing.

Milligan J (2017), *European Union Competition Law in the Airline Industry*, Kluwer Law International.

Mirmina S. (2010), *Regulation on Suborbital Vehicles: One Perspective from the U.S.*, paper presented at conference The Regulation of suborbital flights in the European Context, Leiden, 16.10.2010.

Mohan M. (2014), *Ray of Hope for Airline Alliances: Consideration of Out of Market Efficiencies by the European Commission*, Air and Space Law, 39, 155–162.

Morgera E. (2014), *The EU and Environmental Multilateralism: The Case of Access and Benefit-Sharing and the Need for a Good-Faith Test*, Cambridge Yearbook of European Legal Studies, 16, 109–142.

Mullen L.E. (2013), *The European Union Overstepping its Bounds and Borders: The Extraterritorial Effect of the Emissions Trading System and its Call for Multilateral Action*, University of Pittsburgh Law Review, 74, 783–801.

Nase V. (2012), *Delimitation and the Suborbital Passenger: Time to Prevarication*, Journal of Air Law and Commerce, 77, 747–764.

Nesgos P.D. (1991), *Commercial Space Transportation; a New Industry Emerges*, Annals of Air and Space Law, 16, 393–421.

Northwest. (1992), *Northwest Co-Chair Gave to GOP Prior to Airline Rules*, Denver Post, 6.12.1992.

Nyman-Metcalf K. (1999), *Activities in Space – Appropriation or Use?* Uppsala: Iustus Förlag.

O'Brien Z.N. (2004), *Report of the IISL Space law Colloquium in Vancouver, Canada, October* 2004 [in:] Proceeding of the Forty Seventh Colloquium on the Law of Outer Space, International Institute of Space Law of the International Astronautical Federation, Vancouver, Canada, 4–8.10.2004, 1–17.

O'Connell J.F. (2011), *The Rise of the Arabian Gulf Carriers: An Insight into the Business Model of Emirates Airline*, Journal of Air Transport Management, 17, 339–346.

O'Donnell D.J., Hurtak J.J. (2011), *The Suborbital Private Space Flights May Require a Law Suit to Escape Benefit Sharing*, 54th Colloquium on the Law of Outer Space, Prague.

O'Leary A. (2017), *Transparency and ICAO's Aviation Offsetting Scheme: Two Separate Concepts?* Paper of the Sabin Center for Climate Change Law of Columbia Law School.

Open. (2011), *Open the Skies*, The Economist, 12.11.2011.

Ordyna P. (2010), *Insuring Human Space Flight: An Underwriter's Dilemma*, Journal of Space Law, 36, 231–252.

Oxford Economics. (2011a), *Economic Benefits from Air Transport in the UAE*. www.iata.org/policy/Documents/Benefits-of-Aviation-UAE-2011.pdf.

Oxford Economics. (2011b), *Economic Benefits from Air Transport in Jordan*. www.iata.org/policy/Documents/Benefits-of-Aviation-Jordan-2011.pdf.

Oxford Economics. (2011c), *Economic Benefits from Air Transport in Egypt*. www.iata.org/policy/Documents/Benefits-of-Aviation-Egypt-2011.pdf.

Oxley D. (2017), *Air Passenger Market Analysis – December 2017*, IATA Economics, 1.2.2018, www.iata.org/publications/economics/Reports/pax-monthly-analysis/passenger-analysis-dec-2017.pdf.

Park J.-H., Zhang A. (2000), *An Empirical Analysis of Global Airline Alliances: Cases in North Atlantic Markets*, Review of Industrial Organization, 16, 367–384.

Patel B. (2008), *A Flight Plan Towards Financial Stability – The History and Future of Foreign Ownership Restrictions in the United States Aviation Industry*, Journal of Air Law and Commerce, 73, 487–525.

Pels E. (2008), *Airline Network Competition: Full Service Airlines, Low-Cost Airlines and Long-Haul Markets*, Research in Transportation Economics, 24, 68–74.

Pelton J.N. (2014), *Regulatory Issues for New Global Aerospace Systems* [in:] R. Jakhu, K.W. Chen (eds.), *Regulation of Emerging Modes of Aerospace Transportation*, Montréal: McGill University, 77–100.

Piera A. (2014), *Greenhouse Gas Emissions from International Aviation: Legal and Policy Challenges* (LL.M. thesis), Institute of Air and Space Law, McGill University.

Piera A. (2015), *Addressing Carbon Emission from International Aviation Requires the Recognition of Special Circumstances*, Greenair, 26.2.2015, www.greenaironline.com/news.php?viewStory=2035.

Pineschi L. (2014), *I principi del diritto internazionale dell'ambiente: dal divieto di inquinamento transfrontaliero alla tutela dell'ambiente come common concern* [in:] R. Ferrara, M.A. Sandulli (eds.), *Trattato di diritto dell'ambiente, vol. I*, Milano: Giuffrè, 93–152.

Polkowska M. (2008), *Prawne uregulowania pojęcia 'space debris' a ochrona środowiska kosmicznego*, Jurysta, 7(8), 56–61.

Polkowska M. (2016a), *Prawo kosmiczne w nowej erze działalności w kosmosie*, Cracow: Instytut Allerhanda.

Polkowska M. (2016b), *ICAO – A Platform for Intergovernmental Cooperation in Space*, paper presented at ICAO-UNOOSA Symposium in Abu-Dhabi, 15–17.3.2016.

Polkowska M. (2017), *Organizacja Międzynarodowego Lotnictwa Cywilnego (ICAO) jako platforma dla współpracy państw w zakresie wykorzystania kosmosu* [in:] E. Dynia, L. Brodowski (eds.), *Prawo lotnicze i kosmiczne oraz technologie*, Rzeszów, Poland: Wydawnictwo Uniwersytetu Rzeszowskiego.

Prum D.A., Kisska-Schulze K. (2015), *The Environmentally Conscious Skies: Did the European Union's Game of Brinksmanship Lead to a Viable Global Plan for Emission Trading in Aviation?* Washington University Global Studies Law Review, 14, 1–47.

PwC. (2014), *Overview of Air Transport and Current and Potential Air Connectivity Gaps in the CESE Region.*

Quirico O. (2014), *Primary Sovereignty Rights or Secondary Environmental Duties? Critical International Law Issues Raised by the Extraterritorial Application of the EU Emissions Trading Scheme in the Aviation Sector* [in:] C. Bakker, F. Francioni (eds.), *The EU, the US and Global Climate Governance*, Abingdon, UK; New York, NY: Routledge, 143–160.

Reitzes J., Moss D. (2008), *Thirty Years of Airline Deregulation: A Structure, Conduct and Performance Review*, Houston Law Review, 45, 293–332.

Ricardo D. (1817), *On the Principles of Political Economy and Taxation* [in:] P. Sraffa (ed.) (2005), *The Works and Correspondence of David Ricardo*, Indianapolis: Fund Liberty.

Robinson G.S. (2002), *The Present and Future of Humankind in Space: No Longer a Sanctuary of Transcendent Principles*, Annals of Air and Space Law, 27, 527.

Rosenfield S.B. (1982), *United States Government-Industry Partnership*, The International Lawyer, 16, 473–501.

Rutherford J. (2005), *Networks in Cities, Cities in Networks: Territory and Globalisation Intertwined in Telecommunications Infrastructure Development in Europe*, Urban Studies, 42, 2389–2406.

Ryabinkin C.T. (2004), *Let There Be Flight: It's Time to Reform the Regulation of Commercial Space Travel*, Journal of Air Law and Commerce, 69, 101–138.

Ryngaert C. (2015), *Jurisdiction in International Law*, Oxford: Oxford University Press.

Salazar J.C., Van Fenema P. (2017), *International Air Transport Agreements* [in:] P.S. Dempsey, R.S. Jakhu (eds.), *Routledge Handbook of Public Aviation Law*, Abingdon, UK; New York, NY: Routledge, 252–294.

Sampson A. (1984), *Empires of the Sky: The Politics, Contests and Cartels of World Airlines*, New York: Random House.

Schlangen C.N.W. (2000), *Differing Views of Competition: Antitrust Review of International Airline Alliances*, University of Chicago Legal Forum, 1, 413–446.

Schlumberger C.E. (2010), *Open Skies for Africa: Implementing the Yamoussoukro Decision*, Washington, DC: The World Bank.

Schlumberger C.E., Weisskopf N. (2012), *Is the Arab Take Off Imminent? Opportunities for the Development of the North African Air Transport Sector Following the Arab Spring*, Annals of Air and Space Law, 37, 245–275.

Schmidt-Tedd B. (2011), *Authorisation of Space Activities after the Entry into Force of the EU Reform Treaty* [in:] F.G. von der Dunk (ed.), *National Space Legislation in Europe*, Leiden: Martinus Niihoff Publishers, 297–322.

Schmidt-Tedd B. (2013), *The 1975 Convention on Registration of Objects Launched into Outer Space* [in:] S. Hobe, B. Schmidt-Tedd, K.U. Schrogl (eds.), *Rescue Agreement/Liability Convention/Registration Convention/Moon Agreement (Vol. II, Cologne Commentary on Space Law)*, Köln: Carl Heymanns Verlag, 227–324.

Schnitker R., and Van het Kaar D. (2010), *Aviation Accident and Incident Investigation*, The Hague: Eleven International Publishing.

Scott J. (2016), *Unilateralism, Extraterritoriality and Climate Change* [in:] D.A. Farber, M. Peeters (eds.), *Elgar Encyclopedia of Environmental Law, Vol. I, Climate Change Law*, Cheltenham; Northampton: Edward Elgar, 167–177.

Scott J., Rajamani L. (2012), *EU Climate Change Unilateralism*, European Journal of International Law, 23, 469–494.

Scott J., Rajamani L. (2013), *Contingent Unilateralism – International Aviation in the European Emissions Trading Scheme* [in:] B. Van Vooren, S. Blockmans, J. Wouters (eds.), *The EU's Role in Global Governance. The Legal Dimension*, Oxford: Oxford University Press, 209–223.

Sgobba T. (2010), *Suborbital Space Tourism Regulation: The Safety Perspective*, paper presented at Conference The Regulation of suborbital flights in the European Context, Leiden, 16.10.2010.

Shelton J.R. (1999), *Competition Policy: What Chance for International Rules?* OECD Journal of Competition Law and Policy, 1, 59–71.

Simon S. (2014), *Consolidation in Europe's Airline Industry – The Role of the EU Competition Watchdog*, The Aviation and Space Journal, 13, 2–9.

Sitkol R., Vorrasi K.M. (2012), *The Remarkable 50-Year Legacy of Brown Shoe Co. v. United States*, Antitrust, 26, 47–53.

Skaar R. (2007), *Commercialization of Space and its Evolution: Will New Ways to Share Risks and Benefits Open Up a Much Larger Space Market*, European Space Policy Institute Report, 4, 1–34.

Smith L.J., Kerrest de Rozavel A., Tronchetti F. (2013), *The 1972 Convention on International Liability for Damage Caused by Space Objects* [in:] S. Hobe, B. Schmidt-Tedd, K.U. Schrogl (eds.), *Rescue Agreement/Liability Convention/Registration Convention/Moon Agreement (Vol. II, Cologne Commentary on Space Law)*, Köln: Carl Heymanns Verlag, 83–226.

Stragier J. (1999), *Current Issues in European Air Transport Law and Policy*, Address before the European Air Law Association, 5. 11.1999, http://ec.europa.eu/competition/speeches/text/sp1999678_en.html

Su J. (2013), *The Delimitation between Airspace and Outer Space and the Emergence of Aerospace Objects*, Journal of Air Law and Commerce, 78, 355–378.

Su J. (2014), *Emerging Modes of Aerospace Transportation and the Delimitation between Airspace and Outer Space: A Chinese Perspective* [in:] R. Jakhu, K.W. Chen (eds.), *Regulation of Emerging Modes of Aerospace Transportation*, Montréal: McGill University, 327–342.

Symposium. (2016), *A Market-based Measure for International Aviation: Need, Design and Legal Form*, Carbon and Climate Law Review, 10, 91–163.

Tan A.K.-J. (2010), *The 2004 Damascus Agreement: Liberalizing Market Access and Ownership Rules for Arab Air Carriers*, Annals of Air and Space Law, 35(1), 1–18.

Tan A.K.-J. (2016), *The Future of Multilateral Liberalisation of Air Transport in Asia* [in:] D.T. Duval (ed.), *Air Transport in the Asia Pacific*, Abingdon, UK; New York, NY: Routledge, 275–283.

Tiffany Co. (2000), *Asian Airlines: Flying with a Tailwind, but for How Long?* Salomon Smith Barney, 20.10.2000.

Trepczynski S. (2007), *The Effect of the Liability Convention on National Space Legislation*, Journal of Space Law, 33, 221–244.

Tretheway M., Andriulaitis R. (2015), *What Do We Mean by a Level Playing Field in International Aviation?* Transport Policy, 43, 96–103.

Trimarchi A. (2017), *EU Regulation 868/2004. Report of a Unilateral Approach on Subsidisation and Unfair Pricing Practices and Its Failure*, European Competition Law Review, 38, 72–79.

Truxal S. (2012), *Competition and Regulation in the Airline Industry: Puppets in Chaos*, London; New York: Routledge.

Truxal S., Harris S. (2013), *Airfreight: Regulatory Environment Encourages or Imposes Price Co-Ordination?* Journal of Air Law and Commerce, 78, 541–582.

Turnell S. (2002), *Core Labour Standards and the WTO*, The Economic and Labour Relations Review, 13, 105–126.

Van Antwerpen N. (2007), *Cross-Border Provision of Air Navigation Services with Specific Reference to Europe*, Alpen aan den Rijn: Kluwer Law International.

Van Fenema H.P. (2005), *Suborbital Flights and ICAO*, Air and Space Law, 30, 396–411.

Vasigh B., Tacker T., Fleming K. (2008), *Introduction to Air Transport Economics: From Theory to Applications*, Aldershot, UK; Burlington, VT: Ashgate.

Vissepó V.J. (2005), *Legal Aspects of Reusable Launch Vehicles*, Journal of Space Law, 31, 165–217.

Voigt C. (2011–2012), *Up in the Air: Aviation, the EU Emissions Trading Scheme and the Question of Jurisdiction*, Cambridge Yearbook of European Legal Studies, 14, 475–506.

Von den Steinen E. (2006), *National Interest and International Aviation*, Alphen aan den Rijn: Kluwer Law International.

Von der Dunk F.G. (2007), *Passing the Buck to Rogers: International Liability Issues in Private Spaceflight*, Nebraska Law Review, 86, 400–438.

Von der Dunk F.G. (2013a), *Beyond What? Beyond Earth Orbit?...! The Applicability of the Registration Convention to Private Commercial Manned Sub-Orbital Spaceflight*, California Western International Law Journal, 43, 269–341.

Von der Dunk F.G. (2013b), *Trying to Fit a Square Peg into a Round Hole? Applying Air Law to Manned Commercial Spaceflight – The Case Study of Curaçao*, The Aviation and Space Journal, 12(3), 23–31.

Von der Dunk F.G. (2015a), *Legal Aspects of Private Manned Spaceflight* [in:] F.G. von der Dunk, F. Tronchetti (eds.), *Handbook of Space Law*, Cheltenham; Northampton: Edward Elgar Publishing, 662–716.

Von der Dunk F.G. (2015b), *International Space Law* [in:] F.G. von der Dunk, F. Tronchetti (eds.), *Handbook of Space Law*, Cheltenham; Northampton: Edward Elgar Publishing, 29–126.

Von der Dunk F.G. (2015c), *European Space Law* [in:] F.G. von der Dunk, F. Tronchetti (eds.), *Handbook of Space Law*, Cheltenham; Northampton: Edward Elgar Publishing, 205–268.

Von der Dunk F.G. (2016), *Space Traffic Management: A Challenge of Cosmic Proportions* [in:] IISL (ed.), *Proceedings of the International Institute of Space Law 2015*, The Hague: Eleven International Publishing, 385–396.

Vorwig P.A. (2010), *Regulation of Private Launch Services in the United States* [in:] R.S. Jakhu (ed.), *National Regulation of Space Activities*, Dordrecht; Heidelberg; London; New York: Springer Science + Business Media, 405–419.

Walker M. (2007), *Suborbital Space Tourism Flights: An Overview of Some Regulatory Issues at the Interface of Air and Space Law*, Journal of Space Law, 33, 375–404.

Wall R. (2017), *Time Runs Out for Big German Airline*, Wall Street Journal, 16.8.2017.

Walulik J. (2016), *At the Core of Airline Foreign Investment Restrictions: A Study of 121 Countries*, Transport Policy, 49, 234–251.

Walulik J. (2017), *Progressive Commercialization of Airline Governance Culture*, Abingdon, UK; New York, NY: Routledge.

Walulik J. (2019), Brexit and Aviation Law, Abingdon, UK; New York, NY: Routledge.

Wassenbergh H.A. (1962), *Post-War International Civil Aviation Policy and the Law of the Air*, The Hague: Martinus Nijhoff.

Wassenbergh H.A. (1978), *Innovation in International Air Transportation Regulation (The US-Netherlands' Agreement of 10 March 1978)*, Air Law, 3, 138–162.

Wassenbergh H.A. (1996), *A Launch and a Space Transportation Law, Separate from Outer Space Law*, Air and Space Law, 21, 28–32.

Wassenbergh H.A. (1997), *The Air Transport Industry Comes of Age* [in:] H.A. Wassenbergh, F.G. von der Dunk (eds.), *Deregulation and Regulation of the European 'Airscape'*. Köln: Bundesanzeiger Verlagsges, 21–28.

Wassenbergh H.A. (1998), *Commercial Aviation Law in 1998. Multilateralism Versus Bilateralism*, Air and Space Law, 23, 22–30.

Wassenbergh H.A. (2000), *Regulatory Reform in International Air Transport* [in:] C. J. Cheng (ed.), *Henri A. Wassenberg's Select Essays Over a Period of Fifty Years 1950–2000*, San Francisco; Los Angeles: Regency Publishing Worldwide.

Wereszczetin W.S. (1997), *On the Principle of State Sovereignty in International Space Law* [in:] I.A. Vlasić (ed.), *Public International Air Law I: Documents and Materials*, Montréal: McGill University.

Whalen W.T. (2007), *A Panel Data Analysis of Code-Sharing, Antitrust Immunity, and Open Skies Treaties in International Aviation Markets*, Review of Industrial Organization, 30, 39–61.

Xie F., Levinson D. (2007), *Measuring the Structure of Road Networks*, Geographical Analysis, 39, 336–356.

Yan L. (2011), *Does the Rescue Agreement Apply to Space Tourists?* 54th Colloquium on the Law of Outer Space, Prague.

Yates R.A. (2012), *State Law Limitations on the Liability of Spaceflight Operators*, The Sci-Tech Lawyer, 9(1), 14–16.

Yun Z. (2009), *A Legal Regime for Space Tourism: Creating Legal Certainty in Outer Space*, Journal of Air Law and Commerce, 74, 959–982.

Zhang B. (2017), *Delta, Air France-KLM, Virgin Atlantic, and China Eastern Have Announced a Billion-Dollar Mega-Deal*, businessinsider.com, 27.7.2017, www.businessinsider.com/delta-airlines-air-france-deal-2017-7?IR=T

Zhao Y. (2004), *An International Space Authority: A Governance Model for a Space Commercialization Regime*, Journal of Space Law, 30, 277–296.

Żylicz M. (1992), *International Air Transport Law*, Dordecht; Boston; London: Martinus Nijhoff Publishers.

Żylicz M. (2011), *Prawo lotnicze: międzynarodowe, europejskie i krajowe*, Warsaw: LexisNexis Polska.

List of official documents and materials

A Review of US International Aviation Policy, Hearings Before the House Committee on Public Works and Transportation, 97th Cong, 1st and 2nd Sess. 574, 1982–82.

Addressing Competition Issues: Towards a Better Operating Environment, ICAO Air Transport Symposium (IATS), Montréal, 30–31.3.2016.

Air Carrier Ownership and Control (Presented by the International Transport Workers' Federation), ICAO ATConf/5-WP/75, 26.2.2003.

Air Carrier Ownership and Control Clauses in Bilateral Air Services Agreements, (presented by Ireland on behalf of the EU and ECAC), ICAO AT Conf/6-WP/49, 14.2.2013.

Air Transport Regulation Panel Twelfth Meeting (ATRP/12), Montréal, 26–30 May 2014, ICAO ATRP/12.

An Aviation Strategy for Europe, Communication from the Commission to the European Parliament, the Council, the European Economic and Social Committee and the Committee of the Regions, COM(2015)598 final, 7.12.2015.

Annex to the Summary Record of the 121st Meeting of the Competition Committee held on 18–19 June 2014 – Executive Summary of the discussion on Airline Competition, OECD DAF/COMP/M(2014)2/ANN4/FINAL, 28.10.2014.

Annual Report of the Council, ICAO, 2016.

Aviation: Open and Connected Europe, Communication from the Commission to the European Parliament, the Council, the European Economic and Social Committee and the Committee of the Regions, COM(2017)286 final, 8.6.2017.

Basic Principles of Fair Competition (presented by Ireland on behalf of the European Union (EU) and its member states and other member states of the European Civil Aviation Conference), ICAO ATConf/6-WP/51, 14.2.2013.

Comments of the Department of Justice on the Show Cause Order: Joint Application of Air Canada, et al., DOJ, 26.6.2009.

Commercial Space Flights (Presented by the Secretariat), ICAO LC/36-WP/3-2, 20.10.2015.

Commission Staff Working Document, SWD(2015)261 final, 7.12.2015, Accompanying the document Communication from the Commission to the European Parliament, the Council, the European Economic and Social Committee and the Committee of the Regions, *An aviation Strategy for Europe*.

Competition in International Air Transport (Presented by the Secretariat), ICAO ATRP/13-IP/3, 17.8.2015.

Competition Provisions of Existing Air Services Agreements in Global or Regional Frameworks (presented by the Secretariat), ICAO ATRP/13-IP/2, 24.8.2015.

Consolidated statement of continuing ICAO policies and practices related to environmental protection – Global Market-Based Measures (MBM) Scheme, ICAO Assembly Resolution A39–3.

Consolidated statement of continuing ICAO policies and practices related to environmental protection – Climate change, ICAO Assembly Resolution A38–18.

Consolidated statement of continuing ICAO policies in the air transport field, ICAO Assembly Resolution A38–14.

Consolidated statement of continuing ICAO policies in the air transport field, ICAO Assembly Resolution A39–15.

Consumer Protection and Definition of Passenger Rights in Different Contexts (Presented by the Secretariat), ICAO ATConf/6-WP/5, 7.12.2012.

Developing the agenda for the Community's external aviation policy, Communication from the Commission, COM(2005)79 final, 11.3.2005.

DG Competition Consultation Paper concerning the revision and possible prorogation of Commission Regulation 1617/93 on the application of Article 81(3) to certain categories of agreements and concerted practices concerning consultations on passenger tariffs on scheduled air services and slot allocation at airports, European Commission, 2004.

Draft Articles on Responsibility of International Organizations, International Law Commission, 2011.

Draft Articles on the Responsibility of States for Internationally Wrongful Acts, International Law Commission, 2001.

Emission Reduction Targets for International Aviation and Shipping, European Parliament, Directorate General for Internal Policies, November 2015, Doc. IP/A/ENVI/2015-11.

Etihad Airways Response to Claims raised about State-owned Airlines in Qatar and the United Arab Emirates, before the United States Department of Commerce, Transportation and State, Washington DC, 31.5.2015, Docket Nos. DOC-2015-0001, DOS-2015-0016; and DOT-OST-2015-0082.

EU External Aviation Policy Package, European Commission, MEMO/12/714, 27.10.2012.

European Priorities for the Economic Regulation of International Air Transport (presented by Lithuania on behalf of the European Union and its member states and the other member states of the European Civil Aviation Conference), ICAO A38-WP/63, 13.8.2013.

Fair Competition and Regulatory Cooperation in the Aviation Sector (presented by the United States), ICAO ATConf/6-WP/62, 14.2.2013.

Fair Competition in International Air Transport (Presented by the Secretariat), ICAO ATConf/6-WP/4, 4.12.2012.

Guidance note on ownership and control criteria applicable to applicants/holders of an Operating Licence issued under Regulation (EC) No 1008/2008 on common rules for the operation of air services in the Community, Commission for Aviation Regulation, May 2011.

Guidance on the Commission's enforcement priorities in applying Article 82 of the EC Treaty to abusive exclusionary conduct by dominant undertakings, Communication from the Commission, OJ C 45, 24.2.2009, pp. 7–20.

Horizontal Merger Guidelines, DOJ/FTC, 19.8.2010.

ICAO Global Symposium on Air Transport Liberalisation. The Economic Benefits of Liberalising Regional Air Transport. A Review of Global Experience, ICAO Symposium Paper, No. 3, 2006.

ICAO State letter EC 2/93, AN 11/41-05/83, 12.8.2005.

ILO Declaration on Social Justice for a Fair Globalisation, International Labour Conference 97th Session, Geneva, 10.6.2008.

Impact Assessment accompanying the document Proposal for a Regulation of the European Parliament and of the Council amending Directive 2003/87/EC, Commission Staff Working Document, SWD(2017)31 final, 3.2.2017.

Impact Assessment Accompanying the Document: Proposal for a Regulation of the European Parliament and of the Council on safeguarding competition in air transport, repealing Regulation (EC) No. 868/2004, Commission Staff Working Document, SWD(2017)182 final, 8.6.2017.

Inclusion of international civil aviation in the European Union emissions trading scheme (EU ETS) and its impact ICAO, ICAO C-WP/13790, 17.10.2011.

International Aviation Alliances: Market Turmoil and the Future of Airline Competition, Statement of Deputy Assistant Attorney General R. Hewitt Pate before the Subcommittee on Antitrust, Competition, and Business Rights, Committee on the Judiciary, US Senate, 7.11.2001.

Interpretative Guidelines on Regulation (EC) No 1008/2008 – Public Service Obligations (PSO), Commission Notice, C(2017)3712 final, 8.6.2017.

Interpretative guidelines on Regulation (EC)1008/2008 – Rules on Ownership and Control of EU air carriers, Commission Notice, C(2017)3711 final, 8.6.2017.

Issuance of Annex 20 to the Convention on International Civil Aviation (presented by Bahrain on behalf of Arab Civil Aviation Commission (ACAC)), ICAO ATConf/6-WP/27, 1.2.2013.

Lease, charter and interchange of aircraft in international operations, ICAO Assembly Resolution A23–13.

Liberalisation of Air Cargo Transport, DSTI/DOT(2002)1/REV1, OECD, 2002.

Liberalisation of Market Access (Presented by the United States of America), ICAO ATConf/6-WP/60, 14.2.2013.

Liberalization of Market Access (presented by Ireland on behalf of the European Union (EU) and its member states and other member states of the European Civil Aviation Conference (ECAC)), ICAO ATConf/6-WP/54, 14.2.2013.

List of Routes (178) with Public Service Obligations, European Commission, April 2017.

Manual of Procedures for Operations Inspection, Certification and Continued Surveillance, 5th ed., ICAO Doc. 8335.

Manual on the Regulation of International Air Transport, 2nd ed., ICAO Doc. 9626.

Memorandum of Consultations concerning the US–NL Open Skies Agreement, 1992.

Model Tax Convention on Income and on Capital, OECD, 2014.

Opinion of Advocate General Kokott, Cases C-403/08 and C-429/08, 6.10.2011.

Opinion of the European Economic and Social Committee, European Economic and Social Committee Doc. NAT/710-EESC-2017-1228, 31.5.2017.

Outcome of the Sixth Worldwide Air Transport Conference (Presented by the Council of ICAO), ICAO A38-WP/56, EC/6, 31.7.2013.

Policy and Guidance Material on the Economic Regulation of International Air Transport, 3rd ed., ICAO Doc. 9587.

Proposal for a Regulation of the European Parliament and of the Council on safeguarding competition in air transport, repealing Regulation (EC) No 868/2004, COM (2017)289 final, 8.6.2017.

Proposal for a Regulation of the European Parliament and of the Council amending Regulation (EC) No 1008/2008 on common rules for the operation of air services in the Community, COM(2016)818 final, 21.12.2016.

Proposal for a Regulation of the European Parliament and of the Council concerning protection against subsidisation and unfair pricing practices in the supply of airline services from countries not members of the European Community, COM(2002)110 final, 12.3.2002.

Proposals for Market Access Liberalisation (Presented by Chile), ICAO ATConf/6-WP/28, 13.2.2013.

Reference for a preliminary ruling submitted by the High Court of Justice of England and Wales, Queen's Bench Division (Administrative Court), 22.7.2010.

Regional cooperation and assistance to resolve safety-related deficiencies, ICAO Assembly Resolution A37–8.

Report of the World Wide Air Transport Conference on International Air Transport Regulation: Present and Future, Montréal 23 November – 6 December 1994, ICAO ATConf/4 1994, ICAO Doc. 9644.

Report of the Worldwide Air Transport Conference: Challenges and Opportunities of Liberalization, Montréal 23–24 March 2003, ICAO ATConf/5 2003, ICAO Doc. 9819.

Rio Declaration on Environment and Development, UN Conference on Environment and Development, Rio De Janeiro, 14.6.1992.

Safety Aspects of Economic Liberalisation and Article 83bis (Presented by the Secretariat), ICAO LC/35-WP/3-2, Rev. 30.4.2013.

Safety Oversight Manual, 2nd ed., ICAO Doc. 9734.

Second Review of the Air Transport Annex Developments in the Air Transport Sector (Part Two) Quantitative Air Services Agreements Review (QUASAR), WTO Doc. S/C/W/270/Add.1, 30.11.2006.

Sixth Worldwide Air Transport Conference: Sustainability of Air Transport, Montréal, 18–22.3.2013, ICAO ATConf/6 2013, ICAO Doc. 10009.

State Recognition of the Air Operator Certificate of Foreign Operators and Surveillance of their Operations, ICAO Assembly Resolution A36–6.

Statement of Chairman Robert Pitofsky and Commissioners Janet D. Steiger, Roscoe B. Starek III and Christine A. Varney in the Matter of The Boeing Company/McDonnell Douglas Corporation, FTC Matter No. 971-0051, 5 Trade Reg. Rep. (CCH), 24,295, 1.7.1997.

Stockholm Declaration on the Human Environment, UN Conference on the Human Environment, Stockholm, 16.6.1972.

The Dual Oversight Model for the Interchange of Aircraft from Different States (Presented by 22 Member States, Members of the Latin American Civil Aviation Commission (LACAC)), ICAO ATConf/6-WP/57, 19.2.2013.

The EU's External Aviation Policy – Addressing Future Challenges, Communication from the Commission to the European Parliament, the Council, the European Economic and Social Committee and the Committee of the Regions, COM(2012) 556 final, 27.9.2012.

The Multilateral Agreement on the Liberalisation of International Air Transportation: A Basis for the Future Economic Regulation of Air Services (Presented by New Zealand), ICAO ATConf/6-WP/34, 12.2.2013.

The repercussions of the terrorist attacks in the United States on the air transport industry, Communication from the Commission to the European Parliament and the Council, COM(2001)574 final, 10.10.2001.

Transatlantic Airline Alliances: Competitive Issues and Regulatory Approaches, A report by the European Commission and the United States Department of Transportation, 16.10.2010.

United States – import prohibition of certain shrimps and shrimps products. Recourse to Article 21.5 of the DSU by Malaysia, Report of the Appellate Body, AB-2001-4, WTO Doc. WT/DS58/AB/RW, 22.10.2001.

United States – Measures Affecting Trade in Large Civil Aircraft (Second Complaint): Recourse to Article 21.5 of the DSU by the European Union, Report of the Panel, WT/DS353/RW, 9.6.2017.

Views of Arab States on Fair Competition (presented by the United Arab Emirates on behalf of a group of Arab States), ICAO ATConf/6-WP/32, 12.2.2013.

Working Paper on Concept of Suborbital Flights, ICAO Council, 175th Session, ICAO C-WP/12436, 30.5.2005.

Index

Note page numbers in *italic* type refer to Figures those in **bold** type refer to Tables.